THE DIARY OF VIRGINIA WOOLF

Volume Two:

1920-1924

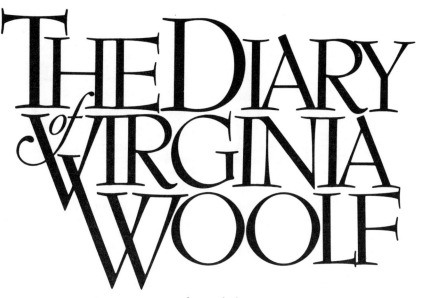

THE DIARY of VIRGINIA WOOLF

Edited by
Anne Olivier Bell
Assisted by Andrew McNeillie

VOLUME TWO
1920-1924

Harcourt Brace Jovanovich

New York and London

Requests for permission to make copies of any part
of the work should be mailed to:
Permissions, Harcourt Brace Jovanovich, Inc.
757 Third Avenue, New York, New York 10017

Printed in the United States of America

Library of Congress Cataloging in Publication Data

Woolf, Virginia Stephen, 1882–1941.
The diary of Virginia Woolf.

Includes index.
CONTENTS: V. 1. 1915–1919.—V. 2. 1920–1924.
1. Woolf, Virginia Stephen, 1882–1941—Diaries.
2. Authors, English—20th century—Biography.
PR6045.072Z494   1977   823'.9'12   [B]   77-73111
ISBN 0-15-125598-9

First American edition
B C D E

CONTENTS

EDITOR'S PREFACE

This second volume of *The Diary of Virginia Woolf* covers five years, from the beginning of 1920 to the end of 1924, a crucial period in her development as an imaginative writer. *Night and Day*, the conventional novel which marks the end of her apprenticeship, had been published towards the end of 1919; earlier in the same year, however, in *Kew Gardens* she had already shown the method—that 'grazing nearer to my individuality'—which she was to use during the years recorded here. Her new approach to fiction was extended in *Jacob's Room*, published in 1922, and further developed in *Mrs Dalloway* which she had finished by the end of 1924. A factor in Virginia Woolf's ability and determination to follow her own path was undoubtedly the Hogarth Press. That which in 1917 had begun as a hobby was now growing fast and becoming a serious business which, though it demanded (and received) a good deal of her attention, also gave Virginia the singular advantage of being able to publish as she wished, without the intervention of alien publishers or their Reader's opinions. *Kew Gardens* and her collection *Monday or Tuesday* were among the first dozen of small books issued under the imprint of Leonard and Virginia Woolf at the Hogarth Press, Paradise Road, Richmond; *Jacob's Room* was the first full-length novel they were to publish.

Concurrently with *Mrs Dalloway* Virginia Woolf was writing the connected series of critical essays assembled in *The Common Reader*, and, during the years 1920-1924, her professional industry was such that she was able to contribute over a hundred articles and reviews to periodical publications. The growing recognition of her talents perhaps also gave her confidence to venture into public controversy. There are of course evidences of her feminism in her earlier books, but in 1920 she was stung by particular examples of masculine complacency into her first purely polemical writing. As these early forays appear to have been overlooked, I have reprinted them here in Appendices II and III.

Virginia and Leonard Woolf had lived in Richmond upon Thames since 1914, always with a country outlet in Sussex. As, however, her mental and physical health stabilised, Virginia grew increasingly resentful of the limitations and inconveniences of a suburban life, and towards the end of 1923 she at last succeeded in overcoming Leonard's resistance, and gained his reluctant agreement to their return to central London. They moved to 52 Tavistock Square, Bloomsbury, in March 1924.

During these years Virginia came to terms with her diary. No longer something which she feels it a duty to keep up regularly, she returns to it, despite gaps and intervals, as though to an old friend in whom she is always free to confide; in its company she unburdens herself unreservedly and unreflectingly. In this Virginia Woolf the diarist differs substantially from Virginia Woolf the letter-writer. As a letter-writer (and as a conversationalist) she for the most part wishes to entertain; she sets out, as it were, to liven things up; she selects, she embroiders, making a good story better if she can, and recklessly sacrifices veracity. But her diary is a rapid and unedited record of the encounters and events, sights and sensations uppermost in her mind when she sat down to write. Like any writer who sets pen to paper she often enough wondered what might become of it; but if she had, as sometimes occurred to her, used her diaries as a basis for those memoirs which she never wrote, there can be little doubt that they would have been drastically transformed.

Some of the gossip which she reports may well not have been true in the first place; but the accuracy of her memory for what she has seen and heard and read is impressive. Her rapid sketches of conversations with Bertrand Russell for example record particulars which can be corroborated in biographical and autobiographical works published long after her death; or again her recollections of a tea-party with Augustine Birrell include details which can be exactly verified, even to the contents of an autograph letter from Charles Lamb that she saw hanging framed upon his wall.

When we consider the accuracy of her record of her own feelings we are confronted with truth of another kind. She does not set out in her diary to reveal her soul or her inner life; but of the honesty of what she does reveal there can be no question. At times clearly she was mistaken in her judgements, when for instance she assures herself that she will not mind what reviewers make of her books; or when one day she may find Desmond MacCarthy's urbanity irritating and time-wasting and on another write that he has no faults as a friend. Undoubtedly in her diary she makes free, in Clive Bell's words, with the 'frailties and absurdities' of her friends; of course she analyses and comments upon them and, because she was so intelligent and perceptive, because her writing is often so brilliant, and so funny, her words can colour our images; and her portraits, even—or particularly—when harsh, tend to remain in the memory. But though acute, she is by no means always *dis*obliging; almost invariably one finds that, having spun off some initial crossness or criticism, she corrects the balance of her observations, either at once or at some later time, and perceives qualities and virtues in her subjects to admire and praise.

The editor of such a personal diary has of course to consider whether or not to omit passages which diminish or dishonour the writer, or which might wound or give offence to the reader. The decision having, rightly or wrongly, been taken that Virginia Woolf's diary merits publication *in extenso*, I do not think it is my function to attempt to beautify her self-portrait by cutting away ugly bits here and there. I should be very sorry to wound or offend anybody, and would, and will, make omissions should I think them essential (there are none in this volume). But this is intended to be a complete and definitive publication of the diary of a rare and remarkable woman, and I incline to follow the advice of one to whom it might well have given pain: 'It is Virginia's truth, not absolute truth, we hope to read; do not tamper with it.'

The manuscript originals of Virginia Woolf's diaries are the property of the Henry W. and Albert A. Berg Collection of English and American Literature in the New York Public Library (Astor, Lenox and Tilden Foundations). The text for the five years included in this present volume is transcribed from Diaries IX-XIII inclusive (see Volume I, Appendix I, in which the whole series is listed). I will here briefly recapitulate the editorial principles and methods used in preparing it for publication.

In the first place, as I have said, nothing has been omitted. On the few occasions where I have been unable to decipher Virginia Woolf's rapid handwriting I have indicated as much by the use of square brackets (reserved for editorial interpolations) and question marks; where she has crossed out or altered words or passages I have followed her reconsidered version, although sometimes, when they seem interesting, the cancelled words are enclosed within angled brackets: ⟨   ⟩.

I have standardised the dating of the entries, which are set out: day, date, month, and italicised thus: *Tuesday 3 January*; the month is repeated in the running headline on each page, together with the year. Virginia Woolf's own dating is inconsistent, and sometimes wrong, and there seems no particular point in reproducing it; but I have indicated when she is mistaken.

Her spelling is so consistently good that her rare aberrations are preserved. Sometimes they are conscious (as in Badmin*g*ton, a family joke), sometimes inadvertent, particularly with proper names where her spelling is often phonetic and where the correct version has been supplied in a square bracket or footnote.

Several autographical idiosyncracies—particularly her habit of forming abbreviations with raised letters as in M.^{rs}, Sq^{re}, 19th, and the like—have, for the convenience of the printer and the reader, been brought as it were down to earth, the stops and dashes omitted; and the variety of marks following the single letter to which she frequently abbreviates names have been standardised to a full point. Her almost invariable use of the ampersand has been retained to suggest the pace of her writing (although unfortunately the symbol in its printed form rather negates this intention), and to give point to the occasions where she chooses to spell out the conjunction.

Inconsistencies of punctuation, in particular a heedless insufficiency of inverted commas, brackets, and of apostrophes in the possessive case, have been minimally amended or supplied. It is not always easy to determine what form of punctuation a single or double mark made at speed is intended to represent, but I have done my best to interpret these appropriately.

Such annotations as I have thought might be helpful to readers are given at the foot of the page to which they relate, and are numbered in sequence *within each month*. (All methods of setting annotations seem to me to have disadvantages, and this is admittedly a compromise solution.) I realise of course that in the matter of footnotes it is impossible to please everyone—though perhaps this is what I have recklessly set out to do. It is my hope that these diaries will be a fruitful source of pleasure and illumination, not only to literary specialists, but to Common Readers everywhere, and for a long time to come. So if for some readers I have spelled out matters which are too well known to require explanation, others may be bored or irritated by references and information useful to the scholarly. It should not need to be said that no one is compelled to read footnotes; but I trust that those unable to resist them may be imaginative enough to appreciate that what they find superfluous may be of service to others.

As so many of the people most frequently referred to by Virginia Woolf in her diary must already be familiar to readers of Volume I (and other works), I have not burdened the text pages with a repetition of biographical information upon them, but this may be found collected together in Appendix I on p. 333. But new arrivals, and less prominent characters, are introduced in footnotes on their first appearance; the index will be the best guide in case of doubt. As before I have attempted, without complete success, to give the full names and dates of everyone mentioned, on the grounds that such matters—people's ages, people's names—did sometimes engage Virginia's attention. The biographical details supplied do not in general extend beyond the period covered by this volume, unless the subject's later history appears to throw some light on his or her present character or situation.

I have where possible identified Virginia's own published writings according to B. J. Kirkpatrick's indispensable *Bibliography of Virginia Woolf*, prefixing the numbers therein by *Kp*. Since Volume I of this *Diary* went to press, J. Howard Woolmer's useful compilation, *A Checklist of the Hogarth Press, 1917-1938*, has appeared, and to this also I have made frequent reference. Had I come across it earlier, I would have saved a lot of time and trouble by using the volume on Virginia Woolf, edited by Robin Majumdar and Allen McLaurin, in *The Critical Heritage* Series; I look forward to being able to lean heavily upon their work in future. On p. 331-2, are listed all the abbreviations I have commonly employed for books and for names; other books are cited by their author, full title, and date of publication in England, except for Virginia Woolf's own works, when reference is made, unless otherwise stated, to the *Uniform Edition* published in London by The Hogarth Press and in New York by Harcourt Brace Jovanovich.

Acknowledgments

It is my pleasure to record my gratitude to many friends, correspondents, officials and institutions, without whose generous and variform help I doubt that this volume would ever have been completed. At the outset, the good will of Dr Lola L. Szladits, curator of the Berg Collection and custodian of the actual diaries, has been a great support to me, as indeed, in a different fashion, has been the Research Fellowship granted me by the Leverhulme Trustees. The custodians of the two other collections of documents to which I have had most recourse, those at the libraries of Sussex University and of King's College, Cambridge, have been invariably helpful. Without the beloved London Library and the aid of its staff I would long ago have given way to despair. The Hogarth Press, and in particular its presiding genius Norah Smallwood, is the most congenial and considerate of publishers; and I have reason also to feel gratitude to Mr John Ferrone of my American publishers, Harcourt Brace Jovanovich.

It has been my good fortune to trail behind Nigel Nicolson and Joanne Trautmann, the fourth volume of whose sovereign edition of

The Letters of Virginia Woolf will shortly be published; my debt to them is great, and gratefully acknowledged.

For the past two years I have been assisted in all aspects of this work by Andrew McNeillie, whose industry, clarity of mind, and sensitivity of understanding have been a powerful stimulus and reinforcement.

I wish I could expatiate on individual kindnesses, but in default, may I offer my warmest thanks to the following, who have gone out of their way to answer questions and provide aid and information:

Barbara Bagenal; Dr Wendy Baron; Mrs Mary Bennett; Sir Anthony Blunt; Lady Campbell of Croy; Angus Davidson; P. N. Furbank; David Garnett; Richard Garnett; Duncan Grant; Dr A. D. Harris; Grace Higgens; Mr George Holleyman; Pat Hodgart; Miss Georgina Howell; Dr Philip Hugh-Jones; Mrs Enid Huws Jones; Milo Keynes; B. J. Kirkpatrick; Paul Levy; Sir Henry Lintott; Dermod MacCarthy; Norman and Jeanne McKenzie; Sir Oliver Millar; Mrs Mary Moorman; Richard Morphet; Raymond Mortimer; Lucy Norton; Bernard O'Donoghue; William Outhwaite; Trekkie and Ian Parsons; Frances Partridge; Mr N. Prinsep; Angela Richards; Mr Michael Robbins; Giles Robertson; Lady Rothschild; Miss Daphne Sanger; Liadain Sherrard; Brenda Silver; George Spater; Dr Graham Speake; Ann Synge; Miss Audrey Withers; Mrs J. D. Wrisdale; Mr H. W. Yoxall.

I also acknowledge the courtesy and assistance I have received from librarians and staff of the following institutions:

The Department of Western Art, the Ashmolean Museum, Oxford; Christ Church, Oxford; East Sussex County Library; Emmanuel College, Cambridge; The Registrar's Office of Manchester University; Merton College, Oxford; Morley College, London; *The Times* Library; the Sussex Archaeological Society; the Theatre Museum of the Victoria and Albert Museum; the Watts Museum at Compton.

The demanding task of typing the transcriptions was carried out with great proficiency by Valerie Gay, Elisabeth Scott, and Imogen Scott; and the even more exacting final copy was typed with truly remarkable accuracy by Sandra Williams.

The joint owners of the copyright in Virginia Woolf's writings are Angelica Garnett and Quentin Bell; their encouragement and approval have been the backbone of this undertaking; and to Quentin, my husband, I owe more than can properly be expressed here: his patience, erudition, and wisdom have been unfailing.

ANNE OLIVIER BELL

xii

1920

1920

In December 1919 first LW and then VW had been ill, and they had been unable to go to Monks House until the 29th; they returned to Hogarth House, Richmond, on 8 January 1920. The entry for 7 January was—as VW indicates—written at the end of her 1919 diary (Diary VIII), but the four pages it covers were torn out and pasted in at the start of her new book for 1920—Diary IX. The first page is headed:

January 1920   Monk's House Rodmell

Wednesday 7 January

To begin the year on the last pages of my old book—the few I've not torn off for letter writing—is all upside-down of course; but of a part with the character of the work.

This is our last evening. We sit over the fire waiting for post—the cream of the day, I think. Yet every part of the day here has its merits—even the breakfast without toast. That—however it begins—ends with Pippins; most mornings the sun comes in; we finish in good temper; & I go off to the romantic chamber over grass rough with frost & ground hard as brick. Then Mrs Dedman comes to receive orders—to give them, really, for she has planned our meals to suit her days cooking before she comes. We share her oven. The result is always savoury—stews & mashes & deep many coloured dishes swimming in gravy thick with carrots & onions. Elsie, aged 18, can be spoken to as though she had a head on her shoulders. The house is empty by half past eleven; empty now at five o'clock; we tend our fire, cook coffee, read, I find, luxuriously, peacefully, at length.[1]

But I should not spend my time on an indoor chronicle; unless I lazily shirked the describing of winter down & meadow—the recording of what takes my breath away at every turn. Heres the sun out for example & all the upper twigs of the trees as if dipped in fire; the trunks emerald green; even bark bright tinted, & variable as the skin of a lizard. Then

1. One of the numerous outhouses in the garden at Monks House had been adapted for VW's use as a study; later her 'lodge' was built in the orchard against the churchyard wall. Mrs Dedman was the wife of William Dedman, the Rodmell village sexton, who also worked in the garden at Monks House; VW described her (*II VW Letters*, no. 1109) as 'an old woman who has borne 11 children & has the sagacity of the whole world since the Flood in her'. Elsie, a village girl, came daily to clean the house.

theres Asheham hill smoke misted; the windows of the long train spots of sun; the smoke lying back on the carriages like a rabbits lop ears.[2] The chalk quarry glows pink; & my water meadows lush as June, until you see that the grass is short, & rough as a dogfishes back. But I could go on counting what I've noticed page after page. Every day or nearly I've walked towards a different point & come back with a string of these matchings & marvels. Five minutes from the house one is out in the open, a great pull over Asheham; &, as I say, every direction bears fruit. Once we went over the cornfield & up onto the down—a dim Sunday afternoon—muddy on the road, but dry up above. The long down grass pale, & as we pushed through it, up got a hawk at our feet, seeming to trail near the ground, as if weighted down—attached to something. It let the burden fall, & rose high as we came up. We found the wings of a partridge attached to [a] bleeding stump, for the Hawk had almost done his meal. We saw him go back to find it. Further down the hill side a great white owl 'wavy' (for that describes his way of weaving a web round a tree—the plumy soft look of him in the dusk adding truth to the word) 'wavy in the dusk', flew behind the hedge as we came past.[3] Village girls were returning, & calling out to friends in doors. So we cross the field & churchyard, find our coke burnt through to red, toast the bread—& the evening comes.

L. has spent most of his time pruning the apple trees, & tying plums to the wall. To do this he wears two jackets, 2 pairs of socks, two pairs of gloves; even so the cold bites through. These last days have been like frozen water, ruffled by the wind into atoms of ice against the cheek; then, in the shelter, forming round you in a still pool. Yesterday I explored towards the house with the white chimneys, finding a grass drive all the way;[4] brooks struck off to the right blue as if with sea water. From one a snipe rose zigzagging across & across, flurried & swift. As I advanced the peewits rose in clouds, one dallying behind, & crying peewit, peewit. Then up in the air across the meadows one sees the (the post—but only Mathew's letter[5]) handful of grain flung in a semi circle

2. Cf. *The Waves*, p 204: 'down in the valley the train draws across the fields lop-eared with smoke'.
3. Cf. George Meredith's poem 'Love in the Valley:'
       'Lovely are the curves of the white owl sweeping
       Wavy in the dusk lit by one large star.'
4. Sutton House on the outskirts of Iford, about a mile from Rodmell up the Ouse Valley.
5. Louise Ernestine Matthaei (1880-1969), classical scholar, Fellow and Director of Studies at Newnham College, Cambridge, 1909-16. She was LW's assistant on the *International Review*.

what birds they are I never know. On the down this afternoon I saw the usual flight go up in front of me, & then half wheeled round t'other way. Bells tinkling as I walked along the valley came from a flock attached to the green side, & there on the top against the sky was a string of three great cart horses, stock still, as on a summers day; for they were beside a corn stack. And this I see is my last page so my threat about counting things to that limit was a true one. Human beings have figured less than the red berries, the suns & the moon risings. Letters have come still, as usual, about N[ight] & D[ay], from Sheppard & Roger; both the kind I like; & old Kitty Maxse sees nothing but stupidity, which don't hurt much—but I'm ashamed of beginning the year with this gossip.[6] Reading Empire & Commerce to my genuine satisfaction, with an impartial delight in the closeness, passion, & logic of it; indeed its a good thing now & then to read one's husbands work attentively. For the rest, the Education of Henry Adams, &—? I wrote my article on English prose for Murry; & now finish Rosetti, taking leave still from the Times.[7]

Saturday 10 January

Ah, that's all very well, but a fate conspires against a solemn opening ceremony. True, I've taken a new nib; but I'm perched high in bug [*sic*] chair, & can't settle to read or write, waiting for Lotty to bring in tin tacks, with which to mend my aged broken down eared arm chair.[8] Entrails years ago burst their barriers, & for the past six months I've sat on a ridge of wood. Leonard suddenly undertakes to confine entrails

6. John Tresidder Sheppard (1881-1968), Lecturer in Classics 1908-33 (and subsequently Provost) at King's College, Cambridge. Katherine (Kitty) Maxse, *née* Lushington (1867-1922), one of VW's early and most socially accomplished friends, upon whose image she was to draw in creating *Mrs Dalloway*. For Roger Fry, see Appendix I.

7. LW's *Empire and Commerce in Africa. A Study in Economic Imperialism* was published jointly by the Labour Research Department and Allen & Unwin on 14 January 1920. *The Education of Henry Adams* (1907) was by the American historian and writer Henry Brooks Adams (1838-1918). VW's review (Kp C183) of *A Treasury of English Prose* edited by Logan Pearsall Smith, appeared on 30 January 1920 in the *Athenaeum*, of which John Middleton Murry (see Appendix I) was editor. The reference to Rossetti has not been elucidated.

8. Lotty (or Lottie) Hope and her friend Nelly Boxall had come to Hogarth House as housemaid and cook in 1916; they had been recommended to the Woolfs by Roger Fry who had employed them at Durbins, his house near Guildford in their home district.

within sacking; but we wait for Lotty. A five minutes walk spreads to 45 with her; she calls on Miss Stanford.[9]

So the New Year is broached; 10 days of it already spent. The 1917 Club has the merit of gathering my particular set to a bunch about 4.30 on a week day.[10] There, returning on Thursday, I found Clive (I heard him from the stairs) Morgan, Fredegond & dim background figures just worth a nod turning out to be Oliviers—varieties of Oliviers.[11] Now Clive showed as gaslight beside Morgan's normal day—his day not sunny or tempestuous but a day of pure light, capable of showing up the rouge & powder, the dust & wrinkles, the cracks & contortions of my poor parrokeet. He makes me feel the footlights myself. The blend of the two was not agreeable; or rather not comfortable. Morgan had a matron waiting for him in Leicester Square. Clive took me in a taxi to Regent Square, after making play with the name of Lytton Strachey. I ran up ahead, & found the room bright & lively; the baby crawling out to fill up a corner, Nessa in her spotted feather hat with the pink plume. I think she thus redeems the rest of her homespun—very successfully. I also think (as Lotty won't come in—my evening wasting—Lindsay [*unidentified*] to read—oh dear) that my charms are beneath the horizon; Mary's about level with the eye; & Nessa's rising resplendent like the harvest moon. Why, otherwise, dwell so rapturously to me on her dress at the party, her beauty, her grandeur?[12] God knows—perhaps to make himself shine brighter. A long yellow lock hung beneath his ear. "I must cut your hair" said V. Whereupon he took his hat off quickly, fingered the long strand, recognised its mission—to cover the bald patch. But it wouldn't stay, & fell back again a little repulsively, lacking grease to keep it in place. Compliments for me: but offered as if he were no longer the privileged purveyor. So home by Victoria, noticing there the hustler in his box.[13]

9. Miss Stanford kept a dairy in Richmond.
10. The 1917 Club was at No. 4 Gerrard Street, Soho.
11. For Clive Bell and Morgan Forster, see Appendix I. Fredegond Shove, *née* Maitland (1889-1949), daughter of VW's cousin Florence (Fisher) and the historian F. W. Maitland; in 1915 she had married Gerald Frank Shove (1887-1947), economist, Fellow of King's College, Cambridge, and an Apostle. The possible varieties of Olivier were Margery, Brynhild, Daphne or Noel, daughters of Sir Sydney Olivier, Fabian socialist, Colonial administrator, and Civil Servant.
12. Vanessa Bell was living at 36 Regent Square, WC1; with her were her three children: Julian (b. 1908), Quentin (b. 1910), and Angelica (b. 1918). For Vanessa Bell, Lytton Strachey and Mary Hutchinson, see Appendix I.
13. An experiment to reduce the time spent by trains at the platform had recently been introduced on the District Railway at Victoria Station: a Station Controller or 'Hustler', mounted on an observation platform, directed operations and sounded a siren after 30 seconds' stop.

Wednesday 14 January

On Sunday the Shoves dined here; Monday nothing; Tuesday Club & talk, almost of an intimate kind, with Gumbo; Bob. T., Fredegond, Alix, the background;[14] Wednesday is the present moment, in from a snatched walk at Kew, awaiting Leonard, & expecting a large party, Doggats, Joshua's &c. at 7-30.[15] So I write as if waiting for a train. I might fill this page & the succeeding ones with the Shoves' gossip, but I have never determined how far it is permitted to go here in indiscretion. I should have to write at length to retail this specimen properly which is the conclusive reason against it. But it referred to the three days of revelation at Garsington; there was a flush of confession it seems, poured into Fredegond's ear. It shows how little one knows one's kind. I should never have expected long fatuous Philip in his leather gaiters, double breasted waistcoat & jewelled buttons to go those lengths. According to Gerald, the general feeling roused in one was pity—such a lonely, in some ways unhappy man. I can't help smiling at the thought of these semi-ducal, (demi-semi at most, I admit) children playing in the suburbs of Ealing & Streatham, living to be insurance clerks or the like, while Garsington lacks an heir. There! The cat's out of the bag.[16]

My intimacy with Gumbo came on the flood tide of her appreciation of N. & D. "So solid—so large—such a great—firm building"—"It belongs to literature—an addition to life". Such sentiments warm one to people. Apart from them, as I think this diary records, I have warmed to her these past years, guessing at a good deal of dreariness, & half expecting that the old light would never blaze again. Now it begins to flicker & that is the origin of her novel. I wonder, parenthetically, whether I too, deal thus openly in autobiography & call it fiction? —Her story is the story of M.S. & J.W. & the conclusion is that she regains happiness,

14. 'Gumbo' was the Bloomsbury nickname for the youngest of Lytton Strachey's five sisters, Marjorie Strachey (1882-1964); she was a teacher. Robert (Bob) Calverley Trevelyan (1872-1951), poet and classical scholar, and an Apostle. Alix Sargant-Florence (1892-1973), educated at Bedales and Newnham College, Cambridge, had been briefly employed by LW in 1917 as a research assistant, since when the pursuit of James Strachey had been her main preoccupation.

15. This dinner party, arranged with J. T. Sheppard, had been postponed from 7 January; see *II VW Letters*, no. 1106, and below, 17 January 1920, n 20.

16. Garsington was the country home near Oxford of Philip Morrell (1870-1943), until 1918 a Liberal MP, and his wife Lady Ottoline, *née* Cavendish-Bentinck (1873-1938), half-sister of the 6th Duke of Portland. They had one daughter. The discovery in 1917 of her husband's infidelities had precipitated a serious breakdown in Lady Ottoline's health, the true cause of which was not then generally known.

though losing the object. My brain at once spins to clothe her story for her,—how happiness is to be represented by a green here; a yellow there & so on. (novelist or not, some instinct of story telling is pretty quick in me). She is to send me her chapters.[17]

Leonard's book is out today. To judge by his calm, you would not think it. Great gales in the way of weather; a French ship sunk in the Bay of Biscay, two days after Bella must have passed through; a Cornish steamer wrecked too off Swanage;[18] & on our windows such a battering at night that we woke twice. Violent gusts leaping out of the heart of complete calm—a suggestion of animal savagery; or human frenzy. But what with glass & brick we human beings do pretty well. I sometimes think with wonder that soon the immense thickness & stability of Hogarth House will be mine to whittle away with a penknife, should I so choose.[19] And here—thank goodness—is L.

Saturday 17 January

Then there was the party, given in skeleton above. Miss Joshua in pale pink, & the shoes of Artemis—laced with silver round the ankles. Doggatt the spruce innocent young man; with eyes like brown trout streams. Sheppard dancing nervously; & Cecil Taylor, to my mind, adequately fitting the part of enlightened schoolmaster.[20] We got through dinner very well on spur of Cambridge & Christianity; things went, to

17. For the M[arjorie]. S[trachey]. and J[os]. W[edgwood]. story, see *I VW Diary* 17 January 1915; her novel on this theme, *The Counterfeits*, was not published until 1927; it was dedicated 'To my Medical Adviser'.
18. Bella Sidney Lock, *née* Woolf (1877-1960), LW's eldest sister and a widow since 1916, was possibly returning to Ceylon where both her first and second husband (W. T. Southorn, whom she married in 1921) had official posts. In the early hours of 12 January the French liner *Afrique*, with 465 passengers on board, sank some 50 miles off La Rochelle; there were only 26 survivors. On 10 January the Cornish boat, the *Treveal*, bound for Dundee from Calcutta with a cargo of jute, was wrecked off Kimmeridge in Dorset with a loss of 36 of the crew of 43.
19. Hogarth House and the adjoining Suffield House, built as one dwelling about 1720, were purchased this month in VW's name from Mrs Brewer of Bayswater for £1950.
20. The party consisted of J. T. Sheppard (see above, 7 January 1920, n 6) and three Cambridge friends of his: Catherine Marie Joshua (b. 1898), Newnham College 1917-20, daughter of the unfortunate Mr Joshua (see below, 15 September 1924, n 4); and two Apostles: James Hamilton Doggart (b. 1900), scholar of King's College who was to become an eminent ophthalmic surgeon; and Cecil Francis Taylor (1886-1955), classical scholar of Emmanuel College, since 1912—and for the rest of his career—a schoolmaster at Clifton College, Bristol.

my taste, lightly & briskly after dinner; & then Bob [Trevelyan] came in. At once we were in another atmosphere. Fantasies were crushed. A Cambridge evening of the 90ties; a Sanger evening;[21] the quality gone; raucous common sense; serious literary criticism, &, what annoyed me, every attempt of a different sort snuffed out directly by Bob's indefatigable snuffer. He wears blinkers, & sees an indisputable stretch of road, but a narrow one. Sheppard ceased dancing; we argued; we vociferated. Alix arrived, pale as clay, & not much lighter in the mind. I lost my balance; my vanity was wounded—in short, I think Bob spoilt the party—but as for seeing that he spoilt it, that vista is shut from him completely. In crept doubts of my liking for S., my liking for Cecil Taylor; the young people one can scarcely like or dislike. So the party ended. Bob stayed. I was gratified by praise of my novel. On this account I suppose, I found the morning more becoming to him than the night. We got back into the Cambridge atmosphere.

Then Ka for the night: now Desmond for the night; tomorrow I go to Roger for the night. All rather heavy going, & cutting up the week into little bits. We had to put off Mrs Clifford; & I'm writing dully, wishing, though I love Desmond, for a solitary night. He has been made successor to Eagle on the Statesman.[22]

Tuesday 20 January

Years ago as a child I made up a wise saw to the effect that if one didn't expect a party to be nice it was & t'other way round. So Desmond's visit was easy, refreshing, & passed without hitch. We had a fine store of talk to keep us going. —The story of his voyage—of Captain Deakes & Captain Haines*; their obscenity that made one sick; the squall at sea;

* [*Haines* crossed out].

21. Charles Percy Sanger (1871-1930), Chancery Barrister, friend and contemporary of Bertrand Russell and R. C. Trevelyan at Trinity College, Cambridge, and like them, an Apostle.

22. Katherine ('Ka') Arnold-Forster, *née* Cox (1887-1938), Newnham College, Cambridge, 1906-10; a kindly, dependable and competent woman, she had been a good friend to the Woolfs, particularly during the long periods of VW's illnesses. Rupert Brooke's death in 1915 had intensified the pain of her unresolved love affair with him, but in 1918 she had married William Edward (Will) Arnold-Forster (1885-1951), an artist, and was now living at Aldbourne in Wiltshire; later in the year they were to move to Cornwall. For Desmond MacCarthy, see Appendix I. For Mrs Clifford, see below, 24 January 1920, n 30. 'Solomon Eagle' was the pseudonym of J. C. Squire, literary editor of the *New Statesman*, 1913-19, and contributor of a weekly page entitled "Books in General'; Desmond MacCarthy was to use the *nom-de-plume* 'Affable Hawk'.

arrival at Cape Town; Mrs Paley's surprise; Paley's greeting 'but we didn't expect you—' His wire 'Desmond sailed' arriving Desmond failed—(as indeed he might probably have done)—all this in the lovely soft voice, with more than the usual freshness & abundance.[23] As for decadence or decay—not a trace of it: fresh & firm & friendly. Then much talk of the New Statesman—projects without number—to be noted down: letters to be written. Secretly, I think, he was much excited & pleased. Five hundred assured; 250 of it dependent on a weekly article, signed Affable Hawk (this is a dead secret). Off we went after tea to Roger's, all across Europe to the Brecknock Arms.[24] Buses pass you bound for Barnet. As we both depend upon holding to a button naturally we did not arrive easily. The house very high & narrow, with many large rooms, & a bright lining of pictures. Roger to my eyes slightly shrunken, aged? Can one use that word of him? And I don't know how much I colour him from my own depression —for I guessed he didn't much care for N. & D. So I went on to fancy him wilful; to trace veins of irrational prejudice in him. He showed freakish by side of D.'s benevolence; old sea captains telling dirty stories not in his line; nor novels either. Yet he professed to find it much superior to the V[oyage].O[ut].

Wednesday 21 January

It would be easy to take up the line that Roger's praise is not worth having, since it is balanced by what appears an irrational prejudice. If the prejudice is on your side, well & good; though even so it sweeps one too far to leave one steady in the head. I sometimes fancy that the only healthy condition is that of doing successful work. Its the prime function of the soul. R.'s work never meeting with the right sort of appreciation, he suffers perpetually from an obscure irritation. The main form it takes is irritation against England; I fancy I can trace it elsewhere also. He is testy without much occasion, & too easily reverts to grievances, how art critics hate him, how its only in France that they care for his pictures— why, he was accusing Clive of taking his ideas & selling them to America

23. George Arthur Paley was a wealthy eccentric who had been at Eton and Trinity with Desmond MacCarthy and, when the latter married in 1906, housed him for several years in a farmhouse on his Suffolk estate. The Paleys now lived in South Africa where Desmond had been to visit them.
24. Roger Fry lived with his sister Margery at 7 Dalmeny Avenue, near Holloway Prison; the Brecknock Arms was a large public house at the junction of Brecknock and Camden roads not far off.

for £200—but on this point I happen to agree with him.[25] If I'm sincere, however, I see that I'm led to infer all this from what I note in my own disposition under a cloud. For one thing, I find it difficult to write. I held my pen this morning for two hours & scarcely made a mark. The marks I did make were mere marks, not rushing into life & heat as they do on good days. Perhaps Roger was the first cloud; Desmond may have contributed a little; & then how many silly things I did yesterday, ending by ringing up the Richmonds at their dinner, & being painfully snubbed by Elena on that account.[26] I should like here to analyse; instead I must wash & dress & dine at the Club & so to Moll Hamilton's party, which I predict will be dull, & more shocks will be administered, & I shall creep cold to bed.[27]

Saturday 24 January

But on the contrary—I didn't creep cold to bed, & the party amused me as a spectacle—I should more truly say astonished me as a pandemonium. Molly can be heard out in the Adelphi; then, as the hostess sets the key, some hundred people, opening their mouths, tried to overcome her, by dint of roaring. I got my station in a corner, between Clive & Norton, & enjoyed the sense of irresponsible amusement.[28] Not a human festival at all. Everyone smiling. As they could scarcely express their pleasure in words this was a necessary device. Margot was there— oh well, unpleasantly disfigured, in a low dress. I tried to turn her periods into laughter. Humour might do more to dissolve her poetry than criticism.[29] Then young Mr Evans confided to me that his admiration

25. Presumably a reference to an article by Clive Bell, 'Order and Authority', first published in the *Athenaeum*, 7 and 14 November 1919, and reprinted in the *New Republic*, New York, 3 and 10 December 1919.
26. Bruce Lyttelton Richmond (1871-1964), editor of the *Times Literary Supplement* and VW's staunchest patron; in 1913 he had married Elena, *née* Rathbone (1878-1964), who had been of the Duckworth-Stephen social circle in Kensington in VW's youth. She was particularly concerned with nursing and midwifery. They still lived in Kensington.
27. Mary Agnes (Molly) Hamilton, *née* Adamson (1882-1966), writer, journalist, and active socialist, lived at 21 York Buildings, Adelphi.
28. Henry (Harry) Tertius James Norton (1886-1937), mathematician and Fellow of Trinity College, Cambridge, and an Apostle.
29. Margot Robert Adamson was the youngest of Mrs Hamilton's three sisters; she was a poet, and had been brought to dine with VW some six months before (see *I VW Diary*, 8 July 1919). 'Young Mr Evans' was probably Charles Seddon Evans (1883-1944), general manager of William Heinemann the publishers.

of N. & D. was personal 'to tell you the truth I'm going through the same thing myself'—poor little man! Yet I was pleased to think my psychology 'intense' & 'modern' & illuminating the crannies of Mr Evan's personal existence.

Oh dear, though, this talk of novels is all turned sour & brackish by a visit to Mrs Clifford.[30] She must have supplied herself with false teeth since I saw her—20 years ago; & her hair frizzed out is surely browned by art; but she remains otherwise the same—large codfish eyes & the whole figure of the nineties—black velvet—morbid—intense, jolly, vulgar—a hack to her tips, with a dash of the stage—'dear' 'my dear boy—Did you know Leonard, that I was only married for 3 years, & then my husband died & left me with 2 babies & not a penny—so I had to work—oh yes, I worked, & sold the furniture often, but I never borrowed.' However the pathetic is not her line. She talks it to fill up space; but if I could reproduce her talk of money, royalties, editions, & reviews, I should think myself a novelist; & the picture might serve me for a warning. I think one may assume it to be more a product of the 90ties than of our age. Again, having years ago made a success, she's been pulling the wires to engineer another ever since, & has grown callous in the process. Her poor old lips pout for a pat of butter; but margarine will do. She keeps her private & very rancid supply on some of the little tables that those distressing rooms are lumbered with (a wooden black cat on the clock, & little carved animals under it): she has a review of herself in the Bookman & a portrait, & a paper of quotations about Miss Fingal. I assure you I can hardly write this down— Moreover, I had a feeling that in these circles people do each other good turns; & when she proposed to make my fortune in America, I'm afraid a review in the Times was supposed to be the equivalent. Brave, I suppose, with vitality & pluck—but oh the sight of the dirty quills [?], & the scored blotting paper & her hands & nails not very clean either—& money, reviews, proofs, helping hands, slatings—what an atmosphere of rancid cabbage & old clothes stewing in their old water! We went away laden with two of the cheap flaring books—'Are you going to take my mangy works! to tell the truth I'm in debt—' Yes, but was that why we were asked to tea? Not altogether, I suppose, but, partly; subconsciously. And now, you see, all colour is taken from my boasting; a

30. Mrs Clifford, *née* Lucy Lane (*c.* 1855-1929), widow of Leslie Stephen's friend W. K. Clifford, FRS, a distinguished mathematician. He died in 1879, leaving her with two young daughters, and she supported her family by writing plays and novels; *Miss Fingal*, her latest, had been published in 1919. She lived at 7 Chilworth Street, Paddington.

2nd edition of the Voyage Out needed; & another of Night & Day shortly; & Nisbet offers me £100 for a book.[31] Oh dear there must be an end of this! Never write for publishers again anyhow.

I've no time or finger power left to describe Desmond in his office; my haul of biographies; luncheon at Gordon Sqre; sitting in the great chairs before Clive's fire afterwards; the apparition of Adrian; affection of Mary, & comparative docility of Clive.[32]

I had tea with Lilian the other evening; we kissed silently: for my errand was to while away an hour of suspense for her while she waits for the verdict on her eyes. She may be blind, I suppose—oh dear; & nothing could be said about it. What courage can make one, at 50, look down the remaining years, with that calamity to darken them![33]

Monday 26 January

The day after my birthday; in fact I'm 38. Well, I've no doubt I'm a great deal happier than I was at 28; & happier today than I was yesterday having this afternoon arrived at some idea of a new form for a new novel. Suppose one thing should open out of another—as in An Unwritten Novel—only not for 10 pages but 200 or so—doesn't that give the looseness & lightness I want: doesnt that get closer & yet keep form & speed, & enclose everything, everything?[34] My doubt is how far it will ⟨include⟩ enclose the human heart— Am I sufficiently mistress of my dialogue to net it there? For I figure that the approach will be entirely different this time: no scaffolding; scarcely a brick to be seen; all crepuscular, but the heart, the passion, humour, everything as bright as fire in

31. James Nisbet & Co of Berners Street, publishers. No more is heard of this offer.
32. The offices of the *New Statesman*, of which Desmond MacCarthy was now literary editor, were at 10 Great Queen Street, WC2. The outcome of VW's haul was 'A Talk about Memoirs' which appeared in the *New Statesman* of 6 March 1920 (Kp C186). Although Clive and Vanessa Bell's joint household at 46 Gordon Square, Bloomsbury, had been given up in the war, Clive retained rooms in the house, which was leased to Maynard Keynes and was now in multiple occupation. For Adrian Stephen, see Appendix I.
33. Lilian Harris (c. 1866-1949), Assistant-Secretary of the Women's Co-operative Guild, and constant companion of the Woolfs' friend Margaret Llewelyn Davies, the Guild's General Secretary.
34. *An Unwritten Novel* was published in the *London Mercury* of July 1920 (Kp C203), and reprinted by the Hogarth Press in the collection *Monday or Tuesday* (1921).

the mist. Then I'll find room for so much—a gaiety—an inconsequence
—a light spirited stepping at my sweet will. Whether I'm sufficiently
mistress of things—thats the doubt; but conceive mark on the wall,
K[ew]. G[ardens]. & unwritten novel taking hands & dancing in unity.[35]
What the unity shall be I have yet to discover: the theme is a blank to
me; but I see immense possibilities in the form I hit upon more or less
by chance 2 weeks ago. I suppose the danger is the damned egotistical
self; which ruins Joyce & [Dorothy] Richardson to my mind: is one
pliant & rich enough to provide a wall for the book from oneself without
its becoming, as in Joyce & Richardson, narrowing & restricting?
My hope is that I've learnt my business sufficiently now to provide
all sorts of entertainments. Anyhow, there's no doubt the way lies
somewhere in that direction; I must still grope & experiment but this
afternoon I had a gleam of light. Indeed, I think from the ease with
which I'm developing the unwritten novel there must be a path for me
there.

Yesterday being my birthday & a clear bright day into the bargain
showing many green & yellow flushes on the trees, I went to South
Kensington & heard Mozart & Beethoven. I don't think I did hear
very much of them, seated as I was between Katie & Elena, & pitched
headforemost into outrageous banter of the usual kind with the Countess.[36]
But the Countess was very affable & jolly, invited me indeed insisted
upon my coming, to tea with her. We turned our money under the new
moon. She vibrated under the pleasure of a compliment—"when Lady
Cromer's there one feels &c &c—" a compliment to her beauty. But the
room was clamorous with South Kensington. Eily Darwin in particular,
fat & decorous & affectionate, yet plaintive as of old, as if protesting
before one spoke against criticism. She told me I had been cruel. I forget
now what I said—something wild & random, as everything said under
those circumstances must be. George Booth took my arm & praised my
book.[37]

35. VW's *The Mark on the Wall* was published by the Hogarth Press in 1917 (Kp
    A2); and *Kew Gardens* in 1919 (Kp A3).
36. During the winter seasons between 1918 and 1921 VW went on her own to a
    number of private subscription concerts at Shelley House, Chelsea, and 23
    Cromwell Houses, South Kensington. The audience contained many friends of
    her youth including the Countess of Cromer (Katie), *née* Katherine Thynne
    (1865-1933), second wife and widow of Evelyn Baring, 1st Earl of Cromer; and
    Elena, Mrs Bruce Richmond (see above, 21 January 1920, n 26).
37. Elinor ('Eily') Darwin (see below, 13 February 1920, n 6) and George Booth
    (see below, 9 March 1920, n 13) were essentially pre-Bloomsbury friends of
    VW.

Saturday 31 January

Here is my calendar: Tuesday the Squires & Wilkinson & Edgar to dinner;[38] Wednesday tea with Elena; Thursday lunch with Nessa, tea Gordon Square; Friday Clive & Mary here; & Saturday sitting over the fire with a morbid & I hope unfounded fear lest certain creatures infesting Lottie & Nelly may begin to twitter beneath my skin. An incident of this sort is like the blackness that used to cross the waves in the bay & make my heart sink when I sat doing lessons at the long table in St Ives drawing room. Sordid—cheap— And the impression was enforced by a visit to Putney.[39] The streets of villas make me more dismal than slums. Each has a cropped tree growing out of a square lifted from the pavement in front of it. Then the interiors— But I dont want to dwell on this. As Leonard said, its the soul of Sylvia in stucco. They were sitting in the dining room with a large table, reading novels— Its partly that I'm a snob. The middle classes are cut so thick, & ring so coarse, when they laugh or express themselves. The lower classes don't do this at all.

It is said that Mr Wilkinson was nearly drunk; that excuse can't serve Mrs Squire though; she has spread more widely; is even more settled into a kind of whitish sediment; a sort of indecency to me in her passive gloating contentment in the arm chair opposite; like some natural function, performing automatically—a jelly fish—without volition, yet with terrifying potentiality. She breaks off into young on the least provocation: Squire is at least direct & honest. I don't like it when he talks about love patriotism & paternity, but on the other hand I can speak my mind to him. Love came into the discussion on account of the Athenaeum.[40] According to Squire the A. denies everything. It is a frost of death for all creative activity. Now the London Mercury provides a very fertile soil. He pressed me to write for the London Mercury. The A. is winning itself a bad name, on account of its hard sceptical tone. I tried to explain to Squire that there is such a thing as honesty & a high standard; his

38. John Collings Squire (1884-1958), from 1919-34 editor of the *London Mercury* and from 1921-31 contributor of a weekly article on books to the *Observer*; he married in 1908 Eileen Harriet Anstruther, *née* Wilkinson, sister of his friend and Cambridge contemporary Clennell Anstruther Wilkinson (1883-1936), journalist and writer of popular biographies. Edgar Sidney Woolf (b. 1883) was LW's third brother.

39. The Woolfs went for a walk in Putney this Saturday afternoon, and called on Edgar Woolf and his wife Sylvia at 7 Castello Avenue.

40. The *Athenaeum* had been resuscitated in the Spring of 1919 under the editorship of J. Middleton Murry. VW had been, and, until towards the end of this year, was to be, a fairly frequent contributor.

retort is & there are such things as poetry & enthusiasm. At present the battle in our circles is between James & Desmond.[41] James wishes to 'stab humbug dead'. Desmond & I wish, on the contrary, to revive it like a phoenix from its ashes. The difference is fundamental; but I am equally able to write for Murry, Squire or Desmond—a proof of catholicity or immorality, according to your taste.

But with us its a question of drains. We are in for a spell of bad luck & find ourselves compelled to spend £200 perhaps on drains, which, six months ago, would have been Mrs Brewer's concern. Still, we had fears for a thousand.

At tea with Elena, in the absence of Bruce [Richmond], we broached, delicately, the subject of the [*Times Literary*] Supplement. She said that people were nice to her in order to influence reviews. She said they made Bruce's life a burden to him. I lightly sketched my interview with Mrs Clifford. It was all known to her, I could see; she knew Mrs Clifford's methods. She dines with Lady Dilke, & hears her japes with Stephen McKenna.[42] I liked Elena for sharing my feeling of repulsion; indeed she is more clearminded & innocent than I am, & regards it through the simple brown eyes of the nicest, most modest, of collie dogs. I liked her better than before, & she sat on a stool, & told me how she does this that & the other for the diseased & the afflicted, & I thought she must be a pleasant sight at a bedside. People who have no brilliance or subtlety seem to take things in directly & sanely in such a way as to abash me, who count myself among the brilliant. There they are, it seems, without exertion or self applause: nor are they much deceived by brilliance. The rest I must skip, since I have 6 biographies to read for Desmond. A letter from a Mr Askew in Staffordshire about N. & D. pleasant; & odd to please the lower classes.

Wednesday 4 February

I had rather catch Leonard's itch than Lottie's—that's my only contribution to lice psychology which still occupies our minds, & wastes our mornings; & poisons our quiet after tea. For according to Fergusson, they turn over in their lairs when warm. No improvement so far—also,

41. James Beaumont Strachey (1887-1967), the youngest child of Sir Richard and Lady Strachey, wrote dramatic criticism for the *Athenaeum*, Desmond MacCarthy for the *New Statesman*.
42. Lady Dilke (1876-1959) was Mrs Clifford's elder daughter Ethel, wife of Sir Fisher Wentworth Dilke, 4th Bt. Stephen McKenna (1888-1967) was a prolific and popular novelist.

so far as I know, no infection. But imagination! By taking thought I can itch at any point on my hundreds of inches of skin. I do it now.[1]

The mornings from 12 to 1 I spend reading the Voyage Out. I've not read it since July 1913. And if you ask me what I think I must reply that I don't know—such a harlequinade as it is—such an assortment of patches—here simple & severe—here frivolous & shallow—here like God's truth—here strong & free flowing as I could wish. What to make of it, Heaven knows. The failures are ghastly enough to make my cheeks burn—& then a turn of the sentence, a direct look ahead of me, makes them burn in a different way. On the whole I like the young womans mind considerably. How gallantly she takes her fences—& my word, what a gift for pen & ink! I can do little to amend; & must go down to posterity the author of cheap witticisms, smart satires & even, I find, vulgarisms—crudities rather—that will never cease to rankle in the grave. Yet I see how people prefer it to N. & D.—I dont say admire it more, but find it a more gallant & inspiriting spectacle.

To Madame Gravé's this afternoon—& found her in her great new house.[2] Maman is getting very trying poor dear. You set her on the stool & she does nothing. Then she wants the stool again—But you've just been there & done nothing maman! Then she calls me cruel—very trying. And when she sleeps her mouth hangs down, as though she were dead. She's getting senile. All this simply, tenderly even, as we wander about the house, looking at the furniture. I like her childishness, & her unquenchable desire to make me another dress which will really be done in a week when she cant finish what's on hand.

Friday 13 February

Again many lapses & the same excuses. For some time now life has been considerably ruffled by people. Age or fame or the return of peace— I dont know which—but anyhow I grow wearied of 'going out to tea'; & yet cant resist it. To leave a door shut that might be open is in my eyes some form of blasphemy. That may be; meanwhile I neither write my diary nor read my Greek. There was a lunch party at the Café Royal

1. Dr D. J. Fergusson of Mount Ararat Road was the Woolf's doctor in Richmond. Lottie's itch seems to have worked its way into 'An Unwritten Novel': cf the unhappy woman who fidgeted as if 'some spot between the shoulders burnt or itched' and her effect on the narrator.
2. Madame Gravé, a dressmaker probably recommended to VW by Mary Hutchinson, and her husband Captain Felix Gravé ('Professor of Fencing'), had recently moved from Fulham to Cornwall Gardens, Kensington.

on the day of Duncan's private view to record: 12 guests; everything handsomely done; I stimulated & fuddled with wine; a queer assortment of the usual & the unusual. There was Mrs Grant, a woman still sailing like a yatcht under the breath of mature charm; Pippa; Adrian; Bunny; Lytton. Lytton had laid out £70 on one of the pictures. Maynard rose & said "To our deep affection for Duncan".[3] I fancy Duncan would rather have done without fuss, & he slunk off after lunch, leaving us to visit the show. It's absurd—my capacity for flooding scenes with irrational excitement; in which mood I say rather more than I mean; or rather what I do mean. Surveying the room with Adrian I thought him despondent, like a man now aware of failure, & contrasting his life with those of his contemporaries. 'How distinguished we all are!' I said; & then it came out—or did I imagine it all?—that he & K[arin]. feel themselves isolated & like people who have been ploughed in some examination. About 35 the lists are posted up for everyone to read. On the impulse of this I invited them to dine; & when they come I shall find myself, I predict, utterly at fault. Meanwhile I say nothing & have nothing to say of Duncan's pictures. They spun in my head like the white wine I'd drunk; so lovely, so delicious, so easy to adore. However I only caught glimpses here & there as well dressed people moved across them. Then tea with Roger at the Burlington, walking across with Maynard; & hearing that his book is now in the 15th thousand; but to the credit of Cambridge he remains unmoved, & is more, instead of less, modest than before.[4]

Next day I bought one of Duncan's pictures; sacrificing a pomegranate coloured dress which much took my fancy.[5] The dress connects itself with tea at Eily's. She disappointed me: slovenly, compromising, slouch-

3. Duncan Grant (see Appendix I) held his first one-man exhibition at the Paterson & Carfax Gallery, 5 Old Bond Street; the private view was probably on Monday 9 February. Duncan's mother, Mrs Bartle Grant, *née* Ethel MacNeil (1863-1948), was a woman of considerable beauty and charm; his cousin Philippa ('Pippa') Strachey (1872-1968), the third of Lytton's five sisters, was Secretary of the National Council for Women's Service until 1951. For Adrian and Karin Stephen, David ('Bunny') Garnett, and Maynard Keynes, see Appendix I.

   VW shared with Charles Darwin an inability to spell 'yacht' correctly (see Gwen Raverat, *Period Piece*, 1952).

4. Keynes's polemic, *The Economic Consequences of the Peace*, had been published for him by Macmillan at the end of December 1919; its initial printing had been 5000. Roger Fry was presumably at the Old Burlington Street offices of the *Burlington Magazine*, of which he had been one of the guiding spirits since its foundation in 1903.

5. Although VW went through the motions of purchasing a watercolour it would seem, in fact, to have been a present from the artist (see *II VW Letters*, no. 1120).

ing through life content at heart with the second best but complaining on the surface—so she struck me; & so matronly & decorous & such a trim smug home, & such commonplace children. Honest Bernard, being honest & of the Darwin ware that never cracks, pleased me much better. He talked about golf & the Waddon Chase dispute. But I shall never see Eily again.[6]

After that, I must skip over forgotten days & alight at Ottoline's last night (I skip tea with Ottoline & Birrell & Tony Birrell the imbecile[7]). Yet I don't know that I can describe an evening party— Philip & I sitting together watched the door open & people come in. There were more of the shady smart sort than of old; or so they looked to me since I did not know them. There were Eliots & Huxleys & Forster &—all the rest. My single diversion was a dialogue with W. J. Turner, an inarticulate rednosed, infinitely modest man, with prominent brown eyes, nice vague eyes, seeming to wish to tell the truth; yet too shy to be ready with it.[8] Squire felt me fathoming his soul t'other night; so he said; Squire respects me immensely; oh well, I'm afraid that had some share in my liking for Turner. At a party now I feel a little famous— the chances are people like Turner whose names I know, also know my name. Moreover, people like Turner are very glad to be praised. That comes always as a surprise. The Eliots gladly dine with us. Murry is affectionate & bantering. I must have one coloured figure though in my black & white; I must spare a phrase for the sealing wax green of

6. Elinor Mary ('Eily'), *née* Monsell (d. 1954), an artist, had married Bernard Darwin (1876-1961) in 1906; he was golf correspondent to *The Times* for nearly forty years, and published a great many books. VW's cousin Florence Maitland had married his father Sir Francis Darwin in 1913 when they were both widowed, and VW had been familiar with this extensive Cambridge circle before her own marriage.

The Whaddon Chase dispute concerned the mastership and future of the Whaddon Chase Hunt. Irate farmers issued 'warning off' notices against the newly-elected master Lord Orkney and his equally new pack of hounds, while Colonel Selby-Lowndes of Whaddon Hall sought to save the pack which had traditionally hunted the country. This contest, conducted in part through the columns of *The Times*, was not settled until the following January.

7. Augustine Birrell (1850-1933), author and Liberal statesman, was an old friend of Lady Ottoline Morrell. He was a widower, and lived with his two sons, the younger of whom, Anthony, though perfectly amiable, was seriously retarded.

8. Walter James Redfern Turner (1889-1946), poet and journalist, was born and educated in Australia, travelled in Europe, and served during the war in the Artillery; his work was included in the third volume of *Georgian Poetry*. He was now music critic of the *New Statesman*, dramatic critic of the *London Mercury*, and soon to become literary editor of the *Daily Herald*.

Ottoline's dress. This bright silk stood out over a genuine crinoline. She did control the room on account of it. Yet I dreamt all night of her disillusioned with a weak pouting face, revealing her inner discontent. If anyone is disillusioned she, so they say, is. Indeed I can't help thinking her unhappy!

Last week end at the Arnold Forsters I've entirely left out.[9]

Sunday 15 February

Partly to obliterate the Webbs, partly to put off for a few minutes reading the Voyage Out I will say that we lunched with the Webbs; had Adrian, Sanger & Hussey to dine last night.[10] But the Webbs! I find the hour of 1.30 on a cold blowy day, precisely fitting to them. As we walk down Grosvenor Road the old papers blow & the middle classes parade in their Sunday clothes. The houses have a red raw look. Factory chimneys face the windows across the river. Owing to Sunday all barges are moored. There is no sun or warmth. But what are they going for? Why should the right pursuits be so entirely hideous? Then theres the mutton & the cabbage & apple tart—all adequate but joyless. Bad cigarettes. A little whisky. The drawing room now a glacial white with water colours hung accurately apart. Mrs Webb displaying shark like teeth. Webb daubed red, & clumsily thick in person. The window in the back room is of frosted glass to conceal back windows. No longer am I frightened; only dreary & dismal, & rasped all over by the sense of so hideous a prospect. Mr Cross of the Foreign Office had brough[t] six portfolios of papers to be looked through.[11] Mrs Webb told me it was wrong to prevent L. from going into Parliament; we want men of subtle intellect &— But what is 'right' & who are 'we'. Frostily friendly she said good bye. One deals with the situation more easily, but the horror of it increases with familiarity. Shall we become like that too? I stamp up & down the platform to warm myself; steep my hands in hot water, crouch over the fire, but still I'm irritated & exacerbated.

9. The Woolfs spent from Saturday afternoon until Monday morning with Will and Ka Arnold-Forster at Aldbourne.
10. Doris Edith Hussey (d. 1951), a friend of Marjorie Strachey, was an independent young woman living in Clifford's Inn and hoping to make a career for herself as a writer. Sidney (1859-1947) and Beatrice (1858-1943) Webb, social historians, political lobbyists and Fabians, lived at 41 Grosvenor Road on the Thames Embankment.
11. Felix Warren Crosse, who was attached to the Foreign Office from 1919-23, carried out research for the Webbs which was incorporated in their survey of *English Prisons under Local Government 1689-1894*, published in 1922.

Wednesday 3 March

So then at the end of that week we went to Rodmell, & are back again two days ago.[1] But I've numbers of old clothes in my dirty clothes basket—scenes, I mean, tumbled pell mell into my receptacle of a mind, & not extracted till form & colour are almost lost. I suppose 'going out to tea' continued; oh, there was a dinner at Gordon Square, when Mary, becoming almost peevish in her bedroom refused to part with hair pins: I made a note of that scene; & have branded her 'stupid'—can one say vulgar? I think not. But dressing for gentlemen induces some disease of the complexion when examined by pure feminine light. Desmond was there: Desmond warm, affectionate, the oldest friend, so I sometimes feel; perhaps the best. I was touched, that is, that he ran along the platform to wish me goodnight. Then we sold Uncle Thoby for £150 to Mr Prinsep: & directly I got the cheque I regretted it—oh dear—again.[2] I'm learning this trick, & wake saying it.

Then there was Roger's speech at the Club & my first effort[3]—5 minutes consecutive speaking—all very brilliant, & opening the vista of that form of excitement not before glimpsed at. Dined with Nessa & Duncan in Soho. Saw the woman drop her glove.[4] A happy evening. Eliot & Sydney dine—Sydney righting himself after our blow about Suffield—not without a grampus sigh or so[5]— Then off to Monks—& here I should write large & bright about the SPRING. It has come. It has been with us over a fortnight. Never did a winter sleep more like an infant sucking its thumb. Daffodils all out; garden set with thick golden crocuses; snowdrops almost over; pear trees budding; birds in song; days like June with a touch of the sun—not merely a painted sky but a warm one. Now we've been to Kew. I assure you, this is the earliest & loveliest & most sustained spring I remember. Almond trees out.

1. The Woolfs went to Rodmell on Saturday 21 February and returned to London on Monday 1 March.
2. One of his two portraits of H. Thoby Prinsep had been given by G. F. Watts to the sitter's devoted niece Julia, VW's mother, before she married Leslie Stephen. It was now sold to a member of the Prinsep family, to which it still belongs.
3. LW's diary for 19 February 1920 records: 'Club tea. RF spoke on Modern Art'— but there is no mention of VW's effort.
4. Cf. *Jacob's Room*, p. 80.
5. T. S. Eliot and Sydney Waterlow (see Appendix I) dined with the Woolfs on Friday 20 February—the evening before they went to Rodmell. Presumably Waterlow had proposed buying the next-door Suffield House—which the Woolfs had just bought and were to sell in May 1921, but they had rejected the idea of such close proximity.

Saturday 6 March

No sooner had I written this [the date] than Madame Gravé appeared, & has left only the wreck of an evening behind her. Still if I don't fill a page now, God knows when I shall again: an endless prospect of un-recorded activity now stretches before me: also behind. Did I say that Desmond & I cheered the return of Mr Asquith to Parliament? I saw a sleek white satiny looking bare head. Also Margot standing up, swaying slightly, & drawing her hands to & from her lips, while a policeman squirmed on the carriage roof—always a touch of the grotesque in these proceedings, though emotions rose like a spring tide, & swept me off my feet, or rather elevated me unconsciously to a parapet, whence I saw the aforementioned bare white head.[6] Tea with Molly & old Mrs MacCarthy; emotions—about the death of a friend; gossip about the Blunts' law suit: Molly wearing 2 minute cows horns above her ears.[7]

Then? —Tuesday & Wednesday here in Richmond printing Hope; & Elena dined with us on Tuesday & made a speech at the Guild,[8] & presented me incidentally with one of those puzzles which I always get wrong I fancy. How far can she be talked to? Is her withdrawal shock or stupidity? Then this 'niceness'; what does it amount to? For seconds she can make me feel crude & provincial; then, as I say, there's the silence—& Heaven knows what goes forward. The machine seems to stop. As for her liking or disliking—I know nothing about it. Her personal presence —so comely, stately & maternal always reduces me—till I grate on the

6. Herbert Henry Asquith (1852-1928), Liberal Prime Minister 1908-16, was defeated in the general election of 1918 but returned to Parliament on 1 March 1920. His progress from his home in Cavendish Square to Westminster was marked by scenes described in *The Times* as 'boisterous to the point of embarrassment'. Near Downing Street the crowd stood six deep and, it was reported, 'The police guard on the roof, with drawn truncheon, saved Mr Asquith from the too pressing attentions of his admirers.' Mrs Asquith (Margot) waved a bouquet 'cheerfully' at the crowds.

7. i.e., Desmond's wife and mother; Molly was deaf. The Blunt lawsuit just con-cluded in the High Court concerned the claim of the Public Trustee and Lady Wentworth against her father Wilfrid Scawen Blunt for possession of the Crabbet Stud of Arab horses built up by Blunt and his estranged wife, Lady Anne, who had died in 1917.

8. *Paris, A Poem* (*HP Checklist* 5) was by Hope Mirrlees (b. 1887). She had been at Newnham with VW's sister-in-law Karin Stephen. The Woolfs had invited her to write something for the Hogarth Press. It was VW's responsibility to provide speakers for the meetings of the Richmond Branch of the Women's Co-operative Guild which took place at Hogarth House.

rocks of (I suppose) her indifference to my enthusiasm. I rather believe that the nice people feel more temperately & universally than we do—& with none of our passion.

Then on Thursday, dine with the Macarthys, & the first Memoir Club meeting.[9] A highly interesting occasion. Seven people read—& Lord knows what I didn't read into their reading. Sydney [Waterlow], to whom the occasion was one of some importance, signified as much by reading us a dream—in reality a parable, to ⟨account for⟩ explain the seeming obtuseness of daylight Sydney by the imaginative power of dreaming Sydney—altogether a queer, self-conscious, self analytic performance, interesting to me. Clive purely objective; Nessa starting matter of fact: then overcome by the emotional depths to be traversed; & unable to read aloud what she had written. Duncan fantastic & tongue—not tied —tongue enchanted. Molly literary about tendencies & William Morris, carefully composed at first, & even formal: suddenly saying "Oh this is absurd—I can't go on" shuffling all her sheets; beginning on the wrong page; firmly but waveringly, & carrying through to the end. "These meagre Welsh, these hard-headed Scots—I detest them—I wanted to be the daughter of a French marquise by a misalliance with—" That was the tone of it—& then "these mild weak Cornishes".[10] Roger well composed; story of a coachman who stole geraniums & went to prison. Good: but too objective. I doubt that anyone will *say* the interesting things but they can't prevent their coming out. Before this by the way, I saw Nessa's new home, no. 50, inspected Pippa's chaos at no. 51; & looked in upon Adrian & Karin doing biology in their dining room. Coming out we ran upon James—such is the rabbit warren nature of the place.[11]

9. The Memoir Club, like its predecessor the Novel Club, was invented by Molly MacCarthy in the hope of inducing Desmond MacCarthy to write something other than journalism. The members—about a dozen old friends—were expected every month, after dining together, to foregather in one or another of the member's houses and each read a chapter of what was to become a full-length autobiography. This proved too ambitious, and the contributions and the frequency of the meetings were reduced. (See *IV LW*, 114; and *Bloomsbury Heritage* by Elizabeth French Boyd, 1976, p 108 ff. VW's (and LW's) diary is evidence that the first meeting in fact took place on 4 March and not on 27 February as proposed by Molly; the Woolfs were at Rodmell then.)

10. Molly's father, Dr Francis Warre-Cornish, Vice-Provost of Eton College, had come from a West Country family of gentleman farmers and clergymen.

11. Vanessa Bell had moved with her children into the upper part of no. 50 Gordon Square as tenant of her brother Adrian Stephen who, with his wife Karin, had embarked on the study of medicine as a preliminary towards becoming psychoanalysts. Lady Strachey and her daughters had moved to no. 51 towards the end of 1919; and James Strachey lived at no. 41.

Poor Mills Whitham yesterday wanted praise of his book, & I hadn't read it—poor man— Sylvia a little depressed—but then with a hu[s]band in brown corduroys, writing country novels—unreadably bad—no wonder.[12]

Tuesday 9 March

In spite of some tremors, I think I shall go on with this diary for the present. I sometimes think that I have worked through the layer of style which suited it—suited the comfortable bright hour after tea; & the thing I've reached now is less pliable. Never mind: I fancy old Virginia, putting on her spectacles to read of March 1920 will decidedly wish me to continue. Greetings! my dear ghost; & take heed that *I* dont think 50 a very great age. Several good books can be written still; & here's the bricks for a fine one.

To return to the present owner of the name: on Sunday I went up to Campden Hill to hear the S[c]hubert quintet—to see George Booth's house—to take notes for my story—to rub shoulders with respectability —all these reasons took me there, & were cheaply gratified at 7/6.[13]

Whether people see their own rooms with the devastating clearness that I see them, thus admitted once for one hour, I doubt. Chill superficial seemliness; but thin as a March glaze of ice on a pool. A sort of mercantile smugness. Horsehair & mahogany is the truth of it; & the white panels, Vermeer reproductions, omega table & variegated curtains rather a snobbish disguise.[14] The least interesting of rooms: the

12. John Mills Whitham (b. 1883), who in 1916 married Sylvia Frances Milman, a youthful friend of the Stephens. They lived in Devonshire. The book referred to was probably *The Human Circus*, published in November 1919.

13. The Booth family was very much part of the intellectual and social world in which VW had grown up; Charles Booth, the shipowner and social scientist and his wife Mary, *née* Macaulay (1848-1939), were friends of Leslie and Julia Stephen; their second son George Macaulay Booth (1877-1971) went into the family shipping business but during the war had been Deputy Director General of Munitions Supply. He and his wife Margaret, *née* Meinertzhagen, a gifted violinist, had built The New House, Airlie Gardens, in 1913-14, incorporating a lofty vaulted music room. Referring to this occasion, Booth noted in his diary: 'English String Quartet. Beethoven Trio. Schubert Quintet. Crowds.' The story for which VW was taking notes was presumably 'The String Quartet' published in *Monday or Tuesday* in 1921 (Kp A5).

14. In 1914 George Booth had commissioned a carpet (which came to be known as 'The Pool of Blood'), and had probably acquired other furnishings for his new house, from the Omega Workshops.

compromise; though of course, thats interesting too. I took against the family system. Old Mrs Booth enthroned on a sort of commode in widows dress: flanked by devoted daughters; with grandchildren somehow symbolical cherubs. Such neat dull little boys & girls.[15] There we all sat in our furs & white gloves. Elena asked us to dine: I (perhaps for this reason) exempt her & Bruce from this censure.

Monday at the Club, which I see I've ceased to describe. Alix; Bunny, Birrell; James; finally Morgan. Alix told me that Florence Darwin—still I call her Maitland—is dead.[16] For a moment I was shocked. Then it seemed to me that her greatest happiness had been with Fred; then I pitied poor old Frank, left for the 3rd time alone. Then an attempt to remember her which I can do rather accurately: the beautiful brown eyes, with the defiant look in them; the brown hair; the colour; the emphatic manner; the exaggeration of her talk—reminding me a little of mother —indeed the manner was much mother's. Always simply dressed in black, I think; & holding herself superbly—in the sense of proudly, tensely; nerves much on edge; but showing so to us only in her dramatic ways; quick movements; beautiful turns & glances, as she protested— Fred treating her with a kind of bantering courtesy, & amusement; which I felt was the cover of a deep understanding between them not unveiled before us. I went one evening into his study to speak to him; opened the door & stood for a second silent; he raised his eyes, thought for a moment that I was Florence, whereupon he looked tender & intimate as I had never seen him—which look of course vanished directly he recognised me. If I now heard that this letter of Fredegond's was untrue, I should try to see her again. But what is it that prevents one from ever seeing people, when years have passed, & there have been deaths & births & marriages?

Thursday 18 March

Strange that this should be my last reflection, since without remembering it, I told Irene Noel-Baker that I dreaded the thought of meeting her

15. Old Mrs Booth had three daughters and more than two dozen grandchildren.
16. For Francis Birrell, see below, 14 October 1922, n7. Florence Henrietta (1863-1920), the eldest of VW's Fisher cousins, had married firstly F. W. Maitland, the historian and biographer of Leslie Stephen, and secondly, after seven years of widowhood, (Sir) Francis Darwin (1848-1925), FRS, already twice a widower. She died at Cambridge on 5 March 1920. Fredegond was the Maitland's younger daughter.

after 6 or 7 years. She said the same thing—but I rather guess this was simulated. Anyhow we met at the Cecils last Sunday;[17] & I see why she dreads meeting me—because I look at her. Oh you little adventuress, I think to myself, so now you've turned matron, & are pushing your way & Philip's way into political circles—witness the bright comprehending chatter she kept up with Ld. R. & Ormsby Gore. & you've got a son, & are proud of nursing him yourself, & you've grown plump, & look less romantic—though the positive search for obvious truths is carried on as pertinaciously as ever. Lady Beatrice daughter of Lord Salisbury, a frank dashing brainless young goddess—who palpably loses divinity if you look at her. Her eyes are of the brightness, hardness, & insensibility of greyblue marbles.

Leonard went on to see Waller upon that curious family crisis which I foresaw some years ago.[18] Still if this diary were the diary of the soul I could write at length of the 2nd meeting of the Memoir Club. Leonard was objective & triumphant; I subjective & most unpleasantly discomfited. I dont know when I've felt so chastened & out of humour with myself—a partner I generally respect & admire. "Oh but why did I read this egotistic sentimental trash!" That was my cry, & the result of my sharp sense of the silence succeeding my chapter. It started with loud laughter; this was soon quenched; & then I couldn't help figuring a kind of uncomfortable boredom on the part of the males; to whose genial cheerful sense my revelations were at once mawkish & distasteful. What possessed me to lay bare my soul! Still, the usual revulsion has now taken place. I saw Nessa yesterday, & she guessed at none of this

17. Irene Noel (d. 1956) had in 1915 married Philip Baker (b. 1889) and joined his name to hers; their son Francis Noel-Baker had been born in January this year. She was the daughter and heiress of Frank Noel of Achmetaga, Euboea, whom the young Stephens had visited during their expedition to Greece in 1906; thereafter VW met or heard of her from time to time in London. Philip Noel-Baker, who had been president both of the Cambridge Union and the Cambridge University Athletic Society, was now working for the League of Nations Secretariat as assistant to Lord Robert Cecil, with whom, and his wife Lady Eleanor (Nelly) Cecil, the Woolfs lunched on Sunday 14 March. The other guests were the Hon. William Ormsby-Gore (later Lord Harlech) and his wife Lady Beatrice, née Gascoyne-Cecil (b. 1891), eldest daughter of the 4th Marquess of Salisbury and a niece of Lord Robert's.

18. The nature of this crisis is obscure, but it had something to do with LW's second sister Clara Woolf (1885-1934). 'Waller' was John Waller Hills (1867-1938), Conservative Unionist MP for Durham City; the widower of VW's half-sister Stella, he was also a solicitor whose firm, Halsey, Lightly & Hemsley, acted for the family.

—which indeed Leonard firmly assured me was a miasma on my part due to late nights &c.[19]

Another late night last night, dining with Lytton, Clive & Nessa at the Eiffel Tower.[20] Lytton stuck in Vic: intimate & cordial, with perhaps a touch of regret. "How seldom we meet!" said Nessa. It was true & yet we all want to meet; & can't do it. They are all speeding south— Nessa, Duncan & Maynard to Italy; Lytton, Carrington & Partridge to Spain.[21]

Saturday 10 April

We sped to Rodmell, which accounts for another formidable break.[1] By the way, Morgan keeps a diary, & in his diary Morgan writes conversation—word for word, when the humour takes him.[2] I dont know that the humour takes me to describe our Easter at Monks House. Through the first week of it I was driven, as with shut eyes, eyes being indeed so intent upon Henry James as to see nothing else.[3] That missive despatched, I got such pleasure out of everything that I keep putting houses & streets—yes & people too—against that background, & seeing them look flat & faded. Clive & Mary last night brought in the loud breezy atmosphere of the Brighton pier. We are getting middle aged. I see him stout, kind—indeed cordial—but so cynical as to be almost

19. No records were kept of the Memoir Club meetings, and it is not usually possible to do more than guess at who read what, when. The first of VW's written Memoir Club papers preserved is that called '22 Hyde Park Gate' (*Moments of Being*, 1976, p 142) which opens: 'As I have said', which suggests it had a forerunner— possibly the 'egotistical sentimental trash' read on this occasion in Vanessa's rooms at 50 Gordon Square on 15 March. (See below, 5 December 1920, n 1).

20. The Eiffel (now the White) Tower Restaurant, 1 Percy Street. Lytton had embarked on preparatory reading for his biography of Queen Victoria early in 1919; it was published in 1921.

21. For Carrington, see Appendix I. Reginald (Ralph) Partridge (1894-1960) had gone from Westminster School to Christ Church, Oxford, in 1913 with a classical scholarship; during the war, he attained the rank of major and was awarded the Military Cross and Bar. In the summer of 1918 he was introduced by his friend, her brother Noel Carrington, to Carrington and thus to Lytton Strachey and, though he returned to Oxford, had been drawn by love of her into a very close triangular union centred on their home at The Mill House, Tidmarsh. They were all now going to visit Partridge's friend Gerald Brenan (see below, May 1923, n 1) in Spain.

1. The Woolfs went to Rodmell on 25 March for a fortnight.

2. E. M. Forster kept an extensive diary from 1903 until his death, though with gaps of several years at a stretch. He did occasionally record conversations *verbatim*.

3. See below, 15 April 1920, n 8.

uninteresting. Poor Mary has little of the Brass Band about her; but much of the mute meretricious fille de joie—I've said that partly for the sake of the m's; but there's truth in it. Then, uncomfortably enough, I kept striking upon something soft & unprotected in her—childish, pathetic almost. She's the mother of children too.[4] I daresay what with one thing & another I'm grown rather brazen—so many compliments (oh, Morgan just now writes to say my memoir was 'splendid'—& dare he ask me to review for the Herald—Desmond sends me stalls for the pioneers tomorrow—[Bruce] Richmond—but enough of quotations[5]). Moreover, I can wince outrageously to read K.M.'s praises in the Athenaeum. Four poets are chosen; she's one of them. Of course Murry makes the choice, & its Sullivan who rates her story a work of genius. Still, you see how well I remember all this—how eagerly I discount it.[6]

To describe Monks House would be to trench upon literature, which I cant do here; since we only slept by snatches last night, & at 4 A.M. turned a mouse out of L.'s bed. Mice crept & rattled all night through. Then the wind got up. Hasp of the window broken. Poor L. out of bed for the 5th time to wedge it with a toothbrush. So I say nothing about our projects at Monks, though the view across meadows to Caburn is before me now; & the hyacinths blooming, & the orchard walk. Then being alone there—breakfast in the sun—posts—no servants—how nice it all is!

I'm planning to begin Jacob's Room next week with luck. (That's the first time I've written that.) Its the spring I have it [in] my mind to describe; just to make this note—that one scarcely notices the leaves out on the trees this year, since they seem never entirely to have gone in —never any of that iron blackness of the chestnut trunks—always something soft & tinted; such as I can't remember in my life before. In fact,

4. Mary Hutchinson had two children, Barbara (b. 1911) and Jeremy (b. 1915).
5. In March and April 1920 E. M. Forster was temporarily acting as literary editor of the *Daily Herald*. Desmond's tickets were for a production by the Pioneer Players of *The Higher Court* by Miss M. E. M. Young at the Strand Theatre; the Woolfs went to this on Sunday evening, and VW's review of the play appeared in the *New Statesman* of 17 April 1920 (Kp C191).
6. For Katherine Mansfield, see Appendix I. In the course of his review of Henry Newbolt's *A New Study of English Poetry* in the *Athenaeum* of 26 March 1920, J. Middleton Murry refers to Walter de la Mare's 'Arabia', W. H. Davies's 'Lovely Dames', Katherine Mansfield's 'Prelude', and T. S. Eliot's 'Portrait of a Lady', 'in each of which' he writes, 'the vital act of intuitive comprehension is made manifest'. Katherine Mansfield's 'Je ne parle pas Français' was reviewed in the *Athenaeum* of 2 April 1920 by J. W. N. Sullivan under the heading 'The Story-Writing Genius', and compared to Chekhov and Dostoievsky.

we've skipped a winter; had a season like the midnight sun; & now return to full daylight. So I hardly notice that chestnuts are out—the little parasols spread on our window tree; & the churchyard grass running over the old tombstones like green water.

Mrs Ward is dead; poor Mrs Humphry Ward; & it appears that she was merely a woman of straw after all—shovelled into the grave & already forgotten. The most perfunctory earth strewing even by the orthodox.[7]

Thursday 15 April

My handwriting seems to be going to the dogs. Perhaps I confuse it with my writing. I said that Richmond was enthusiastic over my James article? Well, two days ago, little elderly Walkley attacked it in The Times, said I'd fallen into H.J.'s worst mannerisms—hard beaten 'figures' —& hinted that I was a sentimental lady friend. Percy Lubbock was included too; but, rightly or wrongly, I delete the article from my mind with blushes, & see all my writing in the least becoming light.[8] I suppose its the old matter of 'florid gush'—no doubt a true criticism, though the disease is my own, not caught from H.J., if thats any comfort. I must see to it though. The Times atmosphere brings it out; for one thing I have to be formal there, especially in the case of H.J.; & so contrive an article rather like an elaborate design; which encourages ornament. Desmond, however, volunteered admiration. I wish one could make out some rule about praise & blame. I predict that I'm destined to have blame in any quantity. I strike the eye; & elderly gentlemen in particular get annoyed. *An unwritten novel* will certainly be abused; I can't foretell what

7. In fact Mrs Ward, who died on 24 March 1920 in her seventieth year, had a tremendous send-off, with condolences from Royalty and the eminent, a *Times* leader, a two-column obituary, and a country funeral at Aldbury. Her coffin was preceded by a detachment of the Hertfordshire Constabulary, and the Dean of St Paul's, Dean Inge, ventured his opinion that she was 'perhaps the greatest Englishwoman of our time.'
8. VW's review of *The Letters of Henry James*, edited by Percy Lubbock, was the leading article in the *TLS* of 8 April 1920 (Kp C190); it was of course unsigned. On 14 April, in his Wednesday column in *The Times*, the critic Arthur Bingham Walkley (1855-1926), in discussing the book, devoted considerable space to the *TLS* article, in which he detected some of the master's 'least amiable mannerisms'. 'The most immaculate of women' he also wrote, '. . . *will* sentimentalise their men friends. . . . Well, if any of these ladies had edited [Henry James's] letters or reviewed them, wouldn't each of the others have said ". . . *she* never understood him poor dear"?' As to Percy Lubbock the editor, Walkley asked if he wasn't 'just a little bleak?'

line they'll take this time. Partly, its the 'writing well' that sets people off—& always has done, I suppose. 'Pretentious' they say; & then a woman writing well, & writing in The Times—that's the line of it. This slightly checks me from beginning *Jacob's room*. But I value blame. It spurs one, even from Walkley; who is (I've looked him out) 65, & a cheap little gossip, I'm glad to think, laughed at even by Desmond. But don't go forgetting that there's truth in it; more than a grain in the criticism that I'm damnably refined in The Times: refined & cordial: I don't think its easy to help it: since, before beginning the H.J. article, I took a vow I'd say what I thought, & say it in my own way. Well, I've written all this page, & not made out how to steady myself when the *Unwritten Novel* appears.

Rain has come—what I mind much more is the black sky: so ugly. Yesterday I think I was unhappy all day long. First, Walkley; then 2 teeth out; then tooth ache all the evening; L. out to speak in Richmond; & couldn't read because of the throb in my gum. The day before I went to the Niggers' show in Chelsea; very sad impressive figures; obscene; somehow monumental; figures of Frenchmen, I thought, sodden with civilisation & cynicism; yet they were carved (perhaps) in the Congo 100's of years ago. Hannay came up.[9] 'Mrs Woolf?' Yes—but who—? We met years ago at the Squires—Hannay. Ah, you do art criticism now? Tell me what I ought to think of the carvings. And these Peruvian bowls— Its the shape, in the bowls. I've lived too long with the carvings. (I don't think this expresses him, though. A man who spaces his words with long silences—a bad critic I'm told. As one would expect of anyone working at the bookshop.) Then I heard Desmond saying O its upstairs —but in he came with a tall lean brown elderly man in frock coat & top hat. Not introduced to me, as though there were a gulf between us. I slipped out into Chelsea Church, & saw the tablet to H.J.—florid & cultivated if you like—spindly letters, & Jamesian phrases. Perhaps by Gosse.[10] So to Madame Gravé's—so to the 17 Club—so home. & then my tooth was beginning.

9. Some thirty pieces of sculpture, mainly from the Ivory Coast and the Congo, were shown at the Chelsea Book Club, Cheyne Walk, in April 1920, a pioneer exhibition which excited great interest and a revision of accepted ideas. Alexander Howard Hannay (1889-1955) was a friend and erstwhile business associate of J. C. Squire, for whose *London Mercury* he was now acting as art critic as well as working at the Chelsea Book Club. He probably met VW at the Squires in 1916 (see *II VW Letters*, no. 810).

10. A wall tablet honouring Henry James, whose funeral took place in Chelsea Old Church in March 1916, speaks of him as 'lover and interpreter of the fine amenities, of brave decisions and generous loyalties'. His ashes were taken to America.

What book can I settle to read? I want something that wont colour my mornings mood—something a little severe. My notion is to write this in chapters straight off; not beginning one unless I can count on so many days clear for finishing it.

Saturday 17 April

The pain from Walkley is dying out, since I've begun Jacob's Room. I can inhibit poor L. as I myself am inhibited. Your trick is repetition, I say: whereupon his pen sticks like a broken machine. To the Bach festival last night; & coincidence led me to run at once into two people I've not met for an age, Noel, for one; then, as I settled into my seat, a voice said Virginia! It was Walter Lamb.[11] The egg shaped man—the billiard ball man—sat by me, & told me a great deal about Bach. Bach was very beautiful, though the human element in the choir always distracts me. *They* aren't beautiful; all in greens, greys, pinks, blacks, fresh from the suburbs & high tea. The hall seemed to suit them better than the music. Home with Walter. "I had such a vivid dream of Thoby the other night" he said. "He came in after beagling, & said, something very important— I can't remember what. Very odd—for I don't think of him often." He was glad to tell me this.[12] I make him tell me about his Royalties. In fact here's a secret that mustn't be repeated—Walter is writing Prince Albert's Academy speech for him.[13] He has a nimble mind, & makes himself much at home in his corner of the world; indeed he's one of the people for whom the world was made the shape it is. I wonder whether admiration of one's own family is snobbish, or somehow the product of love: he seems to love Dorothy & Henry in this particular way.[14]

11. The Bach Festival was at the Central Hall, Westminster, 16-20 April 1920. Noel Olivier (1892-1969) was the youngest of the four Olivier sisters (see above, 10 January 1920, n 11); Adrian Stephen had wanted to marry her, and in consequence she was the one VW knew best. She was now a doctor. Walter Rangeley Maitland Lamb (1882-1968), since 1913 Secretary to the Royal Academy of Arts, had once wished to marry VW. He lived at Kew.

12. Julian Thoby Prinsep Stephen (1880-1906), VW's elder brother, who had died of typhoid fever contracted in Greece; he had been a contemporary of Walter Lamb's at Trinity College, Cambridge.

13. Prince Albert (soon to become Duke of York and later King George VI), second son of King George V, was the guest of honour at the annual Royal Academy Dinner at Burlington House on 1 May 1920. His speech dwelt on village signs and the need for art in the life of the people.

14. Henry was Walter Lamb's younger brother, Dorothy their youngest sister; in 1920 she married John Reeve Brooke, a civil servant.

Tuesday 20 April

Saw the birth of Ka's son in the Times this morning, & feel slightly envious all day in consequence.[15] To the Bach choir last night; but one of our failures. Is it the weather? I'd made out on waking, such a perfect day; & one by one my events missed fire. Such a good morning's writing I'd planned, & wasted the cream of my brain on the telephone. Then the weather; great bouncing gusts all set about with rain soaking one; buses crowded; left typewriting paper in the bus; a long time waiting at the Club—then Bach unaccompanied isn't easy—though at last (after L. had gone home) I was swept up to the heights by a song. Anna Magdalena's song.[16] I walked a few steps beyond Herbert Fisher coming out; followed him across the empty lamplit purlieus of Westminster, saw him step so distinguished, yet to my eye, so empty, into Palace Yard, & so to take part in ruling the Empire. His head bent—legs a little wavering—small feet— I tried to put myself inside him, but could only suppose he thought in an exalted way which to me would be all bunkum. Indeed, I feel this more & more. I've had my dive into their heads & come out again, I think.[17]

I forgot to say how Hussey came on Sunday uninvited, & we took her to Margaret's,[18] & she talked such Stracheyese that I couldn't think much of what she said. Binding Hope now. The books I chose were Berkeley; Maynard; & now they've sent Tchehov's letters, & Barbellion.[19] Never had so few to review—none from The Times (A.B.W[alkley]. perhaps responsible?) none from the Athenaeum; but I've plenty to do all the same.

15. Mark Arnold-Foster was born on 14 April 1920. See also *II VW Letters*, no. 1129.
16. Among the works performed on 19 April by the London Bach Choir were three unaccompanied motets: 'Come, Jesu, come', 'Jesu, priceless treasure', and 'Sing to the Lord'; and the solo 'Bist Du bei mir', no. 25 in the *Klavierbüchlein für Anna Magdalena Bach* of 1725—not by her father J. S. Bach but probably by G. H. Stölzel—sung by Ethel McLelland.
17. Herbert Albert Laurens Fisher (1865-1940), MP, historian, VW's first cousin, had been enticed away from his distinguished academic career in 1916 by Lloyd George to become President of the Board of Education in the wartime Coalition Government; he held the position until 1922.
18. Margaret Caroline Llewelyn Davies (1861-1944), General Secretary of the Women's Co-operative Guild from 1889-1921. She had had a strong influence on the direction of LW's political thought and activity since his marriage to VW, and had been a stalwart friend to both. She lived in Hampstead.
19. 'They' is obscure. George Berkeley (1685-1753), Anglican Bishop of Cloyne in Ireland, philosopher; J. M. Keynes, *The Economic Consequences of the Peace* (1919); a selection of Chekhov's letters translated by Constance Garnett had been published early in 1920; W. P. N. Barbellion's acclaimed *Journal of a Disappointed*

Saturday 24 April

Half blind with writing notices, & corrections in 160 copies of Paris, a Poem, by Hope Mirrlees.[20] Then I've read some Berkeley, whom I much admire, & would like to catch the trick in his style—only I fear its thinking. Reading Maynard too—a book that influences the world without being in the least a work of art: a work of morality, I suppose. Morgan came for a night. Very easy going; as sensitive as a blue butterfly. So I was pleased to write in his birthday book which is one of his tests of niceness.[21] And he's obstinate about 'niceness'—much of a puritan. Tells the truth. I wish I could write his talk down.

I must now write a postcard. Yes, I must really catch the first post if possible. I'll take it myself—Is there time still—I'll tell you what it is. The seat is being painted. The boy is so stupid he'll paint it after its been rained upon. Then it will be ruined.

Nonsense said L. it wont hurt it.

But are you sure? Positive.

Oh then I'll let it alone—if you're quite sure. My mother is having the seat painted green. She wouldn't let me do it, & the boy is dreadfully stupid. I found him putting on the paint without having scraped the old paint off first. &c . . .

This is very like Morgan; so too his reliance on Leonard. "Where d'you get your boots? Are Waterman pens the best."

Wednesday 5 May

We have had a Thursday to Tuesday at Rodmell; which accounts, as I say, making my apology to this book, in which so few pages seem to have been written. As we sat down to dinner on Saturday, Desmond rapped at the door— To follow this up to its source, I should describe dinner at 46: Desmond, Lytton & Mary there; but I don't much like describing dinners at 46.[1] Desmond (this is L.'s saying not mine, & I quote it to avoid speaking grudgingly myself) produces a sense of frowst in the room. It rained; he lay back, smoking cigarettes eating sweets &

Man had appeared shortly before, and his *Enjoying Life* just after, his death in 1919.

20. VW's inked-in corrections are on p 3, a 'St.' inserted before 'John at Patmos'; and on p 22 where the final figure of the inscription '3 rue de Beaune Paris Spring 1916' has been altered to '9'.

21. This was an autograph book, now lost, which Forster invited friends to sign on his birthday.

1. Clive Bell was their host, at 46 Gordon Square.

opening novels which he never read. Being an editor has drugged the remnants of ambition in him, & he is now content. Content is disillusioning to behold: what is there to be content about? It seems, with Desmond now, always afternoon.

We worked at Kot's book. Have I left him out too? His clasp of the hand crushes the little bones: his hand though inches thick is hard as bone, & typifies that dense, solid, concentrated man. He always speaks the truth, & gropes after it in psychology—rather a queer thing to do, & laying waste many a fair garden. As he says a thing, it sounds so convincing. We are publishing Gorki, & perhaps this marks some step over a precipice—I don't know. He analysed Murry in this devastating way. K. is back I suppose;[2] & I amuse myself with playing at the silly game—who's to take the first step: I predict here that perhaps Murry will—if not, we dont meet for a year or two.

But hurry on to the climax— Massingham has offered Leonard Brailsford's post on the Nation—to do the foreign article that is, drawing £400 a year.[3] The drawback is that it means going up every Monday, perhaps Wednesdays, thus ties us tight. If this can be arranged, all else is satisfactory. He could drop his reviewing; do better work; get better pay; & perhaps—my private aim is to drop my reviewing too. But that doesn't matter. I own I like a good compliment to L.: not boastfully; it seems right, I suppose. So now our fortunes look up again. Lytton dined here last night, & seemed confident, happy,—about to begin on Vic. in earnest. Chatto & Windus must have notice in order that they may lay in large stocks of paper in time.

Saturday 8 May[4]

Massingham has postponed seeing L. which may mean that there's some obstacle. Thinking it over, I shouldn't be sorry if it fell through;

2. Samuel Solomonovitch Koteliansky, 'Kot' (1881-1955), an Ukrainian Jew who in 1910 came to study in London and had there remained. He was a close friend of Katherine Mansfield—through whom the Woolfs probably met him—and they had together translated some of Chekhov's papers; he was now collaborating with LW on Maxim Gorky's *Reminiscences of Leo Nicolayevitch Tolstoi* (see *HP Checklist* 10; also *III LW*, 247-53). Katherine had just returned to her and Murry's Hampstead home 'The Elephant' after spending seven months by the Mediterranean because of her ill health.

3. Henry William Massingham (1860-1924), from 1907-23 editor of the Radical weekly *The Nation*, to which Henry Noel Brailsford (1873-1959) regularly contributed articles on foreign affairs. See *III LW*, 185; *IV LW*, 91; also 26 May 1920 below.

4. VW has mis-dated this entry *Sat. May 10th.*

for I cant help suspecting that work of this kind means more of a tie than any money—all the gold of Peru poured into my lap as Miss Mitford says—could repay.[5] Besides, why should I slip the collar round his neck & myself spring free? Partly owing to Lytton, partly to the horror of writing 1, 2, 3, 4, reviews on end, 3 concerning Mitford too, I've been groaning & grumbling, & seeing myself caged, & all my desired ends—Jacob's Room that is—vanishing down avenues. But 1 review weekly won't hurt.

On Wednesday, Walter [Lamb], Adrian & Karin, & Molly Hamilton dined here. A chattering random vivacious evening: I cant remember any scrap of dialogue though. Perhaps with Molly & Karin that's inevitable: Karin deaf of the ears, Molly a little obtuse in the senses. I observe that she scrupulously makes conversation to fill silences with; even though she's nothing to say. Odd to me that life should require 'professional women'. She is reading 500 novels, at 5/- each, for a prize competition; & had a batch of sickly stuff to masticate in the train going home. We discussed politics, A. & I trying to make her define her position; which is visionary. She is bored by the means, but believes in the end. I suppose she'll be Hamilton M.P. one of these days; but the elections go badly for women, & Labour fights shy of them.[6]

Yesterday I had tea with Saxon at the Club; &, remembering old lonely evenings of my own, when the married couple seemed so secure & lamplit, asked him back to dinner. I wonder though whether his loneliness ever frightens him as mine used to frighten me. I daresay office work is a great preservative.[7]

Tuesday 11 May

It is worth mentioning, for future reference, that the creative power which bubbles so pleasantly on beginning a new book quiets down after a time, & one goes on more steadily. Doubts creep in. Then one becomes resigned. Determination not to give in, & the sense of an impending shape keep one at it more than anything. I'm a little anxious.

5. On 5 July 1811 Mary Russell Mitford wrote to her father, Dr Mitford, apropos his financial embarrassments: 'I would not exchange my father, ... for any man on earth, though he could pour all the gold of Peru into my lap.' This is (mis-) quoted by Constance Hill in *Mary Russell Mitford and her Surroundings* which VW reviewed for the *TLS* of 6 May 1920 (Kp C192); for the *Daily Herald* of 26 May 1920 (Kp C192.1); and for the *Athenaeum* of 28 May 1920 (Kp C194).

6. She became Labour MP for Blackburn from 1929-31.

7. Saxon Sydney-Turner (see Appendix I) was a civil servant in the Treasury.

How am I to bring off this conception? Directly one gets to work one is like a person walking, who has seen the country stretching out before. I want to write nothing in this book that I dont enjoy writing. Yet writing is always difficult.

L. is up in London seeing his constituents.[8] Eight gentlemen are waiting on him to learn his views. Then he's having tea with Kot. He has a meeting (I think) won't be home till late. I spent the afternoon typing & setting up Morgan's story.[9] Went out to buy a bun, called on Miss Milan about the chair covers, & when I've done this, I shall read Berkeley. At 2.15 Lady Cynthia Curzon was married to Captain Mosley.[10] Though it was summer till 3.30, it is now brushed with blackness, & I must shut the window & put on my jersey. Nessa comes back on Friday. Clive & Mary are in Paris. Then, I had tea with A. & K. on Sunday & saw all the children—Judith a great lump of a child; Ann with a look of the Watts' drawing of mother; yet both a good deal like Costelloes.[11] I like coming back to Richmond after Gordon Sqre. I like continuing our private life, unseen by anyone. Murry has asked me to write stories for the Athenaeum. No mention of K[atherine]'s wishing to see me.

Thursday 13 May

I open this in order to say that I had tea with Dora at the Club & was introduced to Mr Harold Banks.[12] Who is he? Well, all the voices of the world will thunder in reply Banks! Thats his view of it anyhow.

8. LW was asked to stand for Parliament in 1918 (see *I VW Diary*, 27 July 1918), but didn't; he later agreed to be the Labour Party candidate for the Combined English Universities—all the English Universities other than Oxford and Cambridge—and was adopted later in May; see below, 26 May 1920; also *IV LW*, 33.
9. *The Story of the Siren*, published in July 1920 (*HP Checklist* 9).
10. Miss Milan is metamorphose into a dressmaker in VW's story 'The New Dress'. (See *A Haunted House*, p 46). Lady Cynthia Curzon, second daughter of Earl Curzon of Kedleston, married Mr Oswald Mosley, MP, in the Chapel Royal, St James's, on 11 May.
11. Vanessa Bell had been in Italy with Duncan Grant and Maynard Keynes since the end of March, leaving her three children in the care of the old Stephen family cook Sophie Farrell at 50 Gordon Square—Adrian and Karin Stephen's house. Ann (b. 1916) and Judith (1918-1972) were the Stephen children; their mother was born Costelloe. G. F. Watts' drawing of Julia Jackson as a child belonged to VW.
12. Anna Dorothea (Dora) Sanger, *née* Pease (1865-1955) was of a Quaker family; she had been at Newnham, and was then a teacher before marrying C. P. Sanger in 1900. She suffered from severe arthritis, and was a zealous worker for humane causes. Mr Harold Banks has not been identified.

Figure a sandy florid broad faced man; talking with an American (really Australian) accent. Shirt with black lines. A pleasant smile. Eating steadily. Dora provided bread & butter. 'No thank you I don't smoke . . .' "What *is* your plan exactly Mr Banks?" To tide over the revolution by the cooperation of the middle classes . . . Yes, but thats a little vague— A great many people wish to do that but— Well I'm here to do it Mrs Sanger—I don't want to talk about my Russian experiences. I want to see whether I can get the middle classes with me. If not, I go to Scotland & speak in the streets— A very good idea, I'm sure—but *what* are you going to say? We want a change of government, Mrs Sanger— So many of us feel— Ah, but you English do nothing. You English & the French hold up the whole European movement. When the revolution comes— And when will it come? Within 5 years— you don't believe it?

But why not write this down? I don't believe in writing. I talk to the people. Organisation. Cooperation. Middle classes. The people. I shall do it—I'm going to do it. Organisation— There ought not to be a single horse in the streets— Look at your docks— Then these buildings ought to be turned into homes— What can we do without— The middle classes should come together—I've the programme ready—& Revolution is coming without a doubt.

Why do I disbelieve in Revolution—partly because of Mr Banks perhaps.

Saturday 15 May

Accurately described, today is a fine spring day, not a hot summer day—so L. & I shaded it off, walking up to the Park this afternoon. But Richmond on fine Saturdays is like a lime tree in full flower—suppose one were an insect sitting on the flower. All the others swarm & buzz, & burble. Being residents we don't, of course.

A letter from Madge this morning, asking me to review her novel: a letter from Fisher Unwin offering to give me a copy. Such is the morality of a woman who won't pollute her sons by staying at Charleston.[13] I meant to say how we sat on the grass above the cedars & watched the deer; how I noticed the semi-transparent beauty of a parasol in the sun

13. Margaret (Madge) Vaughan, *née* Symonds (1869-1925), wife of VW's cousin W. W. Vaughan the Master of Wellington College. In her youth VW had romanticised and revered her; but recently Madge had reneged on her agreement to rent Charleston while Vanessa was abroad, as her husband disapproved of Vanessa's liaison with Duncan Grant. Her book, *A Child of the Alps*, was published in 1920 by Thomas Fisher Unwin.

—how the air has this tenderness now that coloured dresses seem to glow in it. A long flattering review of me in the Nation, wiping out Massingham's bitterness, & giving me my first taste of intelligent criticism, so I'm set up—even contemplate thanking the writer.[14]

Flora & George dined here last night, ostensibly to discuss Clara [Woolf], really to tell us the simple fact that she's going to America, & may stay there permanently.[15] Can one imagine anything less desirable than to be a person who may stay permanently in America—& its hoped she does. The slightness of human relations often appals me. One doesn't mind in the least whether she disappears for ever. This doesn't apply to everyone I admit. I'm a little fidgety because Nessa hasn't rung me up— probably she came back last night. I liked George more than I expected. A sandy salty looking youth, unambitious, lean, humorous, decided, content to be a schoolmaster for ever, so long as he doesn't become headmaster. He talked about Sussex, the small owls, & the long eared owls; also the war; he was through it all; never wounded, & saw Damascus. He said the men are very unselfish but boring, because they can talk on so few subjects. How nice, I often think, normal people are!

Tuesday 18 May

Gordon Square begins again & like a snake renews its skin outworn— that's the nearest I can come to a quotation.[16] Gordon Square different —like a looking glass version of 46. You are let in, by a strange servant, go up bare steps, hear children crying at various stages, go up & up—till you reach what is, in the real Gordon Square, servants bedrooms— There's an open door to be passed first, though, & Sophie inside, & one who, beneath a weight of flesh & bone proved to have

14. An unsigned review by Robert Lynd of *Night and Day* appeared in the *Nation* of 15 May under the title 'A Tragic Comedienne'; the reviewer concluded that VW's talent was 'so splendid in its richness and fine in its quality that half of it will go as far as the talents of ten less gifted writers.' VW's grudge against Massingham arose from his 'Wayfarer' paragraph in the *Nation* of 29 November 1919. See *I VW Diary*, 5 December 1919.

15. Flora (1886-1975) *née* Woolf, LW's youngest sister, and her husband George Sturgeon.

16.   'The world's great age begins anew,
        The golden years return,
      The earth doth like a snake renew
        Her winter weeds outworn.'

                        Shelley, *Hellas*, I, 1060

the body of Annie Chart in her.[17] Nessa is right at the top. Well we talked till I left at 8; interrupted though by Lytton, Angelica, & Julian. When Stella came back from Italy there were always a great many presents.[18] So now I was given a hat, a brooch, & paper. Lytton said that James & Alix are to be married in 3 weeks. So after all, she has won.[19] But though satisfactory, I find no excitement in this. They know each other too well to stir one's imagination thinking of their future, as one does with most engagements. Then, talk talk; & as we were despatching the superficial & reaching the easy-intimate, I had to tear off, in the rain, to Wigmore Hall. Sat between Oliver & Saxon; & these musical people dont listen as I do, but critically, superciliously, without programmes.[20]

Today Campbell has been to lunch.[21] Told stories of Palestine. I like thinking I hear men speaking alone. How his general taught him to ride. "No need to say clk clk—you're not talking to a canary." C. dresses like a gentleman, & L. could say to him that he believed nothing without making him deny it. Little romance about the church: then I don't see how they go through with it. How get through the service?—for you can't gibe at God as one does at an editor— The worst of it must be that there's no shop about God—I suppose not at least. Logan came on Sunday, & amused me for an hour. Told us about Christ, & his travels —but if you're not amused by Logan, you're irritated. So, alas, we begin to find; since his book flags & we run risk of losing money by it. A bad

17. Annie Chart had been cook to the Woolfs at Asheham in 1914, and at Hogarth House during VW's illness in 1915; she subsequently became cook to Maynard Keynes at 46 Gordon Square.

18. VW's half-sister Stella Duckworth (1869-97), only daughter of their mother by her first husband, who was rather well-off. Stella had married J. W. Hills in 1897 and died a few months later.

19. See *I VW Diary*, 30 October 1918: 'Alix is ready... to begin her autumn campaign, which Oliver bets that she will win.' Alix Sargant-Florence and James Strachey were married on 4 June 1920, her twenty-eighth birthday. Oliver Strachey (1874-1960), who from 1914 worked as a cryptographer in the Foreign Office, was an elder brother of James and Lytton; at one time he had hoped to become a musician.

20. VW's visit to the Wigmore Hall was probably a consequence of Saxon having had tea at Hogarth House on Sunday; the Franco-Czech programme of works by César Franck, Dvořák and Ravel was given by the Bohemian String Quartet with Fanny Davies at the piano.

21. The Rev. Hon. Leopold Colin Henry Douglas Campbell-Douglas (1881-1940) had been a friend of LW's since University. During the war he had been a Chaplain to the Forces, and was now Vicar of Padbury in Buckinghamshire. In 1937 he was to succeed a brother as 6th Baron Blythswood.

review in the Times, another in Athenaeum; no rush of orders. Hope dribbles along, but she is a negligeable matter.[22]

Thursday 20 May

I'm filling my empty tank as fast as I can—for some reason, I've been in after tea lately, too lazy to read Greek, & rejected by the Times, though not by the Woman's Times, by the by. A light article needed on Psychology of War Widows.[23] All the burden & glory of reviewing falls on L. & I get on with Jacob—the most amusing novel writing I've done, I think; in the doing I mean. Up yesterday with peonies to Nessa; heard of the mysterious letters from the grave (but this story isn't recorded—her maids disasters) also the money difficulties which threaten Maynard & through him, her.[24] Gambling on the exchange is the technical name of it, & things rising for the moment, he loses. The question is how long he can hold out; triumph certain in the end, a crash that is. The war has put its skeleton fingers even into our pockets.

Then I went on with L. to dine with the Coles in Chelsea—[25]The Coles are Webbs in embryo—with differences of course. I'm used to being at ease with clever young men, & to find myself stumped, caught

22. Logan Pearsall Smith (1865-1946), born in New Jersey, educated at Harvard and Oxford, naturalised British in 1913; a 'mandarin of the art of letters'. The Hogarth Press had just published his *Stories from the Old Testament* (*HP Checklist* 11), which was reviewed at length in the *TLS* of 13 May, and briefly in the *Athenaeum* of 14 May 1920—both unfavourably. Reaction to Hope Mirrlees' *Paris, a Poem* ranged from the condemnatory in the *TLS* of 6 May to the more appreciative *Athenaeum* of 21 May 1920.

23. From June 1920 until January 1921 *The Times* published a bi-monthly *Woman's Supplement*, price 1/6. There were no contributions by VW.

24. On Vanessa's return from Italy on 14 May she found her housemaid Mary was in an infirmary having been driven off her head by the sudden deaths, all within a fortnight, of her mother, father, and lover, and the near-death of her brother from pneumonia. She recovered, and returned to work for Vanessa on 18 May. (Letter from Vanessa Bell to Roger Fry, 17 May 1920, CH Camb.) But see also below, 8 June 1920.

   After his resignation from the Treasury the previous summer, Keynes had developed a flair for profitable currency speculation, which he also used for the benefit of Duncan Grant and Vanessa. In Italy, they had spent lavishly on picture frames, furniture and pottery, but on his return to England, Keynes found that an unforeseen upheaval in the world money market had brought them all to the brink of ruin. He did however manage to save their capital.

25. George Douglas Howard Cole (1889-1959) and his wife Margaret Isabel, *née* Postgate (b. 1893), were active socialist intellectuals working for the Labour Research Department. They lived in Bramerton Street, off the King's Road, Chelsea.

out, leg before the wicket at every turn is not pleasant. Never was there such a quick, hard, determined young man as Cole; covering his Labour sympathies, which are I suppose intellectual, with the sarcasm & sneers of Oxford. Then there's a bust of W[illiam]. Morris on the side board, too much to eat, Morris curtains, all the works of all the classics, & Cole & Mrs hopping on the surface like a couple of Cockney sparrows incapable of more than pecks & sips which they do too skilfully for my taste. The whole effect as of electric light full in the eyes—unbecoming at my age. I think the irritation rose partly from a sense that his cleverness was inaccessible. Then they call each other 'darling'. Then there were Mr & Mrs Mair, from Government offices, jokes about Beveridge & Shaw, & David Mair subsiding into complete silence in the background till taken home by his broad browed, loquacious wife in the rag[g]ed [?] petticoat.[26] One can see Mrs Cole rapidly becoming the cleverish elderly fox terrier type of intellectual woman—as it is not a shade or valley in her mind. Cole, grinning like a gutterpipe demon took us to the door—so spry, alert, virile, & ominous.

I have written to Katherine. No answer. Mr Lynd reviewed me in the Nation.[27]

Monday 24 May

A real Bank Holiday—blazing weather—sound of buses unceasing—crowds like queues in the streets—& we spent it properly going to Hurlingham to see polo, of which I must make this rapid note. You get the impression that the turf is india rubber—so lightly do the horses spring—touching it & up again—Captain Lockit galloping down with his stick like a Persian rider with a lance.[28] A large white ball is then thrown in the midst. The horses twirl & dart, dance their paws, twist on their tails like cats; almost like long lean cats their scamper after the ball; only as they come past you hear a roar in the nostrils. But the

26. David Beveridge Mair (d. 1942), Director of Examinations in the Civil Service Commission, and his wife Janet, née Philip (1876-1959), who worked as a temporary civil servant until in 1919 she became Secretary of the London School of Economics, of which her husband's cousin William Henry Beveridge (1879-1963) was Director from 1919-37. This close association culminated in their marriage after David Mair's death.
27. See above, 15 May 1920, n 14. Robert Wilson Lynd (1879-1949), literary journalist and essayist, from 1912 onwards literary editor of the *Daily News* (which in 1930 became the *News Chronicle*), and regular contributor to weekly journals.
28. The Woolfs watched the England polo team's first trial of the season, against the Old Cantabs, at Hurlingham. Major V. N. Lockett played 'back' for England; the result was a 7-goal draw.

bounce & agility of them all knotted together pawing the ball with their feet indescribable; passing in a second from full gallop to delicate ⟨dribbling⟩ trot as the ball is dribbled almost between their feet. This is the game of the officers of England. Each had 8 ponies, & one lasted in this frenzy of freshness only 7 minutes. Anyhow it was well worth seeing. A very large ground. The elect in a shelter; public squatting on grass, or on chairs. The horses become suddenly big when they gallop straight at you & their pace alarming. At a little distance the most graceful & controlled of movements.

Summer has set in two days ago. Yesterday for the first time we lunched out of doors. The Swedes came.[29] Affable conversation. She a painter, a cool friendly Scandinavian, highly enlightened; but I suppose there's some lack of temperament in the enlightened races.

Wednesday 26 May

Running through this I see I've left out one or two important pieces in the mosaic. Massingham has written to ask L. to act as 2nd string in the foreign dept. during vacations, which we interpret to mean that Goldie has taken the 1st string.[30] This suits us on the whole better than t'other. Then L. has been adopted as the Labour candidate of the 7 Universities; may even be writing his letter of acceptance upstairs now. We are having the kitchen re-built at a cost of £80 at Monks House. And the night Morgan & Nessa dined here we saw a fire. Three minutes of excitement—great flames shooting up behind the playground; then a glow as of red yellow gauze, with sparks rising & falling; then a lovely sight when the hose shot into the air, wrapping itself in light & soaring like a rocket. A pouring crackling noise all the time, & now & then wood crashing in. L. went out; & many people came trotting along in mackintoshes; 12 o'clock being struck. The woman next door, wife of the fire-captain, rushed off distracted, & came home in tears, (so the servants say—they sat up, of course). And then I'm reviewed in the New Republic with high praise—indeed no blame.[31] Is this typical of America

---

29. Charlotte Mannheimer, *née* Abrahamson, LW's first cousin on his mother's side, was married to a Swedish MP; she and her daughter Gertrude were visiting England, and lunched with the Woolfs on Sunday.
30. See above, 5 May 1920. Goldsworthy ('Goldie') Lowes Dickinson (1862-1932), Fellow of King's College, Cambridge, teacher, humanist and passionate advocate of international co-operation. He contributed to but did not write regularly for the *Nation*.
31. *The Voyage Out* and *Night and Day* were very favourably reviewed by Constance Mayfield Rourke in the *New Republic*, New York, on 5 May 1920.

—more cordial to the English than we are to ourselves? This morning Katherine writes a stiff & formal note thanking me for my kind post card, & saying she will be delighted to see me, though 'grown *very* dull'. What does this mean—*she* hurt with *me?* Anyhow I go on Friday to find out, unless stopped as is always possible. I praised her story warmly; sincerely too.[32]

Monday 31 May

Back from Monk's an hour ago, after the first week end—the most perfect, I was going to say, but how can I tell what week ends we mayn't spend there? The first pure joy of the garden I mean. Wind enough outside; within sunny & sheltered; & weeding all day to finish the beds in a queer sort of enthusiasm which made me say this is happiness. Gladioli standing in troops: the mock orange out. Kitchen wall battered down. We were out till 9 at night, though the evening was cold. Both stiff & scratched all over today; with chocolate earth in our nails. Then the halt has started again; we went into Lewes for the first time since the war. Gunn rode across the level crossing with his great bob tailed dog. The Thomases were on the platform: poor little draggle tail sisters, scarcely holding to their ladyhood any longer. Thomas affable & kindly to the men, telling them, in a sermonical voice, about the water spout at Louth. "Very se-e-erious, many lives lost, & a quarter of a million damage", as if to conciliate them; no teeth in his upper jaw. Gunn cantered through the water meadows, his mare 'very clever at the gates, but she won't stand still' as the Miss T.'s said, these things interesting them more than water spouts.[33]

I had my interview with K.M. on Friday. A steady discomposing

32. Katherine Mansfield wrote from 2 Portland Villas ('the Elephant'): 'Dear Virginia It's very kind of you to have sent me a card. Yes, I'm back in England until August. I would be delighted if you'd care to come & see me one afternoon, but I am grown *very* dull.' Her story was 'The Man without a Temperament' published in *Art & Letters*, Spring 1920 (reprinted in *Bliss and Other Stories*, 1920).

33. Rodmell and Southease Halt was on the Newhaven and Seaford branch line from Lewes; it adjoined a level crossing. The Woolfs had had to vacate Asheham House in 1919 in order that Frank Gunn, bailiff of the neighbouring farms, might live there. The Rev. Walter Webb Thomas was Rector of Southease (population 69) from 1904-44; he lived with his two sisters. The town of Louth in Lincolnshire had been hit by a freak cloudburst on Sunday 30 May; more than twenty people lost their lives in the floods which resulted, and damage to property was estimated at between quarter and half a million pounds.

formality & coldness at first. Enquiries about house & so on. No pleasure
or excitement at seeing me. It struck me that she is of the cat kind: alien,
composed, always solitary & observant. And then we talked about solitude, & I found her expressing my feelings, as I never heard them expressed. Whereupon we fell into step, & as usual, talked as easily as
though 8 months were minutes—till Murry came in with a pair of blue
& pink Dresden candle pieces: "How *very* nice" she said. "But do fetch
the candles." "Virginia, how *awful* what am I to say? He has spent £5
on them" she said, as he left the room. I see that they're often hostile.
For one thing—Murry's writing. "Did you like C. & A.?" No, I didn't.
"Neither did I. But I thought D. of an I. too dreadful—wrong— Its very
very difficult, often . . ."[34] Then Murry came back. We chatted as usual.
Aldous was our butt. Aldous has brought out Leda: will the public
canonise him too?[35] But Murry going at length, K. & I once more got
upon literature. Question of her stories. This last one, Man without a
T., is her first in the new manner. She says she's mastered something—is
beginning to do what she wants. Prelude a coloured post card. Her
reviews mere scribbling without a serious thought in them. And Sullivan's
praise in the A[thenaeum]. detestable to her.[36] A queer effect she produces
of someone apart, entirely self-centred; altogether concentrated upon her
'art': almost fierce to me about it, I pretending I couldn't write. "What
else is there to do? We have got to do it. Life—" then how she tells
herself stories at night about all the lives in a town. "Its a spring night.
I go down to the docks—I hear the travellers say—" acting it in her
usual way, & improvising. Then asked me to write stories for the A.
"But I don't know that I can write stories" I said, honestly enough,
thinking that in her view, after her review of me, anyhow, those were
her secret sentiments. Whereupon she turned on me, & said no one else
could write stories except me—Kew [Gardens] the right 'gesture'; a
turning point— Well but Night & Day? I said, though I hadn't meant
to speak of it.

'An amazing achievement' she said. Why, we've not had such a thing
since I don't know when—,

34. John Middleton Murry's verse drama *Cinnamon and Angelica* ('why these grocery
names?' asked T. S. Eliot) was published in the spring of 1920; 'The Defeat of
the Imagination' written in 1918 was republished late in 1919 in the collection of
his essays *The Evolution of an Intellectual*.

35. *Leda and Other Poems* by Aldous Huxley was published in May 1920. Huxley
was one of Murry's assistants on the editorial staff of the *Athenaeum* from the end
of April 1919 to October 1920.

36. See above, 10 April 1920, n 6. Katherine Mansfield's *Prelude* had been hand-
printed by the Woolfs and published in July 1918 (*HP Checklist* 2).

But I thought you didn't like it?[37]

Then she said she could pass an examination in it. Would I come & talk about it—lunch—so I'm going to lunch; but what does her reviewing mean then?—or is she emotional with me? Anyhow, once more as keenly as ever I feel a common certain understanding between us—a queer sense of being 'like'—not only about literature—& I think it's independent of gratified vanity. I can talk straight out to her.

Saturday 5 June

Here we are in the prime of the year which I've thought of so often in January & December, always with pleasure; so that even if June's bad, one has had more pleasure from it than from all the other months. Is that cynical? What I believe is that one brings out the taste of the month one's in by opposing to it another. But to think of December now gives me no pleasure. I've gone back into winter clothes; its bitter windy; & the sun sparks & glints instead of burning. It burnt on Derby day though [*Wednesday 2 June*]—the day I lunched with K.M. & had 2 hours priceless talk—priceless in the sense that to no one else can I talk in the same disembodied way about writing; without altering my thought more than I alter it in writing here. (I except L. from this). We talked about books, writing of course: my own. N. & D. a first rate novel, she said. The suppression in it puzzling, but accounted for by circumstances. Then I said 'You've changed. Got through something;' indeed theres a sort of self command about her as if having mastered something subterfuges were no longer so necessary. She told me of her terrific experiences last winter—experience of loneliness chiefly; alone (or only with 'Leslie Moor' alias Ida Baker) in a stone house with caverns beneath it into which the sea rushed: how she lay on bed alone all day with a pistol by her; & men banged at the door. Sydney wrote '*Stick it out*' twice, underlined.[1]

37. Katherine Mansfield had reviewed *Night and Day* in the *Athenaeum* of 26 November 1919 (see *I VW Diary*, 28 November 1919). She had written of it to Murry (10 November 1919): 'I don't like it. My private opinion is that it is a lie in the soul.'

1. Katherine Mansfield had spent four months the previous winter at Ospedaletti on the Italian Riviera a few miles from the French frontier, with Ida Constance Baker (or 'LM') as her ever-faithful but intellectually inadequate companion, literally facing death. A crisis of despair had followed Murry's Christmas visit, when she acknowledged that his support was insufficient for her emotional and physical needs. See *Katherine Mansfield: The Memories of LM*, 1971, and *Katherine Mansfield, Letters and Journals*, edited by C. K. Stead, 1977. Sydney Waterlow was Katherine's cousin; he was lodging with Murry at 'The Elephant'.

Murry sent a balance sheet of his accounts: came at Christmas with plum pudding & curd cheese; 'Now I'm here, its all right'. Then she went to him for assurance; didn't get it; & will never look for that particular quality again. I see what she means, vaguely. She is nervous about her book coming out; fearing lest she hasn't done enough.[2] What she feels exactly for fame & criticism, I don't know; but then in our perhaps too exalted talk, this is not very exactly told. Anyhow, I enjoyed myself; & this fragmentary intermittent intercourse of mine seems more fundamental than many better established ones.

I dined last night with Walter Lamb & Mrs Madan at Hounslow. In this old manor house (cream coloured & black) Miss Arnold used to lie drunk.[3] The high rooms are mostly panelled, or papered with Chinese papers. Outside there is a square garden, all its hair flowing in the wind. It was a cold night, & poor Mrs M. crouched in one room, near the flaring grass, supported by rich volumes, apparently not reading, nor sewing, nor talking, her husband away, & the people of Hounslow vicious & hostile. A kind of echo of great luxury everywhere, as becomes the daughter of Mrs Saxton Noble. Much talk of royalties, she & W. moving in the same sphere. One Princess, Marie Louise, lodges, for months now, in Kent House, & has driven away Mr & Master Noble. She keeps royal state with a maid of honour.[4] The atmosphere of this struck me greatly; the unreality. Then her efforts to join the King's private view of the R.A. Something 18th century in it; a taste of patrons & back stair intrigue. Mrs M. was a sharp shrewd unpretentious young woman, going to have a baby, entirely fed on chopped hay, I should guess, but not servile; only not happy, & never will be, I suppose, since one could detect that her husband filled no important place. They started life in this Hounslow farm 10 months ago. "But what a splendid beginning for married life!" I said. "Indeed it isn't!" she replied. Geoffrey had gone off, & taken the

2. Constable & Co had agreed in February to publish a collection of Katherine Mansfield's stories; *Bliss and other Stories* appeared in December 1920.

3. Mrs Madan, *née* Marjorie Florence Noble, elder daughter of Saxton William Armstrong Noble, the wealthy director of armament firms and his wife Celia, a noted hostess and patron of the arts. In 1919 she had married Geoffrey Spencer Madan (1895-1947); their daughter was born in December 1920. She was living at The Old Manor House (now demolished) at Whitton, near Hounslow, of which the previous tenant had been Miss Ethel M. Arnold, an eccentric younger sister of Mrs Humphry Ward.

4. H.H. Princess Marie Louise (1872-1956), a grand-daughter of Queen Victoria, after the annulment of her marriage in 1900 devoted her life to furthering charitable causes. Towards the end of the war she was offered the use of Kent House, Knightsbridge, by the Nobles, and spent two years there.

key of the port. The discomfort of the third rate (W.L. that is) became acute before the evening was over; like something out of tune. Something slate grey & furtive among innocent leaves.

Tuesday 8 June

It is quite right to think of June in December, save that its a little over-fresh today, almost as if there were Brighton sea round the corner. One of my field days yesterday—National Gallery—there met Clive— ices at Gunters—much of a spectacle—old black & white lady with a confidante observing manners & customs, benevolently, amused. Young man with a back like a clothes' horse hung with perfect grey clothes— lithe women or girls with transparent legs tripping down into the shady caves—ices sucked or sipped in the strangest silence—two young ladies with their mother eating in complete silence: not a spark of life, properly dressed, from the country perhaps. But don't mothers & daughters ever talk? Would a young man have waked them? I could not say what went forward in those mute minds. Dine with Nessa. The whole story of Mary was told me—a complete case of servant's hysteria; all coming, I think, from her wishing to act a day dream, & then, poor creature, stepping too far & believing it, & now babbling in St Pancras Infirmary.[5] The sight of her taken off was sinister; & all the servants were looking from all the windows. What horrid people they are! This made my drive to Waterloo on top of a bus very vivid. A bright night; with a fresh breeze. An old beggar woman, blind, sat against a stone wall in Kingsway holding a brown mongrel in her arms & sang aloud.[6] There was a recklessness about her; much in the spirit of London. Defiant—almost gay, clasping her dog as if for warmth. How many Junes has she sat there, in the heart of London? How she came to be there, what scenes she can go through, I can't imagine. O damn it all, I say, why cant I know all that too? Perhaps it was the song at night that seemed strange; she was singing shrilly, but for her own amusement, not begging. Then the fire engines came by—shrill too; with their helmets pale yellow in the moonlight. Sometimes every thing gets into the same mood; how to define this one I don't know— It was gay, & yet terrible & fearfully vivid. Nowadays I'm often overcome by London; even think of the dead who have walked in the city. Perhaps one might visit ⟨city⟩ the churches.

5. See above, 20 May 1920, n 24. Mary's bereavements had been a complete fabrication. See also *II QB*, 73 and David Garnett, *The Flowers of the Forest*, 1955, pp 211-14.
6. Cf *Jacob's Room*, p 66.

The view of the grey white spires from Hungerford Bridge brings it to me: & yet I can't say what 'it' is.

Thursday 17 June

Today is Cup day at Ascot; which I think marks the highest tide of the finest societies greatest season—all superlatives that mean little to me—save as I catch the hum of wheels in Piccadilly on a fine afternoon, & passing carriages look in & see powdered faces like jewels in glass cases. One must be young to feel the stir of it. We are on the road to Ascot. Open taxis go past; or motor cars like engines on the Great Western Railway. Yet the fine weather gives us too our sudden acceleration: dinner parties; memoir club; invitations; coming one on top of another. And now I cannot describe Mrs Mirrlees, & my dinner at the Rubens Hotel, in the heart of a rich warm hearted British family, untouched in any way since 100 years ago. Civilisation having produced that organism, stereotyped it. Booths are of the same species. I wonder whether its natural for families to keep together. I didn't wonder, though, that night. Unlimited silver flowed out of Sneezer's pockets.[7]

Next day I lunched at Gordon Sqre for Roger's show:[8] got stuffed in the head with wine & talk & sat there not very comfortably. A toast to Roger missed fire somewhat—so, I fear, do the pictures, which fill 3 rooms garishly, as with coloured sheets of tin, not one being yet bought. Lytton & I stood in a window, & looked (at least I looked) at a woman brushing her hair, high up in some by street, & silence descended. "Is there enough to say?" Lytton asked, referring to my gay life. I said no. It scarcely went round. Then he told me how he lived for ambition; he wants influence not fame; not Maynard's influence, but the influence of some old gentleman on whose 80th birthday people present addresses— he wants to deal little words that poison vast monsters of falsehood. This I declared to be unattainable. But I believe it to be what he wishes. Tea at Gunters; dinner at Nessa's; & so home, a little bruised about the lips, thirsty for a great draught of solitude, which was not given me; since we dined next with the Murrys, next with Roger, & last night had the Memoir Club here, of which I'm too sleepy to give any notice. Leonard is dining with the Society, which I believe I enjoy more than

7. Mrs Mirrlees, *née* Emily Moncrieff (d. 1948), was Hope's mother; 'Sneezer' a brother. The Rubens Hotel is in Buckingham Palace Road, opposite the Royal Mews.
8. Roger Fry's exhibition was at the Independent Gallery, 7a Grafton Street; he showed 114 works, and by 20 June had sold one picture and five little studies. See *II RF Letters*, nos. 476-478.

he does, since I shall lie in the shallow light waiting for him; then he will come in; then I shall hear the gossip.

Wednesday 23 June

I lay in the shallow light, which should be written dark, I think, a long time, & then Moore came & took a cold bath at 1 in the morning, consequently I was too muddled next morning to follow his explanation of Berkeley.[9] He has grown grey, sunken, toothless perhaps. His eyes small, watchful, but perhaps not so piercing as of old. A lack of mass, somewhere. He went off to take 'my baby for a walk'. I dont see altogether why he was the dominator & dictator of youth. Perhaps Cambridge is too much of a cave. Yet (I don't attempt to balance this properly) of course there's his entire innocency & shrewdness; not the vestige of falsehood obscuring him anywhere.

I was struggling, at this time to say honestly that I don't think Conrad's last book a good one. I have said it.[10] It is painful (a little) to find fault there, where almost solely, one respects. I cant help suspecting the truth to be that he never sees anyone who knows good writing from bad, & then being a foreigner, talking broken English, married to a lump of a wife, he withdraws more & more into what he once did well, only piles it on higher & higher, until what can one call it but stiff melodrama. I would not like to find The Rescue signed Virginia Woolf. But will anyone agree with this?—anyhow nothing shakes my opinion of a book —nothing—nothing. Only perhaps if its the book of a young person— or of a friend—no, even so, I think myself infallible. Haven't I lately dismissed Murry's play, & exactly appraised K.'s story, & summed up Aldous Huxley, & doesn't it somehow wound my sense of fitness to hear Roger mangling these exact values?[11] Poor Roger has only sold 3 or 4 sketches. There the innumerable pictures hang, like ugly girls at a

9. George Edward Moore (1873-1958), philosopher, Fellow of Trinity College and University Lecturer in Moral Science at Cambridge. His book, *Principia Ethica* (1903) had been a potent influence on his brothers in The Society (the Apostles), the annual dinner of which LW and he had attended on 17 June. He had married in 1916 and his elder son Nicholas was born in November 1918.

10. 'A Disillusioned Romantic', VW's review of Joseph's Conrad *The Rescue*, was published in the *TLS* of 1 July 1920 (Kp C197). In it she draws the conclusion that the novel is not in the final analysis a success 'because Mr Conrad has attempted a romantic theme and in the middle his belief in romance has failed him'.

11. VW did not publish her opinions on Murry's *Cinammon and Angelica* nor Katherine Mansfield's story 'The Man without a Temperament'; her review of *Limbo* by Aldous Huxley appeared in the *TLS* of 5 February 1920 (Kp C184).

dance, & no one bids a penny piece. According to Nessa, he can talk of nothing else, & they're at their wits ends to say the right things— since what is to be said, save that bad pictures don't sell?

I had one of my last teas at 5 Windmill Hill on Sunday, & though it was the last, it was not very agreeable.[12] (That I see is not the way I mean to put it—but a merry go round playing incessantly distracts me). Emphie I suppose interrupted 10 times. Janet reverted to details of selling furniture & the change to the country as if it weighed on her & she sought by making it all sound nice to convince herself. Then in would pop E. with a tea cup or a plated urn for me to look at. "Then we've decided about Cellini & the Bible?" she would ask, which meant more explanations & diversions. I don't know what I wanted to talk about—anything, I suppose, in preference to what was fairly exactly nothing. Then the level downpour of the rain was depressing too; & didn't I come home to find that Nelly had declared herself dying, sent for another doctor, & had entirely ruined poor L.'s evening. She's still in bed, seemingly ill as we were at Xmas; only now cheerful & sensible, & possibly to go home tomorrow, when we go to Monk's House. Each time one looks forward to that more; & its blazing hot; every plant with a frill of red & white even here; the new kitchen to be seen, all of which I must leave to describe later.

Tuesday 29 June

Back from Rodmell, which was disappointing, as if held to our lips the cup of pleasure was dashed from them. We started by cutting down the laurel hedge, enthusiastically, clearing a view of the downs. Next morning L.'s arm was bad again, & so it continued, swollen & irritable, rasping every moment that should have been so delicious. The weather brooded heavy too. One day was consumed by Saxon & Barbara.[13] Poor Barbara has the prominent nose & fixed lines of premature maturity. Such a grind & a drudge her life is as fills me with pity—seeing human

12. Janet Elizabeth Case (1862-1937), classical scholar and teacher, had taught VW Greek at the beginning of the century, and had become a trusted and respected friend. She lived with her sister Emphie in Hampstead, but her poor health had determined her upon removing to the country.

13. Barbara Bagenal, *née* Hiles (b. 1891), a very pretty and good-natured pre-war Slade student who had become a devotee of 'Bloomsbury', and for whom Saxon Sydney-Turner cherished a life-long but ineffectual adoration. She had worked briefly for the Woolfs as a type-setter in the Hogarth Press, and early in 1918 had married Nicholas Beauchamp Bagenal (1891-1974), at that time in the Irish Guards, but who was now finishing his studies at Wye Agricultural College. Their daughter Judith had been born in November 1918.

life a thing to be put through the machine by necessity. For she seemed to have no choice. First Nick, then the child—& all her lines laid down for her for life, by the hand of fate, for she can't leap them. There she treads her road. Our generation is daily scourged by the bloody war. Even I scribble reviews instead of novels because of the thick skulls at Westminster & Berlin. Saxon was airy & sprightly. The kitchen a success I think, but then I'm not a cook. Home yesterday, to find Lottie with her exaggerated forebodings—Nelly taken worse, & so on, all in an alarmist strain, until having secured her sensation she condescended to details which are not very alarming. But the poor wretches seek to protect themselves from faultfinding by so many prevarications that the truth always cowers close to the ground.

Dinner with Nessa last night. My attempt[s] at sensation were over-shadowed by her really great & surprising one—nothing less than the death of a young man at Mrs Russell's dance.[14] They sat out on the roof, protected by fairy lamps & chairs. He crossed, perhaps to light a cigarette, stepped over the edge, & fell 30 feet onto flagstones. Adrian alone saw the thing happen. He called a doctor sitting there, & very calmly & bravely, so Nessa felt, climbed the wall into the garden where the man had fallen, & helped the Dr over. But there was no hope. He died in the ambulance that fetched him. The dance was stopped. Nessa says the younger generation is callous. No one was upset; some telephoned for news of other dances. Aunt Lou bungled everything with her salt American cheerfulness. It was odd how, sitting high up, one began to get a sense of falling. The man was called Wright, aged 21: for some reason he had his birth certificate on him. Only the girl who brought him knew him. The parents, rich country people, come up, were shown the spot & had nothing to say except, 'That was where he fell'—but what could they say? Aunt Lou gave her version of the thing 'not a tragedy—not in the least a tragedy—a stepmother only & seven other children—& its over for him poor boy.' A strange event—to come to a dance among strangers & die—to come dressed in evening clothes, & then for it all to be over, instantly, so senselessly. Pippa had warned them. No brandy was to be had in any of the three houses.

Tuesday 6 July

Too much to write as usual, but we work like navvies at binding

14. The dance was given on 26 June by Alys, née Pearsall Smith (1867-1950) Bertrand Russell's estranged wife and Karin Stephen's 'Aunt Lou', at the Stephen's house, 50 Gordon Square, where Vanessa also lived. VW's report was substantially true.

Morgan, & have no time for frivolity.[1] Festivities get wedged in where convenient. All this comes of choosing a paper that has to be enforced with a lining. It looks as though Morgan might boom, though I dont, as a critic, see altogether what the reason is. And am I a critic? Take Conrad's book. We were at the first Athenaeum lunch—a long single file of insignificant brain workers eating bad courses.[2] Katherine was opposite, & I heard her enthusiastically praising this very book. At last, appealed to, I confessed my perversity, whereupon she hedged—so did I. But which is right? I still maintain that I'm the true seer, the one independent voice in a chorus of obedient sheep, since they praise unanimously. They always begin that when the plays over—thats my view at least. This lunch was a little dingy & professional, a glimpse into the scullery where the Sullivans & Pounds & Murrys & Huxleys stand stripped with their arms in wash tubs. I see the obvious retort; yet I can't rid myself of the feeling that if Lytton, Roger, Desmond, Morgan, Nessa, & Duncan had been there the atmosphere would have been less of the area steps & more of the open air. But I'm rather acid about Murry, on account of his writing I think, & Heaven knows, a story by Katherine always manages to put my teeth on edge. *My* story's out—hailed by Sydney & Mrs Schiff[3]—its odd how one's private circle ceases to attend to these outbursts, & how if praise or blame comes its from the public now. Julian here for the week end; & the weather such constant rain as seldom happens; now & then a torrent that sets streams running in 5 minutes.

Tuesday 13 July

Oh the servants! Oh reviewing! oh the weather! Thus I try to get out of writing my proper account of things. Nelly has vacillated between tears & laughter, life & death for the past 10 days; can't feel an ache anywhere without sending for me or L. to assure her that aches are not certainly fatal. Then she cries. Never, never, never will she get over it,

1. E. M. Forster's *The Story of the Siren*, hand-printed by the Woolfs and covered in marbled paper wrappers, was published in July 1920 (*HP Checklist* 9).
2. The *Athenaeum* offices were at 10 Adelphi Terrace—possibly the lunch took place there.
3. VW is presumably here referring to her own story 'An Unwritten Novel', published in the July number of the *London Mercury* (Kp C203). Sydney Schiff (c. 1869-1944) and his wife Violet, *née* Beddington, were wealthy and discerning patrons of the arts; he provided financial backing for the quarterly *Art & Letters*, and his own novels and translations of Proust were published under the name Stephen Hudson. The Schiffs had made friends with Katherine Mansfield earlier this year when she was in Mentone; both *Art & Letters* and the *Athenaeum* published stories by her in 1920.

she says. The doctor comes. Innumerable pills & draughts consumed. Sweats, sleepless nights, recur. My private wonder is, as usual, how they contrive to live a week—aren't killed by the thunder, like flies. No root in reality is in them; & as for reason, when the mood's on, as soon might one persuade a runaway horse. And nothing the matter save what one of us would call an upset inside & take a pill for. This drives us to accept invitations, since if anyone comes here, the atmosphere lowers. But where have we been? Indeed I see myself cutting covers incessantly. I don't think the boom in Morgan will be sudden though. We are advertising in the Nation.

Now for oh Reviewing!— Three weeks I think have passed without a word added to Jacob. How is one to bring it through at this rate. Yet its all my fault—why should I do the Cherry Orchard & Tolstoy for Desmond, why take up the Plumage Bill for Ray? But after this week I do no more.[4] As for the weather, the sun shines in a modified way at this moment; so I will say no more, save that I don't suppose it will last, or do more than dry the topmost layer of earth upon what must be a swamp. Yet what am I thinking of? That Ka has taken the Eagle's Nest, & that I wish it were mine.[5]

RODMELL

Monday 2 August

Bank Holiday. I'm [in] the middle of baking a cake, & fly to this page for refuge, to fill in moments of baking & putting in my bread. Poor wretched book! Thats the way I treat you! —Thats the drudge you are! Still, take comfort from the thought that I brought you all the way from London, to save scribbling on half sheets which get lost. Our season ended unexpectedly; the blind falling with the light still in the sky. If I were not ashamed of my egotism, I could give a literal meaning to my

4. VW's review of the Arts Theatre production of *The Cherry Orchard* was published in the *New Statesman* on 24 July 1920 (Kp C201); her review of the Hogarth Press's *Reminiscences of Leo Nicolayevitch Tolstoi* by Maxim Gorky appeared unsigned in the *New Statesman* of 7 August 1920 (Kp C204). The controversial Plumage Bill, which sought to restrict the importation into Britain of exotic birds and feathers, after much amendment and delay finally received the Royal Assent in July 1921. VW did take it up for Ray Strachey, who from 1920-23 was editor of the *Woman's Leader*: 'The Plumage Bill' by Virginia Woolf (see Appendix II) appeared therein on 23 July 1920. Rachel Conn Strachey, *née* Costelloe (1887-1940) was the wife of Oliver Strachey and sister of Karin Stephen. She was chairman of the Women's Service Bureau, 1916-34.
5. This was a house perched high on the moors above Zennor in Cornwall, an area which VW regarded almost as her private territory.

metaphor—seeing that I had to leave Nessa's great party at 11 in order to be home, not to disturb L., & be ready for packing & going next morning.[1] (now for the cake). Yes, but the cake & the bread between them have made me write nothing for two days—its now Wednesday 4th, & here we are in from shrooming at Asheham—& I with so much to write (& I must keep an eye on the window to prevent Mrs Dedman from finding L. in his bath in the kitchen) that I cant begin.

Well, the great party: to me the time went in tip toe pirouettes; every minute watched, & some alas wasted. There in the corner I sat with Lady S[trachey]. & we talked of my two grandfathers & the Indian Mutiny.[2] She forges about a room like an unwieldy three decker, benignant, yet easily morose, hoarding some grievance against her family, like most old people, for not reading aloud to her, yet easy with strangers. Then Mr Parker the American—alas, when praise is tracked to the source, as often as not it proves brackish—& so was his. Never heard of me save through Potboilers:[3] but my chief pirouetting was with Mary whose hand I took, held, & kissed, on the sofa with Clive on the other side of me. She said she hated & feared me. I wooed her like a wayward child. Does one speak the truth on these occasions, reach it on tiptoe from where it hangs inaccessible in less exalted moments? Then Nina Turton, flushed, lascivious, imbecile, with the heavy idiot voice, as of old, & yet interesting too, as impure women are to the pure— I see her as someone in mid ocean, struggling, diving, while I pace my bank. One may console oneself though by the brainlessness of the exercise. One dip is all that's needed. Maynard said of her that she'd had more sexual life than the rest of us put together—saw it in her face (here came Mrs Thomsett—& L. stark naked in the kitchen!).[4]

Poor L., utterly driven for a month by Tolstoy & Morgan at last

1. Vanessa's party was on Wednesday 21 July; LW was unwell and did not go.
2. Lady Strachey, *née* Jane Maria Grant (1840-1928), Lytton's mother, belonged to and had married into great Anglo-Indian proconsular families and had always been 'in the counsels of men who governed India'. VW's grandfathers were Sir James Stephen—'Mr Over-Secretary Stephen' of the Colonial Office, and Dr John Jackson, MD, the leading English physician in Calcutta.
3. *Potboilers*, in which Clive Bell wrote of VW as 'one of our three best living novelists' had been published in 1918; Mr Parker has not been identified.
4. Nina Euphemia Lamb, *née* Forrest, had left the painter Henry Lamb two years after their marriage in 1907; they were not divorced until 1927. A woman of compelling beauty and attractiveness, she led a life of wild bohemianism with a succession of lovers, one of whom, whose name she had currently adopted, had been killed in the war. Mrs Thomsett, wife of a Rodmell farm-worker, was acting as cook at Monks House in Nelly's absence.

confessed to feeling tired, & was indeed on the verge of destruction. As a hobby, The Hogarth Press is clearly too lively & lusty to be carried on in this private way any longer. Moreover, the business part of it can't be shared, owing to my incompetence. The future, therefore, needs consideration. This being so, we fled a week earlier than intended, sending Nelly to recover from her vapours, & bring[ing] Lottie down here. On Monday I went up, to say good bye to K.M., was inveigled into a night at 46 & could write many pages on my reflections on sleeping in London again—in Maynard's bed too. I racked my brain to think who had his room when we lived there—how many years ago? The ease & rapidity of life in London a good deal impressed me—everything near at hand, to be compassed between lunch & tea, without setting out & making a job of it. Roger, Duncan, Nessa, Clive, & so on; I seeing it all much composed & in perspective owing to my outsider's vision. K.M. asked me to review her book: I cried off on the ground that to review spoils the reading. She as quick as usual to take the point. They are coming to Eastbourne, so my farewell is deferred. Despicable as I am, I find myself liking to hear her underrated by C[live]. & N[essa]. yet protesting as a writer; & finally harbouring one or two doubts, genuine doubts, as to the merits of her stories, since the two lately printed in the A[*thenaeum*]. have not been good.

And now I can't write my views of Don Quixote as intended, for I've spun my froth off, & have no wits left.

Thursday 5 August

Let me try to say what I think as I read Don Quixote after dinner— Principally that writing was then story telling to amuse people sitting round the fire without any of our devices for pleasure. There they sit, women spinning, men contemplative, & the jolly, fanciful, delightful tale is told to them, as to grown up children— This impresses me as the motive of D.Q., to keep us entertained at all costs. So far as I can judge, the beauty, & thought come in unawares; Cervantes scarcely conscious of serious meaning, & scarcely seeing D.Q. as we see him. Indeed that's my difficulty—the sadness, the satire, how far are they ours, not intended —or do these great characters have it in them to change according to the generation that looks at them? Much, I admit, of the tale-telling is dull—not much, only a little at the end of the first volume, which is obviously told as a story to keep one contented. So little said out, so much kept back, as if he had not wished to develop that side of the matter—the scene of the galley slaves marching is an instance of what

I mean— Did C. feel the whole of the beauty & sadness of that as I feel it? Twice I've spoken of 'sadness'. Is that essential to the modern view? Yet how splendid it is to unfurl one's sail & blow straight ahead on the gust of the great story telling, as happens all through the first part. I suspect the Fernando-Cardino-Lucinda story was a courtly episode in the fashion of the day, anyhow dull to me. I am also reading Ghoa le Simple—bright, effective, interesting, yet so arid & spick & span.[5] With Cervantes everythings there; in solution if you like; but deep, atmospheric, living people casting shadows solid, tinted as in life. The Egyptians, like most French writers, give you a pinch of essential dust instead, much more pungent & effective, but not nearly so surrounding & spacious. By God!—what stuff I'm writing! always these images.

I write Jacob every morning now, feeling each days work like a fence which I have to ride at, my heart in my mouth till its over, & I've cleared, or knocked the bar out. (Another image, unthinking it was one. I must somehow get Hume's Essays & purge myself).

Tuesday 10 August

I have spent the whole afternoon yellow washing the earth closet. I can now reckon up my labours: dining room distempered & cleaned; bannisters painted blue; stairs white; & now the earth closet. Tea comes quick; post (with luck) in the middle of tea; then a lounge in the garden; then Mrs Thomsett round with the plates; green shaded lamp lit, & beneath it we sit ostensibly reading till 10.30: when candles are fetched, & we plod yawning up stairs. Our beds have dents & hollows; but we sleep till Mrs Thomsett calls us. She is one of the most punctual. But then Mr Thomsett is out with his cattle at 5. Perhaps it's his boots that sometimes wake me— The cattle go down to the brooks. Mr Arblaster's motor car pants under the window.[6]

Coming home from Rat Farm on Sunday, a hot still day, Leonard initiated a scheme for the future of the Press. We are going to offer Partridge a share in it, baiting this perhaps minute titbit with the plumper morsel of secretaryship to L.[7] About the middle of dinner L. developed

5. *Le Livre de Goha le Simple* (1919), written in French by two Egyptians, Albert Adès and Albert Josipovici, had been recommended to VW by Roger Fry.

6. Richard Arblaster was a resident of Rodmell. Rat Farm was the Woolfs' name for some deserted farm buildings in the Telscombe Downs.

7. Ralph Partridge, who had originally been a classical scholar, had on returning to Oxford in 1919, obtained a distinction in English Literature; he was now considering what to do, and no doubt the idea of his playing a part in the development of the Hogarth Press had been suggested by Lytton Strachey.

this further: why not install Partridge at Suffield, & buy a complete printing outfit? Why not? Run a shop there too, perhaps. Ramifications spring unceasingly from this centre. The whole depends, however, upon Partridge, who has been invited here. Its a pleasant thing, come autumn, to make plans. Nelly still mysteriously diseased, & that being so we implore her to stay away—

Reading Don Q. still—I confess rather sinking in the sand—rather soft going—so long as the stories aren't about him—but has the loose, far scattered vitality of the great books, which keeps me going—

'Potterism'—by R. Macaulay, a don's book, hard-headed, masculine, atmosphere of lecture room, not interesting to me—[8]

Catherine Wilmot, who went on a tour in 1802—& kept a diary; but I have not yet got in to her—a necessary process.[9] Now to pick sweet peas.

Tuesday 17 August

For the first time in memory, I sit down to this page instead of to the sterner one of duty & profit at some minutes after ten a.m. Damn these aristocrats! damn myself for being such a snob—unable to settle to Jacob's Room because 'about midday' Nelly Cecil in her motor car will descend.[10] 'Driving Bob to Newhaven—may I take bread & cheese with you?' A dull listless morning, too, a little close in the house, yet chilly perhaps under the acacia; & not a spark of colour glowing. My preparations for the aristocracy—but I wrong myself—Molly Hamilton, or Molly MacCarthy or any other Molly—would cause as much stir— consist in pinning a chair cover together & filling the vases with sweet peas & roses. I dont like these civic interruptions into rural life. I didn't like the Clutton Brocks at Charleston.[11] London yesterday I hated. More

8. *Potterism. A tragi-farcical tract* by Rose Macaulay (see below, 18 February 1921, n 10), published in 1920 by Collins.

9. *An Irish Peer on the Continent, 1801-1803: being a narrative of the tour of Stephen, 2nd Earl Mount Cashell through France, Italy, etc, as related by Catherine Wilmot,* edited by T. U. Sadleir (1920). The book is a collection of letters from Miss Wilmot to her brother.

10. Nelly Cecil (1868-1956), *née* Lady Eleanor Lambton, had married Lord Robert Cecil in 1889; they had no children; she was very deaf. She and VW, who first met about 1902, shared a passionate and professional interest in the art and craft of letters.

11. Arthur Clutton-Brock (1868-1924), man of letters and since 1908 art critic of *The Times*; he was the author of *Shelley, the Man and the Poet* (1909) and of other works of a philosophical tendency. A friend of Clive Bell, he had married Evelyn Vernon-Harcourt in 1903.

truly it was not London but a certain yard of the line between Richmond & Mortlake where we stopped for an hour & a half—I, too, due at the dentists with the treat of a lounge through my favourite streets afterwards. I wanted to buy some bright piece of china for the mantelpiece. As it was I scoured the town in taxis, lavished florins, accumulated parcels, swallowed tea, encountered Kot, & then spent 20 minutes at Victoria—however, L. was there, & we could chatter. But as the train swung out into open country life seemed fresher, sweeter, saner. One day I must pay a tribute to the humanity of dentists. Better than journalism for the soul, I told L.—but then, I've a vendetta with Massingham, against whom my arrow was launched.[12] Its true though: I get more & more disinclined for journalism. I've written only half a page of it since coming here—three weeks ago; have refused 3 articles (summing up Jane, Charlotte, & Thackeray) & feel like a drunkard who has successfully resisted three invitations to drink.

Walking with Clive over the instep of Firle Beacon the other night we talked of all this; he seriously advising me for my good to approach America; being, as I always think, an admirable man of business, & doing very well for himself. And we talked about the future of the press & of the novel; he shrewd on both these questions, though perhaps I shall find my own opinions earning good money in his name in America. Through the pheasant wood we came, & by the cornfields; & I made up a sentence about paint with a yellow glaze on it to express the warm deep colours, laid so thickly upon field & down, & overlaid with some varnish so that it glowed, not raw, but under skilful preservation.[13] There was Maynard, Duncan, Nessa; & we broached the new studio,[14] where I sat with the painters all the next morning—talking, talking— till, as I say, the Brocks came, & we turned intelligent & cultured again. I rode home over the fields—one of the few days which are, as I maintain, days: the usual windy rainy weather being the variety & deviation. All being prepared, down to chicken & tongue, Molly H. of course did *not* come—her mother taking the occasion to fall from a ladder.

By opening the garden door I enlarge our garden so far as Mount Caburn. There I walk in the sunset; when the village climbing the hill

---

12. H. W. Massingham, writing as 'Wayfarer' in the Nation of 10 July 1920, had ascribed the recent defeat in Parliament of the Plumage Bill to the vanity of women. For VW's arrow, see Appendix II.
13. Cf. *The Waves*, p 130.
14. A long, low, wooden hut, with the legend 'Les Miserables' painted on it by its previous (military) occupants, had been reassembled beyond the walled garden for use as a studio by Duncan and Vanessa. See *II VW Letters*, no. 1122.

has a solemn sheltering look[,] pathetic, somehow, emblematic, anyhow very peaceful & human, as if people sought each others company at night, & lived trustfully beneath the hills. The old whitehaired women sit on the doorstep till 9 or so, then go in; & the light is lit in the upper window & all is dark by ten o'clock. I had reason to observe nocturnal habits last night, for after my recuperative draught was over, Lottie was still not home; & when 10 struck L. determined to go in search. Bicycling alone along a road in ruts in the dark she might well have fallen—& so forth. I went on foot up to the cross roads; thus passing all the men coming back from the public house, & saying more 'Good nights' than in a week of daylight—proving what I've said of the sociability of night-fall. Then, too, they'd had their lamps lit for them by Mr Malthouse's beer.[15] Presumably every man in the place spends his evenings in the public house of course; & I should like once in a way to hear their talk. (George Sturgeon, who came with Flora on Sunday, has disillusioned me with country talk—his is all of cricket & tennis—coarse shapes of humanity appearing through the haze, all stamped according to their position in Lewes society—I dont think the intelligentzia need fear, either on earth or in Heaven, the competition of these simple natures— for stupidity, buttressing itself with all the conventions & prejudices is not nearly so humane as we free thinkers are). Then the clover smelt sweet up by the corner; & there was Lewes flashing, truthfully speaking with a kind of diamond brilliance, & the sky all powdered (?) with stars, grey with them, since the moon was not up. L. found Lottie at the level crossing, her bicycle punctured, her lamps out, but hilarious & loquacious as a jay in the sun light.

Thursday 19 August

I raise my head from making a patchwork quilt. This is the day of the month when I despatch darning & other needlework, & do in truth more useful work than on days of free intelligence. How shifting & vacillating one's mind is! Yesterday broody & drowsy all day long, writing easily, & yet without strict consciousness, as though fluent under drugs: today apparently clear headed, yet unable to put one sentence after another—sat for an hour, scratching out, putting in, scratching out; & then read [Sophocles'] Trachiniae with comparative ease—always comparative—oh dear me!

We had Nelly Cecil from 12 till 4.30; and how rude & even slovenly

15. Mr Malthouse was the landlord of the Abergavenny Arms, Rodmell.

she made our equipment seem! the rooms diminishing, the silver tarnishing, the chicken drying, & the china dulling. It was hard work; one of us always at her ear, & she, poor woman, receiving words from one or other of us incessantly. Beginning on the very outskirts of intimacy we made progress to the centre. To begin with she's shy, apologetic for the infliction: "I'll stay one hour—oh I'm interrupting—how you must curse me for breaking in on you!" But this went by & her mind, trained to deal with the political situation kept her alert. We had much gossip too, chiefly about Mrs Asquith & her inaccuracies, how the Tennants broke up the old aristocratic world.[16] So to religion. "I have not so much of it as I used to have. When one was young one wished for immortality. And the war made it difficult—oh yes, I go to church still. Bob leads a good, earnest life, & goes on believing." Bob is at Deauville with the Mosley's for a month.[17] Indeed, one guesses at isolation unspeakable; never was there such a look of solitude on any human face as on hers; as if always away from life, alone, forced to bear it, & be grateful for any help. Her body incredibly little & shrunk; eyes slightly fading; cheeks sunk in—

Friday 20 August

Mrs Dedman cajoled us there by calling it a Sussex funeral, & promising that the bearers would wear smock frocks. But only 6 were to be found in the village; so the plan was given up; Mr Stacey was lowered to his grave by black farm labourers, two of whom managed to tumble into the grave as they lowered him.[18] Smock frocks exist however, as she proved by showing us grandfather's, & a fine piece of stitchery it is, with a pattern appropriate to Rodmell, distinct from all other villages. He, who now sits on the bench in the churchyard walk, wore it on Sundays. The entire male population of Kingston village came out of

16. Excerpts from the first volume of Margot Asquith's *Autobiography* appeared in the *Sunday Times* in advance of the book's publication in October 1920. Dealing with her life as Margot Tennant before her marriage to the Liberal politician H. H. Asquith, they attracted a good deal of attention and criticism of the frankness, confusion, and indeed inaccuracy, of her personal memories of well-known or well-connected people.

17. Oswald Mosley, MP, had become parliamentary spokesman for the League of Nations' Union, and at this period he and Lord Robert Cecil worked very closely together.

18. James Stacey, retired farmer, son of James Stacey of Swanborough Manor, died on 17 August 1920, aged fifty and was buried at Kingston, near Lewes, on 20th August. He had begun farming on his own account at Rodmell Place in 1894 and became a leading figure in East Sussex agriculture.

church after the coffin; brown faces, white hairs, showing on top of coal black coats. Four or five meagre girls provided with white handkerchiefs which they used automatically, walked first—one poor old thing with a ribbon of black velvet round her throat. The clergy acted with such portentous gloom that even now I daresay they scarcely feel comfortable. Still glowering like a gargoyle one of them sat in his taxi, waiting to go back to Lewes. The day was cold; a thunder shower purple in the sky. As usual, the service seemed chill, awkward, unmanageable; everyone subduing their natural feelings, & seeming to play a part because the others did. The coffin was a pale grey, wreaths attached by strings. Whether the Catholic form is warmer, I know not; a strange convention this. I saw one man shredding a few grains of dust at the right moment. We stood under a yew tree, by a large tomb. But the ceremonial spirit is entirely absent. We never catch fire. Then the awkwardness of old Sunday coats & hats. Kingston is a fine village, with old bow windowed houses, & the path running to the heart of the hill. I feel Sunday clinging to my clothes like the smell of camphor. —cant write, as I perceive with shame, or rather with amusement.

Wednesday 25 August

For the third time this summer, though no other summer, I went to London [on] Monday, paid 5/- for a plate of ham, & said good bye to Katherine. I had my euphemism at parting; about coming again before she goes; but it is useless to extend these farewell visits. They have something crowded & unnaturally calm too about them, & after all, visits can't do away with the fact that she goes for two years, is ill, & heaven knows when we shall meet again. These partings make one pinch oneself as if to make sure of feeling. Do I feel this as much as I ought? Am I heartless? Will she mind my going either? And then, after noting my own callousness, of a sudden comes the blankness of not having her to talk to. So on my side the feeling is genuine. A woman caring as I care for writing is rare enough I suppose to give me the queerest sense of echo coming back to me from her mind the second after I've spoken. Then, too, there's something in what she says of our being the only women, at this moment (I must modestly limit this to in our circle) with gift enough to make talk of writing interesting. How much I dictate to other people! How often too I'm silent, judging it useless to speak. I said how my own character seemed to cut out a shape like a shadow in front of me. This she understood (I give it as an example of her understanding) & proved it by telling me that she thought this bad: one ought to merge into things. Her senses are amazingly acute—a long description she gave of hosing plants—putting the hose over the high trees, then over the shrubs, then over the mignonette. And Murry said slowly, "You've got it wrong, Katherine. Youth wasn't like that. At least I'm sure mine wasn't." Murry playing tennis all day; an oddly detached couple. She wants to live in an Italian town & have tea with the doctor. It suddenly strikes me as I write that I should like to ask her what certainty she has of her work's merit.— But we propose to write to each other— She will send me her diary. Shall we? Will she? If I were left to myself I should; being the simpler, the more direct of the two. I can't follow people who don't do the obvious things in these ways. I've recanted about her book; I shall review it; but whether she really wanted me to, God knows. Strange how little we know our friends.[19]

So I missed my train; & what I wanted most in the world was to catch it & travel back with L.

Nelly is now going to have her teeth seen to. No talk of her coming back yet. I am quite given up as a reviewer—seriously by the Times I believe—& forge ahead with Jacob, which I wager to finish by Xmas.

Tuesday 31 August

The last day of August—& what a day! November in the city without the lights. Then the schoolchildren singing, & as I write Lottie chatter-chattering—so I'm out of mood. Detestable grey sky—life has too few days to waste them thus. I must walk my temper off upon the downs. But first I've Partridge & Carrington to deal with. Another step has been taken in life: we have a partner & a secretary at a cost of £100. Rash, I suppose; but then what's the point of life if one's not rash? Anyhow we step out bold[l]y, & if the Press is to live, it had better run a risk or two. The young man, aged 26, just left Oxford, is a superb body—shoulders like tough oak; health tingling beneath his skin. Merry shrewd eyes. Since George Sturgeon I'm shy of stupid young men; but P. hasn't that stupidity anyhow. He has been religious; is now socialistic; literature I don't suppose counts for much: he's written an essay on Milton, which C. was not struck by. Happily we had fine weather; & sat in the meadow & watched Squire & Sassoon play cricket—the last people I wished to see— Somehow that the downs should be seen by cultivated eyes, self conscious eyes, spoils them to me. I wish there were nothing but Dedmans,

19. VW did not review *Bliss*. Katherine returned to Mentone on 13 September 1920.

Bottens & Staceys in the world; as they alone people the graveyards.[20] Carrington is ardent, robust, scatterbrained, appreciative, a very humble disciple, but with enough character to prevent insipidity. A little ashamed of P., I thought her. But what shoulders! what thickness of bone! He is an admirer of L.'s. Well, how will it turn out? What shall we print?

[H. G.] Wells has asked us to stay. What other news is there? The time seems to race ahead, broken into halves by the post; & I've such a litter of books to read—though none to review. A cold, disappointing summer. Finished Sophocles this morning—read mostly at Asheham.

Wednesday 8 September

Perhaps a little author's egotism may be allowed—simply that I've taken the plunge of refusing my books from the Times, & dictated conditions for the future—only leading articles, or those I suggest myself. No answer from Richmond, so I don't know his view of it. But, of course, far from being rejected he was respecting my holiday, & suggested a list of victims, Murry & Lawrence among them, at the thought of which I shivered & shuddered, & finally decided to run the risk. At this moment I feel it more of a risk than the day before yesterday, as Lytton, Mary, Clive, came here yesterday, discussed immortality; & I find my bid for it is as letter writer. What about poor Jacob then? & hadn't I better drive my pen through sheets that pay of a morning, in the intervals of writing letters? Oh vanity, vanity! how it grows on me—how detestable it is—how I swear to crush it out— Learn French is the only thing I can think of. Then I didn't like Mary; scented, tinted, lewd lipped, & blear eyed; & the consciousness that its the mean side of me that feasts on such garbage; & resentment with her for making me feed on garbage; & she saying sharp things & then hard, & I unable to say out loud "Well then, why come & sit on my lawn?" Why does she? And I always break off 'poor wretch'—yet not quite magnanimously in her case. L. at tea put me right: M.H. is one of the few people I dislike, I said. No: he replied: one of the many you dislike & like alternately— The bread had not risen—I was worried this morning by school children; & I hate people to compare this to the disadvantage of Asheham—M.H. again. Lytton gave me a lesson in simplicity. If anyone has a right to talk of

20. J. C. Squire, a passionate cricketer, was the organiser of an *ad hoc* team of friends and literary colleagues known as the Invalids, which challenged village teams (and usually lost). Rodmell was a popular fixture thanks to the generous hospitality of Squire's Australian friend J. M. Allison (see below, 15 September 1920 n 7), a local landowner. Siegfried Sassoon shared Squire's love of cricket. Jasper Botten, farmer, lived at Rodmell Place.

immortality he has with his 9 editions & so on. Yet when L. severely told him he had no chance of that, he did not narrow his eyes, shift his hands, or do anything but look calm & animated. It was an amusing talk. How far has our set justified its promise? Lytton maintains that in ourselves we are as remarkable as the Johnson set, though our works may perish—still we're still at the beginning of our works. Then came that about Madame de Sevigné: then Duncan given his chance; I compared E[minent].V[ictorians].'s with Macaulay, & thought Lytton perhaps uncertain about Victoria. Maynard says, however, it should succeed better; indeed is better. Much talk of Athenaeum; Lady Blessington;[1] our printing prospects; before they went. Lytton comes on Friday. After all, isn't he the choicest of us? And now I can go out & look at the downs—where?

Wednesday 15 September

Nelly by the way has now had, I suppose every organ in her body examined, & is pronounced healthy with the exception of her teeth. So that shot of mine seems the true one;—but I confess I don't look forward to the winter. The fact is the lower classes *are* detestable.

Something of that reflection I owe to Lytton who has been with us from Friday to Tuesday, & now that the rain is come, I observe maliciously, is with the Hutches at Wittering[2] (Never does Mary darken my door, or shadow my lawn again, I observe)— And that too comes from Lytton—its a consequence of walking all along the flats with him, on a brilliant evening, so up by Northease farm onto the downs. His admiration of the place made up for all disparagement. But see how many little facts, sayings, points of view I collected from him—that Mary dislikes me 'very feminine', that Clive is a buffoon, that the lower classes are vulgar & stupid, that the Selby Biggs are useless & pretentious,[3] that we only remain—but that the world's very amusing & pleasant, on the whole, society agreeable, 'women essential'; & I think there are one

1. The Irish-born authoress and editor, Marguerite, *née* Power, Countess of Blessington (1789-1849), whose wit and wealth brought her social eminence. Her travels with her husband and her lover Count d'Orsay furnished material for several volumes, including her best-known, *Conversations with Lord Byron* (1834).
2. The St John Hutchinsons had a small holiday house, Eleanor Farm, on the Chichester Canal near West Wittering.
3. Sir Amherst Selby-Bigge (1860-1951), Permanent Secretary to the Board of Education, 1911-25, lived at Kingston Manor; the walk on the downs above Northease had brought Lytton and VW down through Kingston, where they had seen Sir Amherst's daughter-in-law in the road (see *II VW Letters*, no. 1145).

or two doubts of his about the value of his work compared with creating a world of one's own.

Then 'Life is very complex'—this murmured, as if intimate, referring to his own difficulties, which I had explained to me on the Roman Road. A repetition of Nick & Barbara [Bagenal].[4] C[arrington]. lives with P[artridge]. till Christmas, then comes to a decision. And we walked all the way to Kingston, talking, back over the flats, talking. Save for shadows that cross & leave him ruffled, he is now uniformly amiable, & takes pains at table—so that something is always on foot. At night we had the first two or three chapters of Victoria— Disgraceful to say I was twice overcome with sleep, owing to our wood fire; but the liveliness of it is such as to make one forget whether its good or not. I dont know what qualities it has. I suspect it depends too much upon amusing quotations, & is too much afraid of dulness to say anything out of the way. Not at all a meditative or profound book; on the other hand, a remarkably composed & homogeneous book. I doubt whether these portraits are true—whether thats not too much the conventional way of making history— But I think I'm coloured by my own wishes, & experimental mood. A miracle in the matter of condensation & composition I suspect. But we are to read it when done. Blessed with fine weather, I could look from my window, through the vine leaves, & see Lytton sitting in the deck chair reading Alfieri from a lovely vellum copy, dutifully looking out words.[5] He wore a white felt hat, & the usual grey clothes; was long, & tapering as usual; looking so mild & so ironical, his beard just cut short. As usual; I got my various impressions: of suavity, a gentle but inflexible honesty; lightning speed; something peevish & exacting; something incessantly living, suffering, reflecting moods. Still he can withdraw in that supercilious way that used to gall me; still show himself superior to me, contemptuous of me—of my morality, that is, not of my mind. For my own encouragement, I may note that he praised the Voyage Out voluntarily; *"extremely* good" it seemed to him on re-reading, especially the satire of the Dalloways. Night & Day he judges better, on the whole. Well, I can walk & talk with him by the hour.

I should have made more of my release from reviewing. When I'd sent my letter to Richmond, I felt like someone turned out into the open

4. The Roman Road was probably the Woolfs' name for a straight track along the top of the downs. For the Nick-Barbara-Saxon parallel, see *I VW Diary*.
5. See Lot 765 in the *Catalogue of Printed Books . . . the Property of the late Roger Senhouse Esq . . . including a . . . portion of the Lytton Strachey Library*, Sotheby & Co, 20 October 1971.

air. Now I've written another in the same sense to Murry, returning Mallock;[6] & I believe this is the last book any editor will ever send me. To have broken free at the age of 38 seems a great piece of good fortune —coming at the nick of time, & due of course to L. without whose journalism I couldn't quit mine. But I quiet my conscience with the belief that a foreign article once a week is of greater worth, less labour, & better paid than my work; & with luck, if I can get my books done, we shall profit in moneymaking eventually. And, when one faces it, the book public is more of an ordeal than the newspaper public, so that I'm not shirking responsibility. Now, of course, I can scarcely believe that I ever wrote reviews weekly; & literary papers have lost all interest for me. Thank God, I've stepped clear of that Athenaeum world, with its reviews, editions, lunches, & tittle tattle— I should like never to meet a writer again. The proximity of Mr Addison, reputed editor of The Field, is enough for me. I should like to know masses of sensitive, imaginative, unselfconscious unliterary people, who have never read a book— Now, in the rain, up to Dean, to talk about the door of the coal cellar.[7]

Friday 17 September

Oh still in the rain—the green I see through the window has a sulphur tint in it—perhaps the evening sun is sinking behind Falmer—but the rain rains so as to beat the asters to the ground & wet L. through, going & coming from the E.C. We have been into Lewes nevertheless— by train, & walking home with knapsacks. I bought two pairs of stockings, L. a hair brush. We met Mr Thomas at the halt.

Rough weather! said Leonard.

"It is! It is indeed. But then you see, we are already in autumn. And the sea is only three & a half miles away." This he said nervously & eagerly, like a child; & then came out with his measurement, the fame of which has reached Rodmell already: 250 tons of rain fell the other night. But the harvest is in. What other news is there? L. caught a bat in our

---

6. *Memoirs of Life and Literature* by William Hurrell Mallock (1849-1923), author of the satire *The New Republic* (1877), was published in September 1920.

7. James Murray Allison (1877-1929), an Australian who became advertising manager successively of *The Times*, the *Daily Telegraph* and of Allied Newspapers Ltd, owned Hill Farm House and a good deal of land at Rodmell. During the war he had acquired control of the weekly *Land and Water*, which was subsequently incorporated in *The Field*. He was a friend of J. C. Squire and his literary-cricketing coterie (see above, 31 August 1920, n 20). Christopher Dean of the Forge House, Rodmell, was the local builder, wheelwright and general smith.

bedroom & killed it with a towel. I thought the lime tree was on us last night. We were wakened by a clap of thunder. Lottie spent the night at Charleston. I write this as if it were to be my last chance. Eliot comes tomorrow. We do not look forward lightly: but its interesting, which is always something. I've reached the party in Jacob & write with great pleasure.[8]

Sunday 19 September

Eliot is separated only by the floor from me. Nothing in mans or womans shape is any longer capable of upsetting me. The odd thing about Eliot is that his eyes are lively & youthful when the cast of his face & the shape of his sentences is formal & even heavy. Rather like a s[c]ulpted face—no upper lip: formidable, powerful; pale. Then those hazel eyes seeming to escape from the rest of him. We talked—America, Ottoline, aristocracy, printing, Squire, Murry, criticism. "And I behaved like a priggish pompous little ass" was one of his comments upon his own manner at Garsington. He is decidedly of the generation beneath us—I daresay superior—younger, though.

Monday 20 September

To go on with Eliot, as if one were making out a scientific observation —he left last night directly after dinner. He improved as the day went on; laughed more openly; became nicer. L. whose opinion on this matter I respect, found him disappointing in brain—less powerful than he expected, & with little play of mind. I kept myself successfully from being submerged, though feeling the waters rise once or twice. I mean by this that he completely neglected my claims to be a writer, & had I been meek, I suppose I should have gone under—felt him & his views dominant & subversive. He is a consistent specimen of his type, which is opposed to ours. Unfortunately the living writers he admires are Wyndham Lewis & Pound. —Joyce too, but there's more to be said on this head. We had some talk after tea (I put off the Mayors[9]) about his writing. I suspect him of a good deal of concealed vanity & even anxiety about this.) I taxed him with wilfully concealing his transitions. He said

8. Mrs Durrant's party forms Chapter Seven of *Jacob's Room*, approximately half-way through the book.
9. R. J. G. (Robin) Mayor (1869-1947), Principal Assistant Secretary in the Board of Education, had been a Fellow of King's College, Cambridge, and was an Apostle; he had married Beatrice (Bobo) Meinertzhagen (1885-1971), whom VW knew slightly, in 1912. They had taken over Little Talland House, Firle, from VW for use as a country cottage.

that explanation is unnecessary. If you put it in, you dilute the facts. You should feel these without explanation. My other charge was that a rich & original mind is needed to make such psychological writing of value. He told me he was more interested in people than in anything. He cant read Wordsworth when Wordsworth deals with nature. His turn is for caricature. In trying to define his meaning ('I dont mean satire') we foundered. He wants to write a verse play in which the 4 characters of Sweeny act the parts. A personal upheaval of some kind came after Prufrock, & turned him aside from his inclination—to develop in the manner of Henry James.[10] Now he wants to describe externals. Joyce gives internals. His novel Ulysses, presents the life of man in 16 incidents, all taking place (I think) in one day. This, so far as he has seen it, is extremely brilliant, he says. Perhaps we shall try to publish it.[11] Ulysses, according to Joyce, is the greatest character in history[.] Joyce himself is an insignificant man, wearing very thick eyeglasses, a little like Shaw to look at, dull, self-centred, & perfectly self assured. There is much to be said about Eliot from different aspects—for instance, the difficulty of getting into touch with clever people.—& so forth—anaemia, self-consciousness; but also, his mind is not yet blunted or blurred. He wishes to write precise English; but catches himself out in slips; & if anyone asked him whether he meant what he said, he would have to say no, very often. Now in all this L. showed up much better than I did; but I didn't much mind.

Sunday 26 September

But I think I minded more than I let on; for somehow Jacob has come to a stop, in the middle of that party too, which I enjoyed so much. Eliot coming on the heel of a long stretch of writing fiction (2 months without a break) made me listless; cast shade upon me; & the mind when

10. This project developed as Eliot's 'unfinished' poetic drama *Sweeney Agonistes*, the fragments of which were published in *The New Criterion* in 1926-27, and in book form in 1932. 'The Love Song of J. Alfred Prufrock' was first published by the Egoist Press Ltd in *Prufrock and Other Observations* in 1917; but it had been written in 1911. See *Eliot's Early Years*, by Lyndall Gordon, 1977, pp 45-6.

11. The Woolfs had decided if they could to publish Joyce's as yet unfinished novel when it was first brought to them by Miss Weaver in 1918 (see *I VW Diary*, 10 & 18 April 1918). Their own press was far too small for such a task, so LW tried to find a commercial printer to undertake it, but, like Miss Weaver herself, failed: the risk of prosecution for the criminal offence of printing what was undoubtedly classifiable as an 'obscene libel' was too great. *Ulysses* was first published in Paris in 1922.

engaged upon fiction wants all its boldness & self-confidence. He said nothing—but I reflected how what I'm doing is probably being better done by Mr Joyce. Then I began to wonder what it is that I am doing: to suspect, as is usual in such cases, that I have not thought my plan out plainly enough—so to dwindle, niggle, hesitate—which means that one's lost. But I think my 2 months of work are the cause of it, seeing that I now find myself veering round to [John] Evelyn, & even making up a paper upon Women, as a counterblast to Mr Bennett's adverse views reported in the papers.[12] Two weeks ago I made up Jacob incessantly on my walks. An odd thing the human mind! so capricious, faithless, infinitely shying at shadows. Perhaps at the bottom of my mind, I feel that I'm distanced by L. in every respect.

Went to Charleston for the night;[13] & had a vivid sight of Maynard by lamplight—like a gorged seal, double chin, ledge of red lip, little eyes, sensual, brutal, unimaginative: one of those visions that come from a chance attitude, lost so soon as he turned his head. I suppose though it illustrates something I feel about him. Then he's read neither of my books— In spite of this I enjoyed myself: L. came over next day & found me neither suicidal nor homicidal. Home we rode after their inconvenient early tea—Charleston time, invented by Maynard, being an hour before summer time. Summer time, by the way is extended for a month, owing to the threat of a strike which I say won't take place. But what do I know?—can't master these leading articles.[14] Eliot has sent me his poems, & hopes to maintain contact during the winter. This was the text of much discussion at Charleston; & in private, with N[essa]. & D[uncan]. that is, I divulged my intention to deal no more with M.H. They agreed, I think. N. produced further reasons why I should steer clear.

12. Arnold Bennett's collection of essays dealing with contemporary society and in particular with 'women of the top class and of those classes which . . . imitate the top . . . class' was published as *Our Women* in September 1920, and attracted a good deal of attention in the popular press. His general argument was that 'intellectually and creatively man is the superior of woman'.

13. VW went to Charleston on Wednesday 22 September; LW came the next day for lunch and they returned home together after tea.

14. For Lytton Strachey's account of the confusion created by Charleston time, see *Holroyd*, p 805. On 24 September the miners, who earlier in the month had threatened a strike, announced a week's postponement of strike notices. In the next day's *Times* there was a leader on the issue entitled 'Breathing Space'. The same edition carried the government's announcement that 'in view of the possible coal strike' the return from Summer Time to Greenwich Time which should normally have taken place on the night of 26-27 September would be delayed until 25 October.

A hot summer day; too hot standing weeding in the sun. L. is clearing the big bed. Lottie goes tomorrow. Nelly is said to be recovered. No doubt Richmond has something to do with it.

Friday 1 October

Here we are at the last day; the boxes with apples standing open— this book left out by mistake, so that I take the opportunity— Yes; undoubtedly the best summer so far, in spite of execrable weather, no bath, one servant, & an E.C. down a winding glade. To that verdict we both set our hands. The place is enchanting, & though in my jealous moods I've reconnoitred & scrutinised every other house, on the whole I decide that this is best. Even the schoolchildren's voices, if one thinks of them as swifts & martins skirling round the eaves, exhilarate instead of annoying. We now give them apples, rejecting their pence, & requiring in return that they shall respect the orchard. They had already stripped several trees. As I say the time has vanished, & we are back before we have been here. Nelly, by the way, returns. I must try to say nothing sharp, though inclined to. After all, without education,—there are excuses.

I have neither written nor read since Monday, owing to a threatening of headache. It was this, not Eliot I suppose, that broke off Jacob. Very slowly the well, so dry last week, seems to be re-filling. I could invent again— But first I must do Evelyn, then, perhaps, Women. I think Richmond will take as many articles from me as necessary— Murry, I notice, answers nothing; neither prints nor returns my story.[1] Are these the manners of the underworld—what I call 'showing off'? It doesn't much matter. I had my account from Gerald this morning—a little disappointing, I think—I've sold 500 since January—which makes 1600 in all; in 8 months that is. Now it will slack off, & creep very slowly to the 2,000.[2] I don't very much care—but then, it gets more & more doubtful if I shall make enough money this way. Rowntree has quarrelled

1. For VW on Evelyn, see below, 10 November 1920. Her preoccupation with 'Women', kindled by reports of Arnold Bennett's book *Our Women* (see above, 26 September 1920, n 12), was further fuelled by 'Affable Hawk' (Desmond MacCarthy) in the *New Statesman* of 2 October, and took fire in two letters to that journal, which appeared on 9 and 16 October 1920 (see Appendix III). Murry published VW's story 'Solid Objects' in the *Athenaeum* of 22 October 1920 (Kp C207).

2. *Night and Day* had been published by Duckworth & Co in October 1919; the initial printing was 2000, but a second impression of 1000 was in fact issued in 1920. Gerald de l'Etang Duckworth (1870-1937), VW's younger half-brother, was the founder and head of the firm.

with the Contemporary & brought L.'s supplement to an end.[3] We lose
£250 a year—& this is the most serious part of it, for the supplement
was scarcely worth while in that form. We find ourselves free however—
& so speculate about travel—Italy, Greece, France— Oh well, we
rummage in the great bran pie very energetically—Why not install
Partridge, let Hogarth, & kick up our heels? Nessa—did I say—? has
invented Major Grant & his equipage in the basement & thus gets rid
of cooks.[4] All houses will be run like this in a few years. And now its
clearing: blue sky with ice bergs. I must go & see Mr Botten about sending
butter. One of the charms of Rodmell is the human life: everyone does
the same thing at the same hour: when the old vicar performs erratically
on the bells, after churching the women, everybody hears him, & knows
what he's up to.[5] Everyone is in his, or their garden; lamps are lit, but
people like the last daylight, which was brown purple last night, heavy
with all this rain. What I mean is that we are a community.

RICHMOND

Monday 18 October

This is a long break, & perhaps I should not fill it now if it were not
that I am in from the Club, & can't settle to anything. Yet we have been
back seventeen days, have seen a number of people, & harboured more
thoughts than there are words in my mind for: here L. came in, & told
me that Rowntree wants to reconsider the death of the Supplement; will
almost certainly keep it on, with a smaller staff. I'm afraid I wasn't
pleased; for here we are tied again, L. accepting £200 instead of £250;
& no chance of Italy. We argued, & my fears were said to be foolish;
& I daresay they are. Only I'm alarmed, sometimes, to think how easily
L. might devote himself to a cause. I do my utmost to ruin his career.

Who have we seen? The usual people, Nessa & Duncan Clive Mary
Stracheys Stephens, Ka, Arnold Forsters,—Kot, too, who came to bring

3. Since the beginning of the year LW had contributed a 16-page section called *The World of Nations: Facts and Documents* to the monthly *Contemporary Review*, published by Arnold Rowntree's Westminster Press; he in fact continued to do so until December 1921.

4. Duncan Grant's father, the retired army major Bartle Grant (1856-1924), was a man of varied, and on the whole non-military, interests, one of which was cookery. At Vanessa's instigation he organised a central kitchen to supply the several allied households in Gordon Square with meals, which might be collected from no. 50 and transported in hay-boxes to be consumed in the different dining-rooms. The scheme did not last long.

5. The Rev. James Boen Hawkesford had been Rector of Rodmell since 1896.

us Tchehov, & was so excited over it & other projects as to twang like a fiddle, instead of solemnly resounding as usual like a full barrel of beer. We are well launched upon the work of the Press. Partridge— Ralph I should call him—is putting his ox's shoulder to the wheel, & intends to do "hurricane" business. We are bringing out Three Stories by L.: my book; (printed for an experiment by McDermott;) & have in view Tchehov, Eliot, Roger, possibly Lytton's essays; & now little priggish Mervyn A.F. wishes to employ us to print his 'rhymes',— which will be bad, but it is amusing to sell our skill.[6]

Monday 25 October (first day of winter time)

Why is life so tragic; so like a little strip of pavement over an abyss. I look down; I feel giddy; I wonder how I am ever to walk to the end. But why do I feel this? Now that I say it I don't feel it. The fire burns; we are going to hear the Beggars Opera.[7] Only it lies about me; I can't keep my eyes shut. It's a feeling of impotence: of cutting no ice. Here I sit at Richmond, & like a lantern stood in the middle of a field my light goes up in darkness. Melancholy diminishes as I write. Why then don't I write it down oftener? Well, one's vanity forbids. I want to appear a success even to myself. Yet I dont get to the bottom of it. Its having no children, living away from friends, failing to write well, spending too much on food, growing old— I think too much of whys & wherefores: too much of myself. I dont like time to flap round me. Well then, work. Yes, but I so soon tire of work—can't read more than a little, an hour's writing is enough for me. Out here no one comes in to waste time pleasantly. If they do, I'm cross. The labour of going to London is too great. Nessa's children grow up, & I cant have them in to tea, or go to the Zoo. Pocket money doesn't allow of much. Yet I'm persuaded that these are trivial things: its life itself, I think sometimes, for us in our generation so tragic—no newspaper placard without its shriek of agony

6. Of this list the Hogarth Press published, in the course of 1921, LW's *Stories of the East* (*HP Checklist* 16); VW's *Monday or Tuesday* (*HP Checklist* 17); and *The Note-Books of Anton Tchekhov Together with Reminiscences of Tchekhov* by Maxim Gorky, translated by Koteliansky and LW (*HP Checklist* 14). A projected book of Roger Fry's translations from Mallarmé ran into the sand, and eventually appeared posthumously under another imprint in 1936; nothing more by Eliot was published until 1923, and nothing at all by Lytton Strachey. Mervyn Arnold-Forster (1888-1927) was an elder brother of Will's; his 'rhymes' were not printed at the Hogarth Press, but appeared privately and posthumously.
7. A musical play by John Gay, first produced in 1728 and revived with great success at the Lyric Theatre, Hammersmith, in 1920 by Giles Playfair.

from some one. McSwiney this afternoon & violence in Ireland;[8] or it'll be the strike. Unhappiness is everywhere; just beyond the door; or stupidity which is worse. Still I dont pluck the nettle out of me. To write Jacob's Room again will revive my fibres, I feel. Evelyn is done: but I don't like what I write now. And with it all how happy I am—if it weren't for my feeling that its a strip of pavement over an abyss.

Wednesday 10 November

I have walked some way further along the strip of pavement without falling in. Business has kept me stepping out briskly, & then, making an effort, I bought a coat & skirt, & began my social winter at Mrs Samuel Bruce's, between Katie & Elena again, again hearing the same things, & saying the same things.[1] Nelly Cecil spent the night with us, honest, humble, shabby, distinguished. The only people she likes are writers; her own friends she despises a little. De la Mare & Mary Coleridge she respects.[2] Nessa's room at Gordon Square is becoming what the drawing room at 46 was 5 or 6 years ago. I go there & find that astonishing brightness in the heart of darkness. Julian coming in with his French lesson; Angelica hung with beads, riding on Roger's foot; Clive claret coloured & yellow like a canary; Duncan vague in the background, sitting astride a chair, looking with blurred eyes rather dimly. Then we dined with Roger, & with the Sturgeons, & altogether I sometimes feel that not to have a refuge here would be a bad thing—I don't know.[3] Ralph hints at a plan of sharing a London house with us— which tempts me, on some days. All three of us set up L.'s story this afternoon. I've been writing to finish my book; & not a word set to Jacob yet; & I must prepare a chapter for the memoir club; & so, in spite of no reviewing, I don't do as I planned. The house now runs

8. Alderman Terence Joseph McSwiney, Lord Mayor of Cork, 1920, MP for mid-Cork since December 1918, died in the early hours of 25 October in Brixton Prison after being on hunger strike since 16 August. McSwiney had been sentenced by court martial to two years imprisonment for holding a Sinn Fein Court in Cork City Hall.

1. VW went to another chamber concert (see above, 26 January) at Mrs Bruce's house opposite the Natural History Museum, South Kensington, probably on Sunday 31 October.

2. Lady Robert Cecil went to tea and spent the night of 3 November at Hogarth House. Walter de la Mare (1873-1956), poet and man of letters; Mary Elizabeth Coleridge (1861-1907), also a poet, novelist and essayist. Nelly Cecil probably knew them both personally.

3. The Woolfs dined with Flora and George Sturgeon on Friday 5th, and with Roger Fry on Monday 8 November.

very smoothly, indeed melodiously. Didn't I have tea off Nelly's butter?
days fly as usual; & I'm writing a story to ask why—

L. at work on a book for Snowden:[4] endlessly reviewing too; no news
yet from Rowntree about the supt. & that reminds me of the pickle I
got into over Evelyn in the Lit. Supt. last week. 4 mistakes in 4 columns.[5]

Saturday 13 November

This book is badly treated again; & I forget what my excuses are—
no desire to write in it the chief I expect. Now I've finished the Symposium
[Plato] I may relent perhaps. The Waterlows dined last night—Dawks
exactly like a squawking dab chick, waistless, in black, about to bear a
child.[6] She is a persistent, pertinacious woman, & keeps her end up by
force of will. Beauty has not blessed her. Later she complained to me of
her discontent—how she feels small, insignificant purposeless. I sketched
a plan of her life, to which facts do not correspond. Sydney boomed out
in the background that he too was unhappy "of course I'm unhappy—
aren't we all unhappy?—isn't it inevitable, seeing that no one of us has
any satisfactory scheme of things?" This quest for a scheme comes from
living with Murry, who is in pursuit of one very laboriously, hunting
it through the columns of the Athenaeum, for which reason Roger has
broken with him—& that too we discussed, & how he turned Dawks
out of the house. I laughed a good deal, & cheered myself at their discontent. Molly & Desmond seem more seriously in debt than I realised;
& have somehow warded off their creditors by mortgaging old Mrs
MacCarthy's life.[7] Poor Dawks, who has about £1600 a year complains
of John's behaviour, which entirely ruins her day. So they take the

4. 'In 1920 Philip Snowden asked me to contribute a volume to the Independent
   Labour Party's "Social Studies Series".... I wrote a short book with the title
   Socialism and Co-operation, for which I was paid £25' (*IV LW*, 83, 85).
5. VW's review of the *Early Life and Education of John Evelyn, 1620-1641*, with a
   commentary by H. Maynard Smith, was the leading article in the *TLS* of 28
   October 1920 (Kp C208). In the following issue (4 November) Mr Maynard Smith
   set out at length to correct the reviewer on several points, adding the advice
   that 'it is always a waste of time to write on a subject in which you are not interested
   and about which you know very little.' VW, as 'Your Reviewer', replied in the
   issue of 11 November and confessed to 'three slips in four columns.' For these
   'chronological errors' she apologised.
6. Helen Margery Waterlow, *née* Eckhard (1883-1973), Sydney's wife; 'Dawks' was
   her Bloomsbury nickname. Their third child Judith was born on 7 February
   1921; the elder children were Charlotte (b. 1915) and John (b. 1916).
7. Desmond MacCarthy's widowed mother was of French Huguenot ancestry though
   German by birth; she was both rich and mean.

children to the Zoo on Sundays— An odd looking couple—the wrong assortment. Unromantic—terribly unromantic.

L. now translating Tchekov, & I must set to on my share, I suppose.[8] Ralph comes twice a week or so, an indomitable, perhaps rather domineering, young man; loves dancing; in the pink of health; a healthy brain. He described a brothel the other night—how, after the event, he & the girl sat over the fire, discussing the coal strike. Girls paraded before him—that was what pleased him—the sense of power.

Tuesday 23 November

We see too many people for me to describe them, had I the time. I have lived the past 2 weeks methodically, printing till dark, allowing myself a day off, arranging things rather successfully; so my strip of pavement (I bag that phrase for Jacob) widens. O but Ive quarrelled with Nessa & Duncan! I'm standing on my dignity. They choose to tell me lies—very well, I don't go near them till I'm asked.[9] Will they notice? Not in all that shindy of children &c: but I'm cheerful & composed, & conscious of the immense value of my visits. Hope has been for the weekend—over-dressed, over elaborate, scented, extravagant, yet with thick nose, thick ankles; a little unrefined, I mean. That is I like her very much & think her very clever; but I don't like women who are vain & lacking in self-confidence at the same time. It is easily explicable —the rich uncultivated father, brother a trim officer; wealth; health; Jane superimposed,[10] & the greed, like a greed for almond paste, for fame. We talked very well together all the same; & I did my writing (a review of Lawrence sprung upon me) all the same. Why do I dislike unbalanced criticism so much—silliness about Edith Sitwell & Fredegond?[11] As when Ottoline loads her mantelpiece with knick knacks. Old Gumbo in her brown overcoat, spontaneous & emphatic showed up very well

8. LW, with Koteliansky, was translating *The Note-Books of Anton Tchekhov, Together with Reminiscences of Tchekhov* by Maxim Gorky, which the Hogarth Press was to publish in the summer of 1921 (*HP Checklist* 14).
9. The whys and wherefores of this discord remain obscure.
10. Jane Ellen Harrison (1850-1928), the distinguished classical scholar and lecturer at Newnham College, Cambridge. In her old age, Hope Mirrlees became her 'ghostly daughter' and companion.
11. VW's review of D. H. Lawrence's novel *The Lost Girl* appeared in the *TLS* of 2 December 1920 (Kp C210). Edith Sitwell (1887-1964), non-conforming aristocrat and editor of the verse anthology *Wheels* was, as was Fredegond Shove, a poet.

beside her. But I'm exaggerating her defects. She is clever & subtle, & if she hasn't much generosity, I'm not sure that clever people always have.

Then yesterday came Bob for tea, uneasy like a dog who has been roundly beaten for stealing from a butcher's shop, at coming uninvited, & offering to go & leave us to work every 10 minutes. Then we got on to the Poetic Drama & he owned to having begun a new one three days ago. His arguments about the need of writing classical drama, not modern drama, evidently long in use; & I thoughtlessly asked him to write prose[.] "I might as well ask you to write poetry!" he said. Indeed it was unkind. Still he showed up less angular & more considerate & mellow than usual, though L. detected pain in his eye—the legacy of Gladys Deacon perhaps.[12] I like him for praising other writers so unthinkingly—without regard that is to his own position. He praised Eliot's criticism, which had, he said, taken away his own confidence in the poetic drama.[13] I doubt not that under the larches of Leith Hill that will flourish again. The most amusing of his refrains was about Norton. To hear Bob sigh & tread delicately like a hippopotamus holding its breath one would suppose Norton suicidal & maniac.[14] The truth seems to be 'but you must discount what I say—its very difficult to know what impression I'm giving—yet one must say something to his friends; & I *think* its going to be all right now; if we can get over the next few weeks—' The truth is that he has given up mathematics ostensibly on Craig's advice, feels humiliated, & daren't face his friends, poor devil, Gordon Square that is. I think I can trace the crisis far back; his powers proving not quite what he thought; worry; strain; despondency; envisaging failure; thought of boasting; dread of being ridiculous—all that, & then his appearance against him with young women, morbid about sex,

12. Gladys Marie Deacon (1881-1977), a Europeanised Bostonian heiress of whom Proust had said that he had never seen a girl 'with such beauty, such magnificent intelligence, such goodness and charm'; in 1921 she was able to marry the 9th Duke of Marlborough after some ten years' resistance to divorce on the part of his first Duchess, Consuelo, *née* Vanderbilt.

13. T. S. Eliot's *The Sacred Wood: Essays on Poetry and Criticism* was published in November 1920; it contained several essays concerned with Poetic Drama. R. C. Trevelyan lived with his Dutch wife Bessy in a house called The Shiffolds, near Leith Hill in coniferous Surrey.

14. Harry Norton, who had been a brilliant pupil of Bertrand Russell's at Cambridge and of whom much original work in mathematics had been expected, suffered increasingly from feelings of inadequacy and depression; Dr (soon to be Sir) Maurice Craig (1866-1935), Vanessa's doctor, specialised in psychological medicine, and had on occasion been consulted on VW's behalf.

which clearly isn't his strong line; culminating in a kind of breakdown on the motherly housemaid's knee of good Bessy. There he sticks, afraid to issue out, without prospects, a man who has trusted entirely in intellect, & taken his cue from that, given to despising, rejecting, & tacitly claiming an exalted rank on the strength of mathematics which cant be done, & never could be done, I expect. (I quote Maynard) Such an egotist too; never able to see any other face save his own; & worrying out such laborious relationships always b[etw]een himself & other people. Now, poor creature, for I pity him & know his case from my own past, he translates stories from the French, & a book said to want doing by Ponsonby.[15] I can imagine the kind of humility that must be on him, & how he gropes this winter, for some possible method in the future. And here's L. & I can't go on about the Memoir Club!

Sunday 5 December

The Memoir Club was fearfully brilliant—I mean I was; & Leonard so much more impressive with so much less pains; & Morgan very professional; & Mary never laughed once at my jokes. Well, I shall laugh loud at hers next Wednesday to make up.[1] For here I am skipped to December, & only writing now I fear because my brain is tired of reading Coleridge. Why do I read Coleridge? Is it partly the result of Eliot whom I've not read; but L. has & reviewed & praised into the bargain. Eliot & Goldie dined here t'other night—a successful party.[2] A cold in the head made me desperate like wine—nothing seemed to matter. I laughed in the grim marble face & got a twinkle back. What a big white face he has beside Goldie's mobile brown monkey one! A mouth twisted & shut; not a single line free & easy; all caught, pressed, inhibited; but great driving power some where—& my word what concentration of the eye when he argues! We discussed criticism, & I find he thinks himself a poet. A little human laughter comes very welcome to him, as I guess, & I think he would willingly break up his formal ways. His details

15. Probably Arthur Ponsonby (later Lord Ponsonby of Shulbrede) the pacifist politician and author.

1. The Memoir Club meeting had taken place on 17 November, the Woolfs having dined with the MacCarthys beforehand. VW's contribution was probably '22 Hyde Park Gate' (see *Moments of Being*, 1976, p 142). The next meeting was on 8 December.

2. The first essay in T. S. Eliot's *The Sacred Wood* opens with the words: 'Coleridge was perhaps the greatest of English critics'; LW's review of the book appeared under the heading 'Back to Aristotle' in the *Athenaeum* of 17 December 1920. The successful dinner party took place on 1 December.

about his father in law's appendicitis were very precise. My guess is that he wishes to detach himself from sets, & welcomes us as an escape. Then —what? Gerald Duckworth engaged to Miss Chad—does that count as news? dinner at the Toynbees, but I cant go into that.[3] What do I want to go into? How hard we work—thats what impresses me this winter: every compartment stuffed tight, chiefly owing to the press. Whether we can keep it up, I don't know. Then, both so popular, so well known, so much respected—& Leonard 40, & I nearing it, so there's not much to boast of. In my heart, too, I prefer the nondescript anonymous days of youth. I like youthful minds; & the sense that no one's yet anybody. This refers, with shocking slovenliness—but what will you? I cant write 2,000 words an hour carefully—to tea with Miss Hussey at Clifford's Inn. I dont know why I saw my own youth there: she on her own, a journalist, poor, untidy, enthusiastic; & a younger brother coming in, to tea; not so clever, at least not launched; awkward; oh but so young! Both going off to the play, as Adrian & I did, years ago; but perhaps she's happier than I was. Figure a poverty stricken room; gas fire broken; margarine; one table; books, mostly cheap ones; writing table; no ornament or easy chair—(perhaps I had it) dark november day; up several staircases; bath, kitchen behind a dingy curtain, & another woman sharing. We talked about the need of education. "Surely education must achieve something" the brother stammered. She would have none of it—clever, & paradoxical, & flighty—advanced; but I forgive all that for the sake of youth.

Sunday 12 December

Nearing the end of the year. Everything muffled in snow & crisp with frost; streets knobbed & slippery; hands grimy as cold for some reason always makes them. Here we sit over the fire, expecting Roger—whose book is out; as everyone's book is out—Katherine's, Murry's, Eliot's.[4] None have I read so far. I was happy to hear K. abused the other night. Now why? Partly some obscure feeling that she advertises herself; or Murry does it for her; & then how bad the Athenaeum stories are; yet

3. Gerald Duckworth's *fiancée* was Cecil, daughter of Charles Scott-Chad of Pynkney Hall, near King's Lynn; he was fifty, she much younger. The Woolfs had dined with the Arnold Toynbees in Chelsea on 29 November; he was at this time Professor of Byzantine and Modern Greek at King's College, London; his wife Rosalind, daughter of Professor Gilbert Murray the great classical scholar and his wife Lady Mary, was herself a writer.

4. Roger Fry's *Vision and Design* was published late in November 1920; the other books referred to were *Bliss*, *Aspects of Literature*, and *The Sacred Wood*.

in my heart I must think her good, since I'm glad to hear her abused.

Scenes now come to mind. Gordon Square at tea time— All those branches twisting themselves so fluently, like the Laocoon; so I saw them from Ralph's upper room.[5] Then there's Lytton coming round to tea. At once we plunge, even on the cold pavement, into literature. Eliot's book—"serious" far far better than the journalists—disgraceful review by Lynd.[6] "Still he's cut & dried—leaves cut—don't like Milton." — Shall Lytton write to the Nation? What about Vic? So we pace to Nessa's door. And Ralph? Well, I wdn't marry Ralph— A despot. True. But whats to happen to C. She can't live indefinitely with me— Perhaps with him? Door opens, in I go; up I go; children there; sit over the stove; Nessa draws pictures for Angelica. And home again.

Molly Hamilton next. I'm enlarging my sphere, not very widely, but I take pains to accept what's offered. When accepted, I feel that I must make the most. It's not for nothing that I go out to tea. So there we sit, scratching on the match box. "I'm assistant editor to the Review of Reviews—at a salary of £570!" she cried.[7] And so her mother can live in London; & she's launched; poor Molly can do all this by chaining herself to the desk. There the desk was & books laid out as you see them in shops. Did the match burst into flame? Yes, I think so, about happiness, & human beings. I try not to think whether I'm liked for saying things, or what impression I make, only whether I think the things I say. But with another human being this is very difficult—so susceptible am I, so vain. The poetess came in—poor hard boiled egg, duck's egg; going to dine at the Club, taking herself off.

I forget my first view of Molly, going down the Strand the night of the Cenotaph; such a lurid scene, like one in Hell. A soundless street; no traffic; but people marching. Clear, cold, & windless. A bright light in the Strand; women crying Remember the Glorious Dead, & holding out chrysanthemums. Always the sound of feet on the pavement. Faces bright & lurid—poor M.'s worn enough by that illumination. I touched

5. After their marriage in June, James and Alix Strachey had gone to Vienna to study psychology and to be analysed by Freud; in their absence Ralph Partridge had taken over their rooms at the top of 41 Gordon Square. The Woolfs went to tea and met Lytton there on 10 December.

6. Robert Lynd's review, 'Buried Alive', of Eliot's *The Sacred Wood* was published in the Supplement to the *Nation* on 4 December 1920; Lynd called Eliot 'an undertaker rather than a critic' and controverted his view that *Hamlet* 'is an artistic failure'.

7. Mary Agnes Hamilton was about to become assistant to Philip Gibbs, who had taken on the editorship of the *Review of Reviews*, a once redoubtable weekly which it was hoped to revive.

her arm; whereupon she jumped, like some one woken. A ghastly procession of people in their sleep.[8]

Sunday 19 December

This I see will be the last page of the year, since I go to Janet tomorrow for the night; dine in London at a festival party on Tuesday night; & leave for Rodmell on Wednesday. I shan't take this book with me, though if I'm in the mood I might scribble a page to bring back. I ought to say how happy I am, since one of these pages said how unhappy I was. I can't see any reason in it. My only guess is that it has something to do with working steadily; writing things out of my head; & never having a compartment empty. That doesn't mean that I dont stuff the corners with idle moments. I gaze at the fire. I make phrases—well, thats all well known. I can't help suspecting that both Mr & Mrs Woolf slowly increase in fame. That helps to fill compartments. No doubt I like getting letters from publishers: even to be asked to preside over Mr Beresford slightly kindles me.[9] Next year I shall be above all that. I've plucked out my jealousy of Katherine by writing her an insincere-sincere letter. Her books praised for a column in the Lit Sup—the prelude of paeans to come.[10] I foresee editions; then the Hawthornden prize next summer. So I've had my little nettle growing in me, & plucked it as I say. I've revived my affection for her somehow, & don't mind, in fact enjoy. But I've not read her book.

My book seems to me rather good. L.'s book seems to him (so I interpret) rather good. I am entreated to write for the T.L.S. True, I'm not asked to write for the Dial.[11] Lytton is. Lytton dined here the other night; tired, wearied, by C. & P. I suspect, out every night at Gordon Square & pretending doubts about Vic. We discussed Norton's case. L. very loyal to Apostles in distress, & refusing my irreverent analysis. We talk of going to Italy together. Then there was Roger, on a bitter cold night, but we stoked up, & I've been given his book [*Vision and Design*]

8. On 11 November 1920 the Cenotaph in Whitehall had been unveiled by King George V, a solemn ceremony followed by that of the interment of the Unknown Warrior in Westminster Abbey. LW noted in his diary: 'Streets impassable owing to Unknown Warrior'. The next entry is mis-dated 17 December.

9. John Davys Beresford (1873-1947), a prolific and well-regarded novelist; VW reviewed his book *Revolution* in the *TLS* of 27 January 1921 (Kp C213).

10. See *II VW Letters*, no. 1156. Katherine Mansfield's *Bliss and Other Stories* was reviewed in the *TLS* of 16 December.

11. *The Dial* was a literary monthly published in New York; its editor, Scofield Thayer (see below, 22 July 1923, n 16), was a friend of T. S. Eliot.

—a sumptuous book—in return for writing 200 addresses. I think it reads rudimentary compared with Coleridge. Fancy reforming poetry by discovering something scientific about the composition of light!

Then, characteristically, he deposited a bed, bookcases & stained glass windows in our hall; the glass, of course, broken. I observe that I'm soon muzzled; & my depredations in the herd instantly punished. Indeed, Nessa wouldn't have me living next door for something. Indeed, my retort is, I wouldn't live there. I see myself now taking my own line apart from theirs. One of these days I shan't know Clive if I meet him. I want to know all sorts of other people—retaining only Nessa & Duncan, I think.

The Olivers dined here; Ray sitting impassive in the arm chair, rotund, massive, a little surly, in the style of Widow Creighton.[12] Oliver discussed music. She disapproves of abstract questions in a world where there are so many concrete ones. When she dines out she relaxes. A strange life—to believe in that division between reality & unreality. So we reach the end of the year; which is for us cheerful, I think. For one thing we want to get to Rodmell; to see what has happened to the garden. I shall like a soft grey walk. Then the post. Then reading. Then sitting in the chimney corner. I shall walk out on the flats. We take the servants & ensure comfort, for by contriving it, we're now on the best of terms with them. Left to myself I should invite people down. —then probably regret it. But this is dawdling & rambling—never mind—this poor book must take what it can get & be thankful. (I use my new blotter, just given me by L. for the first time.)

Tuesday 21 December

I add a postscript, observing that its the shortest day of the year, &, L. announces, the first of winter. But I want to note these things. I went to Farnham yesterday.[13] Suburban society on the Bus going up. Young man back from city. Young woman been shopping. "Had a good day? Shall I take your parcels." "No; you might run away with them." Arch badinage. Oh terrible country! Like a giant hen run. Half built houses everywhere. Roads scratched. Heath sandy & mangy. Dinner with Cases. Red light on dog legs—leads me to say "How romantic other people's

12. Louise Creighton (1850-1936) was the widow of Mandell Creighton, Bishop of London (d. 1901); the Stephen and Creighton families had known each other in VW's Kensington youth. Oliver and Ray Strachey dined on 13 December.
13. Janet Case and her sister Emphie had moved in the summer from Hampstead to Windmill House, Rowledge, near Farnham, Surrey.

lives are!" Suddenly the waits start. Scene flooded, of course: Janet not eating her maccaroni till they'd done. After dinner sitting over the fire, door half shut as usual. A mouse came out—"A nice gentleman's mouse" I said. Consternation on part of Emphie. "But what are we to do? I'm thinking of that mouse. You can set a trap for rats but not for mice. Seems so craftly." "Well then keep a cat"— "Yes thats nature's way after all—" "Or leave it alone" "Oh dear no. Mice eat books; besides, they're so dirty. Dear me Janet, I wish we hadn't got a mouse." Question why K.M. is indecent—"So silly, I think" says Emphie. "Might as well talk of washing one's hands." Biscuit & chocolate by my bed, on a small white mat, & so on. What else? oh yes: neighbours. Miss Leonard calling. "A name you don't often hear. But theres a bootmaker in Oxford called Leonard. My brother had a pair of boots made there. His wife didn't quite like it oh eh ha ho!" (little laughs like notes of a flute). 'Mr Minchin writes reviews for the Spectator.' said with great awe.[14] Parrot's hot stuff—Parrot's a slack lot. Oh Parrot—Parrot's put a sink in the front kitchen—Everyone abuses Parrot. Emphie has discovered honey at Bat's Corner, unknown to oldest resident.

We should be dining with Nessa &c: but have been put off; & oh dear, I'm glad to sit over the fire—& how could I if I lived in London?

14. Harry Christopher Minchin (1861-1941), a country neighbour of the Cases, contributed reviews and articles to several papers; he had been a schoolmaster but, in the words of his entry in *Who's Who*, 'grew weary of being a whetstone to the wits of others, and took the plunge of independence'. Miss Leonard is not known; Parrot was presumably a builder.

1921

1921

On Wednesday 22 December the Woolfs had gone to Monks House for Christmas, returning to Richmond on 2 January, when VW brings DIARY IX to an end with the following entry.

Sunday 2 January 1921

(The first time I've written 1921. And it shouldn't be written here—should be written on the first page of a new book—but we're just back from Monk's, & I cant settle to anything—must indeed take a bath & wash my head instantly.) I want to scribble notes of the Rodmell social. Talk with Mrs Hawkesford.[1] Cheery looking woman with pimple on end of nose, dressed in dirty ermines. We gentry sat together; rustics tramping up & down the room (the schoolroom) bumping into me; solemn; spiritless—oh infinitely pathetic the 'parties' of the poor! Anyhow not so badly off as clergymen's wives. The first thing she told me, with passion, was that Russell's had sent a plain instead of a fruit cake. "Thats the way they treat you in the country. I can't go 7 miles to complain. None of us like plain cakes. So it won't be eaten. I had to make another cake today. And sometimes they send things so badly packed—in dirty paper too—that they fall to pieces when they're undone—" Then, without preface, to the sorrows of family life. Olive in London, member of the forum, won't stick to anything, now giving dancing lessons with Miss Barker "*using* Miss Barker's name of course. Lady Portarlington is joining.[2] Still, she won't marry, girls dont who take to those ways—& whats to happen in middle life? Thats what I say." Then Bowen. Almost 18 but wont put her hair up— "What am I to do? There's no life for a girl here—no girl friends— She hears Olive talk of London. She'll go next. If she leaves me I dont think I shall be able to stand it. I never sent her to a school so that she mightn't get unsettled. We go to Brighton. She's fond of lectures. She likes chemistry. Olive says she ought to read The Times. We dont take The Times—nor does Mr Allinson [Allison]. He lends us picture papers. But she ought to read the debates.

1. The wife of the Rev. James Boen Hawkesford, Rector of Rodmell from 1896-1928; they had two daughters, Olive and Boen.
2. The Forum was a residential club for ladies in Grosvenor Place; there is no information on the dancing class and its votaries.

Then she could talk to people. Why I can hardly talk to educated people now. One gets out of things. One sees no one. Things happen without one's knowing." She had been in London, & stayed with friends in W. Kensington (where she was brought up) & their house looked over Queens [Club Athletic Ground]. "Always some game going on—ideal I call it". She had made Bowen learn tennis at Tonbridge. "But we were only there for a fortnight—not long enough to learn. She's so shy— People are so stand offish in Lewes. Nothing is ever got up. No tennis parties. Mr Babington (Lord Monk Bretton's people you know) had a lawn at Rodmell Place. Mr Duberly turned his pony on it. Now its given up completely."[3] I offered books, tennis, & The Times. Real unhappiness of course—such isolation too; a cruelty to animals to keep a woman without interests alone in the country to magnify cakes. Still can't go to London because in London a clergyman depends upon pew rents. I should have to pay calls. I should have to make myself nice to people. And we should only get a poor parish. Oh I dont say a word against this—or the people—only for 7 years we've not had a road—its too bad—

VW here starts DIARY X, the title-page of which is inscribed:

HOGARTH HOUSE
RICHMOND
JAN. 1921

Tuesday 25 January

Here have I waited 25 days before beginning the new year; & the 25 is, not unfortunately my 25th, but my 39th birthday; & we've had tea, & calculated the costs of printing Tchekov; now L. is folding the sheets of his book, & Ralph has gone, & I having taken this out of the press proceed to steal a few minutes to baptise it. I must help L. & can't think of a solemn beginning. I'm at a crisis in Jacob: want to finish in 20,000 words, written straight off in a frenzy. And I must pull myself together to bring it off. Tomorrow we ini[ti]ate the Cock Club, Sanger, Pippa, Molly Hamilton & Sidney [Waterlow] dining 'along side' of us.[4] Lytton

---

3. Lord Monk Bretton of Conyboro on the far side of Lewes was a local aristocrat; the other two Rodmell 'gentry'.
4. The Cock Tavern, 22 Fleet Street, was a chop-house with literary associations favoured by the Woolfs ever since they lived in adjacent Clifford's Inn in 1912/13.

has asked to dedicate Victoria to me, which pleases me, & I stipulate, from vanity, for my name in full.[5]

Then, if I had time, I could write a new chapter in Clive's life. Spring has miraculously renewed herself. Pink almond blossoms are in bud. Callow birds crow. In short, he's out of love & in love, & contemplated eloping with a Spaniard in a motor car.[6] "But after all, I said to myself as I walked back, I like to think of my book & my armchair. It's terrible, terrible. I can't give up my old friends after all." The dusky one lives in Chelsea, has a car, no husband, children, & is beautiful as the Southern night. No one has ever seen her, & she, to her credit, has never heard of Maynard Keynes. We speculate about Mary's attitude. Poor parrokeet fallen off her perch, or left to preen & prink in solitude. Then we're just over the crest of a Sydney swell: such a solemn heaving one; the poor man's bosom all clouded & turgid owing to Murry; who sits at Hampstead promulgating doctrines, & caring not at all that S. seriously thinks of leaving wife & children. "I have no solid core. I am unlike everyone else, & probably more unhappy."[7] Indeed his bloodhound eyes drooped & almost spilt tears. We talked sense into him, & the inflated tumour burst. He came down happier to breakfast; & a little less certain of the worth of Murry's goodness. What Murry's goodness amounts to I'm puzzled to say. K.M. (as the papers call her) swims from triumph to triumph in the reviews; save that Squire doubts her genius—so, I'm afraid, do I. These little points, though so cleanly collected, don't amount to much, I think. I read her at the Club last night; then went with L. to the Grand Guignol.[8]

Monday 31 January

Just back from Tidmarsh, from the Club, from Harrison's [Dentist], from losing two books on a bus. Lytton keeps his books amazingly tidy,

5. Lytton Strachey's *Queen Victoria*, published in April 1921, bore the dedication 'To Virginia Woolf' (see *II VW Letters*, no. 1165).

6. Clive Bell's affair with Juana Ganderillas (disobligingly referred to elsewhere as 'the Guano') lasted somewhat less than a year. She was 'very stupid, but so incredibly beautiful' (*II VW Letters*, no. 1176).

7. See *II VW Letters*, no. 1164 of 19 January to Sydney Waterlow: 'Of course I understand that when one feels, as you feel, without a core—it used to be a very familiar feeling to me—then all one's external relations become febrile and unreal.' See also below, 15 November 1921.

8. The 'Grand Guignol' repertory company were giving a programme of six short plays at the Little Theatre, Adelphi. The cast included Sybil Thorndike, Lewis Casson and Russell Thorndike.

like books on the stage. We slept Friday night with Philip at the farm; wet of course; but dryness & comfort within.⁹ A hot bath, linen sheets (oh what a housekeeper I'm becoming!) Poor Philip—so I feel him— worn & dogged, but not much life in him. He is kept at it perpetually, now paying men, now tending a cow with ringworm. We walked to pay woodmen after breakfast through the slim green trees, fading away rather mysteriously, striping the view with their green. The woodmen had their fire in a ditch & were drinking tea. So round to the farm. The cows henpeck the bull, & don't allow his attentions. Philip drove us over [to Tidmarsh], & we sat in the drawing room, lacking life as people's empty rooms do. L. much depressed on Sunday morning & working out how many hours remained, before breakfast. Indeed, Saturday night was hard going. Lytton lapsed into gentle indifference, tired, depressed perhaps. Carrington I think grows older, & her doings are of the sort that age. L. told Murry's story, & we rated him one of those born queer. Carrington had other versions of his machinations with other hypnotised rabbits. Still even this didn't keep us going; & middle age—am I not 39? —brings I fear its dependence upon warmth & books & easy chairs. Next day was better, though of course one never has a [? box] in a strange house, & about 11.30 my eyes feel rough & sore with gazing at the fire. But it was better, undoubtedly. C[arrington]. & R[alph]. tactfully made out lists of summer flowers in the dining room.

"You ought to have dedicated Vic. to C." I said.

Oh dear no—we're not on those terms at all.

"Ottoline will be enraged."

Yes, he thought she might be.

The ms. was there, & once I began reading it, I couldn't stop; or rather had to stop myself. Talk of going to Italy at Easter with the party but— One of the 'buts' is the Press. I sometimes think that L. & I are settling in too soundly. And now, am I to learn Russian with him & Kot? If he can read it & solace his age with it I shall be furious. Talk about Keats & Wordsworth & C. & P[artridge]. Lytton intends to live in Gordon Square permanently; & she is penniless; & P. is possessive— Perhaps after all, said Lytton, one oughtn't to allow these attachments. Our parents may have been right. & so we discussed our parents, & how Ly S. &

9. Lytton Strachey lived at The Mill House, Tidmarsh, with his devoted Carrington as its châtelaine; Ralph Partridge, whom he loved and who was in love with Carrington, normally spent each week-end there. Philip Sidney Woolf (1889-1962), LW's youngest brother, who since demobilisation was training as a farm manager, was at Greenmoor Hill Farm, Woodcote, about six miles north of Tidmarsh.

Lytton (Lord) & Fitzj. would sit talking till 2 A.M.—but what about?[10] So many things could never be said, & the remaining ones coloured by the abstinence. But I'm broiling as I write & can't settle to anything, & detest going away, & vow never to do it, but to work, work, work—

Saturday 5 February

Jealousy or ambition has won the day, & I've just had my first Russian lesson & mortgaged my time to the extent of doing three lessons weekly. L. is mumbling Russian as I write. Have I done a great deal of work in pursuance of my vow? Books begin to drop in, & so long as I can do them every other week I rather like the relief from Jacob. I am beginning the last lap; & it is a sprint towards the end, difficult to keep up.

We had the Memoir Club on Wednesday. Clive & Maynard read; both elaborate & polished, Clive mellow & reminiscent about Mrs Raven Hill (he had her 2 years after his marriage, & for the last time in 1914. She is now imbecile. This was a surprise to me. She coincided with his attachment to me then. But she was a voluptuary. He was not 'in love'.)[1] Maynard, of course, was the solid piece of the evening, so long indeed that we had to leave before the end.[2] I was a little bored by the politics, & a good deal impressed by the method of character drawing. Rosy Wemyss, illegitimate descendant of William the 4th came out very well, —sitting in mock despair at the conference where he presided, unable to answer a question until Maynard had scribbled it for him.[3] Then

10. Lady Strachey had made friends with the new viceroy, Edward Robert Bulwer, 1st Earl of Lytton (1831-1891), on her last visit to India in 1877-79 (she named her son Lytton after him). He returned to England in 1880, and renewed his close friendship with the judge James Fitzjames Stephen (1829-1894), VW's uncle.

1. According to Clive Bell's memoir he first dallied with Mrs Raven-Hill, or Mrs Raven-Hill first dallied with him, in the summer of 1899, when she was 'at once the Aspasia and the Gaby de Lys of North Wilts.' *Née* Annie Rogers, she was the wife of the *Punch* cartoonist Leonard Raven-Hill, and died in 1930.

2. Maynard Keynes' memoir 'Dr Melchior' traces the complicated negotiations with Germany at Paris, Trèves, Spa and Brussels for the second renewal of the Armistice, and describes the characters of many of the leading participants. See *Two Memoirs* (1949). VW wrote the day after the meeting to ask Keynes if he would let the Woolfs have his manuscript so they might read what they had missed. See *II VW Letters*, no. 1166.

3. Rosslyn ('Rosie') Erskine Wemyss (1864-1933), 1st Baron Wester Wemyss, Admiral of the Fleet and First Sea Lord 1917-19, headed the Allied delegation to the Brussels Conference at which Germany consented to the surrender of her merchant fleet as part of the Peace negotiations. The Admiral's maternal grandmother was Augusta, fourth daughter of the Duke of Clarence, later King William IV, by his liaison with Mrs Jordan. See *Two Memoirs*, pp 62-7.

Melchior; & his room, where the three clerks refused to leave off playing the piano. "Smoking isn't allowed until 5" they said; "This is the German revolution" was Melchior's comment.[4] "I was rather in love with him" said Maynard. I think he meant it seriously, though we laughed. Then L.G. at the table, overwhelmed by his own eloquence—denouncing Klotz & 'goold' making a gesture as of a miser sweeping up money bags.[5] All this was very brilliantly told. Mary was there; & I note that one likes her better, partly for showing fight; partly, perhaps, for not being the mistress any longer. I am in hot water for having told Sydney, which I did deliberately, without malice, as conversation, thinking it allowed. Oh what a goose Sydney is! What does he do but march up & congratulate Clive in front of everyone!

Wednesday 16 February

Russian is snatching all the time spared for this book. I can only keep up with L. by running as hard as I can. Everyone prophecies an early end. But I feel myself attached to an express train. With Kot & Leonard dragging me, I must be pulled through somehow. Six months continued at this rate—Russian from 12.15 to 12.45 & from 5.30 to 6. from 9.30 to 10, & on the way to Waterloo & back again must have some result. So far the chief one is as I say that I don't write here. Let me think how many occasions I have let slip.

We have dined twice at the Cock, repairing afterwards to Hussey's— no Hussey has married the dullest man in England—to Niemeyer's room;[6] the gas fire is broken. We balance on hard chairs. But the atmosphere is easy & pleasant; the dinner modest, solid, & somehow in keeping with our clothes. More & more do I become in a state of undress. I believe this affects my writing—or its the other way about. Pale, marmoreal Eliot was there last week, like a chapped office boy on a high stool, with a cold in his head, until he warms a little, which he did.

---

4. See *Two Memoirs*, pp 48-9.
5. 'Lloyd George had always hated him and despised him; and now saw in a twinkling that he could kill him. Women and children were starving, he cried, and here was M. Klotz prating and prating of his "goold" '. *Two Memoirs*, p 61.
6. Doris Edith Hussey married Ralph Roscoe Enfield (1885-1973) on 5 February 1921; educated at Bedales and Christ Church, Oxford, he had joined the Ministry of Agriculture in 1919 and became a leading agricultural-economist. Otto Ernst Niemeyer (1883-1971), created KCB in 1924, was a colleague and superior of Saxon Sydney-Turner in the Treasury; he had beaten Maynard Keynes into second place in the Civil Service Entrance Examinations in 1906. He had presumably taken over Hussey's set of rooms in Clifford's Inn.

We walked back along the Strand. "The critics say I am learned & cold" he said. "The truth is I am neither." As he said this, I think coldness at least must be a sore point with him.

Then there was Murry's farewell dinner at 46.[7] Clive gritty & bawling, Lytton observant & mute. The rest much as usual. I sat next Murry, & let my prejudices run away with me for the first half. He posed, I thought; looked anguished & martyred. Yet the dinner was at his request. I kept thinking how he summed up us & held us worthless. Then, at the end, I asked after Katherine. Poor man! he poured himself out. We sat on after the others had gone.

"But I lacked imagination, he said. I never saw. I ought to have understood. I've always held one was free to do as one likes. But she was ill, & that made all the difference. And it was nothing—nothing at all."

This referred of course, without names, to the Bibesco Scandal, with which London, so they say, rings.

"And I adore Katherine— She's absolutely the most fascinating person in the world—I'm wholly in love with her."

Apparently she is worse—dying? God knows. This affair seems to have brought on a crisis. She is desperately depressed, thinks her book bad, can't write; accuses herself; I imagine, is beside herself with jealousy. Murry asked me to write to her. She feels herself out of things, left alone, forgotten. As he spoke with great feeling, & seemed to be very miserable, & anxious to apologise (was it for this that he wished to see us all—to prove that there was nothing in it?) I liked him, felt with him, & I think there can be no doubt that his love for Katherine anyhow is sincere. All the rest seems of no great importance beside it. Sydney's version is of course absurdly over emphatic. We went upstairs & told stories about Ottoline. Desmond was the chief performer. He gets his edges too blurred for my taste. Humanity can be due to laziness, as well as kindness. He refuses to think—seems to trust to natural niceness to float him through personal affairs—or so I feel; & thus gets nothing very sharp or thrilling. At anyrate, when Lytton & Roger came to facts they painted a far more

7. In November 1920 Katherine Mansfield, miserably ill and lonely at Mentone, had heard of Murry's philandering with Princess Elizabeth Bibesco (*née* Asquith); he had undertaken to end the relationship but the publication of a story by Elizabeth Bibesco in the *Athenaeum* of 14 January 1921 had precipitated a fresh access of bitterness and despair and, with the paper losing money, Murry had decided to rejoin Katherine. In February the *Athenaeum*, which he had edited for two years, was merged with the *Nation* (see F. A. Lea, *The Life of John Middleton Murry*, 1959, pp 80-1). The dinner at 46 Gordon Square took place on Friday 11 February.

⟨splendid⟩ vivid figure, Owing to Leonard, it may be, or to natural good taste, I find 46 a little blaring & brazen always, & didn't much mind catching the last train home. Lytton slipped out with us & whispered his horror & repulsion in the hall. *Never* would he dine there again. Clive *too* appalling. L. agreed. So did I. For the truth is no one can speak in their natural voice. Clive was telephoning to Gavrillana (or how does she call herself)? for twenty minutes. An envelope addressed to her lay in the hall. He plumes himself on the affair, which might be conducted on the moon for all I believe in it. I imagine her as stupid as a pearl tie pin.

I skip lots of people, lots of doings. We now think of Cornwall at Easter, with Lytton's troupe. My book is an eyesore, & I wake in the night twitching with horror at the thought of it. Now to Dorothy Wordsworth—a quiet evening for once. We have taken to dining out, for some reason.

Friday 18 February

I have been long meaning to write a historical disquisition on the return of peace; for old Virginia will be ashamed to think what a chatterbox she was, always talking about people, never about politics. Moreover, she will say, the times you lived through were so extraordinary. They must have appeared so, even to quiet women living in the suburbs. But indeed nothing happens at one moment rather than another. The history books will make it much more definite than it is. The most significant sign of peace this year is the sales; just over; the shops have been flooded with cheap clothes. A coat & skirt that cost £14 in November went for 7 perhaps 5. People had ceased to buy, & the shops had to dispose of things somehow. Margery Strachey who has been teaching at Debenhams foretells bankruptcy for most of the shopkeepers this very month.[8] Still they go on selling cheaply. Pre-war prices, so they say. And I have found a street market in Soho where I buy stockings at 1/ a pair: silk ones (flawed slightly) at 1/10. A hundred yards down the road they ask 5/6 to 10/6 for the same things, or so they seem. Food has fallen a penny here, a penny there, but our books scarcely show a change. Milk is high, 11d a quart. Butter fallen to 3/- but this is Danish butter. Eggs—I dont know what eggs are. Servant girls aged 20 get £45 wages. And the Times pays me 3 guineas instead of £2.2 for a column. But I think

8. Debenham & Freebody, the drapery and fashion department store of Wigmore Street; such large emporiums normally took responsibility for the housing and instruction of the greater number of their female employees.

you'll find all this written more accurately in other books, my dear Virginia: for instance in Mrs Gosse's diary & Mrs Webb's.[9] I think it true to say that during the past 2 months we have perceptibly moved towards cheapness—*just* perceptibly. It is just perceptible too that there are very few wounded soldiers abroad in blue, though stiff legs, single legs, sticks shod with rubber, & empty sleeves are common enough. Also at Waterloo I sometimes see dreadful looking spiders propelling themselves along the platform—men all body—legs trimmed off close to the body. There are few soldiers about.

To change the subject, Rose Macaulay dined here last week—something like a lean sheep dog in appearance—harum scarum—humble—too much of a professional, yet just on the intellectual side of the border. Might be religious though: mystical perhaps. Not at all dominating or impressive: I daresay she observes more than one thinks for. Clear pale mystical eyes. A kind of faded moon of beauty: oh & badly dressed. I don't suppose we shall ever meet for she lives with Royd Smith, & somehow won't come to grips with us.[10]

Monday 21 February

To fill in an awkward space between Russian & dinner I take up this book. I ought to notice the long drawn spring afternoon—tea easily by daylight—Ralph able to set up 8 lines afterwards. Leonard's book will be printed by the end of the week perhaps. Massingham would be grateful if I would review D. Richardson for him.[11] This amuses & slightly gratifies me—especially as I refuse. We dined with Roger the other night; & found Sydney still a grudging reluctant convert—still remembering his master, not his own man or Roger's man. After dinner we

---

9. Mrs Gosse, *née* Ellen Epps, was the wife of the prominent man of letters Edmund Gosse, who contributed a weekly article to the *Sunday Times*; and Beatrice Webb, who *did* keep a diary, large extracts from which were published by her in 1926 and 1948, and by Margaret Cole in 1952 and 1956.

10. (Emilie) Rose Macaulay (1881-1958), dutiful if rebellious daughter in a large family; her father ended his career as a Cambridge don. She published her first book in 1906, since when two books of poetry and nine more novels, including *Potterism* (see above, 19 August 1920), had appeared. She contributed to the *Westminster Gazette* and became a protégé of its literary editor Naomi Gwladys Royde-Smith (d. 1964), in whose house, 44 Princes Gardens, Kensington, she now lived when in London, and for whose celebrated weekly literary parties she acted as joint hostess. Rose Macaulay had become an Anglo-Catholic before the war.

11. Dorothy Richardson's *Deadlock* (1921), the sixth volume in her novel sequence *Pilgrimage*.

turned over sketches in the studio—not the pleasantest occupation for a cold night. Still old Roger has a quality of imagination which attracts me—loose & warm & genuine, in contrast to the costive judicial Sydney, who was catching us out all the time. Sydney looks melancholy; is touched with grey. This gives him an air of distinction. I daresay his face has been one of his horrors. The looking glass always confirming the Apostles.[12] Then we had Quentin & Julian for Sunday, packed Julian home with a temperature, & I put him to bed. Quentin ran in to see Angelica; came up saying she was better but very white. I liked to think of all this set going in the younger generation.

Saxon & Matthew for dinner—a successful combination. A tyrannous old mother has again devastated a daughters life.[13] I see how easily one says of course the daughter must look after her—of course she does, & gives up her dream—only of Geneva—still it was a dream; & must now teach music in Maida Vale until the old tyrant dies.

Tuesday 1 March

I am not satisfied that this book is in a healthy way. Suppose one of my myriad changes of style is antipathetic to the material?—or does my style remain fixed? To my mind it changes always. But no one notices. Nor can I give it a name myself. The truth is that I have an internal, automatic scale of values; which decides what I had better do with my time. It dictates 'This half hour must be spent on Russian' 'This must be given to Wordsworth.' or 'now I'd better darn my brown stockings.' How I come by this code of values I dont know. Perhaps its the legacy of puritan grandfathers. I suspect pleasure slightly. God knows. And the truth is also that writing, even here, needs screwing of the brain— not so much as Russian, but then half the time I learn Russian I look in the fire & think what I shall write tomorrow. Mrs Flanders is in the orchard. If I were at Rodmell I should have thought it all out walking on the flats. I should be in fine writing trim. As it is Ralph Carrington & Brett have this moment gone; I'm dissipated; we dine & go out to the Guild. I cant settle as I should to think of Mrs Flanders in the orchard. Brett is gay, pink, brown, vivacious. Why did I think her a moping

12. The fact that he had not been elected to the Apostles whilst at Cambridge was the source of perpetual mortification to Sydney Waterlow.

13. Louise Ernestine Matthaei was LW's assistant on the *International Review*, and subsequently on the *Contemporary Review*. Later in 1921 she did succeed in going to Geneva where she joined the agricultural service of the ILO. Her mother was a teacher of music.

figure in the chimney corner? Ott's insinuations, I suppose. She told me that she has an inner view of Ottoline unguessed by the rest of us. Deafness, she says, makes one a judge of truth. You become an expert in faces.[1]

We came back from Rodmell yesterday; & Rodmell was all gold & sunshine. The one dismal element was provided by the human race. We went to tea at the Rectory, & found, alas, a roomful of dressed women, including Mrs Allinson, & Mr Fisher, & Mr & Mrs Shanks. This surly poet, so we judged him (and his poetry is Squire's poetry) proposes to live in the village. We shall meet him. He will look in. Oh dear—no more dreaming & rambling for me—always the risk of a recall to editions & royalties, & what Sylvia Lynd thinks of Tomlinson. Our garden becomes a suburban garden.[2] Anything would be better than a poet—than one of Squire's poets. I would rather have Gerald Duckworth himself—& he is to be married tomorrow.[3]

It is settled that we go to Zennor with the Lytton company on the 23rd. Before that we go to Manchester. So the summer is on us. Already I feel time broken up. I must buy some clothes. & I note with pride that I have just received £45 from America for the V[oyage]. O[ut].[4] Then Violet Dickinson came to tea here—grown half a foot taller, but otherwise unchanged; wrists a little coarse & even dirty; pearls & emeralds round her neck; asking questions, never listening, rapid, intuitive,

1. The Hon. Dorothy Eugénie Brett (1883-1977), painter, elder daughter of the 2nd Viscount Esher, was a contemporary of Carrington's at the Slade; she had spent a good part of the war with the Morrells at Garsington, but now lived in her own house at Pond Street, Hampstead. She was deaf. For Mrs Flanders in the orchard, see *Jacob's Room*, pp 14-15.
2. The tea-party at the Rectory was by invitation of the Rev. and Mrs Hawkesford; Mr Fisher is unidentified; Elsie Allison was the wife of J. M. Allison (see above, 15 September 1920); Edward (Richard Burton) Shanks (1892-1953), history scholar of Trinity College, Cambridge, was the first winner of the Hawthornden Prize 1or Imaginative Literature with his third book of poems, *Queen of China*, in 1919; from 1919-22 he was assistant editor on Squire's *London Mercury*; in 1921 he and his wife took Charnes Cottage, separated from Monks House garden only by the church path; this marriage came to grief, and he remarried in 1926. Sylvia Lynd, *née* Dryhurst (1888-1952), wife of the journalist and essayist Robert Lynd, was herself a novelist and poet. Henry Major Tomlinson (1873-1958), war correspondent and writer, was literary editor of the *Nation* from 1917-23.
3. Gerald Duckworth's marriage to Cecil Alice Scott-Chad was solemnized at St Mary Abbot's, Kensington, where his sister Stella Duckworth had been married to Jack Hills in 1897.
4. George H. Doran Company published both *The Voyage Out* and *Night and Day* in the course of 1920. (In 1925 the American rights in both titles were sold to Harcourt Brace & Co.)

humorous in her slap dash way, careering about to tea parties marriages & sick beds & keeping up her connection with lunatics & institutions, like a woman of the 90ties. One of the lay sisters who go about doing good, & talking gossip, almost improved out of existence nowadays I suppose; a survival from the 19th Century are of individual goodness.[5]

My book is back from the printer, who has added the final eyesore—a brown back. There it is in masses, & I can't read it, for fear of howlers, printers as well as writers. L.'s stories are today, bating a line or two, done. Now Clive proposes we should bring out his private poems.[6] Morgan goes to India, & I think for ever. He will become a mystic, sit by the roadside, & forget Europe, which I think he half despises. In thirty years time he may turn up again, give us an amused look, & return to the East, having written a little unintelligible poetry. He has no roots here. And the news made me melancholy. I like him, & like having him about. But we shan't see him again. He sails on Friday.[7]

Sunday 6 March

But perhaps I colour my view of Morgan from my painter's box. At any rate, Bob at the Cock the other night made it all seem very reasonable & desirable— "a trip to India just the thing for him—a relief after his . . . well, his mother is trying sometimes—very fond of him, of course; devoted to him & he . . ." This in the usual Bob style, hinting little defects & mysteries with one corner of his mouth, praising with the other.

We had a Cock on Friday—perhaps not quite so good, though vociferous & noisy. Marjorie dines out seldom, I fancy, likes society,

5. Violet Dickinson (1865-1948) came from a well-connected family on the Wiltshire-Somerset borders whose country neighbours included the Duckworths and the Thynnes. VW met her first in 1902 when she was twenty and Violet thirty-seven, and for many years depended very much on her loving friendship, but time and circumstances had by now loosened the bonds of intimacy. She was some 6 feet tall, and lived with her younger brother Oswald when in London at Manchester Street, or in her country house, Burnham Wood near Welwyn.

6. *Monday or Tuesday* (Kp A5) was produced for the Woolfs by a Richmond jobbing printer, Mr McDermott, owner of the nearby Prompt Press; he had been extremely helpful to the tyro LW on printing matters, and this was the first job to be entrusted to him. The result was 'one of the worst printed books ever published' (see *III LW*, 239-40). LW's own *Stories of the East* were hand set and printed at Hogarth House; Clive Bell's *Poems* were also to be produced there by December 1921 (*HP Checklist* 12).

7. On 4 March 1921 E. M. Forster set off on his second visit to India, this time to act as Private Secretary to the Ruler of the state of Dewas Senior; he returned to England towards the end of the year.

throws herself into it, & dresses in salmon pink, short skirt & white stockings: like all Stracheys undoes her premedi[t]ated care by unpremedi[t]ated outbursts—hugs her legs till you see—well, all there is. Then I was locked with Bob; had my brain wrung dry by his horny conscientious hands. He starts so well; means so well; is a man of such seriousness & integrity—touched with white on the temples to lend him dignity too—so that to begin with I both like & admire. Oh yes: I end with that too; & yet the steam roller has gone over me—he takes criticism say, or the verse drama, & by the time its over, everything is tight tied in knots; nothing illuminated. He has a shrewd way with him; but why he ever applied himself to an art which wants invention, richness, abandon, originality I really cant say. Poor Bobo was a little stupid as she expressed it: dumb, I should have said; brooding ineffectively over the sorrows of the world. Poor Betty . . . poor someone else, left with a bastard. Then she can't, as she says 'find my form', whether its to be realism, romance, comedy, tragedy. I was more interested in poor Betty, who has come a cropper, which as I explained, is what one likes people to do.[8] She lost £200 on her play the other day (Wilde, Bottomley & Fielding: unrecorded) got no notices, no praise, can get no work, has spent all her money; is financed by the Mayors, but they cant make a great actress of her, provide her with a chin, or curtail her nose. She flames with the most melodramatic ambition. Nothing short of a great part, a great audience, a great success will satisfy her. She refuses to accept whatever it is she might have, leaves dreadful notes on the hall table for Bobo—who in her turn writes plays, can't find her form, & is rejected by stage managers. One sees indeed, without much difficulty why the type is an unmarketable one. All is too soft & emotional. Now for writing or anything I believe you must be able to screw up into a ball & pelt straight in people's faces. They vagulate & dissipate.

We parted on an island in Kingsway: she saying to me, looking out from her great dark eyes under her wide hat, hair looping down, a little wild, yet infinitely soft—even woolly, "I see this evening that I must give up writing" or words to that effect. What she meant, I dont know. Was it a compliment to me? as I should like to think. How pleasant to

8. Elizabeth Meinertzhagen (1892-1948) was one of Beatrice Mayor's five sisters; their mother had been one of nine Potter sisters (another was Beatrice Webb), and Betty Potter was the name she adopted for her stage work. She had appeared as Goneril in the 1920 Players' production of Gordon Bottomley's *King Lear's Wife* at the Kingsway Theatre, in a programme which also included *A Florentine Tragedy* by Oscar Wilde and *The Virgin Unmasked* by Henry Fielding. The Woolfs saw it on the afternoon of 22 February.

have ruined someone's life all in one evening! But she is one of those who only drift a little way in desperation: she is anchored in niceness & general muddle. So I daresay, is Betty, to whom I've just written.

Nessa approves of Monday or Tuesday—mercifully; & thus somewhat redeems it in my eyes. But I now wonder a little what the reviewers will make of it—this time next month. Let me try to prophecy. Well, the Times will be kindly, a little cautious. Mrs Woolf, they will say, must beware of virtuosity. She must beware of obscurity . . . her great natural gifts &c. . . . She is at her best in the simple lyric, as in Kew Gardens. An Unwritten Novel is hardly a success. And as for A Society, though spirited, it is too one-sided. Still Mrs Woolf can always be read with pleasure. Then, in the Westminster, Pall Mall, other serious evening papers I shall be treated very shortly, with sarcasm. The general line will be that I am becoming too much in love with the sound of my own voice: not much in what I write: indecently [?] affected; a disagreeable woman. The truth is, I expect, that I shan't get very much attention anywhere. Yet, I become rather well known. Now L. may have considerable success.

Thursday 10 March

Mr Chancellor has been here trying to make us discontented with our offer for Suffield—not that it is an offer: we have stated terms; will take £1400. Now Chancellors say at auction we might get £17 or £1800.[9] But this is doubtful; & an amusing example of the tug of war between business men, & the shady shifts they resort to to poach each others game.

For news, what is there? I lunched with Nessa & Duncan the other day, & dashed my pleasure by losing my Roman brooch. Duncan has a large proper studio with a gallery, a deserted place, very silent, off Haverstock Hill, where a murder might take place, or a dead body be found. On the contrary, they were very cheerful, having been to Cambridge, seen the Greek play, heard Roger lecture, & ravished their eyes on several beauties—for there are beauties now, not seekers after truth, as in my day.[10]

9. Chancellors were the Richmond Estate Agents through whom the Woolfs had originally bought Hogarth House in 1915, and who were now handling the sale of Suffield House for them.

10. The Oresteian Trilogy, produced by J. T. Sheppard with a cast of undergraduates, was performed at the New Theatre, Cambridge, from 2-9 March 1921; Roger Fry's lecture, on 'Composition', was given to the Heretics' Society on Sunday evening, 6 March.

Norton has descended. Bob, of course, muddled it all up. Norton can lunch at any rate at 46; & proposes to live there; yet is desperate; verging on suicidal; can talk of nothing but himself; & will, Nessa thinks, hang about them all like an old decomposing albatross. There's a new suggestion Dr who can make your hair curl, & unravel every knot in your nerves as far as 20 years back—but Norton can't be made to face him. So Craig goes on rubbing in the suggestion that Norton can't work; & he can't work; & now proposes to get employment with the Webbs. What other news? Singularly little in the way of letters this week, not that I ever write them.

Sunday 13 March

Well our terms for Suffield have been accepted of course; & of course we feel, or I feel, slightly defrauded—great nonsense, as we are sure of our money this way, save on the auction, & at most could only have made another £150, I suppose. Still it was the gambler's chance that I liked. People called Turner have bought it, old & deaf, which appears to be necessary should you live at Suffield.[11]

We dined with the Sangers заңувров on Friday. No one there, or came in afterwards, but Molly [MacCarthy]; & all our grey heads over the fire made me feel a little greyheaded. We discussed death, a sore subject with Dora, I suspect; one of her morbidities. She cant face it. But then death, as I made out for myself at the age of 12, coming at the end of illness is altogether different from death as one sits over the fire. Charlie a little silent as this went forward, as at the display of a wifes complexes husbands mostly are. Molly was very deaf, resigned, but intermittently deaf only. Charlie not very encouraging about Russian— at least he says the literature is scarcely worth the trouble. Nothing but the great novels, & these adequately translated. But I doubt whether any English pupil can judge of this. A person with my taste shut up in a library might unearth treasures. Anyhow this is provision for old age. Also we talk of Russia next year—also language helps one to understand writers atmosphere, like seeing their country. And then Kot will pull us through; & vanity urges. Kot, poor honest somehow wounded man let out by chance that Katherine lost 3 ms books he [word missing] of Tchehov's letters.[12] He patiently sets to work to write them out again.

11. Suffield House was purchased by C. G. Turner, a Richmond Solicitor, for £1400.
12. Katherine Mansfield had collaborated with Koteliansky, who was a close friend of hers, in translating a number of Chekhov's letters which were published in the *Athenaeum* in 1919.

Unless she has some very good excuse this seems to me wanton cruelty on her part. She is a tidy methodical woman. How could one lose 3 books lent one by a man who gets his bread by writing? But she never abused Kot; as he does them.

Time is a good deal broken just now by the journey to Manchester next Wednesday. We come back on Friday, then to Cornwall on Wednesday. So what am I to write? What am I to read? I have scribbled an article for Desmond;[13] tomorrow I distemper the kitchen rose pink & leaf green. I can't begin Dorothy Wordsworth, nor start Jacob's travels to the East. Still, I generally put in my pen & pick out something.

In the way of history the Germans have gone back to Germany.[14] People go on being shot & hanged in Ireland. Dora described mass going on all day in Dublin for some wretched boy killed early on Monday morning. The worst of it is the screen between our eyes & these [?] gallows is so thick. So easily one forgets it—or I do. For instance why not set down that the Maids of Honour shop was burnt out the other night?[15] Is it a proof of civilisation to envisage suffering at a distance—& then the faculty of seeing that laws matter—the constitution of Cheko-Slovakia for example—is that an important one?[16] Anyhow very little bestowed on me.

Eliot dines here tonight, alone, since his wife is in a nursing home, not much to our regret. But what about Eliot? Will he become 'Tom'? What happens with friendships undertaken at the age of 40? Do they flourish & live long? I suppose a good mind endures, & one is drawn to it & sticks to it, owing to having a good mind myself. Not that Tom admires my writing, damn him.

Nessa has influenza; slightly; & I'm glad to see how solicitous dear old Duncan is, waiting on her, & taking thought for her, better I think than Clive ever did. That little man postpones his poems till the autumn, meaning, I daresay, to add one or two in praise of his dusky lady. I am told that poor Moll Hutch. found the separation intolerable, & has come

13. No signed article by VW appeared in the *New Statesman* in March 1921.
14. The German delegation to the Reparations Conference in London (1-7 March, 1921) returned to Berlin on 8 March, their proposed modifications to the amount and manner of payment of the German war indemnity having been rejected by the Allies. See *A Revision of the Treaty* (1922) by J. M. Keynes.
15. 'Maids of Honour' were small sweet spicy tarts to be had at Billett's, 3 Hill Street, Richmond, called after the ladies in waiting of Caroline of Anspach, wife of King George II, whose summer residence was at Richmond.
16. The interim constitution of the newly-created Czechoslovak state issued on 13 November 1918 had been replaced on 29 February 1920 by one instituting a centralised rather than a federal state.

back to platonic intercourse; strictly platonic. How the pismire survives the tug of war; or whether he sucks pleasure from it I cannot say. Anyhow he dines out nightly, 'not been in, I suppose, since the night you dined with us,' he boasts; & mixes with society 'which, thank God, he doesn't bring here' says Nessa. I trace some anxiety on her part for his welfare. Perhaps one doesn't like the father of one's children to dissolve into pure lust & gluttony & pleasure & vainglory. She hopes, anyhow, that he will return to Charleston this summer & write his book on Civilisation. His views on that subject will be on lines agreeable with her present life, I suppose. Will the lady have taught him a fresh version of the old story? I fancy when he began the book, 15 years ago, he was a Moorite. Well, I suppose there are Moors in Spain. Now the light fades (though I am just becoming brilliant) & I must tackle the aspects [of Russian verbs] & the Labour party programme—one of L.'s triumphs.[17]

Friday 18 March

Just back from two days at Manchester. I fancied myself writing this account, & how good it would be; what lots of things I had to say; & now the pen brings blankness. Well I was kept awake by business men talking in low steady almost continuous voices in the room above till 1-30: & we were up early, breakfasted & caught a train, & so home, travelling all through the great rocky moors of Derbyshire—bald moors; the strangest looking places. So solitary they might be 18th Century England, the valleys cut by a thread of water falling roughly from heights; great sweeps of country all sunny & gloomy with bare rocks against the sky, & then behold a row of east end slum houses, with a strip of pavement & two factory chimneys set down in the midst. The houses are all stone, bleak, soot stained, different from our cottages; not cottages at all, but streets. Suddenly, in the palm of a wide valley you come on a complete town—gasworks, factories, & little streams made to run over stone steps & turn engines I suppose. Now & again no houses but wild moors, a thread of road, & farms set into the earth, uncompromising, since nothing like flowers, long grass, or hedges grow round them.
"Yes, I said to Mrs Unwin, Derbyshire is a very fine country." We were standing in a pit at the University, a table beneath a light below us, & a row of chairs, on which sat Professors Unwin, Findlay, Goldman (a financier) & Weiss. Leonard then got up & made his speech, a very

17. Perhaps a reference to the programme LW proposed to offer as Labour Party candidate for the Combined Universities, on the eve of his visit to Manchester.

vigorous one. We sat round on hard benches, with ink pots, or the holes for them, in front of us.[18]

All Manchester streets are the same, & all strung with tramlines. These follow each other at a few yards distance, making the roads mechanical & unsociable. You hear bells striking all the time. Then there are no tea shops, but great cafés; & no little shops, but all big drapers. We lodged (paying 18/ each for bed only) at the Queens Hotel, in a large square; but whats a square when the trams meet there?[19] Then there's Queen Victoria, like a large tea cosy, & Wellington, sleek as a mastiff with paw extended; none of this was quite English, or at least London. The people were lower middle class, no sprinkling of upper class.

But my observation of the university type was more profound. Mr & Mrs Weiss gave a dinner in the refectory before L.'s second speech; & there they all were—professors & wives, elderly people, depressed looking, like the inferior branch of a profession, with the manner of dons, but not the extreme confident eccentricity of first rate brains. But how supercilious I thought myself, & ultimately how much pure merit seemed in them, with the very thinnest coating of decorum. The women were dowdy; oh yes, but they too had fought for the right—which is a phrase I distrust, but how use any other of people, struggling along just decently on so many pounds a year, & sacrificing it, as a matter of course, for their views. P. Unwin told me he had been arrested 3 times for attending seditious meetings during the war. Mrs Weiss said her husband had resigned because the University refused to accept a C.O. upon which they thought better of it. And yet there is no surface brilliancy; not a scrap of romance. It is a little familiar professional society, trying to keep up the standards, which (perhaps wrongly) I suppose must be hard work in Manchester, or am I merely snobbish in thinking it harder to say clever things & write clever books in Manchester than in Cambridge? I applied the test of father's name twice; but neither Unwin or Weiss had heard it. The women had their activities not so pronounced as in Cambridge, pleasanter perhaps; common efforts to get up bazaars; enquiries about health; shabby best clothes. Old Mrs ⟨Findlay⟩ Herford

18. George Unwin (1870-1925), Professor of Economic History; Joseph John Findlay (1860-1940), Professor of Education; Frederick Ernest Weiss (1865-1953), Professor of Botany, all of the University of Manchester. The financier was not on the staff of the University and has not been identified. Mrs Herford (see below) was the German wife of the Professor of English Literature, Charles Harold Herford (1858-1931).

19. The Queen's Hotel stands on the corner of Piccadilly and Victoria Square, Manchester. See also *II VW Letters*, no. 1169 of 17 March to Vanessa Bell.

(I distributed the husbands & wives all wrongly) & Professor Finlay sat patiently looking at the tablecloth with nothing to say, like two old horses who have been working in the fields all day together.

L., in the large room after dinner, was emphatically first rate; I don't mean his clothes; nor yet his speech; but its a question of being the master. Now all the professors know that they're not masters. I think L.'s remark that he did not wish to be elected rather flabbergasted them; & I fancy they asked themselves afterwards why the Woolves had taken the trouble to come—"Are you a politician?" they asked me. "Do you do much organising work?" I said I listened. Mrs Findlay shook her head. Why was I there then? Oh for the fun of spending £10 in Manchester & seeing the Zoo. Lord! what a scatterbrain I am! But they'd none of them read my books. So we went to the Zoo; & I daresay I could write something interesting about that—a pale stone desert given over to charwomen & decorators: a few bears, a mandrill, & a fox or two—all in the desolation of depression.

Tuesday 22 March

Here we are on the verge of going to Cornwall. This time tomorrow —it is now 5.20—we shall be stepping onto the platform at Penzance, sniffing the air, looking for our trap, & then—Good God!—driving off across the moors to Zennor— Why am I so incredibly & incurably romantic about Cornwall? One's past, I suppose: I see children running in the garden. A spring day. Life so new. People so enchanting. The sound of the sea at night. And now I go back "bringing my sheaves"— well, Leonard, & almost 40 years of life, all built on that, permeated by that: how much so I could never explain. And in reality it is very beautiful. I shall go down to Treveal & look at the sea—old waves that have been breaking precisely so these thousand years. But I see I shall never get this said , & Lottie is chattering.

We had Eliot to dinner on Sunday & went to Love for Love, he & I in the Pit; L. upstairs, with a ticket from the New Statesman.[20] Eliot & I had to drive in to Hammersmith in a taxi, having missed our train. We passed through dark market gardens. 'Missing trains is awful' I said. "Yes. But humiliation is the worst thing in life" he replied. "Are you as full of vices as I am?" I demanded. "Full. Riddled with them." "We're

20. Congreve's *Love for Love* was performed by the Phoenix Society at the Lyric Theatre, Hammersmith, on Sunday evening, 20 March; it was VW who was to review it for the *New Statesman* (see 2 April 1921, Kp C217).

not as good as Keats" I said. "Yes we are" he replied. "No: we dont write classics straight off as magnanimous people do." "We're trying something harder" he said. "Anyhow our work is streaked with badness" I said. "Compared with theirs, mine is futile. Negligible. One goes on because of an illusion." He told me that I talked like that without meaning it. Yet I do mean it. I think one could probably become very intimate with Eliot because of our damned self conscious susceptibility: but I plunge more than he does: perhaps I could learn him to be a frog. He has the advantage of me in laughing out. He laughed at Love for Love: but thinking I must write about it I was a little on the stretch. We saw George Moore talking to Eddie Marsh, on some steps; a little obese, dim eyed, weak, inconsiderable.[21] I was disappointed. There was no rakish poll to be seen. As for Clive he dresses as effectively as any beauty, & poses like someone at a first night. Mary was there. "Tom", she said, "you must come and see the boat race." Well, these women's emotions, which I don't trouble to write out, are amusing; not very serious in my case. Then we met Nessa & Duncan, as shabby as old moths, making off home together. I bought a pair of boots yesterday for 33/6, which were made for another & fit me precisely. The truth is my foot is shaped like a snake. I have muddled away these 3 days, as far as writing is concerned, & intend to write nothing in Cornwall; but to read the classics. Candide: Shakespeare—historical plays: Adolphe: Keats' Letters: Thomas Hardy: & perhaps Hudibras. I shall find some old biography or 10th rate novel & read only that. Never mind.

Leonard is an impulsive man. He has lent Monks House to Mrs Martin.[22] She goes there tomorrow. As she is a complete zany, has no husband, no control over anything, & floats down stream, I see no reason why she should ever get out of Monk's House. How are we to turn her out? And somehow I see her laying eggs diffusively all over the garden —an amorphous jelly of a woman, German too.

I had tea with Nessa yesterday & heard a pack of troubles. Poor Ann has inherited Karin's disease of the ear & must be operated on.[23] They have notice to leave Charleston. And Clive, as she remarks, is not much

---

21. Edward Marsh (1872-1953), an Apostle, civil servant, and private secretary to Winston Churchill; he was a notable patron of painters and poets, and edited the five volumes of *Georgian Poetry*. The George Moore he was talking to was the writer, not the philosopher.

22. Mrs Martin was the sitting tenant of Suffield House; in order to get her to vacate the house so that the new owner Mr Turner might move in, LW offered her the temporary use of Monks House.

23. The impending operations did not in fact take place for some years.

help at Easter. Adrian came in to tell me that Desmond wanted me, to demand my article instantly. Adrian wears a short red-brown moustache, reminding me in a ghastly way of the hair that grows after death. So distinguished I always think him, but (to me) so repressive.

As for other news, I think I have never said that Lytton stays at home with Lady Strachey, who has taken to fainting on the floor.

The Woolfs went by train to Penzance on Wednesday 23 March and drove out to Ponion, near Zennor, where they lodged with Mrs Hoskings within walking distance of the Arnold-Forsters at Eagle's Nest; they returned to Richmond on Thursday 31 March. The following entry, mis-dated 28 March, is written on two sheets of loose-leaf paper attached to the main diary pages with stamp-paper.

Wednesday 30 March

This is the last evening, & L. is packing, & I'm not in the mood for writing, but feel superstitiously that I should like to read something actually written in Cornwall. By looking over my left shoulder I see gorse yellow against the Atlantic blue, running up, a little ruffled, to the sky, today hazy blue. And we've been lying on the Gurnard's Head, on beds of samphire among grey rocks with buttons of yellow lichen on them. How can I pick out the scene? You look down onto the semi-transparent water—the waves all scrambled into white round the rocks —gulls swaying on bits of seaweed—rocks now dry now drenched with white waterfalls pouring down crevices. No one near us, but a coast-guard sitting outside the house.

We took a rabbit path round the cliff, & I find myself a little shakier than I used to be. Still however maintaining without force to my conscience that this is the loveliest place in the world. It is so lonely. Occasionally a very small field is being ploughed, the men steering the plough round the grey granite rocks. But the hills & the cliffs have been given over as a bad job. There they lie graceful even in spite of all their stones & roughness, long limbed, stretching out to sea; & so subtly tinted; greys, all various with gleams in them; getting transparent at dusk; & soft grass greens; & then one night they burnt the heather at Tregerthen, the smoke rolling up over the crest, & flame shining. This we saw from Ka's. The Eagle's Nest stands up too much of a castle-boardinghouse to be a pleasant object; but considering the winds, firm roots are needed. Endless varieties of nice elderly men to be seen there, come for climbing.

Friday 8 April

10 minutes to eleven a.m. And I ought to be writing Jacob's Room;
—I can't, & instead I shall write down the reason why I can't—this
diary being a kindly blank faced old confidante. Well, you see, I'm a
failure as a writer. I'm out of fashion; old; shan't do any better; have
no head piece; the spring is everywhere; my book [*Monday or Tuesday*]
out (prematurely) & nipped, a damp firework. Now the solid grain of
fact is that Ralph sent my book out to the Times for review without
date of publication in it. Thus a short notice is scrambled through to
be in "on Monday at latest", put in an obscure place, rather scrappy,
complimentary enough, but quite unintelligent. I mean by that they
don't see that I'm after something interesting. So that makes me suspect
that I'm not. And thus I can't get on with Jacob. Oh & Lytton's book
is out & takes up three columns: praise, I suppose.[1] I do not trouble to
sketch this in order; or how my temper sank & sank till for half an hour
I was as depressed as I ever am. I mean I thought of never writing any
more—save reviews. To rub this in we had a festival party at 41 [Gordon
Square]: to congratulate Lytton; which was all as it should be; but then
he never mentioned my book, which I suppose he has read; & for the
first time I have not his praise to count on. Now if I'd been saluted
by the Lit. Sup. as a mystery & a riddle, I shouldn't mind; for
Lytton wouldn't like that sort of thing, but if I'm as plain as day, &
negligible?

Well, this question of praise & fame must be faced. (I forgot to say
that Doran has refused the book in America[2]). How much difference
does popularity make? (I see pretty clearly, I may add, after a pause in
which Lottie has brought in the milk & the sun has ceased to eclipse
itself,[3] that I'm writing a good deal of nonsense.) One wants, as Roger
said very truly yesterday, to be kept up to the mark; that people should

1. The half-column review, in the *TLS* of 7 April 1921 (see *M & M*, pp 87-8)
though of course unsigned, was written by Harold Child, whose favourable notice
of *Kew Gardens* in the *TLS* of 29 May 1921 had allowed VW 'as much praise . . .
as I like to claim' (see *I VW Diary*, 10 June 1919). Excerpts from both these
notices were reprinted at the back of *Jacob's Room* where favourable and unfavourable press opinions of VW's published work were judiciously intermingled. Lytton
Strachey's *Queen Victoria* was reviewed over some 2¾ columns in the *TLS* of 7
April, and the praise was pretty well unqualified.
2. What George H. Doran Company refused, Harcourt, Brace and Co. accepted;
and *Monday or Tuesday* was published by them on 23 November 1921.
3. The solar eclipse of 8 April 1921 was visible from 08.35 a.m. to about 11.05 a.m. in
the London area.

be interested, & watch one's work. What depresses me is the thought that I have ceased to interest people—at the very moment when, by the help of the press, I thought I was becoming more myself. One does *not* want an established reputation, such as I think I was getting, as one of our leading female novelists. I have still, of course, to gather in all the private criticism, which is the real test. When I have weighed this I shall be able to say whether I am 'interesting' or obsolete. Anyhow, I feel quite alert enough to stop, if I'm obsolete. I shan't become a machine, unless a machine for grinding articles. As I write, there rises somewhere in my head that queer, & very pleasant sense, of something which I want to write; my own point of view. I wonder, though, whether the feeling that I write for half a dozen instead of 1500 will pervert this?— make me eccentric,—no, I think not. But, as I said, one must face the despicable vanity which is at the root of all this niggling & haggling. I think the only prescription for me is to have a thousand interests—if one is damaged, to be able instantly to let my energy flow into Russian, or Greek, or the press, or the garden, or people, or some activity disconnected with my own writing.

But, honestly, I need not pull a very long face yet. Roger is staying with us. I think he has the nicest nature among us—so open, sincere, & entirely without meanness; always generous, I think, & somehow hearty? He throws out a tremendous laugh. We went to the Bedford Music Hall last night, & saw Miss Marie Lloyd, a mass of corruption— long front teeth—a crapulous way of saying 'desire', & yet a born artist—scarcely able to walk, waddling, aged, unblushing.[4] A roar of laughter went up when she talked of her marriage. She is beaten nightly by her husband. I felt that the audience was much closer to drink & beating & prison than any of us. The coal strike is on.[5] If I weren't crowded & hurried & distracted I would bring my Gordon Square gossip up to date. Juana Ganderilla has been seen—a lady in the continental style, lovely, composed, simple, illiterate, emotional, going into trances.

4. Marie Lloyd (1870-1922)—the stage name of Matilda Wood—was nearing the end of her illustrious career as a cockney entertainer on the music-hall stage; she had first appeared in 1894. She had been married three times, and her matrimonial troubles were notorious. The 'New Bedford' was in Camden Town.
5. The coal strike had in fact been 'on' since 1 April, when, according to *The Times* of 2 April, 'The production of coal in Great Britain to all practical intent ceased . . .' VW presumably meant that it was still on following the breakdown of talks on 7 April between the government and the miners who refused to start pumping operations to save endangered pits as a preliminary to meeting the owners. See below, 12 April 1921 n 9.

Sunday 10 April

I must note the symptoms of the disease, so as to know it next time. The first day one's miserable: the second happy. There was an Affable Hawk on me in the New Statesman which at anyrate made me feel important (& its that that one wants) & Simpkin & Marshall rang up for a second fifty copies.[6] So they must be selling. Now I have to stand all the twitching & teasing of private criticism which I shant enjoy. There'll be Roger tomorrow. What a bore it all is!—& then one begins to wish one had put in other stories—or left out the Haunted House, which may be sentimental. Anyhow next week there'll be Tchekhov & Leonard as well as me. And suppose every one (that is to say the 6 people who matter) praise Leonard, shall I be jealous—but, mark my word, all of this will be forgotten in 6 weeks time.

Pernel dined here: they dress badly, as I think I've said before. I think perhaps she grows a little pensive; but I'm not good at judging my friends' moods. Then Roger came in—utterly unwearied—in spite of standing on a ladder for 8 hours restoring Mantegnas.[7] He draws people here in shoals—yesterday, just after Kot had gone, in came Mr & Mrs Reece, & tomorrow there'll be Pippa—always some slave or other attending; & as we're in the middle of the rush we get whelmed, & I can't write sense or nonsense, & must devote all this week to reviewing. —I want to read Victoria & Swift.

Tuesday 12 April

I must hurriedly note more symptoms of the disease, so that I can turn back here & medicine myself next time. Well; I'd worn through the acute stage, & come to the philosophic semi depressed, indifferent, &

6. Desmond MacCarthy's 'Books in General' page, calling attention to the Hogarth Press and VW's work but mainly devoted to her *Monday or Tuesday*, appeared in the *New Statesman* on 9 April 1921. Simkin, Marshall, Hamilton, Kent & Co, in the City, were wholesale booksellers and the foremost distributors of books.

7. (Joan) Pernel Strachey (1876-1951), fourth of Lytton's five sisters, was Vice-Principal of Newnham College, Cambridge, and, from 1923-41, its Principal. Roger Fry had been asked in 1912 to advise on, and subsequently to undertake, the cleaning and restoration of the nine great ruined Mantegna canvases representing the *Triumph of Caesar* in the Royal Collection at Hampton Court. He was now completing his work, which had been interrupted by the war, and found it convenient to spend several nights at Hogarth House. The Reeces are unidentified.

spent the afternoon taking parcels round the shops, going to Scotland Yard for my purse, when L. met me at tea & dropped into my ear the astonishing news that Lytton thinks the String Quartet 'marvellous'. This came through Ralph, who doesn't exaggerate, to whom Lytton need not lie; & did for a moment flood every nerve with pleasure, so much so that I forgot to buy my coffee & walked over Hungerford Bridge twanging & vibrating. A lovely blue evening too, the river sky colour. And then there was Roger who thinks I'm on the track of real discoveries, & certainly not a fake. And we've broken the record of sales, so far. And I'm not nearly as pleased as I was depressed; & yet in a state of security; fate cannot touch me; the reviewers may snap; & the sales decrease. What I had feared was that I was dismissed as negligible.

Roger again last night, scraping at his woodcuts while I sewed; the sound like that of a large pertinacious rat.[8] We live in stirring times. Here is Ralph saying that Michael Davies has enlisted to protect the country, against the miners, & McIver is offered £1 exs. by government for himself & car, which he will accept.[9] Yet no one—so far as I know —really believes that we are in for anything. It will be tided over. Our cellars will be full; our larders too. Nothing is going to upset us. People in a century will say how terrible it all was. And I walked past Downing St yesterday & saw a few men in cabs, a few men with despatch boxes, orderly public watching, wreaths being laid on the Cenotaph. Lytton's book already selling 5 thousand copies, & the weather perfect.

Wednesday 13 April

Now I note the latest symptom—complete absence of jealousy. What I mean is that I shall feel instantly warm & pleased (not only after an hour & a sharp pang) if there's a long & sound & appreciative review

8. In December 1921 the Hogarth Press published *Twelve Original Woodcuts* by Roger Fry (*HP Checklist* 13).
9. Michael Llewelyn Davies (1900-1921), nephew of Margaret and adoptive son of J. M. Barrie; Alan Squarey McIver, contemporary and close friend of Ralph Partridge in the army and at Oxford. His father was a Liverpool shipowner, and he eventually became managing director of the family business. They had presumably joined one of the 'Defence Units' formed by the government against the threat of a general strike. The creation of these emergency units, which motorists were encouraged to join, was announced in the House of Commons on 8 April, On that day the Triple Industrial Alliance had warned the government that if negotiations between miners and coal owners were not resumed it would organise strike action from midnight on 12 April.

of L. in the Lit Sup tomorrow. I think this is perfectly true. Most people, though, would not have to write this down. I suppose I had a qualm or two. No time for more than this interesting & important statement. Rather to our respite, Roger is away for the night after a fair bust up yesterday—Ray Pippa Saxon all together—& I must read my book. A strike now proclaimed for Friday, & we had just planned to go to Monks.

Friday 15 April

I have been lying recumbent all day reading Carlyle, & now Macaulay, first to see if Carlyle wrote better than Lytton, then to see if Macaulay sells better. Carlyle (reminiscences) is more colloquial & scrappy than I remembered, but he has his merits.—more punch in his phrase than in Lytton's. I don't count this as my judgment though, since I was half asleep, & haven't done more than half Vic yet. Lytton rang up this morning to ask for Roger, & I asked him about his book. "Are you smothered in laurels" "Well, rather depressed," he said, & so he sounded. "I'm in the middle; & then I shall write to you about it" "And I'm writing to you about yours" he answered. "We will be candid" I said. "When shall I see you? Never, presumably." Anyday next week would do, he said,—he is coming to tea & dinner on Wednesday. So fame hasn't done him much harm. He's sold, so they say, 5,000 copies this week, & another edition is printing. I have sold just 300. Well, but that doesn't prove my immortality, as I insinuate. The truth is I have no notion of my standing, or of Lytton's. One ought to write more of this occasion, since I suppose in 20 years' time the publication of Queen Victoria will be thought an important matter; but these things aren't important to us. They say he's been given a bust of Prince Albert & a photograph of the Queen by a spectacle maker. And Max Beerbohm is doing a caricature of him,[10] & altogether he's a solid celebrity, one of our leading writers, not merely the hero of one book which might not be repeated. Ralph seems willing to go on with our printing, though orders have again sunk low. No review of Tchekhov or L. yet; only shorter mention by donkey

10. Max Beerbohm drew 'Mr Lytton Strachey trying* hard to see her with Lord Melbourne's eyes' in November 1920; to enable Max to 'verify his impressions' after the publication of *Queen Victoria*, Lytton called on him at the Charing Cross Hotel on 13 April 1921. The finished drawing was exhibited at the Leicester Galleries in May and June, with Max's postscript: *'—and contriving—M.B. 1921' added in the catalogue; it was reproduced in *A Survey*, published by Heinemann in 1921.

Dalton I suppose in the Lit. Sup.[11] This is the first free time for reading I've had for an age,—I shall lavish it all on Q.V. & must now go & fetch her, since of course Roger borrows her to read o'nights.

A queer sort of stillness seems already settling down on us, as of Sunday. This is the foreboding of the General Strike. We have put off going to Rodmell. Marjorie's party is put off. L. has just come in with a paper which says that nothing has been done to patch up the strike. Therefore at 10 tonight, unless something happens meanwhile, all trains, trams, buses, mines, & perhaps electric light works come to an end. The servants have been to the Coops & brought back a weeks groceries. We have a bundle of candles. Our most serious lack is coal, as Nelly forgot to order any. We burn coke in the drawing room & cook on gas. Still, Heaven knows why, I don't believe the strike will happen.

Sunday 17 April

And I was perfectly right. The strike didn't happen.[12] About 7 o'clock L. rang up Margaret & heard that the Triple Alliance had split: the railwaymen & transport workers refusing to go on with it, & leaving the miners by themselves. Nothing is yet accurately known. Presumably the miners will have to give in,* & I shall get my hot bath, & bake home made bread again; yet it seems a pity somehow—if they're to be forced back & the mine owners triumphant. I think this is my genuine feeling, though not very profound. It is fairly obvious that working people are well enough satisfied to prefer going on working; I remember the pleasure of the railwaymen when they started running about platforms & leaning out of engines again.

* They haven't given in yet. May 9th

Yesterday we had our avenue walk—the first for a long while; & L. explained the plan of his new book—a revised version of the Wandering Jew. Very original & solid, it seemed to me; & like a good business man, I pressed him to promise it for the press. Its true that sales & reviews flag, & I much doubt if M. & T. will sell 500, or cover expenses.

11. Frederick Thomas Dalton (1855-1927) was the principal editorial assistant on the *TLS*. The 'mention' of LW's *Stories of the East* appeared under 'New Books and Reprints' in the issue of 14 April 1921. Of the three stories 'The Two Brahmans' was judged the best 'because it is the most simply told'.

12. The proposed strike by the combined forces of the railway and transport workers and the miners—the Triple Industrial Alliance—came to nothing, largely because of a failure of co-operation between the union leaders, and chiefly because Frank Hodges, the miners' leader, in conducting independent talks with backbench MPs, had apparently dispensed with accepted national negotiating machinery.

But I want to push on with it nevertheless; & a solid big book like L.'s is essential. We discussed all this walking down the Avenue; looking in at the iron gates of Ham House, & so home to tea, & a Russian lesson with Kot, & now I must write to Lytton & polish off a review.[13] Always these last paragraphs floor me.

Monday 18 April

Just back from lunching with a Cabinet Minister. I mean, of course, Herbert Fisher. We think he asked us in order to apologise for—everything. He said he had neither the physical force nor the combativeness to carry things through. He said he hated Parliament. A political life is dull, & wastes all one's time he said; one is always listening to dull speeches, frittering time away. He leaves home at 10, gets back at 11 P.M. & then has a bundle of papers to go through. The upshot of it all was that he couldn't be blamed for his conduct about Ireland.[14] And then he was careful to explain that the public is ridiculously in the dark about everything. Only the cabinet knows the true spring & source of things he said. That is the only solace of the work. A flood tide of business flows incessantly from all quarters of the world through Downing Street; & there are a few miserable men trying desperately to deal with it. They have to make tremendous decisions with insufficient evidence on the spur of the moment. Then he pulled himself up, & said, solemnly, that he is going to Geneva to initiate peace—disarmament.[15] "You are the great

13. The formal grounds of the seventeenth-century Ham House, which faces the Thames near Petersham, are enclosed by very fine high iron railings with central gates between stone piers. For VW's letter to Lytton Strachey on his *Queen Victoria*, see *II VW Letters*, no. 1174.

14. This was the period of the most horrific violence between the Irish Republican Army and the Government forces, which was bringing deep discredit upon British rule. VW's cousin H. A. L. Fisher, President of the Board of Trade, a Liberal and a supporter of partition and Home Rule for Ireland, was one of the six members of the Coalition Cabinet's Irish Committee, and as such was, if reluctantly, party to the decision to send the Black and Tans into Ireland in March 1920, and to form the Auxiliary Division of the Royal Irish Constabulary some six months later—'one of those hateful necessities which in exceptional times must be accepted as the lesser of two grave evils' (*An Unfinished Autobiography*, 1940). The Peace Treaty with the Sinn Fein was not signed until December 1921.

15. H. A. L. Fisher attended the annual meeting of the Council of the League of Nations at Geneva, 17-28 June 1921, the proceedings of which he reported to the House of Commons on 5 July.

authority upon that, I understand", he said to Leonard. Anyhow I confess it seemed to me, sitting opposite to Leonard in that brown ugly room with its autotypes of Dutch pictures & Aunt Mary on a donkey,[16] that Leonard was an authority & Herbert a thin-shredded thread paper of a man, whose brain has been harrowed in to sandy streaks like his hair. Never was there a thinner lighter airier specimen I thought; his words without body, & his head cocked at a queer angle, & his hands gesticulating, & his eyes so blue, but almost vacant, & cheerful colourless words, slightly mannered & brushed up in conformity with some official standard of culture—I daresay Mr Balfour talks something like that.[17] But after mouthing his meaning behold; it flew away like thistledown, & it appeared that this Cabinet Minister & representative of Great Britain in whose hands are armies & navies was dry & empty again—& asking me colloquially whether I remembered Aunt Mary on the donkey, which I did. 'The donkey is too small', I said 'And the horse has no ears,' he added. 'Watts has come down in the world' I said, feeling astonishingly young & juicy beside him.

"Yes, he said. I daresay: But I feel that the man who painted that picture was a great man—not a great painter, perhaps, but a great man." After which he descended as usual to badinage about the arts; & praised a Mr Munnings: wonderful pictures of horses; landscapes in the 18th century style behind them. "Thats what I like—the 18th century style —old Crome & Cotman. Well, Munnings is that style—worth going to the Royal Academy to see—quite a young fellow—fought through the war."[18] But modern art he didn't care for; & we walked down Victoria Street to the House of Commons; & he said he was reading Southey's Letters—"first rate reading. There's a beautiful description of winter.

16. Fisher's London home was at 28 Ashley Gardens, Westminster; his mother—VW's Aunt Mary—had been portrayed as Una by G. F. Watts in his representation of Spenser's 'Una and the Red Cross Knight'. A preparatory drawing and the painting, for which Mary Jackson sat in 1862 shortly before her marriage to Herbert Fisher, was given to her by the artist, and is still in the possession of her family. George Frederic Watts, OM (1817-1904) had been a protégé and neighbour of Mary Jackson's aunt Sara Prinsep, and frequently called on members of her family—famous for its female beauties—to sit for him.

17. Arthur James Balfour (1848-1930), philosopher and statesman, was like Fisher (who admired him immensely) a member of Lloyd-George's coalition cabinet, being at this time Lord President of the Council.

18. Alfred James Munnings (1878-1959), a Suffolk miller's son, was to become President of the Royal Academy in 1944. He had been an official war artist attached to the Canadian Cavalry Brigade, and between the wars achieved a tremendous celebrity as a painter of horses and country scenes.

Now who are our promising litterateurs?" I said Joyce. Never heard of Joyce. So we parted, Herbert very amiable, grey & distinguished, in his pea-jacket, going to tackle the liquor bill, & envying us very much, he said, writing books at Richmond.[19] And then we ran into Will Vaughan at the London Library, portly & hearty, & keeping up a laugh like an old sea-captains all the time he talked. Indeed, we had nothing to say.[20]

Friday 29 April

A great deal to say, I suppose: a great many portraits to sketch; conversations to write down; & reflections to work in—had I time; which I have not (& that sentence reminds me that I mean to read Marvell.) But every afternoon for a week I've been up to the AEolian Hall; taken my seat right at the back; put my bag on the floor & listened to Beethoven quartets.[21] Do I dare say listened? Well, but if one gets a lot of pleasure, really divine pleasure, & knows the tunes, & only occasionally thinks of other things—surely I may say listened. We are just back from the 5th: & I had my hand clasped by Lady Cromer in the street: we had tea with Lytton, Carrington & Ralph.

I ought to say something of Lytton. I have seen him oftener these last days than for a whole year perhaps. We have talked about his book & my book. This particular conversation took place in Verreys: gilt feathers: mirrors: blue walls & Lytton & I taking our tea & brioche in a corner: we must have sat well over an hour.

"And I woke last night & wondered where to place you" I said. "There's St Simon & La Bruyère.

Oh God, he groaned.

And Macaulay I added.

"Yes, Macaulay" he said. "A little better than Macaulay."

But not his mass, I insisted. More civilisation of course. And then you've only written short books.

I'm going to do George the IVth next, he said.

Well but your place, I insisted.

19. H. A. L. Fisher acted as a Government spokesman on matters relating to the Liquor Control Board, established under the Home Office in 1915 as a wartime measure. On 27 April the Government, abandoning a proposed new Licensing Bill, invited the Control Board to continue its existence for another 12 months.

20. William Wyamar Vaughan (1865-1938), now Master of Wellington College, Headmaster of Rugby 1921-31, VW's first cousin.

21. During a Beethoven Festival Week, 25-30 April, at the Æolian Hall, the London String Quartet played, in chronological order, all 17 Beethoven string quartets.

And yours he asked

"I'm the 'ablest of living women novelists' " I said— So the British weekly says.[22]

"You influence me" he said.

And he said he could always recognise my writing though I wrote so many different styles, "which is the result of hard work" I insisted. And then we discussed historians: Gibbon: a kind of Henry James, I volunteered. Oh dear no—not in the least he said.

"He has a point of view & sticks to it" I said. "And so do you. I wobble." But what is Gibbon?

Oh he's there all right; Lytton said. Forster says he's an Imp[?]. But he hadn't many views. He believed in 'virtue' perhaps.

A beautiful word, I said.

But just read how the hordes of barbarians devastated the City. Its marvellous. True, he was queer about the Early Xtians—didn't see anything in them at all. But read him. I'm going to next October. And I'm going to Florence, & I shall be very lonely in the evenings.[23]

The French have influenced you more than the English, I suppose, I said.

Yes. I have their definiteness. I'm formed.

I compared you with Carlyle the other day, I said. I read the Reminiscences. Well they're the chatter of an old toothless grave digger compared with you: only then he has phrases.

Ah yes, he has them, said Lytton. But I read him to Norton & James the other day, & they shouted—they wouldn't have it. I'm a little anxious though about 'mass'. That's my danger is it?

Yes: You may cut too fine I said. But its a magnificent subject—George the IVth—& what fun, setting to work on it.

And your novel?

Oh I put in my hand & rummage in the bran pie. Thats whats so wonderful. And its all different.

Yes. I'm 20 people.

But one sees the whole from the outside.

The worst of George IVth is that no one mentions the facts I want. History must be written all over again. Its all morality—

& battles, I added.

22. The *British Weekly* says: 'Virginia Woolf in the opinion of some good judges is the ...'; this was in the course of a review of the Hogarth Press's Gorky/ Tchekhov translation (*HP Checklist* 14) in the issue of 23 April 1921.

23. In May 1921, a few weeks after the publication of *Queen Victoria*, Lytton set off with his sister Pippa to stay with the Berensons in Florence.

And then we walked through the streets together, for I had to buy coffee.

Tuesday 3 May

Hamilton Fyfe in the Daily Mail says that Leonard's story P. & S. will rank with the great stories of the world.[1] Am I jealous? Only momentarily. But the odd thing is—the idiotic thing—is that I immediately think myself a failure—imagine myself peculiarly lacking in the qualities L. has. I feel fine drawn, misty, attenuated, inhuman, bloodless & niggling out trifles that don't move people. 'Limbo' is my sphere; so they say in the Daily News.[2] Then Romer Wilson has brought out a novel—to which Squire will certainly give the Hawthornden prize, thus robbing Katherine of it: so
he did
I have some cause for pleasure.[3] I write this purposely, to shame it out of me. A full stop in Jacob, owing partly to depression. But I must pull together & finish it off. I can't read it as it is.

We had Oliver & Saxon to dinner on Sunday; & I went to tea with Nessa on Saturday; & yesterday we were in London at the New Statesman office: & I bought Eliot on Prose;[4] & Romer Wilson;—all of which I note to put off doing my Russian; I suppose: for I see I am going to say nothing sensible or witty or profound. And yet I comfort myself

1. H. Hamilton Fyfe (1869-1951), author and journalist, was at this time the literary editor of the *Daily Mail*. In the paper's edition of Monday 2 May 1921, Fyfe opened his review 'A Batch of Spring Fiction' with the judgment: 'Among the famous short stories of the world I think "Pearls and Swine" [one of LW's *Stories of the East*] will certainly find a place.' He also described it as 'a corker' and concluded that if LW could do this often he would 'gain a "first" in fiction very soon.'

2. VW's *Monday or Tuesday* was reviewed in the *Daily News* of Monday 2 May 1921 under the title 'Limbo', by R. Ellis Roberts. Singling out 'The Haunted House' as 'by far the best thing in the book' the reviewer concludes '... all this bereft world of inconsequent sensation is but a habitation for those lonely, dishevelled souls who are driven about by the great wind which blows through Limbo'.

3. Romer Wilson was the pen-name of Florence Roma Muir Wilson (1891-1930); she had studied Law at Girton before the war, and had worked as a temporary civil servant. On 29 June 1921 she was awarded the Hawthornden Prize (£100 and a silver medal) for her third novel *The Death of Society*, which the *TLS* on 5 May described as 'rapturous and transcendental' and 'an ecstasy in five convulsions'.

4. The April 1921 number of the monthly miscellany *The Chapbook*, published by the Poetry Bookshop, contained T. S. Eliot's essay 'Prose and Verse'.

with the reflection that there's no knowing what won't interest old Virginia one of these days.

Monday 9 May

Well, but I assure you, when Virginia's old, no one will be talking of Romer Wilson. What a book! What a perfect example of the faux bon: every attitude, scene & word, I should say matched in the old word shop of the minor poets: never a single thing seen for herself, or dared; & yet by taking all the scenery & supplying the appropriate words she has Squire, Lynd, & Turner by the heel: another proof that what people dread is being made to feel anything: a certain kind of rhapsody makes them feel wild & adventurous; & they then make out that this is passion & poetry—so thankful to be let off the genuine thing.

Yesterday I had tea with Lady Cromer, & I observe that she's more Lady Cromer in her own drawing room than met casually in the street.[5] Supported by her pretty chinzes, large airy rooms, family portraits by Watts & Sargent—green stained wood, parquet floors, & young bumpkin Greek God dragoon of a son she is the English Countess again: thus rather a bore, I've come to think. Do I travel to Finchley Rd on a Sunday missing my chocolate cake merely to exchange views with Lady Cromer upon the niceness of the Bruce Richmonds, the charm of St John's Wood, the good qualities of the French—to hear Mr Keynes called 'very clever' & Lytton Strachey 'very clever' & myself very good to have come there? I cant get it right though. Time was when I thought this breeding & personality so distinguished & somehow celestial that it carried everything off. Now I'm more exacting: after all shes a little middle class: & then the personal goodness attitude restrains me. Doing good to peoples cooks if you're Lady Cromer seems to me an easy way to waste time agreeably. Barbara at the club today, stunned with the problem of life, thoroughly in for it, & scarcely able to deal with it, appeared to me more interesting—thats it perhaps—than Lady Cromer swimming over the waves. But she's a nice woman: a character: beautiful too: so upright, firm, possessed—& then that queer old way of bending her head on one side & falling half absentminded as she talks, looking out of the window; her voice so charmingly accented, her eyes half closed. I

5. Lady Cromer lived at 29 Marlborough Place, St John's Wood, to reach which VW probably travelled by the North London Railway from Richmond to Finchley Road. Her son, the Hon. Evelyn Baring (1903-1973), was still at New College, Oxford.

got home to find Mr Brenton of Barnes; & according to his code one asks people kindly after their health, & comes back to shake hands, very punctiliously; & the poor man is sunk cheeked, spotted, ugly: drab: yet L. says interesting, & he should judge having had 3 hours of him! An order for 25 stories of the East today from S[imkin]. & M[arshall].

Sunday 15 May

Whit Sunday—dull, wet, & cold; so that on the whole we dont blame the coal strike for keeping us here over the fire instead of Monks House. Moreover, L. has a chill in his inside, & sits rather dismally with his head in his hand, poor man, allowed no tea or coffee. Its that I should mind—all the romance of the day dulled. By this time I think Carrington will have made up her mind one way or t'other. She must have had an odious Sunday. But still she *must* make up her mind. So I told Ralph on Friday, broaching that topic after all these months of silence. He did it himself, rather, by telling me of his gloom of the night before: his loneliness. "I wished for my mother" he said. "Though she irritates me, & I could tell her nothing." He was very shrewd & bitter about C. "She thinks herself one of the little friends of all the world" he said. Then he said she was selfish, untruthful, & quite indifferent to his suffering. So people in love always turn & rend the loved, with considerable insight too. He was speaking the truth largely. But I expect he was biassed; & also I expect—& indeed told him—that he is a bit of an ogre & tyrant. He wants more control than I should care to give—control I mean of the body & mind & time & thoughts of his loved. There's his danger & her risk; so I don't much envy her making up her mind this wet Whit Sunday.

I read 4 pages of sneer & condescending praise of me in the Dial the other day.[6] Oddly enough, I have drawn the sting of it by deciding to print it among my puffs, where it will come in beautifully. The Dial is everything honest vigorous & advanced; so I ought to feel crushed. L. went on selling all last week. I very slowly dribble. Tchekhov is at a standstill. But we hear that never was there such a season for all commodities, in proof of which not a picture at the London Group was sold

6. The New York *Dial*, in its May issue, published 'The Modern English Novel Plus', a review of *Night and Day* and *The Voyage Out*, by Kenneth Burke. On balance the 'condescending praise' is reserved for *The Voyage Out*, the 'sneer' for *Night and Day*. The Woolfs were to quote a long extract from the more disobliging passages on *Night and Day* at the back of the first edition of *Jacob's Room*. See also above, 8 April 1921, n 2.

2 days ago, though many are worth buying.[7] And did I say?—we propose to spend £1000 a year upon a tea shop, book shop, gallery in Bond Street. After all, why not? I like rummaging in the great Bran pie, as I've said before: thus we rout middle age for one thing; for another, such queer specimens come out of it. There was Mr Reginald Morris on the hearthrug the other day—a very bad poet from Hounslow.[8]

Monday 23 May

So Carrington did make up her mind to become Partridge—no, that is precisely what she is determined not to do; & signs herself aggressively Carrington for ever. If people ever took advice I should feel a little responsible for making up Ralph's mind. I mean I am not sure that this marriage is not more risky than most. Certainly she is not in love; & he has the obdurate Anglo Indian in him.[9] But still, if she couldn't face the prospect of a week end breach, or of a journey alone to Italy, she had no alternative. So they were married on Saturday. The day before Michael Davies was drowned bathing at Oxford.[10] Life does this sort of thing too habitually—I begin to feel bored, like a passenger thrown from side to side of a ship. I dont describe what I feel: something of anger at the unreason of it; & something of—not indifference, no: but as if one knew by this time how things go: first these marriages, at the same moment deaths. Just from not knowing how to swim he pulled another young man down, & now at the age of 21 it's all over for both of them. And then in this fine weather too. We have been to Rodmell, & as usual I come home depressed—for no reason. Merely moods. Have other people as many as I have? That I shall never know. And sometimes I suppose that even if I came to the end of my incessant search into what people are & feel I should know nothing still. I mean I go on thinking in the belief that if one thinks about it enough one comes to some conclusion. That I begin to judge doubtful. I was thinking about this in the Strand today—wondering whether I am after some play or novel, as I go on ferreting away. But I'm too scatterbrained to get it right. I was up in

7. The 14th exhibition of the London Group was shown at the Mansard Gallery at Heal's, 196 Tottenham Court Road, from 9 May–4 June 1921.
8. Possibly a Reginald Morris whose *Poems* were published by the author at St Margaret's-on-Thames in 1932.
9. Ralph Partridge's father had been in the Indian Civil Service.
10. Michael Llewelyn Davies drowned at Sandford Pool on the Thames near Oxford on 19 May. He was twenty-one years old and an undergraduate at Christ Church. Rupert Buxton, a fellow undergraduate, lost his life in attempting to save his friend who, according to the evidence, 'could hardly swim at all'.

the Strand with 12 copies of Monday or Tuesday; so that sells a little; & 2 goslings, to be sent to Lewes; & my review of Patmore for the Times;[11] & then caught a train home, put my great lupins & peonies in water, & should now settle with concentration to my book. But which book? I've a notion of reading masterpieces only; for I've read literature in bulk so long. Now I think's the time to read like an expert. Then I'm wondering how to shape my Reading book;[12] the more I read of other peoples criticism the more I trifle; can't decide; nor need I just yet. But how I enjoy the exercise of my wits upon literature—reading it *as* literature. And I think I can do this the better for having read through such a lot of lives, criticisms, every sort of thing.

We had dinner to report Desmond's talk the other night. He talked admirably for the purpose, but less intimately which was natural; & yet I hate people to talk admirably, as if they were dining out. There was Roger, & Molly & good Miss Green. That's my d——d condescension —I cant help condescending to very plain poor serviceable women, & then they bob up as happy as grigs & twice as able as I am.[13]

Thursday 26 May

My evening being ruined by Gravé as usual—I mean by non-Gravé— I mean she said she was coming at 6 & its 6.30—I may as well wreak my temper, write out my fidgets, in this book. Such is the constitution of my brain that I can settle to nothing if I'm waiting. This doesn't want settling to. Haven't I schooled my diary well? It takes what it can get & is thankful.

I sat in Gordon Square yesterday for an hour & a half talking to Maynard. Sometimes I wish I put down what people say instead of describing them. The difficulty is that they say so little. Maynard said

11. VW's review of *Courage in Politics and Other Essays* by Coventry Patmore appeared in the *TLS* of 26 May 1921 (Kp C221).
12. This is the first reference in the *Diary* to what was to become the *Common Reader*.
13. This dinner party on 18 May, designed to record the inimitable quality of Desmond MacCarthy's conversation, was perhaps inspired by a book which VW had read in 1919: *Eleanor Ormerod, LLD, Economic Entomologist* (1904), in the introduction to which the editor Robert Wallace describes how a shorthand writer was to be concealed behind a screen in her dining room to take down Miss Ormerod's reminiscences. In this instance Miss Green, LW's secretary at the *Contemporary Review*, was the recorder. Family tradition has it that Desmond was completely unaware of the arrangement (see also *II Roger Fry Letters*, no. 501), but VW's text seems to suggest otherwise; the same tradition insists that his conversational brilliance did not survive transcription.

he liked praise; & always wanted to boast. He said that many men marry in order to have a wife to boast to. But, I said, its odd that one boasts considering that no one is ever taken in by it. Its odd too that you, of all people, should want praise. You & Lytton are passed beyond boasting —which is the supreme Triumph. There you sit & say nothing. I love praise, he said. I want it for the things I'm doubtful about. Then we got upon publishing, & the Hogarth press; & novels. Why should they explain what bus he took? he asked. And why shouldn't Mrs Hilbery be sometimes the daughter of Katherine. Oh its a dull book, I know, I said; but don't you see you must put it all in before you can leave out. The best thing you ever did, he said, was your Memoir on George.[14] You should pretend to write about real people & make it all up— I was dashed of course. (& oh dear what nonsense—for if George is my climax I'm a mere scribbler). What else did we talk about? He was going to some official dinner. He gets £120 for an article—[15]

Thursday 2 June

But this was written a week ago, today being the day after Derby Day, the very height of the season, I suppose: anyhow of leaf & flower.

People turn up regularly though with little planning on our part. Madge [Vaughan] on Friday; Kot on Saturday; Roger; Fredegond; Mr Reginald Morris. Will these names recover anything in 10 years time of the last week of May 1921? I wish I had the same record of 10 years back, when I was a young woman—only then one can't scribble. One takes thought. One gets it too literal.

Madge asked to come; so we had her. She is curiously changed. She has become ordinary. Middle age has thickened her lines, & deepened her colour. In her mind she is grown cheerful, & commonplace. I notice now that her forehead is oddly pinched at the top. She said of herself that she was stunted—which expresses it. She has never grown up, but lived somewhere under shelter, unchastised, talking a great deal about life, but not facing it. Oh she did talk about life—always with reference to herself, which makes the mind squint. She sees nothing in itself. So we vacillated between 'life' & Will: 'my life': 'my odd nature', 'I have no brain' 'I am very psychological'. But then I ought to have broken away, & so on; but as it is quite obvious that she is rich, successful, &

14. i.e., '22 Hyde Park Gate' (*Moments of Being*, p 142) probably read on 17 November, 1920 (see above, 5 December 1920).
15. Five long articles by Maynard Keynes appeared in the *Sunday Times* this summer, and he contributed regularly to the *Manchester Guardian*.

happy, these complaints which make the staple of her talk, lack substance; & she easily slides into gossip, & repetition. Indeed you can't keep her to poetry, kitchen, love, art, or children for more than a minute. Yet she has her gaiety & her vitality which protect one from the worst boredom. But not Leonard nor Roger. They were out of hand with misery. And this was the woman I adored! I see myself now standing in the night nursery at Hyde Park Gate, washing my hands, & saying to myself "At this moment she is actually under this roof."

Fredegond came, all in black (& she dresses very badly). Uncle Hervey is dead, she said.[1] And she was off to bury him, but couldn't find a train (the strike, you see, is still on.) Hervey Fisher was the genius of our youth; & the only fruit of it is a volume of stories which are neither better nor worse than what one reads on a journey in a Red Magazine. They said he was dropped by his nurse; & so for 52 years, poor man, he has been plagued with illness; has been mad; has never done anything he liked, I suppose, even his marriage being called off by Aunt Mary.

Sunday 5 June

Poor Hervey Fisher has been buried a week, & is as if he had never been, I suppose: though if I chose I could imagine some feelings on the part of Adeline. Fredegond told us that he once lost his temper with Herbert, walked up to him & licked his eyelashes!

We went to Miss Royde Smith's party on Thursday to discuss Ireland. Never did I see a less attractive woman than Naomi. Her face might have been cut out of cardboard by blunt scissors. I fixed her with my eye. She fixed me with hers. But I got to the bottom of hers & jumped on the rock in a second. She is slightly furred too; dressed à la 1860; swinging ear rings, skirt in balloons; & a body that billows out but perfectly hard. There she sat in complete command. Here she had her world round her. It was a queer mixture of the intelligent & the respectable. There were two clergymen. They made jokes, which were well

1. Hervey Fisher (1873-1921), seventh of VW's Fisher cousins, died at Sheringham on 26 May. Since childhood he had suffered from crippling spinal tuberculosis and consequent mental derangement, but with tremendous heroism—both his own and his family's—he overcame his disabilities to the extent of being able to lead an active intellectual life. After the death of his mother in 1916 he was looked after by his sister Adeline Vaughan Williams. His one published book was *A Romantic Man and Other Tales* (1920). The fortnightly *Red Magazine* contained nine or ten stories and an instalment of a serial.

within the bounds of decency. My translation of their attitude would be "See how free & playful & advanced we are—yet we have not sacrificed niceness. We are people of the world. Very open minded. Not mere intellectuals—no—look how nicely we dress." Lady Rhondda was more plain dealing I thought; a solid bull dog, something after Ray's pattern.[2] I detest the mixture of ideas & South Kensington. Then Rose [Macaulay] chipped in with her witticism all in character at which the clergyman, Duncan Jones, said 'Oh Rose!' & everyone laughed loud, as if Rose had done the thing they expected.[3] Yes, I disliked it all a good deal—& the furniture & the pictures—the marriage of conventionality & the Saturday Westminster. I talked to Robert Lynd—& I didn't much care for him. He is a true journalist—all spent in clever words, elongated, exhausted, voluble, with the cloudy shifty look in the eyes which comes of catering perpetually for the Daily News. I can fancy him much liked. There's no bite about these people. I tried to be elderly & broad minded. I thought of Bloomsbury. But then in Bloomsbury you would come up against something hard—a Maynard, or a Lytton, or even Clive.

Murry has written against our Tchekhov in the Nation.[4] As for Kot, yesterday he couldn't keep his seat for fury. He verged on the voice & language of the public house— He said the sort of thing I've heard men say before they kick each other out. Is Murry "a damned swindler"? Suppose we admired Murry's writing, would he change his tune? In my theory he's all parched for praise—run mad for lack of it. Yet it goes against my psychology to think people scoundrels. Moreover they're more interesting if you can keep the stew on the boil. I think he's a greater mix than the rest of us. I don't know—at this moment I incline to think him a damned swindler—only a swindler so plausible that he'll become Professor of English literature in the University of Oxford.[5]

2. Margaret Haig Thomas, Viscountess Rhondda (1883-1958), succeeded to her father's title by special remainder in 1918; she was a militant member of the Women's Social and Political Union, and in 1920 founded (and from 1926 edited) the weekly *Time and Tide*.

3. Probably Arthur Stuart Duncan-Jones (1879-1955) at that time Vicar of St Mary's, Primrose Hill, and later (1929) Dean of Chichester.

4. In his long review in the *Nation & Athenaeum*, 4 June 1921, of LW and Koteliansky's translation of Gorky's *The Notebooks of Tchekhov*, Murry wrote that he believed it to be 'almost a crime to make public fragments of an author's manuscripts which he obviously did not mean to show the world', and feared this publication would 'strengthen a tendency that is already much too prevalent among those who meddle with letters—the tendency to approach an author by the backstairs'.

5. J. M. Murry gave a series of lectures, published as *The Problem of Style* (1922), at Oxford during the Trinity Term, 1921.

Tuesday 7 June

About an hour after writing this in came Eliot, & the first or third thing Eliot said was "Murry has been having tea with me—in fact he stayed a very long time, rolling another cigarette, & trying to say something, but he did not say it." So then L. burst out, & told him about the Tchekhov article; & this was no news to Eliot, who said "When we first knew each other we seemed to be becoming very friendly; but then we realised that we were fundamentally antagonistic— We had nothing to say today. There seemed to be nothing to be said."

"What did you say?" I asked.

"He talked mostly about himself. He said the Athenaeum had almost done for him. He got nothing from going into society except exhaustion— "I shan't do anything till I'm 50 or 60" he said". Eliot rolled his head & his eyes in imitation of Murry at this. "He can't hold his own with other people. Thats why he doesn't like going out." I repeated my phrase "He's parched with vanity;" "He will be very successful" said Eliot. "He's been giving 6 lectures on style at Oxford—as though it were a duty. He takes the crown as soon as he's offered it. But he's not satisfied with that."

"No, he wants us & you & Lytton to praise his poetry;"

"I've talked to him about his writing: I've never been able to praise it."

Literature is the devil, I said (meaning for the character).

He agreed.

Leonard said how he'd never met a worse man than Murry. That was the gist of what Eliot said; I think indeed his opinion is black at all points; & he knows him, & his methods better than we do. Strange to know a bad man!

The thing is that he is always trying to bias himself against his bad-ness—hence his confessions, his poses, & also, so Eliot said, these hysterical admirations for great men who have what he lacks.

"But never for his contemporaries—" I said.

"He used to lament the decay of D. H. Lawrence" Eliot said.

"He is a damned swine"—said L. & L. has written in this sense on a postcard to Sydney inviting him to play chess & discuss Murry.

Eliot, by the way, saw no truth in Murry's article.

"He is extremely clever" he said.

"But you don't mean that in a good sense", I said.

"Oh no: not at all."

Now I think its true that Eliot had wished us to open our eyes about

Murry. He certainly agreed to all criticisms, & made me feel that he could stress them & add facts if he chose. I think it probable that one of Murry's devices was to crab us both to Eliot, in his oblique way; & to insinuate that my writing was trivial, & so on.

"No one has any scope"—that was one of his phrases.

It will be interesting to watch his career to the high seat of authority. Unless, as L. says, he commits a felony. Probably in one word Eliot thinks him dishonest through & through.

And Eliot astounded me by praising Monday & Tuesday! This really delighted me. He picked out the String Quartet, especially the end of it. "Very good" he said, & meant it, I think. The Unwritten Novel he thought not successful: Haunted House "extremely interesting". It pleases me to think I could discuss my writing openly with him. And I was stoical; & I write without cringing (allow me these words of commendation!) Ulysses he says is prodigious.

On 10 June VW went to a concert, and that night could not sleep; next day she had a headache and stayed in bed, the beginning of two months of what LW called 'a severe bout' of ill-health, the fluctuations of which he noted in his diary. He took her to Rodmell from 17 June to 1 July; back at Hogarth House, she was able to see some visitors, but spent a lot of her time in bed, and it was not until after their return (by hired car) to Rodmell on 18 July that she was able to get through a night without a sleeping draught.

MONKS HOUSE, RODMELL

Monday 8 August

What a gap! How it would have astounded me to be told when I wrote the last word here, on June 7th, that within a week I should be in bed, & not entirely out of it till the 6th of August—two whole months rubbed out— These, this morning, the first words I have written—to call writing—for 60 days; & those days spent in wearisome headache, jumping pulse, aching back, frets, fidgets, lying awake, sleeping draughts, sedatives, digitalis, going for a little walk, & plunging back into bed again—all the horrors of the dark cupboard of illness once more displayed for my diversion. Let me make a vow that this shall never, never, happen again; & *then* confess that there are some compensations. To be tired & authorised to lie in bed is pleasant; then, scribbling 365 days of the year as I do, merely to receive without agitation of my right hand in giving out is salutary. I feel that I can take stock of things in a leisurely way.

Then the dark underworld has its fascinations as well as its terrors; &
then sometimes I compare the fundamental security of my life in all
(here Mrs Dedman interrupts for 15 minutes) storms (perhaps I meant)
with its old fearfully random condition—

Later, I had my visitors, one every day; so that I saw more people
than normally even. Perhaps in future I shall adopt this method more
than I have done. Roger, Lytton, Nessa, Duncan, Dorothy Bussy,[1]
Pippa, Carrington, James & Alix—all these came; & were as detached
portraits—cut out, emphatic, seen thus separately compared with the
usual way of seeing them in crowds. Lytton, I note, is more than ever
affectionate. One must be, I think, if one is famous. One must say to
one's old friends "All my celebrity is nothing—nothing—compared
with this" And that was what he did say too. We were talking about love.
He said he had suffered tortures from D[uncan]. & H[enry]. L [amb].
had wished to marry them & settle down, had been refused; & now can
love no more. "It is madness—" he said. "One cannot treat lovers like
rational people" this was said of Ralph's vagaries. "That won't happen
to us again" "Yet it is love that still matters—for look at you, you've
got fame enough—I sometimes see my name in the papers—yet that is
nothing." "You mean this—he said—indicating the 3 of us sitting in
the window— Oh yes, this is what matters—one's friends."

Tuesday 9 August

Then, as I say, there was Roger, with 20 holes in his teeth to be
stopped; & I thought his teeth were all of soulless bone, as some of
mine are; & now I hear that he has mercurial poisoning from these
stoppings in Paris. There's no doubt we are a weakly set of people; but
then they i.e. Nessa &c have had a splendid summer of dissipation. I
dont envy it: I dont want it; far far away it seems; I want nothing but
quiet & an active brain. Indeed I am reading Hardy for my famous
article—the one I'm always talking about.[2] I ransack public libraries &
find them full of sunk treasure. Yet I have a worm of uncertainty moving
at the foundations of this pleasant life—Allison, when we asked him to
cut a branch in the field, replied that he has sold the field for building

1. Dorothy Bussy, *née* Strachey (1866-1960), one of Lytton's elder sisters, had
   married the French painter Simon Bussy in 1903; they lived at Rocquebrune, but
   normally came to England each summer. She was a gifted writer and translator,
   particularly of the works of Gide.
2. On 14 February 1919 Bruce Richmond had written to VW: 'My next suggestion
   will, I hope, be many years before it comes to anything; but would you be ready
   with an article on Hardy's novels whenever the evil day comes?' (MHP, Sussex).

purposes to a friend. So I shall have Jack Squire in a poetical villa within a hundred yards. As it is I see Shanks' paper stand at his cottage window when I walk down my garden path; & cultivated voices & a cultivated dog barking wake us on Sunday mornings. The truth is, Rodmell is a colony for Georgian poets, & though I am all for letting live, & not reading their works, it is hard & indeed intolerable that I should have to let them live next door to me. We have even answered an advertisement about a house near Arundel; & paced out a meadow with a wonderful view, & imagined a house there. But L. says we are too old to build a house.

If one goes into the matter, & considers the good of the majority, Allinson's descent upon Rodmell is probably a benefit. He puts up gates & hedges, mends cottages, ploughs fields, owns a telephone, gives teas in the barn, & I suppose finds work & does kindnesses when old Stacey would have been stingy & too much of a rustic to imagine a better state of things. Old Stacey it is said drank himself to death, & had to be buried straight away—which will not happen to Allinson. However for my purposes farmers who drink, & lounge about like Mr Smith, muddy & ruddy & obsolete are far preferable to Allinson who looks as if he had been dressed by one of the advertisers in his own *Field*.[3]

Wednesday 10 August

But how is one to arrive at the truth? I have changed the Daily News for the Morning Post. The proportions of the world at once become utterly different. The M.P. has the largest letters & the double column devoted to the murder of Mrs Lindsay;[4] anglo Indians, Anglo Scots, & retired old men & patriotic old ladies write letter after letter to deplore the state of the country; applaud the M.P., the only faithful standard bearer left. They lament the downfall of England, which is flourishing

3. J. M. Allison had a financial interest in the hunting-shooting-fishing, country-gentleman's weekly *The Field* which had absorbed his own paper *Land and Water*; the Field Press had launched the *London Mercury*; hence the wealthy, hospitable landowning Allison became a magnet for Squire and the 'Georgian poets' by whom VW felt threatened. David Smith farmed at Little South Farm, Rodmell.

4. Mrs Lindsay of Coachford in Co. Cork, described by the *Morning Post* as a 'Southern Unionist', had been abducted from her home by the IRA on 17 February 1921 and executed as a spy. Nothing was known of her fate until her sister, a Mrs Ethel Benson of Dublin, received a letter dated 29 July from Cathal Bruga, the Dail Eireann Minister for Defence, telling her that Mrs Lindsay had been executed 'some months ago. . . .' The *Morning Post* carried a double-column article on the affair in its edition of Monday 8 August.

as usual in the D.N.; hardly spotted at all in the D.H. The heroes of the day in the Herald are the unemployed who rioted.[5] The M.P. ignores them altogether. But the D.N. has become a vivacious scrapbag. News is cut up into agreeable scraps, & written in words of one syllable. I may well ask, what is truth? And I cant ask it in my natural tones, since my lips are wet with Edmund Gosse.[6] How often have I said that I would never read anyone before beginning to write? The book came at breakfast, & I fell. He is one of the respectables. If Shelley had come before him now G. would have been distressed, though interested in young men of good birth. But how low in tone it all is—purred out by the firesides of Dowagers. That is not quite true, seeing that he has some sturdiness, some independence, & some love of letters. The peculiar combination of suavity, gravity, malignity & common sense always repels me. Once he sat next me & did not speak until he had an audience. Lytton, meeting him in ducal society, says he is very amusing.

Of private news, I have little, yet a thousand small events seem in progress. The time flies. I look at my watch & find it eleven. I've wasted 30 minutes gossiping with Mrs Dedman. L. has his rash on his arm from clearing the horrid little arch of ivy. We have bought the Dedmans' chickens. I find the eggs with a thrill of [*word illegible*]—warm, smooth, with a feather or so stuck to them. The servants, or rather the angelic couple of attached familiars, return tomorrow; & are welcome for the first time. Allison (for he is neither Addison nor Allinson) is away. I pray daily for his bankruptcy, or that his wife may being dishonour upon his name.

Thursday 11 August

A fortnight already gone. It goes too quick—too quick. If only one could sip slowly & relish every grain of every hour! For, to speak the

---

5. The rioting occurred on the morning of Monday 8 August 1921 at the timber yard of Messrs J. Gliksten & Co in the East End of London. Because of a potential labour dispute the company had over the week-end advertised for 'hands'. Some 4000 men from up and down the country responded to the advertisement, but in the meantime Gliksten's had resolved its difficulties and thus did not now have the vacancies it had anticipated. The men, in the words of the *Daily Herald*, 'became angry'. Mounted and foot police were used to drive them from the company's premises, after which action fire broke out in the 21 acre yard causing damage estimated at £1 million. The *Daily Herald* of Tuesday 9 August carried a full front page story on the incident.

6. Edmund Gosse's *Books on the Table* (1921) was a selection from his regular *Sunday Times* articles.

truth, I've thought of making my will for the first time during these past weeks. Sometimes it seems to me that I shall never write out all the books I have in my head, because of the strain. The devilish thing about writing is that it calls upon every nerve to hold itself taut. That is exactly what I cannot do— Now if it were painting or scribbling music or making patchwork quilts or mud pies, it wouldnt' matter.

The first thing that happened when we came here was that a branch blew down off Allison's tree. It lies with its branches standing up in the air, on a sloping part of the meadow, & the children of the cottages collect every morning & swing from rope, or are twirled round & round, till dark. A girl of 12 superintends, & I see her at work swinging the small children hour after hour. Sometimes they cry; sometimes quarrel; but the amusement lasts them. I suppose Julian & Quentin would soon be tired of it. No nurse would consent to stand there swinging them.

In the evening sometimes there's a game of stoolball.[7] I caught them at it, as I stood in the road beneath, pink & blue & red & yellow frocks raised above me, & nothing behind them but the vast Asheham hills— a sight too beautiful for one pair of eyes. Instinctively I want someone to catch my overflow of pleasure.

Saturday 13 August

"Coleridge was as little fitted for action as Lamb, but on a different account. His person was of a good height, but as sluggish & solid as the other's was light & fragile. He had, perhaps, suffered it to look old before its time, for want of exercise. His hair was white at 50; & as he generally dressed in black, & had a very tranquil demeanour, his appearance was gentlemanly, & for several years before his death was reverend. Nevertheless, there was something invincibly young in the look of his face. It was round & fresh-coloured, with agreeable features, & an open, indolent, good natured mouth. This boy-like expression was very becoming in one who dreamed & speculated as he did when he was really a boy, & who passed his life apart from the rest of the world, with a book, & his flowers. His forehead was prodigious,—a great piece of placid marble;—& his fine eyes, in which all the activity of his mind seemed to concentrate, moved under it with a sprightly ease, as if it was a pastime to them to carry all that thought.

7. A game with bat and ball, something of a cross between rounders and cricket, believed to be peculiar to Sussex where it is still played in many of the country villages.

"And it was pastime. Hazlitt said, that Coleridge's genius appeared to him like a spirit, all head & wings, eternally floating about in etherialities. He gave me a different impression. I fancied him a good natured wizard, very fond of earth, & conscious of reposing with weight enough in his easy chair, but able to conjure his etherialities about him in the twinkling of an eye. He cd. also change them by thousands, & dismiss them as easily when his dinner came. It was a mighty intellect put upon a sensual body; & the reason why he did little more with it than talk & dream was, that it is agreeable to such a body to do little else. I do not mean that C. was a sensualist in an ill sense. . . ." which is all that I can take the trouble to quote from Leigh Hunt's memoirs vol 2 page 223, supposing I should want to cook this up again somewhere. L.H. was our spiritual grandfather, a free man. One could have spoken to him as to Desmond. A light man, I daresay, but civilised, much more so than my grandfather in the flesh.[8] These free, vigorous spirits advance the world, & when one lights on them in the strange waste of the past one says Ah you're my sort—a great compliment. Most people who died 100 years ago are like strangers. One is polite & uneasy with them. Shelley died with H.'s copy of Lamia in his hand. H. wd. receive it back from no other, & so burnt it on the pyre. Going home from the funeral? H. & Byron laughed till they split. This is human nature, & H. doesn't mind owning to it. Then I like his inquisitive human sympathies: history so dull because of its battles & laws; & sea voyages in books so dull because the traveller will describe beauties instead of going into the cabins & saying what the sailors looked like, wore, eat, said; how they behaved.[9]

Lady Carlisle is dead. One likes people much better when theyre battered down by a prodigious seige of misfortune than when they triumph. Such a stock of hope & gifts she set out with, & lost every-

8. James Henry Leigh Hunt (1784-1859) and VW's *great*-grandfather James Stephen (1789-1859) were almost exact contemporaries. The above passage, accurately transcribed, is taken from Chapter XVI, 'Keats, Lamb, and Coleridge' of the three-volume, 1850, edition of *The Autobiography of Leigh Hunt*; and the passages quoted in the following footnote are from Chapter XIX of the same.
9. 'A body had been washed onshore, near the town of Via Reggio, which by the dress and stature, was known to be our friend's. Keats's last volume also (the *Lamia*, etc.), was found open in the jacket pocket. He had probably been reading it when surprised by the storm. It was my copy. I had told him to keep it till he gave it me with his own hands. So I would not have it from any other. It was burnt with his remains.' 'The barouche drove rapidly through the forest of Pisa. We [Hunt and Byron] sang, we laughed, we shouted. I even felt a gaiety the more shocking, because it was real and a relief. . . .'

thing (so they say) & died of sleepy sickness, her 5 sons dead before her, & the war crushing her hope for humanity.[10]

Wednesday 17 August

To while away the time till L. comes in, from London, Fergusson, office, &c, I may as well scribble. Really I think my scribbling is coming back. Here I have spent the whole day, off & on, making up an article—for Squire perhaps, because he wants a story,[11] & because Mrs Hawkesford has told Mrs Thomsett that I am one of the, if not the, cleverest women in England. It's not nerve power so much as praise that has lacked, perhaps.

Yesterday I was seized with the flux, as the Bible has it, Dr Vallence was fetched, came after dinner, & paid a call.[12] I wish I could write down his conversation—A mild, heavy lidded, little elderly man, son of a Lewes Dr, has always lived here, existing on a few broad medical truths learnt years ago, which he applies conscientiously; he can speak French, as it were, in words of one syllable. As both L. & I knew a good deal more than he did we got upon general topics—old Verrall, & how he starved himself purposely to death.[13] "I could have had him sent away," said Dr. V meditatively "He had been away once. His sisters away to this day—quite crazy, I believe— A bad family—very bad. I sat with him in your sitting room. We had to sit right into the chimney to get warm. I tried to interest him in chess. No. He didn't seem able to take an interest in anything. But he was too old—too weak. I couldn't send him away." So he starved himself to death, pottering about this garden.

Crossing his knees, & touching his little moustache meditatively now & then, V. then asked me if I did anything? (He thought me a chronic invalid, & fine lady). I said I wrote—"What novels?—light things?"

10. Rosalind Frances Howard, Countess of Carlisle (1845-1921), widow of the gentle artistic 9th Earl, and grandmother of Rosalind Toynbee, was a dominating woman of tremendous ability largely directed towards temperance reform, women's political rights, and Irish Home Rule. She had six sons and five daughters.

11. Nothing by VW was published in Squire's *London Mercury* between 'An Unwritten Novel' (Kp C203) in July 1920 and her 'Lives of the Obscure' (Kp C244) in January 1924; but see below, 10 September 1921: 'I started an article upon the obscure.'

12. Dr Herbert Vallance, MRCS, LRCP (Lond. 1893), of 23 High Street, Lewes, was in practice until the second World War.

13. Jacob Verrall (1844-1918) was the previous owner of Monks House; further information about him is given in *III LW*, 63-4.

Yes, novels. "I have another lady novelist among my patients—Mrs Dudedny. I've had to buck her up—to fulfil a contract, a contract for a new novel— She finds Lewes very noisy. And then we have Marion Crawford. . . . But Mr Dudedny is the puzzle king.[14] Give him any puzzle—he'll tell you the answer. He makes up the sort of puzzles shops print on their menus. He writes columns in the papers about puzzles."

"Did he help to answer puzzles in the war?" I asked.

"Well I dont know about that. But a great many soldiers wrote to him—the puzzle king." Here he crossed his legs the opposite way. Finally he went, & invited L. to join the Lewes chess club, which I should very much like to attend myself, these glimpses into different groups always fascinating me intolerably, for I shall never join the party of Dr Vallence & the puzzle king.

I shall never . . . has a kind of meaning, alas. For L. has been to see Allison, & there is no doubt that our fate is the worst possible. Ted Hunter is going to build his cottage, so far as we can tell, right against the orchard wall. He is going to make a proper road, & so far as I can see, the flats will be untenable. What to do we cannot decide. And this just as we were getting settled in to our liking—& with the added bitterness that we might, twice over, have bought the field & the terrace & saved the loveliest of views for ever.[15]

Thursday 18 August

Nothing to record; only an intolerable fit of the fidgets to write away. Here I am chained to my rock: forced to do nothing; doomed to let every worry, spite, irritation & obsession scratch & claw & come again. This is to say that I may not walk, & must not work. Whatever book I

14. Henry Ernest Dudeney (1857-1930), mathematical puzzle expert, author of *Amusements in Mathematics* (1917), *The Canterbury Puzzles* (1907, 1919) and later *The World's Best Word Puzzles* published by the *Daily News* in 1925. His wife Alice (d. 1945) was a prolific author of popular novels and stories. They lived at Castle Precincts House, Lewes. Francis Marion Crawford was a very well-known author, but he lived in Italy, not Lewes, and was in any case dead (1854-1909).

15. Monks House garden on the edge of Rodmell village was bounded on the south by the church path and on the north by the orchard wall, beyond which was Allison's field, so that Hunter's proposed cottage would have obstructed the Woolfs' view of and access to the open Ouse valley 'flats'. In the event the cottage was not built, and LW was later able to buy the field and double the extent of his garden. Edward Hunter was a London solicitor, a partner in Hunter and Haynes.

read bubbles up in my mind as part of an article I want to write. No one in the whole of Sussex is so miserable as I am; or so conscious of an infinite capacity of enjoyment horded in me, could I use it. The sun streams (no: never streams floods rather) down upon all the yellow fields & the long low barns; & what wouldn't I give to be coming through Firle woods, dusty & hot, with my nose turned home, every muscle tired, & the brain laid up in sweet lavender, so sane & cool, & ripe for the morrows task. How I should notice everything—the phrase for it coming the moment after & fitting like a glove; & then on the dusty road, as I ground my pedals, so my story would begin telling itself; & then the sun would be down, & home, & some bout of poetry after dinner, half read, half lived, as if the flesh were dissolved & through it the flowers burst red & white.

There! I've written out half my irritation. I hear poor L. driving the lawn mower up & down, for a wife like I am should have a label to her cage. She bites! And he spent all yesterday running round London for me. Still if one is Prometheus, if the rock is hard & the gadflies pungent, gratitude, affection, none of the nobler feelings have sway. And so this August is wasted.

Only the thought of people suffering more than I do at all consoles; & that is an aberration of egotism, I suppose. I will now make out a time table if I can to get through these odious days.

Poor Mdlle Lenglen, finding herself beaten by Mrs Mallory flung down her racquet & burst into tears. Her vanity I suppose is colossal. I daresay she thought that to be Mdlle Lenglen was the greatest thing in the world: invincible, like Napoleon.[16] Armstrong, playing in the test match, took up his position against the gates, & would not move, let the bowlers appoint themselves, the whole game became farcical, because there was not time to play it out.[17] But ⟨Achilles⟩ Ajax, in the Greek play, was of the same temper. —which we all agree to call heroic in him. But then everything is forgiven to the Greeks. And I've not read

16. Mlle Susanne Lenglen (d. 1938) was lawn tennis champion of both France and England for five years from 1919. During her American debut, in New York in 1921, she came literally to grief against the American champion Mrs Mallory, breaking down in the manner described by VW early in the second set of the Women's Championship.

17. In the closing stages of the Fifth Test Match at the Oval (15-17 August), W. W. Armstrong the Australian captain, a somewhat controversial figure capable of exciting the crowd to what *The Times* described as 'un-English' behaviour, was reported to have taken up his position 'on the farthest boundary . . . and declined to move either at the end of an over, or when the ball came his way'. The match resulted in a draw, the series being won by Australia.

a line of Greek since last year, this time, too; But I shall come back, if its only in snobbery; I shall be reading Greek when I'm old; old as the woman at the cottage door, whose hair might be a wig in a play, its so white, so thick. Seldom penetrated by love for mankind as I am, I sometimes feel sorry for the poor who dont read Shakespeare, & indeed have felt some generous democratic humbug at the Old Vic, when they played Othello & all the poor men & women & children had him then for themselves. Such splendour, & such poverty. I am writing down the fidgets, so no matter if I write nonsense. Indeed, any interference with the normal proportions of things makes me uneasy. I know this room too well—this view too well—I am getting it all out of focus, because I cant walk through it.

Saturday 10 September

My handwriting is getting detestable. But I have done with fidgets long ago, & sat in the sun at Bishopstone, & at Chalvington, & at Telscombe Cliffs. I recovered, & we took to seeing houses—without the least success, except that the rides to & from were successful. My only grievance is that one runs off the edge of the lovely into hideousness too soon. Newhaven is spot & rash & pimple & blister; with the incessant motor cars like active lice. Much more important (to me) than anything else, was my recovery of the pen; & thus the hidden stream was given exit, & I felt reborn. I started an article upon the obscure, & should have finished it today, according to calculations, had not Lytton come;[1] & it is impossible to write, unless the brain is unstirred completely by anything save the usual routine. However I gained by the exchange. We talked & talked; & always dislodged some new nugget, the deeper we went. Of course, his friendships are now, as mine are, fearfully important to him—all the more, as I daresay I have said, because he has been offered all the thin shining substitutes which his fame procures—ladies & lords without stint. But what did we talk about? (oddly enough I could write more freely after tea: this is the colourless morning hour, the mist driving across the flats, & rain come at last on the sudden wind.) First we skirmish round with trivialities; next we ascertain how we stand; we recognise that our position is sound; then begin on *our* writing; then on books—but its all easy enough, & interspaced. He is going to write a play, "I am going to meet my Waterloo"—that is to say he is going to have a shot at the creative. If that fails, he dooms himself to

1. See above, 17 August 1921, n 11.

history for ever—perhaps a history of English literature. Writing is an agony, we both agreed. Yet we live by it. We attach ourselves to the breath of life by our pens. The exciting illusion begins. Clive says we pour out brandy & so make romance, which does not exist. Clive came suddenly into view yesterday, in white flannel trousers, & open flannel shirt. He seemed bursting through; & his neck a series of rings of fat, like the Chess Queen's body. A dowager would hide this with a dog collar. And the heat had sopped his hair, so that he looked debauched & rubbed by dissipation. He was obviously nervous, & instead of boasting of his triumphs, as he did a few months back, almost deprecated them. "Did Lytton think the great world dull? Was he going to give it up? Well, perhaps it *is* too dull— One should live in the country & work" I'm glad to say that the repentant mood gave out; & up bubbled his natural man. The New Republic—America—money—&c &c &c—

I see that I shirk giving an account of Lytton's talk—for one thing, I dont like the appearance of writing what will interest Mr Gosse or Mrs Asquith in 50 years' time. Then, it needs a screw of the brain. I ought to note, though, for my good, that I must get out of the way of minding what people say of my writing. I am noted for it. It breeds discomfort. For instance, when Lytton was telling me of Max [Beerbohm]'s tastes in literature, he thought it necessary to explain that Max had not read me—which was uncomfortable. My dislikes of M.H. is attributed to her low opinion of my writing. So I must give up drawing attention to 'my writing'. One slips into the way of it; & a little slip is magnified soon. But that was the one awkward moment. In the old days there would have been a thousand.

Monday 12 September

It is true that we are alone again, but I cannot take up my pen, partly, I think, from superstition. I said goodbye to James & Alix at 9 this morning: therefore the whole day is contaminated. Freud has certainly brought out the lines in Alix.[2] Even physically, her bones are more prominent. Only her eyes are curiously vague. She has purpose & security; but this may well be marriage. James remains precisely where he was—the only human being, Alix says, fit for the contemplative life,

2. Since their marriage, James and Alix Strachey had been living and studying psychoanalysis in Vienna under Sigmund Freud; they were taking a holiday in England.

which is the highest. To look on comprehendingly is, she says, better than to create. But James claims no such eminence. He is the least ambitious of men—not ambitious even of being a character—low, muted, gentle, modest. I suspect that his points show in the shade—which Alix certainly provides. I can fancy him very considerate—selfish, of course, but not blind-selfish, not at all possessive, masculine, or dominating. The worst of it, as I should feel, is the greyness; nothing is worth doing; & his mind is capable enough to make out a case for anything, or against. I daresay his monotony is partly due to us. I fancy that in private he may be as gay as a small boy; perhaps they have a private language. Perhaps they go for treats. Perhaps he is the easiest & gayest of companions. Here he leapt on to my bed, directly I left it, & lay reading Jane's pamphlet.[3] There's Noel, too, in the background. Noel, for James, as for Adrian, the unattainable romance, though she has married Jones or Richards, & is romantic no more.[4] I caught Alix in profile & saw her old, masterly, advanced; always in the same coat & skirt, which indeed renews itself as if it were her natural covering.

Lytton, by the way, talked about s——y; & agreed that the b's are all namby pambies & sentimentalists. He is himself, he said. To be a b. one must be un-virile, unpossessive, very nice indeed, but tending to be sentimental. And then their tastes become so degraded.

I have finished the Wings of the Dove, & make this comment. His [Henry James's] manipulations become so elaborate towards the end that instead of feeling the artist you merely feel the man who is posing the subject. And then I think he loses the power to feel the crisis. He becomes merely excessively ingenious. This, you seem to hear him saying, is the way to do it. Now just when you expect a crisis, the true artist evades it. Never do the thing, & it will be all the more impressive. Finally, after all this juggling & arranging of silk pocket handkerchiefs, one ceases to have any feeling for the figure behind. Milly thus manipulated, disappears. He overreaches himself. And then one can never read it again. The mental grasp & stret[c]h are magnificent. Not a flabby or slack sentence, but much emasculated by this timidity or consciousness or whatever it is. Very highly American, I conjecture, in the determination to be highly bred, & the slight obtuseness as to what high breeding is.

3. Jane Harrison's *Epilegomena to the Study of Greek Religion* was published by the Cambridge University Press in 1921; 'with psychologists Freud and Jung as authority, she treats of the things that have lain, and still lie implicit, in all forms of religion.'

4. On 21 December 1921 Noel Olivier had married a fellow doctor, William Arthur Richards of Llanelly, at St Martin's in the Fields.

Sept 12. 21.   Charleston

My dear Virginia,

I should be sorry if Jack Squire were to suppose that he had seriously put me out; also, I can't swear to the phrase "put them right", though I'm sure it was nothing less impertinent; & so I hope you will say nothing about it. You don't guess how much I enjoyed my outing to Monks, or how much I like the society of you & your husband. You have created an atmosphere different from, perhaps better than, any I know. It seems odd, considering that we all started much alike in many ways; but I suppose, as they get older, people who start at all peculiar get more & more distinct. Anyhow, what I want to say is that the pleasure of seeing you both besides being great is particular. I am half tempted to suggest some sort of reunion either here or on the downs (weather permitting) for Friday—my birthday—only Mary will be with us and, owing to some absurd misunderstanding, she, I gather, is in your black books. So perhaps we had better wait till the following week.

                                                     Yrs
                                                     Clive.

P.S. On the ballet Murry is ignorant & silly.[5]

Wednesday 14 September

Now there's a chapter in a novel! First: I suspect that Jack Squire rejected the article: then I suspect that Clive, with one of his violent, lovable, revulsions—& yet he's a snob too—has turned against Coalbox, Jacks, & Lavatory, & wishes to secure his place in intellectual society;[6] & finally, partly from the same reasons, he is determined to contrive so that Mary is on visiting terms with us. The little man is all a bubble, all a muddle; & I could have foretold the whole thing, which has been brewing, I believe, ever since I refused to be one of the ladies at his tea party; & Leonard's abilities have become known; his star is in the ascendant; & when a star ascends, sure enough Clive will be frantically

5. See the *Nation & Athenaeum*, 10 September 1921: 'The Art of the Russian Ballet' by J. Middleton Murry: 'The chances are that the Russian Ballet will be an irrevocable memory fifty years hence.'
6. Coalbox = Lady Sibyl Colefax, *née* Halsey (d. 1950), an indefatigable hostess and collector of 'interesting' people; Lavatory = probably Hazel (d. 1935), the second wife of Sir John Lavery, RA, the highly successful and fashionable portrait painter; a beautiful red-haired Irish-American from Chicago, she became a prominent figure in London Society, and entertained liberally at 5 Cromwell Place. Jacks = Jack Squire?

rushing after. But I say much of this is praiseworthy. Leonard demurs. He is one of those dogs that cringe, he thinks. Anyhow, to continue my comment on the text, its plain that Mary & I are to be coupled together. No gentle gliding apart into mists. Yet why? I reply that I will see her & settle what the quarrel is about if she likes; since I have heard many versions.

There was a very great storm 3 nights ago—on Sunday 11th Sept. to be exact. I had to light my candle for support. Next morning our plum tree was down, & a great tree snapped some feet from the ground in the churchyard. Several graves are under leaf; & a wreath of immortelles lies under glass undamaged. The cottagers have been busy snatching up the twigs; the larger branches belonging, perhaps, to the Rector. More rain fell that night than in the 3 previous months, yet L. is not satisfied. Our garden is a perfect variegated chinz: asters, plumasters, zinnias, geums, nasturtiums & so on: all bright, cut from coloured paper, stiff, upstanding as flowers should be. I have been planting wallflowers for next June.

Thursday 15 September

It is the loveliest of evenings—still; the smoke going up straight in the quarry; the white horse & strawberry coloured horse feeding close together; the women coming out of their cottages for no reason, & standing looking; or knitting; the cock pecking in the midst of his hens in the meadow; starlings in the two trees;[7] Asheham fields shorn to the colour of white corduroy; Leonard storing apples above my head. & the sun coming through a pearly glass shade; so that the apples which still hang are palish red & green; the church tower a silver extinguisher rising through the trees. Will this recall anything? I am so anxious to keep every scrap, you see.

I have been dabbling in K.M.'s stories, & have to rinse my mind—in Dryden? Still, if she were not so clever she couldn't be so disagreeable.

A letter from Morgan this morning.[8] He seems as critical of the East as of Bloomsbury, & sits dressed in a turban watching his Prince dance,

---

7. Two large elms stood on the far side of Allison's field; the Woolfs called them Leonard and Virginia.
8. In a letter of 8 August 1921 E. M. Forster wrote to LW describing himself celebrating the birthday of Lord Krishna, 'in a turban, shirt and dhoti, but with no enthusiasm' watching 'his highness dance before His God'. He said that he was disappointed by Lytton Strachey's *Queen Victoria*, found it 'flimsy' in effect, and thought Strachey's 'skippy butterfly method' a limiting one. Although, he added, 'I expect he *has* written an important work....' See MHP, Sussex.

quite unimpressed. He is not impressed by Q.Vict. either. Flimsy, he says, compared with Macaulay, which was perhaps what I meant.

There is one woman of genius among the cows. She has decided to leave the herd & eat the branches on the fallen tree. She has now one disciple. The rest utterly condemn. She is a Roger Fry. I heard from Roger the other day, all in a hubblebubble about Murry's sneering pin-pricking article.[9] He is so angry that he can talk of nothing else, (the cow has 2 disciples). We must go on doing what we like in the desert Roger says, & let Murry climb the heights, as he certainly will.

The birds are moving about like nets full of fish; they turn sideways & vanish; sideways again, & become full of black spots.

Monday 19 September

Miss Green has been for the week end, & a more comfortable guest does not exist. One need not bother about her; yet, at meal times, she proves brisk & fresh. Her father was a professor, or teacher, of geology at Oxford. Her mother a Unitarian, & a liberal, with a great admiration for Gladstone. When Minna was 9 her father died. She has been secretary to Lady St. Davids.

"I consider you as my child" said Ly St D, & underpaid her. Then to Beerbohm Tree for 3 weeks. He walked about the room, behaved like Malvolio, & discoursed to an invisible audience about life. Minna found this trying, especially as it took place late at night in the dome of His Majesties. He used to say "Am I to give this autograph?"— Then she was with Heinemann. But his lack of courage annoyed her; he was afraid to publish Norman Angell; &, not having a penny in the world, Minna was too good a pacifist to stay— So she went on to the U.D.C.[10] In this way she has lived all over England; & is fearfully independent—marches about, protected by her extreme plainness, unmolested, & unnoticed; yet has a strong will of her own; & observes, & won't be put upon. She is

9. In May Roger Fry had given a lecture to the Institute of British Architects, which was published by Chatto & Windus as *Some Architectural Heresies of a Painter*; Murry's article upon it, 'Mr Fry among the Architects', was published in the *Nation & Athenaeum* on 27 August 1921. Fry's letter to VW—which he considered 'absolutely my masterpiece', written on his way to St Tropez, does not appear to have survived (see *II RF Letters*, no. 506).

10. Miss Green's employers were successively a Viscountess and hereditary Baroness; the famous actor-manager and owner of His Majesty's Theatre; the publisher; and the Union of Democratic Control. After her work for LW on the *International* and *Contemporary* Reviews ended, she worked on the *New Leader* and then *Foreign Affairs*.

one of that regiment of the wage earning women's republic. She eats up everything on her plate, very thoroughly; does not keep accounts; spends nothing on dress, & I daresay subscribes to the Russian Famine Fund. Now she is off to spend a fortnight in Germany—a country which she thinks very beautiful. I said there were too many signposts & plaster statues. She would have none of it. But then her thick legs, laced boots, wooden face, flaxen hair (scanty) & red cheeks, would be respectable there; ludicrous in Italy or France.

Wednesday 28 September

Eliot's visit passed off successfully, & yet I am disappointed to find that I am no longer afraid of him—[11]

[*Wednesday 2 November*]

This was the very last thing I wrote at Rodmell—so I suppose. And today is the 2nd of November; Wednesday to be exact; 10 to 7; & Dorothea just left the house for five years & a half.[1] But I like old Kate; who cant see, & picks up butter in mistake for bread. Dorothea surely is a survival from the glacial period. I felt her great nose sawing up and down; she has very powerful mandibles; & little pig eyes. Very soon we should have got across each other. I felt come over me the old aversion. She persists; prods; brutally tramples; & speaks with a kind of measured sweetness, such as people use in boarding houses to servants. Well we had no time to fight; since they took 2 hours to come; & had to catch a train. She salaamed to me. She said that the fruit of her Indian stay might be another book. She said "My book had a very long review in the Times." "Oh? I said. I never knew you'd written a book." "It was a very stupid review" she began with furious egotism, gnashing her teeth; & began eagerly to quote. So our minutes passed.[2]

11. Eliot's visit to Monks House was at the week end of 24 September; the Woolfs returned to Hogarth House on Thursday 6 October and LW almost at once got 'flu and stayed at home for a week.

1. VW's cousins, Dorothea Jane Stephen (1871-1965), a teacher of religion in India, and Katherine Stephen (1856-1924), Principal of Newnham College, Cambridge, 1911-20, were respectively the youngest and eldest children of Sir James Fitzjames Stephen. See also *II VW Letters*, nos. 1199, 1200, 1201, and particularly 1204.

2. The review of *Studies in Early Indian Thought* by Dorothea Jane Stephen in the *TLS* of 13 February 1919, concluded that the book seemed inadequate, being 'one-sided as a statement and unsatisfying as a picture of the Indian mind.'

But I ought to run over the 5 weeks or so left out; & really cannot; for I have seen so many people of sorts; & so much has happened; though we are where we are. A printing machine is waiting at Richmond Station, & will be delivered at 8 a.m. tomorrow.[3] Ralph is putting his back to the wheel, a very solid obdurate back. Some of our luncheons have been stormy, or rather silent, with sudden raps of opposition from the third party. My belief is that he has to dig his feet in vigorously in order to make any impression against L.'s superior mobility. But we have got along so far; & yielded, not reluctantly, about Tchekhov's letters.[4] In two days time—during the week end at any rate—I hope to finish Jacob. I have asked for books from the Times to compell myself to break off. And one of these days I must read it. We go to Rodmell on Friday. I see I can think of nothing worth saying. It has been a November day: soft, dark, as wet as the tropics, with a great funeral (Dr Gardiner's) passing the window—[5]

Clive hopes to see more of me. He sups with Gandarilla; & Betsy Bibesco wishes me to review her book.[6]

Tuesday 15 November

Really, really—this is disgraceful—15 days of November spent & my diary none the wiser. But when nothing is written one may safely suppose that I have been stitching books; or we have had tea at 4 & I have taken my walk afterwards; or I have had to read something for next days writing, or I have been out late, & come home with stencilling materials, & sat down in excitement to try one. We went to Rodmell, & the gale blew at us all day; off arctic fields; so we spent our time attending to the fire. The day before this I wrote the last words of Jacob—on Friday Nov. 4th to be precise, having begun it on April 16 1920: allowing for 6 months interval due to Monday or Tuesday & illness, this makes about

3. This was the second-hand Minerva treadle printing machine, which LW bought for £70.10s. (In 1930 VW gave it to Vita Sackville-West, and it is still at Sissinghurst Castle.) See *IV LW*, 72-3, also for Ralph Partridge's employment in the Hogarth Press.

4. This may refer to the abandonment of a proposal to publish Koteliansky's translations of a selection from Chekhov's letters—a publication undertaken by Cassell & Co in 1925.

5. Dr Matthew Henry Gardiner (1856-1921), senior partner of the Woolfs' Richmond doctor, Dr Fergusson; he died on 28 October, of a heart attack. See *II VW Letters*, no. 1201.

6. *I Have Only Myself to Blame*, a collection of stories, was Elizabeth Bibesco's first published book.

a year. I have not yet looked at it. I am struggling with Henry James'
ghost stories for The Times; have I not just laid them down in a mood
of satiety?—[7] Then I must do Hardy; then I want to write a life of
Newnes;[8] then I shall have to furbish up Jacob; & one of these days, if
only I could find energy to tackle the Paston letters, I must start Reading:[9]
directly I've started Reading I shall think of another novel, I daresay.
So that the only question appears to be—will my fingers stand so much
scribbling?

We dined with Clive on Friday. Aldous & Mary & Maynard there.
All the time I felt Mary solicitous, even affectionate; & sure enough, as I
left she took my hand, said "I don't like this plan of quarrelling" &
asked me to come & see her. So far nothing has happened—for was I
to ring her up, or she me—& what's it all about?

Molly came to tea. Lilian came to lunch. Poor Lilian—poor Margaret.
They sit beside the corpse of the Women's Guild; the blinds are drawn;
they are sad & white, brave, tearless, but infinitely mournful.[10] I see
what has happened. When one leaves a life work at 60, one dies. Death,
at least, must seem to be there, visible, expectant. One ought to work
—never to take one's eyes from one's work; & then if death should
interrupt, well, it is merely that one must get up & leave one's stitching
—one won't have wasted a thought on death. Margaret says in her work
one gets superannuated. One must give it up. A very cruel work then;
& she is left without husband or child. So we dragged Lilian over
Richmond; but she saw nothing but the ground. Very unhappy she said
she was. And Janet wants to sell her odious house & move to the

7. VW's article entitled *Henry James' Ghost Stories* appeared in the *TLS* of 22
   December 1921 (Kp C225).
8. Sir George Newnes (1851-1910) made his fortune with the popular journal *Tit
   Bits*, and thereafter founded the *Strand Magazine*, the *Westminster Gazette*,
   Country Life and many other newspapers and magazines. He financed the South
   Pole expedition of 1898, and his philanthropic acts included the presentation
   of a library to Putney and the construction of cable railways in Devon and Derbyshire. His mother makes a brief appearance in 'The Lives of the Obscure' (Kp
   C244).
9. *The Paston Letters, 1422-1509*, re-edited and published by Dr James Gairdner
   in 1904 in six volumes (not four, as VW's footnote to her published essay states),
   was a collection of over 1000 letters concerning the affairs—domestic, feudal,
   political and legal—of a well-to-do Norfolk family. VW's essay 'The Pastons
   and Chaucer' appeared in *The Common Reader*, which at this time she referred to
   as 'Reading'.
10. In 1921 Margaret Llewelyn Davies and Lilian Harris retired from their respective
    posts of General Secretary and Assistant Secretary of the Women's Co-operative
    Guild, to which they had devoted over thirty years' voluntary service.

New Forest.[11] I can't say that elderly group has met with the fate it deserves.

Molly was dressed in Mrs Freshfield's velvets.[12] A skirt is enough for an ordinary dress I daresay. "Have we quarrelled with Desmond?" we asked. Dear dear no. We seem to him cranky & crusty? Oh nonsense. Oh well thats all right then— Desmond is merely lazy. He is very uncommunicative just now. He tells me nothing. You have heard about the Waterlows? Sydney has become quite intolerable. He plants red flowers & they come up blue. She can do *nothing* nothing right. He grumbles all the week end. So at last she forbade him to come down. But he couldn't stand another Alice walking out of the house. They have been abroad for 6 weeks. She broke down & told me the whole thing. We must just go on disliking each other as other couples do, she said.[13]

Wednesday 16 November

Can I make out the Waterlow's tragedy from this telegraphic scrap? I see I scribbled too quick to put in the quotation marks. Anyhow this was what Molly said the other day, & as I have a collection of Sydneyana I add this. I ought to be about to set off to the Wigmore Hall to hear Bach: & nature has intervened; & I am, with my usual economy, asking myself how I can get the utmost possible pleasure out of my evening, which I spend alone, since L. is dining with the Webbs, to meet Fabians.[14] Shall I read King Lear? Do I want such a strain on the emotions? I think I do. It is pouring; but we say Thank God it is warmer. It has been freezing for a week. We go to bed under red blankets, quilts, fur coats; & I cant get up till I hear the quarter struck. But now, as I say, it is raining. I take in the Westminster Gazette. For some politics are beginning to interest me, as I suppose they interest City men—like a football match. One might become a virulent Socialist—or a Conservative? It is a game. I mean by that that I don't think of ends (nor does any one else) but of

11. Janet and Emphie Case built a house at Minstead in the New Forest and moved there from Surrey towards the end of 1922.
12. Augusta Charlotte Freshfield, *née* Ritchie, was Molly MacCarthy's aunt; she had died in 1911.
13. This 'bit of gossip' was given more extended treatment in a letter to Vanessa written two days earlier (see *II VW Letters*, no. 1204). Alice, *née* Pollock, had been Sydney Waterlow's first wife.
14. LW's diary entry for Wednesday, 16 November reads: 'Dined Webbs, Laszki, C. H. Lloyd etc. New Fabian Essays scheme.'

means. The American offer about the Navy has set me off on this.[15] I get no letters nowadays, so I read my paper. Clive's poems have gone today to the Reviewers; our publishing day being December the 1st. Did I describe the advent of the Press? Nelly panic struck, thinking it would come through the kitchen floor. How do you invent these fears? I asked her. Indeed, if she were as ingenious in her cooking we should do well. "Don't go & take the wire off the larder windows, for goodness sake" she said, "or we shall be having robbers."

But never have we been so peaceful domestically for so long.

What other news is there? I have left out everyone for a month— everything. How Lady Cromer came to tea, in a charwoman's bonnet, & cut great chunks of bread for herself. "My dear Virginia, when one is old one sees how absurd it is to think that sort of thing—I know my nieces accuse me of it—& I never give it a thought." This was when I told her how Kitty [Maxse] was worldly, & wished me to marry into South Kensington. She spoke with that old mellow worldly benignancy, as if all her thoughts were easy & shabby & loose, which I find so charming. In my house I like her better than in hers. She is trying to keep her son not a snob: "but he'll get among those kinds of people" she said. The Barings were horrified when she sent him to Winchester. "You send a boy to school in order to make friends" they said "The right sort".

Friday 25 November

L.'s 41st birthday; & he has just caught a mouse in his hands. My apology for not writing is quite truthfully, the Hogarth Press. Roger's woodcuts, 150 copies, have been gulped down in 2 days. I have just finished stitching the last copies—all but six. L. has been dismissed & taken on in another capacity by the same post; & now, this afternoon, he has been sketching a plan to Green, who is stranded, by which she may become our secretary.[16] The Hogarth Press, you see, begins to out-grow its parents.

Last week end we spent at Tidmarsh. We must have talked our 12

15. It was announced on 15 November that Britain had accepted, at an arms limitation conference in Washington, the principle of equality of naval strength with the United States.

16. LW had edited the international supplement of the *Contemporary Review* since it had superseded the *International Review* at the beginning of 1920; he was now asked to contribute instead a signed article on 'Foreign Affairs' each month, beginning in the new year. Miss Green, though she undertook typing jobs for VW, found work under Brailsford on the new *New Leader*.

hours, I suppose—& I remember so little: for with old, worn, creased, shabby, intimate friends, it runs so easily; no rapids, or waterfalls; room for everything; & no damned brilliance. We laughed over the letter of the mad negress, I remember. And it was all very warm & the details— such as cups & plates—were exquisite. Carrington & Ralph have a gigantic 4 poster bed. The geese shriek in the early morning. You see, I can't remember a thing—except that I was warm & communicative. Monday, though, I had a headache. I thought how foolish I had been to ask Richmond for books: & now I have 4 articles to write, & my brain is recovered, & I feel able to polish them all off, rather slap dash.[17] But I wake in the night & think that I haven't written Hardy; & I shall open my paper & find him dead— So we go on.

Last night Saxon dined here, & behold, here is a postcard, "Mr & Mrs Patteson in 1831" which tells me a good deal. They were drowned. & Lord Houghton wrote a poem about em, & Saxon thought they were Prinseps;[18] & this came of talking about the river Wye, & Barbara, & Sweden & the Finns, & Sydney & Desmond, & how no one will be read 100 years hence save Shaw; which Ralph said to me at tea today, you dont quite like. This is an unwonted subtlety on his part; though hs is apt to be more subtle when he's severe. He was 27 yesterday.

Saturday 26 November

Kot just gone after hearing Leonard his Russian; & so I have an odd half hour to fill up, & reach for this book. I have been cross examining Kot upon the quarrel between Dostoevsky & Turgenev, & find him stuffed with facts, & of course passionate severe & uncompromising. For once in a way I shall have some truth to put in my article.[19] We have spent the day mostly indoors, labelling Roger this afternoon. A

17. These were four contributions to the *TLS*, namely her essay 'Henry James' Ghost Stories' (Kp C225, published 22 December); and reviews of *Legends of Smokeover* by L. P. Jacks (Kp C224, 15 December); *The Two Friends and Other Stories* by Ivan Turgenev (Kp C223, 8 December); and *Fyodor Dostoyevsky: A Study* by Aimée Dostoyevsky (Kp C226, 12 January 1922; see below, 26 November 1921).

18. 'The Tragedy of the Lac du Gaube in the Pyrenees', commemorating the death of a honeymoon couple, was published in 1840 in *Poetry for the People and Other Poems* by Richard Monckton Milnes (1809-85), 1st Baron Houghton. Saxon had spent his summer leave in Finland.

19. VW made use of the information imparted to her by Koteliansky in her review of *Fyodor Dostoyevsky: A Study* by Aimée Dostoyevsky in the *TLS* of 12 January 1922 (Kp C226; reprinted in *Books and Portraits*, 1977) where she takes the writer to task for suppressing evidence.

yellow, prickly kind of day, with the quiet which comes of fog, & is accentuated, as it happens, by the road being up. It is said that we are to have wood pavement. Today we raised the servants wages by £2 each; & Nelly, for a joke pretended that we had raised her & not Lottie, & I believe this has taken away Lottie's pleasure. I believe she suspects that we perhaps meant this, or preferred Nelly. At any rate, we have had no thanks.

As for Mary I am playing a fine diplomatic game. I have no time— 7.30 draws near—to detail the stages. But I aim at not seeing her; at being friendly; for ever planning to meet; & never never never coming to grips. As if to emphasise this, my nib here dropped into the pot & is clogged with black ink. I can't help suspecting that this is her game too. What could we say to each other alone?

Saturday 3 December

The diplomatic game is being played with considerable finesse, & I fancy I shan't meet Mary face to face (which comes, I think from Crossing the Bar[1]) at all. I shan't cross that bar. Oddly enough, I feel sceptical & disillusioned about Clive and his doings. I've said so often enough out of spite; but this seems normal & true. His poor old brain has run down; as at 40 it very well may, if you drink too many cocktails, & sit too long with pretty Mrs Jowett. "Can it be Mr Jowett's fault, Madame?" said Gravé to me the other night. But I can pass no judgment upon the potency of Mr Jowett.[2]

I dined with the Sangers last night, & enjoyed society. I wore my new black dress, & looked, I daresay, rather nice. That's a feeling I very seldom have; & I rather intend to enjoy it oftener. I like clothes, if I can design them. So Bertie Russell was attentive, & we struck out like swimmers who knew their waters.[3] One is old enough to cut the trimmings

1. The last stanza of Tennyson's *Crossing the Bar*:
    'For though from out our bourne of Time and Place
        The flood may bear me far,
    I hope to see my Pilot face to face
        When I have crossed the bar.'
2. Lesley Jowitt, *née* McIntyre (d. 1970) was the wife of William Jowitt, a rapidly rising barrister, soon to become KC, a Liberal MP, and later Attorney-General and Lord Chancellor under Labour administrations, and an earl. She took an active interest in the arts.
3. The Hon. Bertrand Arthur William Russell (1872-1970), grandson of Lord John Russell, twice Prime Minister, and heir-presumptive to his earldom; philosopher, mathematician and pacifist; at Trinity College, Cambridge, he and C. P. Sanger were both Apostles. VW and Russell came to dine without their spouses: LW

& get to the point. Bertie is a fervid egoist—which helps matters. And then, what a pleasure—this mind on springs. I got as much out of him as I could carry.

"For I should soon be out of my depth" I said. I mean, I said, "all this" & I waved my hand round the room, where by this time were assembled Mr & Miss Amos, Rosalind Toynbee, a German, & Mrs Lucas—[4] "All this is mush; & you can put a telescope to your eye & see through it."

"If you had my brain you would find the world a very thin, colourless place" he said

But my colours are so foolish I replied.

You want them for your writing, he said. Do you never see things impersonally?

Yes. I see literature like that; Milton, that is.

The Choruses in Samson are pure art, he said.

But I have a feeling that human affairs are impure.

God does mathematics. That's my feeling. It is the most exalted form of art.

Art? I said.

Well theres style in mathematics as there is in writing, he said. I get the keenest aesthetic pleasure from reading well written mathematics. Lord Kelvin's style was abominable.[5] My brain is not what it was. I'm past my best—& therefore, of course, I am now celebrated. In Japan they treated me like Charlie Chaplin—disgusting.[6] I shall write no more

---

was seeing his constituents in the north; Russell's wife, Dora Black, with whom he had spent the previous academic year in China and had married in September following his divorce from his first wife Alys, had given birth to their son on 16 November. Russell was at this time earning his living in London by journalism and lecturing.

4. Maurice Sheldon Amos (1872-1940), jurist, was a friend and contemporary of both Sanger and Russell at Trinity; his sister was called Bonté and was a doctor. Rosalind Toynbee, *née* Murray (1890-1967), wife of the historian Arnold Toynbee, daughter of Professor Gilbert Murray and granddaughter of the formidable Lady Carlisle, was herself a novelist. Mrs Lucas was probably Emily Beatrice Coursolles Jones (1893-1966), not long married to the Cambridge don F. L. Lucas (see below, 3 January 1922, n 3); in 1919 she had reviewed *Night and Day* in the *Cambridge Magazine* (see *I VW Diary*, p 310, fn).

5. William Thomson, first Baron Kelvin of Largs (1824-1907), Professor of Natural Philosophy in Glasgow for over 50 years, mathematical physicist and fecund inventor; his papers were published in 5 volumes, 1882-1911.

6. On their way back from China in July Russell and Dora Black had visited Japan where they had been pursued by journalists. See *The Autobiography of Bertrand Russell*, Vol. II (1968), pp 133-5.

mathematics. Perhaps I shall write philosophy. The brain becomes rigid at 50—& I shall be 50 in a month or two. I have to make money.

Surely money is settled upon Russells by the country, I said.

I gave mine away years ago, to help promising young men who wanted to write poetry.[7] From 28 to 38 I lived in a cellar & worked. Then my passions got hold of me. Now I have come to terms with my self: I am no longer surprised at what happens. I don't expect any more emotional experiences. I don't think any longer that something is going to happen when I meet a new person.

I said that I disagreed with much of this. Yet perhaps I did not expect very much to happen from talking to Bertie. I felt that he had talked to so many people. Thus I did not ask him to come here— I enjoyed it though a good deal; & got home & drank cocoa in the kitchen; & at 7.30 this morning traced a smell of shag in the house & found L. smoking his pipe by the kitchen fire, having come back safe. There was no meeting at Newcastle; a very small one at Manchester; rather more at Durham; but it was an absurd effort for such results, & L. has spoken to Miss Green to that effect severely.

Sunday 11 December

Yes, I ought to be doing the beds; but Leonard insists upon doing them himself. Perhaps that's Lottie on the stairs? Ought I to go out & scold her for not staying in bed? Is the hot water on? Well, soon it will be time to go out & eat a plate of meat in the restaurant in the passage. In other words, both the servants have German measles, & for 3 days we have been servants instead of masters.

Excuse this scrawl therefore;—surely that is Lottie washing up?

Well, what news can I get in?

We went to Heartbreak House with the P[artridge]s. & Lytton. Lytton had just bought a manuscript by Mde du Deffand.[8] Lytton is ripe like a peach in the sun. Carrington wears his old overcoat cut down. Partridge laughs at the wrong jokes.

7. As a consistent pacifist Russell gave £3000 worth of debentures in a firm making armaments to T. S. Eliot whom he describes as being 'desperately poor'. Years later the poet returned the debentures. See *The Autobiography of Bertrand Russell*, vol. II (1968), p 19.

8. Bernard Shaw's *Heartbreak House* was showing at the Court Theatre. Lytton's purchase was probably the book *Reflexions, Sentences et Maximes morales* by A. de la Houssaye, Paris 1725, which contained Mme du Deffand's signature. See lot 732 in the *Catalogue of Printed Books . . . the Property of the late Roger Senhouse Esq . . . from the Lytton Strachey Library, Sotheby & Co, 20 October 1971*.

There was John & Mrs John slightly gross & elderly: wine making his lines thick; & her face more substantial.[9]

Kot dined here. Why did I go to bed with the gooseflesh after hearing discourse of Sullivan Gertler & Sydney Waterlow?[10] They have grease in their texture. And they despise women. And now & then Kot talks like a man of the underworld. No—I cannot make anything of this, what with one thing & another.

I mark that for perhaps the 50th time, I am frustrated as I mean to write poor T. Hardy. I pray that he sits safe & sound by his fireside at this moment. May all bicycles, bronchitises, & influenzas keep far from him.[11]

Sunday 18 December

Here it is practically the end of the year, & more pages left blank than seems to me altogether wholesome. But my diary dwindles, perversely enough, when the stuff for it is most abundant. There was Roger here for tea & dinner yesterday; the day before I had to go plundering the shops for presents after tea (we have tea at 4 now to suit Ralph). The day before, Thursday, I had to put in semicolons to my Hen James article while talking to Ralph over my shoulder & then to rush to catch a train to Hampstead to dine with Brett & Gertler. Tomorrow we dine with Adrian. But in thus accumulating facts I am shirking my business of describing them. Well, Brett's salon need give no one the gooseflesh. I thought to myself, as I sat in my black dress by the anthracite stove in the studio that if Sydney, Kot, Gertler, Brett, Miln, & Sullivan with one voice denounced me, I should sleep the sounder.[12] It is a group

9. Augustus John (1878-1961), as renowned for his bohemianism as for his art, and his beautiful wife Dorelia (1881-1969); VW had met them before her marriage in Lady Ottoline Morrell's company.

10. Koteliansky and Waterlow adhered to a social group in Hampstead which included Brett and Murry (and Katherine Mansfield when available) as well as Sullivan and Gertler. John William Navin Sullivan (1886-1937), scientist, biographer and journalist, had been a colleague of Murry's in the War Office and became a close friend and his assistant editor on the *Athenaeum*. Mark Gertler (1891-1939) the painter, who VW had known for several years (see *I VW Diary*), had since Carrington's marriage to Partridge finally subdued his long, passionate and unrewarded love for her. He had recently spent six months in a sanatorium with tuberculosis.

11. Hardy took to cycling in the 1890s, when it enjoyed great popularity as a pastime, and remained an indefatigable cyclist into his old age.

12. Herbert J. M. Milne, a classical scholar, was an assistant keeper in the Department of Manuscripts at the British Museum; he had lodged with Murry in Katherine's absence.

without teeth or claws. For one thing they have no faith in each other. In my day groups were formidable because they coalesced. But there was Gertler dismissing Sydney as an old bore (not to his face) & Kot detecting faults, "yes very serious faults—no you misunderstand my character—I do not find fault with the people I really like—I never discuss them—" & Miln is a moonfaced cipher—what they call, justly, a quiet man—& Sullivan is too much of the indiarubber faced, mobile lipped, unshaven, uncombed, black, uncompromising, suspicious, powerful man of genius in Hampstead type for my taste. Anyhow, the hours wore rather thin, & Gertler was the chief stimulant. He has grown fat; his hair stands upright; he has the same tightly buttoned face as of old —little eyes—hard cheeks—something small & concentrated about him which makes me repeat, however foolhardily, that I don't believe he can paint a picture—though his pertinacity would bore holes in granite, if *that* helped. However to balance this, I must add that he's more spontaneous than most: has an alert mind, & is, I should say, in defiance of Ralph, something of a Puritan. Sydney shocks him. Sydney says "Now what do you do about women's society? Do you copulate with your models?" And again, "Did you think that Marg made a bloody fool of herself the other night?"

Brett is soft, docile, & small. She danced before Q. Victoria.[13]

Roger's visit went off specially well. I mean we are grown rather intimate, & sit talking at our ease—practically of everything. This was not so a year ago. It is partly the good effect of having friends in common —not, as used to be the way, my seeing Roger alone, while Leonard stayed at home. I see in this one of the good effects of middle age. Roger had Benda in his pocket & read a passage aloud which started us off, & Leonard made him stand to his guns; & then on to all the usual things.[14] Roger grudges every minute now that he doesn't paint. So we reflected upon these strange, on the whole merciful, dispensations, by which Roger always sees masterpieces ahead of him & I see great novels— We have our atmosphere of illusion, without which life would be so much duller than it is. Here am I at last starting on Hardy, & saying to myself,

13. Dorothy Brett and her younger sister Sylvia, daughters of the 2nd Viscount Esher, used to attend a dancing class held weekly at Windsor Castle by the renowned Mrs Wordsworth for some of Queen Victoria's grandchildren and their cousins; the Queen used to watch them.

14. Julien Benda (1867-1956), French philosophical writer. Among his published works at this date were *Le Bergsonisme ou une Philosophie de la mobilité* (1912) and *Belphégor* (1918). *La Trahison des clercs*, the work for which Benda is now best known, did not appear until 1927.

not for the first time, This at least is going to be first rate. We discussed Proust, & Clive &, since I like to trace these things, I was interested to see how far apart Roger & Clive are now compared with what they were—Roger suspects Clive's friendships: had not yet been to see him.[15]

And before this Rosalind & Arnold T[oynbee]. appeared with a kitten & the manuscript of her new novel. She is a wisp of a woman, with the eyes of a kind sensitive thoughtful nature, which can't, I am afraid, produce much in the way of art. She can't by any possibility write a long book, she said; & she only made £10 by her last; & altogether she seems rather shelless & defenceless, though she is Gilbert Murray's daughter. I'm glad at least I'm not that, with a dash of aristocracy to refine still further.

Our luck seems, at last, to be in again. At least these are all good signs. Allison is tired of farming: the Americans want to have L.'s Contemporary articles; 37 copies of Tchekov were ordered yesterday; & the Labour Monthly wants L. to write another article. If each of these letters had been written the other way round we should have been very dismal, so we ought to be very cheerful. With luck we may have £400 instead of £250; & we might buy a motor car; & we might buy the meadow; & we might run up another lodge, & we might take in a new strip of garden. & so on & so on.

Monday 19 December

I will add a postscript, as I wait for my parcels to be wrapped up, on the nature of reviewing.

"Mrs Woolf? I want to ask you one or two questions about your Henry James article—"

First (only about the right name of one of the stories.) And now you use the word 'lewd'. Of course, I dont wish you to change it, but surely that is rather a strong expression to apply to anything by Henry James. I haven't read the story lately of course—but still my impression is—

Well, I thought that when I read it: one has to go by one's impressions at the time.

But you know the usual meaning of the word? It is—ah—*dirty*— Now poor dear old Henry James— At anyrate, think it over, & ring me up in 20 minutes.

So I thought it over & came to the required conclusion in twelve minutes & a half.

15. Roger Fry had been in France all autumn, but was back in London by December 1921, when he gave a series of lectures in the North of England.

But what is one to do about it? He [Bruce Richmond] made it sufficiently clear not only that he wouldn't stand 'lewd', but that he didn't much like anything else. I feel that this becomes more often the case, & I wonder whether to break off, with an explanation, or to pander, or to go on writing against the current. This last is probably right, but somehow the consciousness of doing that cramps one. One writes stiffly, without spontaneity. Anyhow, for the present I shall let it be, & meet my castigation with resignation. People will complain I'm sure; & poor Bruce fondling his paper like an only child dreads public criticism, & is stern with me, not so much for disrespect to poor old Henry, but for bringing blame on the Supplement.

And how much time I have wasted!

We dined with Adrian & there was Hope; & we sat in the high draughty cold room with all the empty spaces, shouting at each other—till I felt the light in my eyes, in my brain—all of me exposed & desolate. These deaf women make society impossible. It is like shouting in a high wind on the Brighton parade.

We had been buying presents, & sitting in the Club wedged between Kot & Bob. Kot persisting, enforcing, emphasising, analysing, rubbing in—how we are to publish Russian books—how L. is to give up the Contemporary—no, you misunderstand me—I did not say I consider your life to be worthless— Bob on the other side unusually calm & even sensitive. He is having his arteries manipulated in order to finish his play. He groaned sadly that he could not write. Desmond tells him that he is not dramatic. What with the Duchess & Desmond he has come to a full stop:[16] & said that he felt an old fogey, & he said this simply & I felt sorry for him; still, he seems to believe in his arteries, & once they start flowing, he will take us all by surprise— Nor do I, at least, insist upon more plays.

To add to Leonard's trophies, the Webbs have asked him to edit a book; the League of Nations Union offer to reprint Inl. Government; & the Village in the Jungle is sold among other rare first editions at 6/-. All very good.

16. Cf *II VW Letters*, no. 1210 to E. M. Forster: 'His love for the Duchess (this is Gordon Square gossip) has subdued and softened him' (a reference to Gladys Deacon, lately married to the 9th Duke of Marlborough; see above, 23 November 1920).

1922

1922

Tuesday 3 January

It is a good resolution that sends me to this page so early—only came back from Rodmell last night—but it is parsimony—a gloomy forecast that makes me use the odd leaves at the end of poor dear Jacob. Blank leaves grow at the end of my diaries.[1]

Home, as I say, last night, after 10 or 11 days at Monks House—days when the wind blew from every quarter at the top of its voice, & great spurts of rain came with it, & hail spat in our fire, & the lawn was strewn with little branches, & there were fiery sunsets over the downs, & one evening of the curled feathers that are so intense that one's eyes see nothing for 10 seconds afterwards. Mr Shanks had the double pneumonia, & was prayed for in Church, as indeed I thought advisable when I saw Dr Vallance's face at the window. We drank tea at the Rectory, & I was knocked over by the blast of crude emotion which that festival always releases. In the morning I wrote with steady stoicism my posthumous article upon Hardy. No more reviewing for me, now that Richmond re-writes my sentences to suit the mealy mouths of Belgravia (an exaggeration, I admit) & it is odd how stiffly one sets pen to paper when one is uncertain of editorial approval.[2] That—my dependence upon Printing House Square—is the true reason why I give up; joined with the economic reason that I make as much by other means. Leonard planted, pruned, sprayed, though the cold & the wet & the wildness made his behaviour a heroism to be admired, not comprehended. And last night, on top of our arrival, came to dinner Peter & Topsy.[3] Her face

1. For more precise detail concerning this parsimony, see *I VW Diary*, Appendix I, XI.
2. Bruce Richmond had coerced VW into substituting the word 'obscene' for 'lewd' in her *TLS* article *Henry James' Ghost Stories*; see above, 19 December 1921. For the article upon Hardy, see above, 9 August 1921, n 2.
3. Frank Laurence ('Peter') Lucas (1894-1967), a classical scholar of Trinity College, Cambridge; his undergraduate studies were interrupted by four years' war service, but, graduating in 1920, he was offered a fellowship in classics, and later in English, at King's College. He was an Apostle, and the following reference to his brothers' surprise at his marriage relates to his fellow members. In February 1921 he had married the novelist E. B. C. ('Topsy') Jones (1893-1966). She and VW had common friends, and she was probably the Mrs Lucas met at the Sangers on 2 December 1921 (see above, 3 December 1921).

is unnaturally elongated. It looks as if it had been caught in a door as a child. Why, we asked, did he marry her?—but we did not ask it quite so amazedly as his brothers do. He is a romantic: an innocent; a resolute boy; & she, I suppose, had a deeper experience of life, & somehow vouched for all sorts of things which, with this innocence & scholar's unworldliness, he was ready to take on trust. Fundamentally I guessed her to be sadder & more strained than he is; but also much less disinterested & sincere. So the evening passed; & I vacillated between liking & disliking, feeling pretty sure that I should never take to her warmly, but welcoming the spruce shining mind. With Peter one might be intimate, save that he is so young, so fresh: & not, after all, a born writer. We talked about Fredegond's religious mania; about Cambridge; youth; our set; theirs; the past; Romer Wilson (whom I denounced, & won some agreement) & finally the Greeks & the Romans, upon which Lucas, who can answer straight off any such question & becomes definite & exact in his replies, instead of merely gentle & modest, said they must return to Blackheath.[4] In the hall Topsy (May I call you Topsy? I asked in the hall) explained why they must return to Blackheath too volubly for my taste. But there's 6 o'clock striking, & its my evening with the Pastons. Tonight my reading begins.

Sunday 22 January

'Tonight my reading begins' did I say? And two nights later I was shivering over the fire & had to tumble into bed with the influenza. How describe the fortnights lapse? Happily, it has been a mitigated lapse —not complete like the summer's. Again I have a gallery of little bright portraits hanging against the wall of my mind—Nessa—Bobo [Mayor]— Bob—Kot—Pippa—to be exact; Nessa just back from France, alighting for a fortnight, & then off again, leaving the children, who have meanwhile got influenza, to Paris.[5] But what am I to say about her? All very gay in French boots, hat, & check skirt; with that queer antique simplicity of surface which I compare to the marble cheeks of a Greek statue. I mean her attitude to Clive.

4. The Shoves, like the Lucases, lived in Cambridge, both men being fellows of King's. Fredegond Shove, after her mother's death in 1920, became increasingly preoccupied by religion; she was to be received into the Roman Catholic Church in 1927. During the war Topsy Jones had shared a flat with Romer Wilson, winner of the 1921 Hawthornden Prize, when both were working as temporary civil servants in London.
5. Vanessa Bell, with Duncan Grant and her three children, had followed Roger Fry to St Tropez in mid-October, 1921.

"Its a great pity" she said. "Mary is a stupid little woman. There she was at the station to meet us. They've settled down together completely. I never thought it possible after the Guano. She's a very nice woman—quite simple & straightforward."

"Its ruining him" I said. "He talks about writing like a fashionable man, now. And if Mary's there, he's intolerable."

"Yes" said Nessa. Her acceptance of all this is complete; perfectly open, unresentful, philosophic.

But can I bind myself to go through my hoops—Bob & Bobo & the rest?

I'd rather try a general "account of my friends" to match one I made two or three years ago.[6]

Suppose I visualise them as a group of marbles with myself in the midst? —& now one drawing near, & then another rolling off into a corner? It's Desmond that has rolled into the corner this time. I dont know how it came about. Fundamentally, it is chance; that I was ill, & he in Ireland, & then he dines out, & has to be at the office, & so on & so on. Only there are seasons when he breaks through these hindrances persistently, & even has to be warded off (by Leonard that is for I never manage that); whereas, now, for the past 8 months, since the dinner when we hid Miss Green behind a screen, we have never seen him. Eight months—& life consists of how many months? That's what I begin to say to myself, as I near my 40th birthday. The machinery for seeing friends is too primitive: one should be able to see them by telephone—ring up, & be in the same room. Only there is loneliness to be considered too—this exacting brain—this spirit which wont entirely accommodate itself to company. One person one must have, like air to breathe; but—as for the rest? Still I don't like missing Desmond; & I blame myself a little for writing sharply in the N.S. (but I was right) about women;[7] & I find myself condemning him for a penny a liner on good terms with his public.

Lytton's marble is very close. I think he has determined, partly owing to his fame, to stick tight to one or two rocks, & his friends are one of them. So we are asked to Tidmarsh, & meetings are very carefully cherished, when they occur. His flame burns very pure. No masses of superfluity intervene. We have burnt up all that long ago. (Here mercifully I am compelled to stop in order to rule some blue lines. This is still influenza writing, or I'm inhibited by [Dr] Fergusson's prohibition.

6. This was begun precisely three years earlier, on 22 January 1919. See *I VW Diary*.
7. VW's letters to the *New Statesman* in 1920 about women are reprinted as Appendix III.

No work for 2 or 3 weeks, he says. But I fancy I shall finish Hardy tomorrow.)

And I could only find a black pencil. But the truth is that when one is seeing people often & intimately one cannot say very much about it. I don't see Lytton far enough away to have a clear view of him.

On the other hand, Sydney has almost vanished into the fog. Yesterday he loomed up again—for the first time since —? He hasn't been here for 9 months perhaps. He wants to come back. But as during his absence, I have had reports of his infidelity I'm going to hum & haw a little. I doubt that he is faithful or unfaithful. And he lives in the pigsty—by which I mean the Murrys & the Sullivans & the Gertlers.

I've no quarrels to record. Now I come to think of it I'm on excellent terms with Clive, with Maynard, with Mary, for anything I know to the contrary. We should get on admirably on a desert island, if Mary could go behind a rock; but London, this January 1922, is not a desert island, & though we meet each other in the street now & again, the conditions don't make for intimacy. There's Saxon—at the end of the telephone. Infinitely weary, bored, irritable, even yawning audibly as he spoke, was he last night—grudging other people, so I thought, even their influenzas. What one envies more than anything is simply life. We all live, this way or that: Saxon has never quite got the hang of it—nor Adrian either, I fancy, though Karin obscures Adrian rather effectively. We dined there, perhaps I forgot to record, & bawled like Margate boys.

The Pope is dying today; & the Irishmen have come to terms.[8] The church bells ring, & though it is 10 minutes to eleven I can't see the face of the clock, nor even the trees in the garden. The birds wake us with their jangling about 7 o'clock; which I take to be a sign of spring, but then I am always optimistic. A thick mist, steam coloured, obscures even twigs, let alone Towers Place.[9] Why do I trouble to be so particular with facts? I think it is my sense of the flight of time: so soon Towers Place will be no more; & twigs, & I that write. I feel time racing like a film at the Cinema. I try to stop it. I prod it with my pen. I try to pin it down.

8. Pope Benedict XV had in fact died at 6 am that morning. Michael Collins (the Sinn Fein leader) and Sir James Craig (representing Ulster) had issued a joint statement on 21 January that agreement had been reached between the Irish Free State and Northern Ireland concerning the settlement of the boundary, the boycott of Belfast, and other controversial issues.
9. Towers Place was a small lane parallel to Paradise Road at the end of the garden to the rear of Hogarth House.

Saturday 4 February

Another fortnight spent in bed. Indeed, almost as I put down my pen I was seized with a second attack, lay in bed like a piece of timber, & am still in bed, sitting up, looking at the fire, the tree twigs hung with drops of aquamarine, & my temperature a shade above normal. I think this second attack was more wearisome than the first, & I have seen very few people. Nessa came again. How painful these meetings are! Let me try to analyse. Perhaps it is that we both feel that we can exist independently of the other. The door shuts between us, & life flows on again & completely removes the trace. That is an absurd exaggeration. The truth is she was a little depressed, ostensibly because no one had mentioned painting to her in the course of three weeks. "I have seen all the cleverest people, she said, & not one asked me about the South of France. Nobody mentioned painting. I hung two of our latest paintings in Maynard's room, & he never noticed them."

"Surely Clive?" I said.

"Oh Clive knows nothing whatever about it" she replied. All this tends to make her turn to Paris as her dwelling place. But then there are the children, Julian at school, Quentin coming home nightly.[1] And then there is Duncan. "And after all there is nothing binding in our relationship", she said. "Its quite different from yours."

And so this ruffled me: donkey that I am—am susceptible to the faintest chord of dissonance twelve fields away. I set out to prove that being childless I was less normal than she. She took offence (the words are too strong). Told me I shouldn't enjoy café life in Paris. Told me I liked my own fireside & books & my friends visits; implied that I was settled & unadventurous. Implied that I spent a great deal upon comfort. As we had only 2 hours together, & she left for Paris next morning, & perhaps I shant see her till May, anyhow not continuously, I felt a sort of discontent, as the door closed behind her. My life, I suppose, did not very vigorously rush in.

Indeed, we are at the moment a little tremulous again. What to do about Ralph?—about the Press? Mrs Manning Sanders forges ahead.[2] She has reached the printing off stage, which means that Ralph works in the basement, & leaves the machine dirty. We had tea at 4 yesterday,

1. In January 1922 Julian Bell was sent as a boarder to Leighton Park School near Reading; and Quentin went as a day boy to Peterborough Lodge preparatory school at Swiss Cottage.
2. *Karn*, 'a new long poem by a short fat poetess' (*II VW Letters*, no. 1213), Ruth Manning Sanders, was printed by the Hogarth Press and published in May 1922 (*HP Checklist* 23).

& I made myself agreeable. "And the type will be dry for me tomorrow?" I said, having dissed wet type laboriously all the afternoon.

"No it is not washed yet" he said. Then vanished.

L. was struggling with the fire. When the door shut I understood— L. was white with rage—that R. had slipped off leaving L. to go down & clean up. If he had apologised, this would have been bad enough; but to slink away, like a shamefaced schoolboy, was outrageous, & I was furious. L. had been at work all day; & now had another hour in the cold.

Upon this crystallised all our grumblings of the past— They are to the effect that he is lazy, undependable, now industrious, now slack, unadventurous, all corroded by Lytton, can't praise, yet has no view of his own—the old story, which one has heard so often from the victims of the old serpent, but rather a serious detraction from his merits, as a partner in an enterprise. Should the enterprise be modified? Should we part company? Should we hire a woman drudge? I suspect that the work is not possible for an educated & vigorous young man: but I am being charitable.

Monday 6 February[3]

What a sprightly journalist Clive Bell is! I have just read him, & see how my sentences would have to be clipped to march in time with his.[4]

Mrs Manning Sanders is a bob haired, wide mouthed woman, dressed in a velvet dressing gown, plump, sandy-haired with canine brown eyes far apart. We liked her. But to Ralph her Fitzroy St origin was against her—this is his rule of thumb measure—for God knows, he said nothing, & is hard & angular as a block of wood. However, we had Mrs M.S. from 5 to 7.15.

Tuesday 14 February

So far had I written that Monday when Fergusson came in & pronounced that my eccentric pulse had passed the limits of reason & was in fact insane. So I was laid in bed again, & set up my state in the drawing

3. VW has written 5 instead of 6 February.
4. Clive Bell's latest article 'The Creed of an Aesthete' (an attack on Bernard Shaw's play *Back to Methuselah*) had appeared in *The New Republic*, New York, on 25 January 1922. It is probable—but impossible to be certain—that he had sent it to VW to read.

room, where I now write sitting up in bed, alongside the fire, with a temperature a shade below normal, & a heart become naturally abnormal, so that perhaps I shall be up & creeping this time next week. I am reading Moby Dick: Princesse de Cleves; Lord Salisbury: Old Mortality; Small Talk at Wreyland;[5] with an occasional bite at the Life of Lord Tennyson, of Johnson; & anything else I find handy. But this is all dissipated & invalidish. I can only hope that like dead leaves they may fertilise my brain. Otherwise, what a 12 months it has been for writing!—& I at the prime of life, with little creatures in my head which won't exist if I dont let them out. K.M. bursts upon the world in glory next week;[6] I have to hold over Jacob's Room till October; & I somehow fear that by that time it will appear to me sterile acrobatics. Nevertheless, such is life, that I am very tolerably amused; see a good many people, Elena [Richmond], Kot, Adrian, Lytton today; & drowse off comfortably. It is illness at its best. We dine over the fire. L. has his tray on a little stool. We are as comfortable as cottagers (looked at through the window) & this morning dropped from the blue (yes it is blue, & frost on the roofs, & Ralph skating at Tidmarsh; & Mrs Sanders not sent her proofs) £114.18., unexpected payment by Mitchells, in whom I lost, so I thought, £600.[7] This is mercy indeed; for we were very low at the bank, having bought type; & would have had to sell out, for our travels & printers bills. God after all does exist; for always some wind brings down an apple at the critical moment.

Elena has grown solid, like a tree trunk. She keeps her mystery. A performing seal—one doesn't know what is instinct, what intellect. I find her sympathetic—so maternal, quiet, kindly; & liking literature as a lady does; & saying such unexpected things about it, as a lady does. She doesn't like representation in fiction; can't stand Wells & Bennett; attempts Dorothy Richardson; is puzzled; reverts to Scott; hasn't heard of Joyce; comfortably waves aside indecency; I should guess that she represents the top layer of the ⟨Mudie⟩ general public very accurately. She is modest, even reserved, about her own doings, which gives her charm. Would have like a country life—dogs, garden, village charities,

5. *Moby Dick* by Herman Melville, published 1851; *La Princesse de Clèves*, the novel by Mme de La Fayette, published in 1678; the first two volumes of the *Life of Robert, Marquis of Salisbury* by his daughter Lady Gwendolen Cecil which appeared in 1922; *Old Mortality* by Sir Walter Scott, 1816; and *Small Talk at Wreyland* by Cecil Torr (1857-1928), published in 3 volumes, 1918, 1921, 1933.

6. Katherine Mansfield's *The Garden Party and Other Stories* was published by Constable in February 1922.

7. VW had held shares in Mitchell Bros (London) Ltd, which went out of business in 1919; this windfall was a final disbursement of the company's assets.

county committees, Gunby & Stephen Massingberd I suppose, best of all;[8] & hates London, where she has had however her great successes. Like my father, I am attracted by the simple & affectionate & womanly. Not that she now dresses with beauty or has much to boast. She is a handsome du Maurier matron, with a double chin, settled complexion; & she dresses in a pepper & salt tailor made, wears spats, & has something of the American bust. I like chattering to her about literature. On Saturday when she comes again, I shall try to discuss the Lushingtons.

And Adrian is so happy & genial that I am really pleased. I don't want to make him out a failure even. An unambitious man, with good brains, money, wife & children is, I daresay, the most fortunate of us all. He need not protect himself by any illusions. He sees things as they are. He is humorous, contented; free to enjoy without envy or uneasiness. "Oh well", he said talking of his medical career, "it's something to do." "Its easier now to go on than to stop" he said. He has his ya(t)cht, & as the years pass, he will ripen into a delightful father. Moreover, like the whole family, he has this distinguished, cool, point of view, which always makes him good company, & admits him to any society—if he wished for any society, which needless to say, he doesn't.

Saxon's father is dead; & Saxon controls two houses of lunatics, some with broken legs, others with the influenza; which will make a man of him, so all is for the best in the best of all possible worlds.[9]

I did not enjoy Molly [MacCarthy]'s visit. She is so deaf; so wandering; grown as plump as a ptarmigan; inconclusive more than ever; given to sudden vacant pauses, with her head dropped down; yet very affectionate in her flittermouse way; with that charming irresponsible heartlessness, which always amuses me. She wakes from a pause & raps out something quite to the point & even prosaic. She told me how she had loved the Governor of Madras, & refused Desmond for him, & was very glad now she had married Desmond, who suits her exactly she said. Why did I not enjoy Molly's visit then? Well, she never concentrates upon me, I suppose.

I meant to make some notes of my reading (which should include Peacock by the way) but Lottie's interminable gossip with the old witch wood woman frets me. Talk—talk—talk—wonder expressed—loud laughter—agreement—wood woman's voice claps [?] more & more

8. Gunby Hall in Lincolnshire (built 1700; now National Trust property) was inherited by Stephen Langton Massingberd (1869-1925); he married Kitty Maxse's sister Margaret Lushington; she died in 1906.
9. Dr Alfred Moxon Sydney-Turner, MRCS, LSA, JP, of Ventnor Villas, Hove, had been the proprietor of a private home for mental patients.

emphatic—Nelly there too—Talk with them a kind of muscular activity I think, for they never say much: repeat one thing over & over.

Goodbye goodbye—don't forget.

Ah! at last! And now Lottie must compare notes with Nelly downstairs.

Wednesday 15 February

I thought to myself, as Lytton was talking, Now I will remember this & write it down in my diary tomorrow. And as I thought that, everything melted to mist. People don't say things, except in biographies. True, Lytton was smooth & mild & melancholy beyond his wont; but with intimates, when talk is interesting, one sentence melts into another; heads & tails merge; there is never a complete beast. These I remember as opinions: Lady Gs. life of Salisbury is extremely good: Salisbury was a perfect aristocrat. The point about him was that he was a man of action simply & solely. Lady S. was stuck up & pert; they discussed travelling second class. And what else can I remember? Absolutely nothing? 'Latest Racine' he had read on the posters at Waterloo; thought it referred to Masefield; then re-read Racing.[10] But he was back again in his old pre-Eminent Victorians despondency, partly, I guessed, because the publishers are chilly about his essays; partly because he can't think of a plot for a play. When I told him a history of George IVth was quite good enough, I think he was pleased. How these writers live in their work— How ambition consumes them! Everything radiates from this in Lytton, & I fancy loneliness leaks in through the chinks. He gave me the first edition of a book by Beckford [not traced]; a very characteristic present, & the first he ever gave me, or I him.

We disagreed violently about Percy Lubbock's book;[11] & I traced poor dear Ralph's swift unerring insight to the original source. Its annoying to me—as if Lottie picked up my gold watch & gave it a scouring with Bluebell polish (this utterly inappropriate image comes from the irritation she is just now causing me by scrubbing door plates, & turning on the electric light.) All Lytton's subtleties & allusions come out spick & span blown through brass.

10. John Masefield's play, adapted and partially translated from Racine's biblical tragedy *Esther*, had been reviewed at length in the *TLS* of 9 February 1922. Strachey's long essay on Racine was about to reappear in his collection *Books and Characters* (1922).

11. Percy Lubbock's book, *The Craft of Fiction* (1921), was to be discussed in VW's lead article 'On Re-reading Novels' (Kp C228) in the *TLS* of 20 July 1922. See below, 23 June 1922.

Of my reading I will now try to make some note.

First Peacock; Nightmare Abbey, & Crotchet Castle. Both are so much better than I remember. Doubtless, Peacock is a taste acquired in maturity. When I was young, reading him in a railway carriage in Greece, sitting opposite Thoby, I remember, who pleased me immensely by approving my remark that Meredith had got his women from Peacock, & that they were very charming women, then, I say I rather had to prod my enthusiasm. Thoby liked it straight off. I wanted mystery, romance, psychology I suppose. And now more than anything I want beautiful prose. I relish it more & more exquisitely. And I enjoy satire more. I like the scepticism of his mind more. I enjoy intellectuality. Moreover, fantasticality does a good deal better than sham psychology. One touch of red in the cheek is all he gives, but I can do the rest. And then they're so short; & I read them in little yellowish perfectly appropriate first editions.[12]

The masterly Scott has me by the hair once more. Old Mortality. I'm in the middle; & have to put up with some dull sermons; but I doubt that he can be dull, because everything is so much in keeping—even his odd monochromatic landscape painting, done in smooth washes of sepia & burnt siena. Edith & Henry too might be typical figures by an old master, put in exactly in the right place. And Cuddie & Mause are as usual, marching straight away for all time, as lusty as life. But I daresay the fighting & the story telling business prevent him from going quite ahead with his gun as in the Antiquary;

Thursday 16 February

to continue— Certainly the later chapters are bare & grey: ground out too palpably: authorities, I daresay, interfering with the original flow. And Morton is a prig; & Edith a stick; & Evandale a brick; & the preachers dulness I could take for granted. Still—still—I want to know what the next chapter brings, & these gallant old fellows can be excused practically anything.

How far can our historical portrait painters be trusted, seeing the difficulty I have in putting down the face of Violet Dickinson, whom I saw, for 2 hours yesterday afternoon? One hears her talking in a swinging random way to Lottie in the hall, as she comes in. "Where's my marmalade?— How's Mrs Woolf? Better eh? Where is she?" meanwhile

12. The first editions of *Nightmare Abbey* and *Crotchet Castle* were published in 1818 and 1831; VW's copies, probably inherited from her father, were sold at Sotheby's on 27 July 1970. Meredith was Peacock's son-in-law.

putting down coat & umbrella & not listening to a word.[13] Then she seemed to me as she came in gigantically tall: tailor made; with a pearl dolphin with red tongue swinging from a black ribbon; rather stouter; with her white face; prominent blue eyes; nose with a chip off the end; & small beautifully aristocratic hands. Very well: but her talk? Since nature herself could give no account of it—since nature has wilfully left out some screw—what chance is there for me? It touches Mr Bevan; bounces off to Wild Dayrell & the nurse who cut out a bit of the curtain, which was found after three hundred years to come from the curtain at Littlecote: Mrs Bevan kept hordes of goats. Mr Bevan has escaped with a Frenchwoman. His taxi—a Daimler car—went from Victoria to the Emporium & back again: away again—then to the aerodrome.[14] Such nonsense putting old Ribblesdale & Horner on Boards—Ly.R. was an Astor & refused to let a penny of hers be invested— Your friend Miss Shreiner has gone to Bankok.[15] Dont you remember all her boots and shoes in Eaton Square? To tell the truth I remembered neither Shreiner, her boots, or Eaton Square. Then Herman Norman is back & says things are in an awful mess at Teheran.

'He's my cousin' I said.[16]

Hows that? Off we went on to Normans. Leonard & Ralph were having tea meanwhile & sometimes intercepted a whiff of grapeshot. Now all this, properly strung together, would make a very amusing

13. See *II VW Letters* nos. 1206, 1216, reminding Violet Dickinson that VW was keeping some home-made marmalade for her.

14. A somewhat distorted summary of the story in part recorded by John Aubrey in his *Brief Lives* under 'Sir John Popham'. The piece cut from the curtain is said to have served to identify and bring to justice William Darell, owner of the Littlecote estate in Wiltshire, who had a midwife brought blindfold to his house to deliver a child which he then cast on the fire. The Littlecote estate was conveyed in 1587 by 'Wild Dayrell' to Mr Justice Popham, before whom he stood trial. The current tenant of Littlecote, Mr Robert Lee Bevan, a prominent city man, had hurriedly left the country the previous week following the liquidation of two of his concerns. He was eventually apprehended in Vienna, brought to trial for fraudulent conversion, and sentenced to seven years penal servitude.

15. There are references to this unknown lady, who was clearly *not* a friend of VW's, in *I VW Letters*, nos. 486 and 507, written in 1909; it is equally clear she can not have been Olive Schreiner, the celebrated authoress, who was not in Bankok but dead. Lord Ribblesdale (1854-1925), and Sir John Horner (1842-1927) of Mells in Somerset, were pre-eminently landowning country gentlemen; the former's second wife was Ava, widow of the immensely wealthy American, Colonel J. J. Astor.

16. Herman Cameron Norman (1872-1955), diplomat, was British Minister in Teheran, 1920-21; he was a grandson of Julia Margaret Cameron and thus a second-cousin of VW's.

sketch in the style of Jane Austen. But old Jane, if she had been in the mood, would have given all the other things—no, I dont think she would; for Jane was not given to general reflections; one cant put in the shadows that appear curving round her, & giving her a sort of beauty. She quiets down—though believing the old doctrine that talk must be incessant—& becomes humane, generous; shows that humorous sympathy which brings everything into her scope—naturally; with a touch of salt & reality; she has the range of a good novelist, bathing things in their own atmosphere too, only all so fragmentary & jerky. She told me she had no wish to live. "I'm very happy" she said, Oh yes, very happy— But why should I want to go on living? What is there to live for? Your friends?— My friends are all dead. Ozzie? Oh he'd do just as well without me.[17] I should like to tidy things up & disappear.

But you believe in immortality?

"No: I don't know that I do—Dust & ashes, I say."

She laughed of course; & yet, as I say, has somehow the all round imaginative view which makes one believe her. Certainly I like—is love the word for these strange deep ancient affections, which began in youth, & have got mixed up with so many important things? I kept looking at her large pleasant blue eyes, so candid & generous, & hearty & going back to Fritham & Hyde Park Gate.[18]

But this doesn't make a picture, all the same. I feel her somehow to be the sketch for a woman of genius. All the fluid gifts have gone in; but not the boney ones.

Friday 17 February

I've just had my dose of phenacetin—that is to say a mildly unfavourable review of Monday or Tuesday reported by Leonard from the Dial, the more depressing as I had vaguely hoped for approval in that august quarter.[19] It seems as if I succeed nowhere. Yet, I'm glad to find, I have acquired a little philosophy. It amounts to a sense of freedom. I write what I like writing & there's an end on it. Moreover, heaven knows I get consideration enough.

Molly Hamilton sits for her portrait today. Her portrait, to be sure,

17. Oswald Eden Dickinson (1869-1954), Violet's youngest brother, was Secretary to the Home Office Board of Control in Lunacy; they lived together.

18. VW's close friendship with Violet Dickinson dated from 1902, when, as an old friend of Stella Duckworth's, she stayed with the Stephens in the New Forest at Fritham House which they had rented for the summer.

19. LW's report was of a brief unsigned review of Monday or Tuesday in the February issue of the Dial (New York). See below, 18 February 1922, n 25.

was a little shadowed by the fact that, but for her, I should have had Lytton in the chair, & should have got more for my money. She is a crude piece of work by comparison. One of the strugglers; & thus a good deal of time must be wasted upon facts—how she is to get a job— what she can live on &c. Besides, the strugglers are all worn & muscular with struggling. She is bitter against people—seems to me to snap, as a dog does with a thorn in his foot. And something of her pleasure in seeing me is the charwoman's pleasure in talking of her bad leg: by a grate which she need not polish, & with tea things which she need not wash up. However, to give her her due, she is a warm, courageous, bustling woman; & I like her spirit, & the trophies she brings me of buffeting & rejection—'real' life; if one chooses to think it so. Never was anyone more on their own; & I think she means it when she wishes the motor omnibus would swerve in her direction; but cant be bothered to step to meet it. "And then I'm so angry with myself. I have a good howl & start afresh." I shouldn't like to come in from the Strand, grudging the omnibus its good guidance, find my fire out, no one there, & perhaps a business letter from a firm or an Editor—something severe & impersonal. A dull man wants to marry her. Why not marry a nice man? I asked.[20] "After being on one's own for eight years its impossible to marry any-one" she told me. "One gets into the habit of being free to do as one likes." She had been the guest of Lady Rhondda in the South of France; & Lady R. who is a good able superficial woman, had psychologised her divorce proceedings all the time, which was boring Molly said;[21] & Lady R. is a feminist, & Molly is not. But the lady Rs. ought to be feminists, I said; & you must encourage them, for if the rich women will do it, we neednt; & its the feminists who will drain off this black blood of bitterness which is poisoning us all. So we talked; the fire dying out; all in shadow, which is the best light for women's nerves once they're passed 40. I observe that my women guests of that age— Molly & Elena, move to have their backs to the window, on some excuse or other. Old Violet who has passed that stage, faces light composedly.

I meant to write about death, only life came breaking in as usual. I like, I see, to question people about death. I have taken it into my head that I shan't live till 70. Suppose, I said to myself the other day this pain

20. Mrs Hamilton's marriage in 1905 had been unhappy and brief. She did not remarry.
21. Lady Rhondda (a viscountess in her own right) was the wife of Sir Humphrey Mackworth, 7th Bt; their interests proved incompatible, and she divorced him in 1923.

over my heart suddenly wrung me out like a dish cloth & left me dead?—
I was feeling sleepy, indifferent, & calm; & so thought it didn't much
matter, except for L. Then, some bird or light I daresay, or waking
wider, set me off wishing to live on my own—wishing chiefly to walk
along the river & look at things.

Saturday 18 February

Three dozen eggs at present prices work out at 10/6. Three dozen = 36.
Four eggs for breakfast work out at 28 a week. This leaves 8 over for
cooking. I have an egg now every night for dinner. I make these calculations not with a view to an essay upon national economy, though that
comes in. My weekly books—these are in my mind—the very top layer,
to be shifted off here most conveniently. For according to the papers,
the cost of living is now I dont know how much lower than last year;
whereas my books remain about the same. You cant question Nelly
much without rubbing a sore. She threatens at once to send up a
cheap meal "& Mr Woolf wont like that." There! Not a very grievous
itch; & quelled by the sight of the new Byron letters just come from
Mudie's.[22]
Once more my mind is distracted from the thought of death. There
was something about fame I had it in mind to say yesterday—oh I think
it was that I have made up my mind that I'm not going to be popular,
& so genuinely that I look upon disregard or abuse as part of my bargain.
I'm to write what I like; & they're to say what they like. My only interest
as a writer lies, I begin to see, in some queer individuality: not in strength,
or passion, or anything startling; but then I say to myself, is not 'some
queer individuality' precisely the quality I respect? Peacock, for example:
Borrow; Donne; Douglas, in Alone, has a touch of it. Who else comes
to mind immediately? FitzGerald's Letters.[23] People with this gift go on
sounding long after the melodious vigorous music is banal. In proof of
this, I read that a small boy, given a book by Marie Corelli for a Sunday
school prize, at once killed himself; & the coroner remarked that one of
her books was not what he himself would call "at all a nice book". So

22. *Lord Byron's Correspondence*—some 350 hitherto unpublished letters mostly to
Lady Melbourne, John Cam Hobhouse, and Douglas Kinnaird—was edited and
published by John Murray IV on 16 February 1922.
23. Norman Douglas's *Alone*—'not so much a book of travel as the book of a
traveller,—had been published late in 1921. VW possessed the 7 volumes of the
Letters and Literary Remains of Edward Fitzgerald edited by W. Aldis Wright,
1902 (see *Holleyman*, MH II, p 5).

perhaps the Mighty Atom is dwindling away,[24] & Night & Day arising—though the Voyage Out seems at the moment most in esteem. That encourages me. After 7 years next April the Dial speaks of its superb artistry.[25] If they say the same of N. & D. in 7 years I shall be content; but I must wait 14 for anyone to take Monday or Tuesday to heart.

I want to read Byron's Letters, but I must go on with La Princesse de Cléves. This masterpiece has long been on my conscience. Me to talk of fiction & not to have read this classic! But reading classics is generally hard going. Especially classics like this one, which are classics because of their perfect taste, shapeliness, composure, artistry. Not a hair of its head is dishevelled. I think the beauty very great, but hard to appreciate. All the characters are noble. The movement is stately. The machinery a little cumbrous. Stories have to be told. Letters dropped. It is the action of the human heart & not of muscle or fate that we watch. But stories of noble human hearts have their moments unapproachable in other circumstances. There is a quiet understated profundity in the relations between Madame de Cléves & her mother, for example. If I were reviewing it, I think I should take for my text beauty in character. Thank God though I am not reviewing it. Within the last few minutes I have skimmed the reviews in the New Statesman; between coffee & cigarette I read the Nation: now the best brains in England (metaphorically speaking) sweated themselves for I don't know how many hours to give me this brief condescending sort of amusement. When I read reviews I crush the columns together to get at one or two sentences; is it a good book or a bad? And then I discount those 2 sentences according to what I know of the book & of the reviewer. But when I write a review I write every sentence as if it were going to be tried before 3 Chief Justices: I cant believe that I am crushed together & discounted. Reviews seem to me more & more frivolous. Criticism on the other hand absorbs me more & more.

But after 6 weeks influenza my mind throws up no matutinal fountains. My note book lies by my bed unopened. At first I could hardly read for the swarm of ideas that rose involuntarily. I had to write them out at once. And this is great fun. A little air, seeing the buses go by, lounging by the river, will, please God, send the sparks flying again. I am suspended

24. *The Mighty Atom* by the immensely popular novelist Marie Corelli (1855-1924) was published in 1896.
25. The *Dial* review of *Monday or Tuesday* (see above, 17 February 1922, n 19) said that 'In her present volume of sketches Mrs Woolf becomes much more arty than in her novels, although she never surpasses the technical superbness of *The Voyage Out*'.

between life & death in an unfamiliar way. Where is my paper knife?
I must cut Lord Byron.

Monday 6 March

The cat lets this mouse run a few steps once more. I have walked for
10 minutes only, according to the directions of Dr Sainsbury, who after
examining me for an hour said—many things; among them that we can't
go abroad.[1] But I am back again, after 2 months this very day, sitting
in my chair after tea, writing; & I wrote Jacob this morning, & though
my temperature is not normal, my habits are: & that is all I care for.
No more lounging & drowsing & doctors visits of a morning, I hope.
Yet I no longer feel very trustful. And Ralph may be in any moment to
stop these reflections.

Sunday 12 March

This book dwindles, now that I draw my stream off in the morning.
Were it not for the irritation of suspense—Nelly & Lottie: the hospital;
the operation, & my own raging toothache—by which I designate my
desire to be writing out the preface to Reading,[2] I should let this page lie
blank. Yet many portraits are owed to it— I have seen people—&
people. Eliot, Clive, Violet,—if no one else. Of these Eliot amuses me
most—grown supple as an eel; yes, grown positively familiar & jocular
& friendly, though retaining I hope some shreds of authority. I mustn't
lick all the paint off my Gods. He is starting a magazine; to which 20
people are to contribute; & Leonard & I are among them![3] So what
does it matter if K.M. soars in the newspapers, & runs up sales skyhigh?

1. Dr Harrington Sainsbury, a distinguished heart specialist of 52 Wimpole Street,
   to whom VW had been referred by Dr Fergusson. (For his opinion, see *II VW
   Letters*, no. 1224.) The Woolfs had been planning to go to Italy this spring.
2. See MHP/B 11d, Sussex. This consists of some forty pages of heavily revised type-
   script headed 'Preface', altered to 'Introductory. Byron & Mr Briggs', which
   internal evidence suggests was completed before 26 March 1922. VW sets out to
   discover the value of a reviewer 'taking it for granted that he has no method,
   but only a personality—that he is in short much nearer the ordinary reader, of
   whom there are multitudes, than the critic of whom, with great luck, there is one
   in a century'. Dr Johnson's 'common reader', it is stressed, is 'a person of first
   importance', someone 'not to be despised'.
3. T. S. Eliot's aspirations to edit a literary magazine of his own were to be realised
   with the appearance in October 1922 of the first number of his quarterly *The
   Criterion*, financed by Lady Rothermere. VW did become a contributor; there are
   no contributions by LW.

Ah, I have found a fine way of putting her in her place. The more she is praised, the more I am convinced she is bad. After all, there's some truth in this. She touches the spot too universally for that spot to be of the bluest blood.

"I've ceased even to think about Murry. I've forgotten all about him" said Tom.

What, then, did we discuss? He has written a poem of 40 pages, which we are to print in the autumn.[4] This is his best work, he says. He is pleased with it; takes heart, I think, from the thought of that safe in his desk. Clive, via Mary, says he uses violet powder to make him look cadaverous. Thus it appears that Mary is not on good terms with Tom; & that I am seeing Clive rather frequently. He comes on Wednesdays; jolly, & rosy, & squab: a man of the world; & enough of my old friend, & enough of my old lover, to make the afternoons hum. One a week is probably enough. His letters suggest doubts. But, oh dear me, after 9 weeks claustration, I want to vault the wall, & pick a few flowers. The ethical code of Bloomsbury allows poaching; & I'm amused to see how far their ethics are merely theoretic. Moreover, & more seriously, a change of relationship, a middle aged relationship, offers new experiences.

Then I hit Morgan on the wing. He had come to London that very day, & so came here, & was, we thought, depressed to the verge of inanition. To come back to Weybridge, to come back to an ugly house a mile from the station, an old, fussy, exacting mother, to come back having lost your Rajah, without a novel, & with no power to write one —this is dismal, I expect, at the age of 43.[5] The middle age of b——s is not to be contemplated without horror. But he was charming, transparent; & told us as much as we could get out. A years absence fills one too full for many drops to issue upon turning the bottle upside down. He told us about the sparrows that fly about the Palace— No one troubles about them. "I used to shout at them sometimes. One got caught in the electric wire. There it hung, until it wrenched its claw off & flew away. The squirrels sat on the piano. There is a great quarrel between the elder branch & the younger branch. The younger branch

4. This was *The Waste Land*, which the Hogarth Press was to publish in September 1923 (*HP Checklist* 28).

5. E. M. Forster had recently come back from India to his mother's semi-detached suburban villa at Weybridge. He had for six months been private secretary to H.H. Sir Tokoji Rao III, Ruler of Dewas Senior, a small central Indian state he had previously visited in 1912-13 (see E. M. Forster, *The Hill of Devi*, 1953). His projected novel had run aground, and the eventual completion of *A Passage to India* owed a great deal to LW's encouragement.

came to the festival of the God. He treated me very nicely, & hoped to see more of me. "If I thought they would treat you with decent politeness, I should be only too glad that you should go" the Rajah said. I used to row on the lake which was nice. The Indians were too heavy to row. There were black hills. A very nice climate, but dull. There were sparrows only. In other parts the birds were so lovely—I thought of you Virginia (which pleased me). I dont believe in native states any more. Agitators don't exist there. If they come, they disappear. It is a very nice life; but one wants other people to talk to. It is much nicer than this. I felt no enthusiasm at seeing my native cliffs again." That was obvious. Off he went, carrying a very heavy metal plate, to dine with Aunt Rosalie at Putney.[6]

Friday 24 March

I write in order to drown the voice of the canary bird—Leonard's typewriting I mean. I cannot read it down, but I can write it down. Gravé is imminent. I have nothing special to add as to my circumstances. Still invalided, I sit & receive visitors almost daily; & say nothing about them here. I am writing the first chapter of Reading with the usual fabulous zest. I have never enjoyed any writing more. How often have I said this? Does the pleasure last? I forget— I *say* I shall write the book in 6 months,—under the year, at any rate. For this reason, people are neglected, & accumulate, up & up & up: I cannot see them now—Nessa, Duncan, Toynbees, Bobo, Goldie, Mason,[7] Roger, Clive, Clive, Clive, Ray. Clive is the most persistent; we talked from 4.30 to 10.15 the other day. It is clear that I am to rub up his wits; & in return I get my manners polished. I hear of supper parties; elicit facts about drink & talk & goings on. Viola Tree starts singing Mozart with a great hole in her stocking: Christabel "a little lump of passion": Mary—mum; Shearman confiding at 3 A.M. his distaste for life.[8] Off we go—C. & I—upon our

6. Rosalie Alford, *née* Whichelo (1866-1957) was Forster's mother's sister, and his favourite among his many aunts. The plate was probably Bidar-work from Hyderabad State, where he had stayed with his friend Masood; (Forster owned several pieces himself).

7. J. H. Mason (1875-1951), a scholarly printer and typographer, was a friend of Roger Fry, who brought him to lunch with the Woolfs on 15 March.

8. Viola Tree (1884-1938), eldest of the three daughters of the great actor-manager Sir Herbert Beerbohm Tree; two books by her were to be published by the Hogarth Press. Christabel, the Hon. Mrs Henry MacLaren, *née* Macnaghten (1890-1974), who on the death of her father-in-law in 1934 became Lady Aberconway.

relish for it. He enjoys *every*thing—even the old hag in the doorway.
There is no truth about life, he says, except what we feel. It is good if
you enjoy it, & so forth. Obviously we reach no heights of reason.
Nor do we become completely intimate. A little colour is added to taste.
We have our embrace; our frill of sentiment. Impossible, as Nessa says,
to talk without it. But I perceive, chiefly through his letters, that once a
fortnight is the pitch of our relationship.

Nelly & Lottie have talked till the sky seems nothing but a dish cover
echoing their changes of mind. They go home for the week end to settle
the matter, & eat birthday cakes, & I guess that she won't go to hospital
after all. Refer back to some other scene of the kind if you wish to know
how many hours have been wasted; how many reflections upon the lower
classes formulated; & how often L. has approached me before I order
dinner with a pained, solicitous appearance, begging me on no account
to say this or that, strongly advising me at all costs to make something
else plain.

Betty Potter loves me; is in despair; & I have to see her rehearse in
order to keep her from suicide. How can anyone be such a fool as to
believe in anyone?

Thursday 30 March

They have decided for the operation; or rather Johnston has decided
for them; & no one can overrule his finding, as he alone had the materials.
Now Emma Gilman is in the house, & we have just presented a rose
coloured dressing jacket.[9] The atmosphere is a little tremulous, with that
kind of significance in trivial sayings which is moving & uncomfortable.
It is snowing now, large loose watery flakes; they fall straight; there is
no wind: four turned to large drops hang on the branch against the
window; (but I am thinking out tomorrow's writing—or even skipping
to the end of the book, & thinking what I shall say about Shaw). Muddy
water is in the evening sky, & we began summer time last Sunday, so

Sir Montague Shearman (1857-1930), KC and picture collector. They were
interested in the arts and moved—as did Mary Hutchinson and indeed Clive
Bell—in a relaxed post-war society wealthier and more sophisticated than that of
the Woolfs.
9. The subject of Lottie's internal disorder was a regular accompaniment of everyday
life this year. Mr James Johnstone, surgeon of Richmond and the London Homeo-
pathic Hospital, was Nelly and Lottie's doctor. Emma Gilman was one of Nelly's
nieces.

the evening sky is prolonged. The poor Vaughans will find it very difficult to get through the long evening; & Emma will take a turn in Kensington Gardens, or will say, as she once said to me, "One always expects something of the summer; but somehow, it never seems to happen." This she said some time in 1908 in Russell Square, one evening.[10]

I am shirking Bobo's rehearsal, which I meant to describe.[11] Miss Craig is a rosy, ruddy 'personage' in white waistcoat, with black bow tie & gold chain loosely knotted.

Stop those monkey tricks, do Saunders—& let us have some light.

Miss Craig (Saunders stands right up to the footlights & shouts through her hollowed hands:) "There's a short on the battens, Miss Craig."

Lets have the floats then. . . .

Now, all of you. I want you to listen *carefully* to the music. Make the movements that suggest themselves to you.

Beautiful lady, you go up to the balcony. Can you step to the left? No: I won't take risks. Young man, Dunlop, you walk straight—straight I say—straight— Can't you move that table? No? Well then to the right. Miss Potter (this with some acerbity) *you* needn't dance.

Poor Betty looked like the skeleton of a sheep. She is at one of her crises, & may be dismissed the stage over this affair.

But it is, as usual, the atmosphere I want to get. The supple, candid, free & easy good sense of theatrical manners, as I noted them at tea. "My dear boy," drinking out of the same cup. Little Lanchester said, when I asked if she walked in her pyjamas, "Oh do stop being funny"— I dont think one could use one's brain without being warned off. Still, it don't much matter. I walked with Miss Litvinne, mother of an illegitimate child, down Longacre, & found her like an articulate terrier—eyes wide apart; greased to life; nimble; sure footed, without a depth anywhere in her brain. They go to the Cabaret; all night dances; John Goss

10. VW is referring to her spinster cousins, Margaret (1862-1929) and Emma (1874-1960) Vaughan, who still lived in Kensington, and with whom she now had very little contact.

11. The rehearsal was of three plays to be performed by the Playwrights Theatre on Sunday 2 April at the Kingsway Theatre. Two of the plays were by Beatrice Mayor: *The Girl in the City*—a monologue delivered by her sister Betty Potter, with music adapted from Lord Berners and a dream-sequence of mute figures; and *Thirty Minutes in a Street*, with a cast of twenty-one. Edith Craig (1864-1947), the producer, was Ellen Terry's daughter. Elsa Lanchester (b. 1902), whose first appearance on the professional stage this was, had previously organised and taught The Children's Theatre, and ran an unlicensed night-club-cabaret called The Cave of Harmony in Gower Street; she was to marry Charles Laughton in 1929.

sings.[12] She was communicative, even admiring I think. Anyhow, I like Bohemians. Then we went into the theatre, & there was the light on, the group significant, (Bobo's children) gold tissue; something stimulating & unreal.[13]

The Woolfs went to the public performance of Beatrice Mayor's plays at the Kingsway Theatre on Sunday 2 April; two days later there was a Memoir Club meeting; and on Friday 7 April, the day before Lottie's opera-tion, the Woolfs went to Monks House, returning to Richmond on Thursday 27 April, when they also visited Lottie in hospital.

Thursday 27 April

Just back—not from the Club, but from Lopokhova & Rodmell, & fingers are so cold I cant close them on my pen.[1] It is blackening for another downpour. This is the worst spring on record. 27 days of bitter wind, blinding rain, gusts, snowstorms, storms every day. So Rodmell was mitigated joy, & to this was added Nelly's diversion so that we had to carry coals ourselves. She left us after a week, unable to stand the bi-weekly journey to Lottie in hospital.

We saw Mayors, Nessa, & Cecils.[2] Lady G. Cecil is much like a terrier dog in coat & skirt: worried, untidy, insignificant; ardent, masculine in

12. Rachel (Ray) Litvin (d. 1977), an actress whose portrait Vanessa Bell painted at about this time and who late in life was to become a painter herself, had the part of a housewife in *Thirty Minutes in a Street*. John Goss (1894-1953), after a succession of menial dead-end jobs, had in 1920 adopted singing as a career, and was to become a highly successful and popular baritone soloist.

13. Susan Mayor had a speaking part in *Thirty Minutes in a Street*; Beatrice Mayor's other two children formed part of the crowd.

1. In 1921 the Russian ballerina Lydia Lopokova (b. 1891) had returned to London with the Diaghilev company, and had enjoyed great personal success in its summer and winter seasons. Maynard Keynes, who had fallen in love with her, persuaded her to live in Gordon Square among his friends, and it may have been there that VW encountered her. She was however now dancing twice daily with Massine in *The Cockatoo's Holiday*—a divertissement performed as an adjunct to a film called *Love* in a programme designed by the impresario Walter F. Wanger to stimulate the English palate for films, and to secure the permanent conversion of Covent Garden Opera House into a cinema.

2. The Woolfs went to lunch with Lord and Lady Robert Cecil at their house Gale, Chelwood Gate, on 25 April; his sister, Lady Gwendolen (1860-1945), had recently published the first two volumes (it was never completed) of the *Life* of their father, the statesman Robert Cecil, 3rd Marquess of Salisbury, which VW had been reading (see above, 14 and 15 February 1922).

talk; a terrier on a chain; a great lady much snubbed & reduced: where, I wonder, do her lines & cavities come from? The 8oties was her heyday, when she went to Glasgow with Ld Salisbury & there were 10,000 people in the station who cheered like one man—(the Gordon crisis I think). Jimmy & Hugh & I spent all our pocket money & more—Jimmy was in debt for 3 years, getting up an agitation about Gordon—hiring halls & speakers.[3] Where's that spirit now? The whole of politics is dominated by one personality in whom no one believes. Gladstone was a dishonest man if you like—but he was a great man. He had a policy. This man [Lloyd George] has nothing. Hugh tells me there's no politics now as there was in our youth. Its a different thing. Your husband says the same. All spites & personalities. Very bad for the country— We faced each other standing still in the woods to deliver these views.

VW was again ill, and in bed for some days, early in May; and on 26 May had three teeth extracted, but went the next day to Tidmarsh for the week-end. Lottie returned to work on 28 May. On 31 May the Woolfs went to Monks House for Whitsun, returning to Richmond on 10 June.

Sunday 11 June

   Disgraceful! disgraceful! disgraceful!
   From the 27th day of April to this, the eleventh of June, not a word has been recorded. And I only write now to excuse myself from copying out a page or two of Jacob for Miss Green. The depression of a return from Rodmell is always acute. Perhaps this continued temperature—I lost 3 teeth in vain the other day—may be some sort of cause for my ups & downs. Yet the 10 days at Rodmell passed smoothly. One lives in the brain there—I slip easily from writing to reading with spaces between of walking—walking through the long grass in the meadows, or up the downs; &—well I need not talk about June. Perfection is such that it becomes like a normal state. Such is 'weather'; & happiness is not strange but normal too— And so of course, coming back from Rodmell,— blank—reason for blank forgotten as well as blanks contents. If I give my reason, I shall waste my time & energy.

3. The description of Lord Salisbury's reception in Glasgow in September 1884 is given on p 114 of the third volume of Lady Gwendolen's *Life* of her father, which was not published until 1931. James (1861-1947, who succeeded his father as 4th Marquess of Salisbury in 1903) and Hugh (1869-1956) Gascoyne-Cecil were the eldest and youngest of her five brothers.

Friday 23 June

I was telling lies to Dorothy Bussy the other day about this very book—how I lived in writing—& wrote & wrote in the streets—& coming home floated it off here. I think I've been working too hard; talking too much; to open this book. Working at copying Jacob after tea. That, of course, deserves a page or two—my premonitory shivers. As for the talk, it has been all about love & lies with Ralph.[1] We have had a mad bull in the house—a normal Englishman in love; & deceived. My comments could fill a book, & perhaps *will* fill a book. I don't find it possible to excuse all, as tradition exacts, & Ralph agrees that it should exact. In short, I don't like the normal when it is at 1000 horse power. His stupidity, blindness, callousness, struck me more powerfully than the magic virtues of passion. And yet it was interesting—very genuine, on his part; save for the flimsy disguise with which he tried to excuse himself. I began by believing his story—that C. had lied in matters of such importance that their relations were now forever damaged. But he concealed some essentials; how he had treated her, so as to foster lies. She supplied some very queer facts, one, that he flew into a passion (& his passions are like those in books) because she got naked with V. Dobrée. And he thinks this fine. "But I am like that." "You're a maniac" I said. Indeed I shouted it in the train coming back from Roger's lecture.[2] I lost my temper. We bellowed across the trains rattling. He foxes his eyes; turns rose pink; looks like taking aim at a rabbit. Shouts louder & louder. "I should have left you if you had treated me like that." He does not answer. That is his good point. Old Victorian sherry drinking Squire though he is, one can launch out at him, & he is trained enough to stand fire. She is far sub[t]ler & more civilised; a lier, I daresay; but then one must lie to children. After this, & I think a little on account of my bellowing, a reconciliation took place. At least he chatters again today, & won't allude to it. Lytton is gone, & so is Valentine. But I sketch this, partly from discretion, partly from haste, & so leave out

1. Ralph Partridge, who had been unfaithful to Carrington with Valentine Dobrée, had discovered that she, Carrington, had been unfaithful to him with Gerald Brenan. These convoluted affairs may be followed in *Holroyd*, p 863ff; *Carrington. Letters & Extracts from her Diaries*, 1970, p 216; Gerald Brenan, *Personal Record, 1920-72*, 1974, p 42ff (where for *Bollard* read *Dobrée*). Valentine, *née* Brooke-Pechell (1894-1974) was the wife of Bonamy Dobrée, the writer and literary scholar. She was a painter, and had been a great friend of Carrington's.
2. In June Roger Fry gave three public lectures—on Rubens, Rembrandt, and Poussin—at the Mortimer Hall, Mortimer Street, W.1; the Woolfs went to the one on Rembrandt on the evening of 21 June.

the links. It was the stupidity of virility that impressed me—& how, having made those convenient railway lines of convention, the lusts speed along them, unquestioning. She is not in love—with anyone, I expect; though Lytton has the afterglow of any passion she has. & this queers R.'s pitch.

Now I have little time for anything else. We have seen a great many people. Roger's lectures provide a rendezvous. Eliot dined last Sunday & read his poem. He sang it & chanted it rhythmed it. It has great beauty & force of phrase: symmetry; & tensity. What connects it together, I'm not so sure. But he read till he had to rush—letters to write about the London Magazine—& discussion thus was curtailed. One was left, however, with some strong emotion. The Waste Land, it is called; & Mary Hutch, who has heard it more quietly, interprets it to be Tom's autobiography—a melancholy one. Yes, Mary kissed me on the stairs. That was after the Memoir Club.[3] Lytton & Morgan read; & our standard is such that little is left for me to hint & guess at. They say what they mean, very brilliantly; & leave the dark as it was before. Then Mary crossed the room & purred in my ear. Molly grows very deaf, & I scold myself for not sitting next her. She puts her chin on her hand & looks wistfully round: says random rather disconsolate [things]. Morgan, who is now out & about again, thanks to Leonard's advice, very calm, serene, like a kettle boiling by some private fire, a fire at Weybridge, spent the night here after the Dinner, & then we sat round the table & discussed his book.[4] Our list grows more & more distinguished, but why is there no boom in Tolstoi? No one buys Karn, or Fredegond; but Bunin sells now fairly well.[5] Jacob, as I say, is being typed by Miss Green, & crosses the Atlantic on July 14th. Then will begin my season of doubts & ups & downs. I am guarding myself in this way. I am going to be well on with a story for Eliot, lives for Squire, & Reading, so that I can vary the side of the pillow as fortune inclines. If they say this is all a clever experiment, I shall produce Mrs Dalloway in Bond Street as the finished product. If they say your fiction is impossible, I shall say what about Miss Ormerod, a fantasy. If they say, You can't make us care a damn

3. The Memoir Club meeting was on 19 June; the Woolfs dined at 46 Gordon Square.
4. The Apostles' (Society) dinner was on 15 June.
5. In addition to Ruth Manning-Sanders' *Karn* (*HP Checklist* 23), the Hogarth Press had in May and June published Koteliansky and LW's translations of *The Autobiography of Countess Sophie Tolstoi* (*HP Checklist* 25) and of I. A. Bunin's *The Gentleman from San Francisco and Other Stories* (*HP Checklist* 19); and Fredegond Shove's poems *Daybreak* (*HP Checklist* 24).

for any of your figures—I shall say, read my criticism then.[6] Now what *will* they say about Jacob? Mad, I suppose: a disconnected rhapsody: I don't know. I will confide my view to this book on re-reading. On re-reading novels is the title of a very laborious, yet rather gifted article, for the Supt. And Leonard is going to make £3,000 a year, via Mr & Mrs Holt, an incredible couple, who spent an incredible afternoon with us at Monks.[7] "He sells everything—he'll be selling me next" she says, very arch.

Mr Holt half winked, & cocked his head.

"Little woman, little woman" said Mr Holt.

"He's the straightest boy that ever lived" said Mrs Holt, not without emotion.

"No there's nothing to be done with books. Henry isn't at all keen I should try. Henry made £30 by an hours work this morning. He keeps his mother, & his orphan sister & her child in a semi detached house with two maids. Everything as nice as it can be."

Mr Holt looked L. straight in the eyes—liked to talk business alone—praised the house & garden too lavishly. Very much in the style of a best seller himself. Perfectly unreal, sentimental, & not, in spite of Mrs Holt, very straight, I should say.

Monday 17 July

Back from Garsington, & too unsettled to write—I meant to say read; but then this does not count as writing. It is to me like scratching; or, if it goes well, like having a bath—which of course, I did not get at Garsington.[1] But Julian said at breakfast this morning that she wanted to be rich in order to have hot baths. Philip replied that they are now laying on water. Then Julian said she wanted to put milk in her bath, if it kept her complexion. She didn't mind being a fine lady. She wanted to come to London; but "mummy only goes for operations & horrid

6. Both 'Mrs Dalloway in Bond Street' (Kp C238) and 'Miss Ormerod' (Kp C257) were to be published in the New York *Dial*, in July 1923 and December 1924 respectively; and 'On Re-reading Novels' (Kp C228) in the *TLS* on 20 July 1922.

7. Henry Holt, of Exmouth, Devon, wrote to LW on the strength of Hamilton Fyfe's view expressed in the *Daily Mail* (see above, 3 May 1921) that 'Pearls before Swine' (one of LW's three *Stories of the East* published by the Hogarth Press in 1921) was one of the greatest stories he had ever read, to suggest that, were LW to rewrite it with "an American flavour", he could sell it (and further stories) very profitably in the USA. Nothing came of his proposals (see *IV LW*, 88-90). Mr and Mrs Holt had been to Monks House on 8 June.

1. VW went, without Leonard, to Garsington on Saturday 15 July, and returned to London on Monday morning. Julian was the only child of Philip and Lady Ottoline Morrell; she was born in May 1906.

things like that. I did once stay with Brett, but they wouldn't let me go again." O. & P. stood by with their long cold noses peering into letters assiduously.

But this was the last 10 minutes of my stay. I don't know that any incident burnt through the long windy cold day. I liked old Birrell's stories. He is a very well matured vintage: the barrel round & tight & mellow; & the wine within bright & sweet, & not lacking tang either. At least he laid down the law very briskly about Logan's character: "nasty"—& Lady Colefax—a bore "I prefer Sir Alfred who makes all the money. When fat old gentlemen like myself go to the house, those rogueish Sitwell boys sit at the window opposite & cry through a megaphone 'The Ambassador from Sweden'. . ."[2] His account of the society into which Logan introduced me the other day was not rosy. A general distrust, hidden satire, gorging of pate de fois gras in public, improprieties, & incessant celebrities. Birrell does it—sits there, I suppose, by way of distraction; & pays for his tea by talk. Ottoline has her little green book room with the gilt pillars stuffed with pretty yellow books. There I sat, crouching over the fire, & we talked, rather on our guard—a little toothless, perhaps. Much disillusioned she said she was, but now indifferent to disillusionment. So we had the case of Aldous Huxley—a pretty poor one "mere marionettes, not you at all—mere marionettes—why should mere marionettes destroy a long & cherished friendship? Yours very affectionately Aldous Huxley."[3] But mere marionettes have destroyed it. There is Murry pleading & whining to be taken in at the Bailiffs house, with a view to Oxford honours, so Birrell shrewdly said. Still we were low in tone—had she not an operation on her bladder two days before? But energy ran like whips through her. Tea was a long rambling meal— I had Mrs Seligman [*unidentified*] to talk to; & plunged into her hidden tragedy—a boy undeveloped; & a girl dead. Her poor wretched hunted hare face lit it all up. The boy, she says, has, she knows, a most remarkable

2. Sir (Henry) Arthur Colefax (1866-1936), a Yorkshireman of considerable and varied attainments, had studied natural sciences at Strasbourg and Oxford; he became a KC and from 1918-30 held the appointment of Solicitor-General to the County Palatine, Durham; but he was primarily a specialist at the Bar in patent and trade mark law. He had married Sibyl Halsey in 1901; they lived and entertained at Argyll House which faced across the King's Road, Chelsea, towards 2 Carlyle Square, home of the Sitwell brothers, Osbert (1892-1969) and Sacheverell (b. 1897), and their sister Edith (1887-1964), poets and literary controversialists.

3. Aldous Huxley's novel *Chrome Yellow*, a barely disguised picture of Garsington and its chatelaine, had been published in November 1921. Huxley's disingenuous reply to Lady Ottoline's letter of protest is reprinted in *Ottoline at Garsington, 1915-18*, edited by Robert Gathorne-Hardy, 1974, pp 216-7.

mind, but cant read at 11. Sheppard was there with his shiny Homers beneath his arm, depressed, & O. sought to raise his spirits by calling him the happiest of men.

P. drove me into Oxford this morning; & there was Miss Margesson on the platform. This takes me back to last week; my party at Logan's: at Mary's; at the Squires.[4] Yes: I saw Lady Colefax & likened her to hard red cherries on a cheap black hat. And Lady Lewis was there, who remembered my mother before she married my father & thought her the most beautiful, the most delightful, of women"—you're very good looking, too, but not like her".[5]

One gets flattered & stimulated at these places; & I found myself thinking of fame, & seeing doors open before me; but I was too much of a coward to walk in to Kent House the next day to meet la Princesse de Polignac, Lytton Strachey, & others.[6] But one of these days no doubt I shall. But to make one love literature—this is the way. I have skimped all this disgracefully, & here vow to stitch myself a new book, & start fresh at Rodmell.

The 1917 Club has opened its new rooms, & is infested with Mayors & Husseys, (who has written a book in the style of Lytton).[7]

Leonard has been offered Brailsford's post on the Nation; & has taken it, short of note writing.[8] He is quit of The Contemporary in January.

4. Catherine Margesson (b. 1887)—a granddaughter of the 7th Earl of Buckingham-shire—and her parents apparently mistook VW for someone they knew. (See *II VW Letters*, no. 1262). VW took tea with Logan Pearsall Smith at St Leonard's Terrace, Chelsea; on 12 July she dined with Mary Hutchinson at River House, Hammersmith, where LW joined her before going on to the Squires' party which was near by at Swan House, Chiswick.

5. Elizabeth, *née* Eberstadt (1845-1931), widow of the eminent Victorian solicitor Sir George Lewis; their house at Portland Place had been a meeting place for all the leading literary, artistic and musical personalities at the end of the nineteenth century. VW's parents were married in 1878.

6. The Princesse de Polignac, *née* Winnaretta Eugenie Singer (1865-1943), widow of Proust's friend Edmond de Polignac. Eldest daughter of the founder of the Singer Sewing Machine Company, she devoted her immense wealth to the encouragement of science, art, and in particular, music. Kent House was the Knights-bridge home of Mrs Saxton Noble, also a noted hostess and patroness of the arts.

7. In 1922 the 1917 Club extended its premises at no. 4 Gerrard Street, Soho, to no. 5 next door. *A Lady of the Salons. The Story of Louise Colet* by D. E. Enfield (Doris Hussey's married name) was published in 1922.

8. H. N. Brailsford became editor of *The New Leader*, the organ of the Independent Labour Party, in 1922; he had been leader-writer and specialist on foreign affairs on the *Nation*.

Philip is back, & installed at Waddesden.[9]

I am finishing Jacob's Room.

Grizzel [*a dog*] now belongs to us.

I have seen Hope, Logan, Lady Cromer, Hussey, Duncan, & I don't know who all this last week, but have said nothing.

We dine in the drawing room—the dining room being given over to print & Ralph (he annoys us both considerably). My temp. goes on, as usual, & Dr Hamill thinks that my right lung is suspicious.[10] Fergusson says no. And perhaps I shall have to see Sainsbury to settle it.

Wednesday 19 July

I will seize the opportunity of tea being done, Ralph gone, & Leonard writing letters, to pay some of my dues here. I put aside Mary to write about. One very cold wet night last week, or week before, she dined with me, alone, Leonard out, no servants; rain making the streets swim. I opened the door, & there she was with her white Pierrot face, black satin, orange shawl, laced shoes—the whole outfit merely to dine with me in the rain. She is an impulsive generous woman, whose generosity still exists; but subterraneously I think, floored over by her society varnish, & only let issue by people who don't compete. She started off upon her treatment by Vanessa, & this was the object of her visit, I suspect; to get me, I mean, to act ambassador. But, at my age, I tend to believe in the moment, more than in posthumous reflections. She was nice enough to me, chattering about her new dress for Chrissie [MacLaren]'s party; &, whether I was deluded or not I dont know, but she seemed able to put up some defence against my literary observations. That she may repel me with Tom's arguments is no doubt true. All I maintain (& I maintain this against Nessa & Leonard) is that she showed up well on that occasion; & indeed I suspect that Nessa unintentionally flattens her more than she suspects. The situation is against nature. Nature outs, under disguise, which of course complicates. Sitting at the kitchen table at no. 50 I had this out with Nessa; & I remember how pleased I was to be taking my ease there, & not tiptoeing in the cold at Lady

9. Philip Woolf was back from India, where he had gone in March; he now took up the post, which he was to hold for thirty years, of estate manager to James de Rothschild of Waddesdon Manor, Buckinghamshire, who was married to a cousin of the Woolfs, and got married himself, to Marjorie ('Babs') Lowndes.

10. Dr Philip Hamill was another Harley Street specialist to whom VW had been referred because of her continuing temperature and indisposition. She had seen him on 26 June.

Colefax's—to meet the Princesse de Polignac. Nothing can be done says Nessa. Moreover, nothing needs to be done, since in October Clive sets up at no. 50, & can entertain Mary there.[11] In fact, says Nessa, all this palaver about friendship with N. is merely a selfseeking device to improve M.'s own position, which, in the autumn, may need re-inforcing. And M. has set Clive against Lydia, & so turned off Maynard; & then one night she kissed Roger, & set afloat the usual contrary stories; altogether, her character is too much in holes for this last attempt to patch it up, & my embassy was fruitless. The truth is, as I am fond of beginning my sentence, that alliances of this kind always cut grooves somewhere or other—being contrary to all passion; & you cant, even in 1922, do what Plato & Shakespeare couldn't do. No intelligence bridles the old hag—nature, to wit.

Ralph's old hag is temporarily under control. Today he has a story that Maynard & Lytton are to buy the English Review from Austin Harrison, set him up as drudge, pay their contributors £10.10. a thousand words, & beat all rivals.[12] If Ralph wants it, then I think Lytton may agree; not otherwise. At Garsington they were getting up a subscription to give Tom £300, & so free him from journalism.[13] These two bits of gossip seem to belong together; & there was a third—that the Nation contributors have signed a Round Robin asking that Murry be removed —which leads naturally to Sydney Waterlow the other night— Yes, he dined here, in his pearl tie pin. I thought him sweeter, more reasonable, than usual. He has lost his last shreds of belief in Murry, save in Murry's Criticism, but as this too, depends upon spites & whims, I don't think even that can be saved from the wreck. Sydney is very proud of his lawn & his fruit trees. He wishes his children were bigger. The little boy promises to be intelligent. Parents never mask their pride successfully. How proud Philip & Ottoline were because Julian could say Prufrock by heart! But bitterness struggles with Ottoline's pride. "Half a dozen

11. Since early in 1920 Vanessa Bell had rented the upper part of 50 Gordon Square from the Adrian Stephens; she now relinquished these rooms to Clive, who had them redecorated and refurbished, and moved herself and her children to 37 Gordon Square.

12. The literary monthly *The English Review* had been founded by Ford Madox Hueffer in 1908; the present editor, Austin Harrison (1873-1928) now wished to give up.

13. Since 1917 Eliot had essentially depended for his livelihood upon his job in the Colonial and Foreign Department of Lloyd's Bank, Queen Victoria Street. This is VW's first reference to the scheme, in which she was to become involved (see below, 27 September 1922 and *II VW Letters* from 1 August), to provide an assured income which would set him free to concentrate on his creative writing.

tennis balls are quite enough. You only leave them out in the wet."
"I dont leave them out in the wet, Mummy",—typical of many breakfast
talks, no doubt. But Sydney is softer, for the moment, & did not blow
& bellow as much as usual.

Now, I never talked to Hussey (who is Mrs Enfield) about her book,
though she accosted me in the Club for that purpose, for these reasons.
She doe[s]n't praise my writing. She imitates Lytton. And she doesn't
know the art of reading. Never, for goodness sake, set yourself to read
Balzac through & talk about it. If you must do these athletics, do them
in the bathroom. Somehow the connection between life & literature must
be made by women: & they so seldom do it right. There was Hussey
stalking beside me to the London Library (though I wished to be alone)
& mincing out highly intelligent remarks beneath the horses noses,
about seeing things like God & setting the cap on, & I so much rather
she'd talk about her cat, her cook, or her weekly bills. But, of course,
she didn't praise me. And she marries the dullest man in London, &
they travel in Italy. What is worth while? Only feeling things for yourself—& this, I dont think poor Hussey dares do. One might feel, for
example, that Ralph [Enfield] was a bore, & Balzac sometimes dull. Can
you like Balzac if you like Ralph? That's what I ask myself when I talk
to Hussey. She is an ironmongers daughter, & thus the chain of Lytton
galls her neck.

Saturday 22 July

My conscience drives me again to write.
"This is real rain" says L. at the window.
"Mrs Thomsett wont have to go right up somewhere to get pails of
water" says Lottie.
It is pouring heavy, straight, thick. Puddles stand in the garden. It is
stuffy, dirty skyed. A white mist of rain blows off the roofs. One poor
plant is bent over. We have just had Saturday tea, at
Yes he does in   which we read the weeklies, & abused poor cur Murry.
Friday Nights   He slobbers over Garnett this week, which suggests
that Garnett has slobbered over him.[14] You can't write
criticism without being a good man, so I maintain. One always sees the
soul through words.

14. Murry's adulatory review of Edward Garnett's collection of essays *Friday Nights*
appeared in the *Nation & Athenaeum* of 22 July 1922. At the beginning of his
chapter entitled 'Tchekhov and his Art', Garnett refers to Murry as being 'alike
the most serious and the most illuminating' of English writers on Tchekhov,
and quotes at length from his 'eloquent pages' in *Aspects of Literature* (1920).

Clive came to tea yesterday, & offered me only the faded & fly blown remnants of his mind. He had been up late. So had I—at the pictures.[15] For my own part, all my strings are jangled by a night out. Dissipation would rot my writing (such as it is, I put in, modestly). Words next day dance patterns in my mind. It takes me a week to recover from Lady Colefax—who by the way invites me for Friday. Col-fox = black fox. This is from my Chaucer reading.[16] The question yesterday was about Lytton & the English Review. Would it be good or bad for his writing? Ralph says that he is depressed; blocked by the play he can't write—& never will be able to write, say I; & if he lubricated himself with journalism, he might reel off some history or biography, & so pass by the play unmoved; & this is his line, & a good one, too, I say. But Leonard thinks that my view & Ralph's are temporal compromising views, to which Lytton ought not to listen. Partly I am influenced by a wish for the fun of the thing—12 numbers of a new review written by the most brilliant of the age—myself among them, paid double: London Mercury killed, &c. &c. But James is spending this wet Sunday at Tidmarsh; & James will addle the egg.

If Lytton takes it, Ralph is to be business manager, & leave us. Well? We are polite, but we don't sigh. And here is a long letter from Dobree, opened by mistake, showing that R. is in mischief again. His spirits are down, & even the servants notice his surliness. Poor young man! For really he was never meant for intellectual whirlpools. No: he was meant for punts in backwaters, gramophones, ices, flirtations, a pretty wife, large family, & interests in the City. Nature is perpetually driving him to convert Tidmarsh into the likeness of this, & so everything goes athwart him. We have bad luck with our prentices. Next time we must stipulate for eunuchs.

Hamill sticks to it that my right lung is wrong. Fergusson finds nothing. Pneumonia germs have been discovered. And my case is to be laid before Sainsbury on the 9th—all rather a bore.

Wednesday 26 July

Just in from tea with the Mirrlees; who are vulgar, L. says: & I think I agree. They have vulgar friends. "Pocky"—the girls name was, to

---

15. LW and VW dined at Gordon Square with Vanessa and Duncan on 20 July and then went to the cinema.

16.   'A col-fox, ful of sly iniquitee,
        That in the grove hadde woned yeres three'
                Canterbury Tales, The Nun's Priest's Tale

whom Hope & I talked. She & the second housemaid had been carrying a salmon about London. She told us the story of her cornelians. Her mother now keeps her jewels, because she can't be trusted. Her mother calls her 'little girl'; & her nostrils opened too wide, & she was self-possessed, & crude & cut a dash, & had no mind, & had the shingles in her hair, & would sit on gossiping with Hope, who seemed to like it all better than I thought right. Rub off the top varnish—life, youth, colour, wealth (which we grant Pocky) & what remains? A dull old woman.

On Sunday L. read through Jacob's Room. He thinks it my best work. But his first remark was that it was amazingly well written. We argued about it. He calls it a work of genius; he thinks it unlike any other novel; he says that the people are ghosts; he says it is very strange: I have no philosophy of life he says; my people are puppets, moved hither & thither by fate. He doesn't agree that fate works in this way. Thinks I should use my 'method', on one or two characters next time; & he found it very interesting, & beautiful, & without lapse (save perhaps the party) & quite intelligible. Pocky has so disturbed my mind that I cannot write this as formally as it deserves, for I was anxious & excited. But I am on the whole pleased. Neither of us knows what the public will think. There's no doubt in my mind that I have found out how to begin (at 40) to say something in my own voice; & that interests me so that I feel I can go ahead without praise.

Friday 28 July

The affairs of the P[artridge]s. have engrossed us for 2 hours again;[17] & a postscript had to be added to Lytton on the telephone. I'm afraid its a sordid business, as C. said. Nor do I like to see women unhappy. P.'s conduct is that of the village Don Juan. Again, he behaves like a bull in a garden. And with it he is malicious. He is a male bully, as L. says. I am reminded of the tantrums of Adrian & Clive. There is something maniacal in masculine vanity.

August. 1922   *Rodmell*

Thursday 3 August

Owing to the change of ink & the change of place, I here begin a new page. Twice a year I make good resolutions—in August & October.

17. Carrington came to tea with the Woolfs on 28 July.

My good resolution for August is to work methodically, yet with the grain not against it. Often, my wisdom teaches me, good resolutions wither because forced. And modern science teaches us to respect pleasure, or that is my reading.

I should make one of my little addings up of days, since there is a break. On the whole a good summer; by which I mean that pleasures—dining out, seeing people,—were rather successfully combined with reading & writing & staying at home. On the whole, L. & I are becoming celebrities. L. would deny this; but then he did not go to Logan's tea party, nor to Garsington. Still I draw my observation from other sources. Reputation seems to accumulate, though we published nothing this year. Mrs Nicolson thinks me the best woman writer—& I have almost got used to Mrs Nicolson's having heard of me.[1] But it gives me some pleasure. Again, I am on freer terms with my little world, & have the chance I think to expand it, only no money to buy clothes. I am horribly in debt for Joyce & Proust at this moment, & must sell books directly I get back to London.

We ended our season last Monday at the Commercio, with Clive & Roger.[2] Roger came in with his hair flying & his coat flying carrying canvases—his mouth open, his eyes searching round—& we had our usual talk. Clive had his bits of gossip; & did I not by my evil eye inspire one of them? Mrs Shanks (so they say) has left the Georgian poet.[3] But Tom, coming round to Gordon Square afterwards, was by no means so certain of this as I could wish. Tom was sardonic, guarded, precise, & slightly malevolent, as usual. Clive, of course, on his good behaviour. He sounded me as to a visit to Wittering.[4] Nessa had the mumps downstairs. Duncan drifted in, soft haired, vague, gentle as usual. And Roger undid his canvases, & leant 2 portraits of Logan against the sofa.[5]

1. The Hon. Victoria (Vita) Nicolson, *née* Sackville-West (1892-1962), only child of the 3rd Baron Sackville of Knole and his wife Victoria, illegitimate daughter of his uncle Lionel Sackville-West, 2nd Baron, and the Spanish dancer 'Pepita'. A compulsive writer since childhood, Vita Sackville-West had already published two novels, a book of stories, and a quantity of poetry. In 1913 she had married Harold Nicolson of the Diplomatic Service; he was now attached to the Foreign Office in London. Her opinion of VW was no doubt retailed by Clive Bell who knew the Nicolsons.
2. A small Italian restaurant in Frith Street, Soho.
3. Rodmell village gossip confirmed this rumour; see *II VW Letters*, nos. 1266, 1273, 1277.
4. i.e., to Mary Hutchinson's holiday house, Eleanor Farm, on the Chichester Canal near West Wittering.
5. Of these portraits one was shown at the 17th London Group Exhibition in October 1922 (no. 18), but their present whereabouts is unknown.

"Yes, I think that is the best portrait I have done so far" he said. "I think I have never carried anything quite so far as that head." He is 55 I suppose; & still thinks he is about to begin to paint as he should—a merciful dispensation—a carrot to lure him across the desert. But it is no desert to Roger. Every faculty is used & burnished, & some fairly on the way to be worn out. He suffers, consults doctors, aches & shivers, but eternally goes on. The perfect man, as I told him, & as indeed I believe him to be. He is off to spend the summer painting with Derain. It is his obsession now—to paint, paint, paint. Nothing else is worth doing. Pamela is marrying, or failing to marry, her Roumanian Jew.[6]

Yesterday I walked to the top of Asheham hill, & found colonies of mushrooms on the way. The house now looks a little rigid & fixed, the country shut in, & severe compared with this. But the garden here, with the outhouses & their ivy down, is a lovely patch—open & airy with views of the hills; & so far Ted Hunter remains quiescent. The rot has set in, I hope, & I pray that Ted Hunter's wife may now elope with Mr Belloc. Allison will then lose his fortune, &, Bowen being with child by Shanks, the Hawkesfords will leave, & the Woolves be left by themselves in chastity & glory.[7]

I must broach a new page to announce the beginning, the true not spurious beginning, of Reading this morning. I shall write next that I have never enjoyed any writing more, or felt more certain of success. Jacob's Room is crossing the Atlantic.

Wednesday 16 August

I should be reading Ulysses, & fabricating my case for & against. I have read 200 pages so far—not a third; & have been amused, stimulated, charmed interested by the first 2 or 3 chapters—to the end of the Cemetery scene; & then puzzled, bored, irritated, & disillusioned as by a queasy

6. Roger Fry returned to St Tropez and spent September and October there, painting and attempting, through diet and rest, to cure his chronic internal pains. André Derain (1880-1954) usually spent the summer months painting in the Midi near Toulon, but there is no record of the two friends meeting at this time. Roger's daughter Pamela (b. 1902) who had this year been studying painting in Paris, and Micu Diamand, a Roumanian painter, had fallen in love; they were to marry in February 1923.

7. VW's sense of her privacy being threatened by the agglomeration in Rodmell village of friends and associates of the wealthy and gregarious J. M. Allison gives rise to this hopeful fantasy. The writer Hilaire Belloc (1870-1953), had acted as military commentator on Allison's weekly *Land and Water* during the war and had become a friend; he lived at Horsham.

undergraduate scratching his pimples. And Tom, great Tom, thinks this on a par with War & Peace! An illiterate, underbred book it seems to me: the book of a self taught working man, & we all know how distressing they are, how egotistic, insistent, raw, striking, & ultimately nauseating. When one can have the cooked flesh, why have the raw? But I think if you are anaemic, as Tom is, there is a glory in blood. Being fairly normal myself I am soon ready for the classics again. I may revise this later. I do not compromise my critical sagacity. I plant a stick in the ground to mark page 200.

For my own part I am laboriously dredging my mind for Mrs Dalloway & bringing up light buckets. I don't like the feeling I'm writing too quickly. I must press it together. I wrote 4 thousand words of reading in record time, 10 days; but then it was merely a quick sketch of Pastons, supplied by books. Now I break off, according to my quick change theory, to write Mrs D. (who ushers in a host of others, I begin to perceive) then I do Chaucer; & finish the first chapter early in September. By that time, I have my Greek beginning perhaps, in my head;[8] & so the future is all pegged out; & when Jacob is rejected in America & ignored in England, I shall be philosophically driving my plough fields away. They are cutting the corn all over the country, which supplies that metaphor, & perhaps excuses it. But I need no excuses, since I am not writing for the Lit Sup. Shall I ever write for them again?

I see I have said nothing about our day in London [on 9 August]— Dr Sainsbury, Dr Fergusson, & the semi-legal discussion over my body, which ended in a bottle of quinine pills, & a box of lozenges, & a brush to varnish my throat with. Influenza & pneumonia germs, perhaps, says Sainsbury, very softly, wisely & with extreme deliberation. "Equanimity—practise equanimity Mrs Woolf" he said, as I left; an unnecessary interview from my point of view; but we were forced into it by one step after another on the part of the bacteriologists. I take my temperature no more till Oct. 1st.

Meanwhile, there is the question of Ralph. This—it is the old question of his lumpiness, grumpiness, slovenliness, & stupidity versus his niceness, strength, fundamental amiability & connections—has been forced on us by one of Roger's suggestions—a man called Whittal, wants to come in: young, intelligent, with a motor car, well dressed, sociable, & critical; living in London, & not pressed for money. I am a little alarmed by the social values of Mr W. for we don't want the Press to be a

8. The first essay in *The Common Reader* is 'The Pastons and Chaucer'; the second 'On Not Knowing Greek'.

fashionable hobby patronised & inspired by Chelsea. Whittal lives only two doors off Logan.[9]

Tuesday 22 August

On this day, I don't know how many years ago, 1897 to be precise, Jack came to Hindhead & was accepted by Stella in the moonlit garden.[10] We wandered about the house till she came in & told us. Thoby thought they were tramps. I tried to describe the little trees in the moonlight.

Jack was accepted in Tyndall's little study on that bare heath $\dfrac{\begin{array}{c}1922\\1897\end{array}}{25}$ twenty five years ago. As she died so soon after, somehow it still seems to me like a real thing, unsmothered by the succeeding years.

But I always have to confess, when I write diary in the morning. It is only 11.30 to be honest, & I have left off Mrs Dalloway in Bond Street; & really why is it? I should very much like to account for my depression. Sydney Waterlow spent the week end here; & yesterday we had a days outing at Brighton. At Brighton I saw a lovely blue Victorian dress, which L. advised me not to buy. Sydney reproduced in his heavy lifeless voice exactly the phrases in which Murry dismisses my writing "merely silly—one simply doesn't read it—you're a back number." Then Squire rejected Leonard's story; & perhaps I dont like seeing new houses built all about; & get edgy about our field. So now I have assembled my facts —to which I now add my spending 10/6 on photographs, which we developed in my dress cupboard last night; & they are all failures. Compliments, clothes, building, photography—it is for these reasons that I cannot write Mrs Dalloway. Indeed it is fatal to have visitors, even like Clive for one day, in the middle of a story. I had just got up steam. All that agony now has to begin again. And Sydney, however one may discount him beforehand, is always a feather bed on a hot night—

9. James Whitall, son of Logan Pearsall Smith's cousin John, head of the glass manufacturing business in New Jersey from which the family derived its money; he had come to England before the war to complete his cultural education, and was living at 21 St Leonard's Terrace, Chelsea; Logan lived with his sister Alys Russell at number 11. See *English Years* by James Whitall, New York 1935.

10. To be more precise, it was in 1896 that the Stephen family were lent Hindhead House, Haslemere, by the widow of Leslie's old acquaintance the eminent natural philosopher John Tyndall. See *Sir Leslie Stephen's Mausoleum Book*, Oxford 1977, p 100. For VW's recollections of that night of 22 August, see *Moments of Being*, pp 49-50, 100-101.

ponderous, meritorious, stuffy. The stuffing is now provided by Kot & Sullivan, who have provided him with a new outfit. Everything is conscientiously revised by their not, to me, penetrating flame; & if the process is done in one's presence it becomes, I don't know why, curiously enervating, humiliating & depressing. Some rooms always smell mouldy —good well built rooms too. No one ever suffered so acutely from atmosphere as I do; & my leaves drooped one by one; though heaven knows my root is firm enough. As L. very truly says there is too much ego in my cosmos.[11]

In fact, Sydney was lighter in hand than I have known him. He had made a vow, for at 45 he makes vows, not to discuss his personal affairs. A deep groan intimated so much when we approached the delectable subject. No: he must refrain. We passed the door. And he got naked & bathed, & made the river look many sizes too small. He is a soft pink mass when naked. We talked too much about Murry. Still, it would have been as[c]etic not to, considering our lack of subjects of equal value. Yet Sydney considers that he can talk about literature. He *can* pick up a pencil doubtless; but the chances are he picks up half a dozen. I am thinking of Thoreau, whose fineness of touch was proved by some dealing of his with pencils.[12] I mean that Sydney is entirely without fineness of touch. His grandmother was a ratcatcher's daughter: his grandfather a printer's devil: both facts which he profoundly regrets. And so do I.[13]

I am once more writing off the fidgets. Ah, but how divinely happy we were until 12.30 on Thursday when Clive boarded the enchanted island with news from the world of Mary & Colefax! Never have I been so happy in my life. The day was like a perfect piece of cabinet making—beautifully fitted with beautiful compartments. It rained (I

11. LW was adapting Rudyard Kipling, *Life's Handicap* (1891), 'Bertram and Bimi'. It was rather a favourite of his. See *Nation & Athenaeum*, 3 November 1923, 'The World of Books' by LW: ' "There is too much ego in your cosmos" says the fat German to the enraged gorilla in one of the best stories Kipling ever wrote.'

12. Henry David Thoreau (1817-1862), American poet, philosopher, and naturalist. His father owned a lead pencil factory at Concord, Mass., with which Henry was associated. VW had written on Thoreau on the hundredth anniversary of his birth (*TLS*, 12 July 1917; Kp C80).

13. Sydney Waterlow's paternal grandfather at fourteen was bound apprentice for seven years to a printer; subsequently, with his brothers, he built up the great family firm of printers and stationers which he was to direct; he became an MP, Lord Mayor of London, immensely wealthy, and a noted philanthropist. When he was twenty-three he married his first and only sweetheart who came from Kent where her father had a house; he was said to be a London merchant and manufacturer.

think) things must have happened in the same way & same order as today; but how differently! I could hardly keep my temper ordering dinner this morning—& so on. But I shall walk to Asheham & try to start the machine again. The odd thing is that neither of us wishes for visitors. Of course they threaten us from all sides—Partridges, M[olly]. Hamilton, Americans, Lytton, Morgan, Tom, Sangers—no: leave me, leave me, is all I say: to work my brain.

Boen [Hawkesford] came to tea on Sunday—a cheap piece of crockery, for her nose reminds one of a tea pot spout; her mouth is like a slot in coarse china. She is changing; reading Bliss under Shanks' orders; wishes to live in London in order to work; not dance; & hurried off to play tennis with him, I suppose. I surprised them on the river bank swimming the great sheep dog "They got him from a shepherd here" says Boen, with a strange accent or tremor on they, as if 'they' were past, yet not dead; & so, under pretext of exercising the dog, the walking out which Mrs Dedman so strongly disapproves, goes on; leading according to Sydney, to a life of misery for Shanks, Boen getting her claws into him, clinging to him, drawing him under.

"Rot!" I said. Poor man. I look forward to his Collins.[14] Tuesday cont.

Slowly the cloud withdraws. Not that I can put pen to paper at this moment; but the waters, which that great grampus dislodged, meet together again. I am once more washed by the flood, warm, embracing, fertilising, of my own thoughts. I am too feeble to analyse the psychology, which I guess to be interesting. Its as if some foreign body had dispersed reality for the moment; the foreign body being of some gross material, inimical to thought. And if I can only protect this for the present, I shall be able to write. So the question for me is, how far to withdraw from unsympathetic society in the future? Is this cowardly, or merely good sense? For instance, here is Brett already inviting us into the heart of the enemies camp—Hampstead Thursday evenings. If I go I shall be rasped all over, or at any rate dulled & blunted, by the presence of Sullivan, Kot & Sydney. If I don't go shall I soften & rot in the too mild atmosphere of my own familiars? Perhaps the best plan would be to live in a neutral territory—neither friend nor foe, & by this means sink the exacting claims of egoism. Is there such a society possible though?

I have ordered the blue silk dress, & must now save 10/- a week towards it. —six weeks that is. But if I save the money here, I waste

14. i.e. a letter of thanks after a visit—a bread-and-butter letter—so called after Mr Collins's in *Pride and Prejudice*.

it at the other end, so I have imposed this task upon myself with some amusement.

The way to rock oneself back into writing is this. First gentle exercise in the air. Second the reading of good literature. It is a mistake to think that literature can be produced from the raw. One must get out of life—yes, thats why I disliked so much the irruption of Sydney—one must become externalised; very, very concentrated, all at one point, not having to draw upon the scattered parts of one's character, living in the brain. Sydney comes & I'm Virginia; when I write I'm merely a sensibility. Sometimes I like being Virginia, but only when I'm scattered & various & gregarious. Now, so long as we are here, I'd like to be only a sensibility. By the way, Thackeray is good reading, very vivacious, with 'touches', as they call them over the way at the Shank[s]es', of astonishing insight.

I have so many letters to write: to Jacques[15] (& he praised Monday or Tuesday highly; & I like to please Jacques; yet Jacques' praises never outweigh dull donkey Sydney's dispraises) to Ka; to Carrington; to—I forget; & shan't bother, but shall now rock myself into literature by reading Ulysses!

Wednesday 23 August

A headache: no writing; so I will copy.

Aug. 21 1922

My Dear Virginia,

The atmosphere was extraordinarily propitious; such an effluence of beauty from the landscape & the air, with that healing touch that I've always found in those parts, but there was more than that. As the hours slipped by, so few & so fast, I felt more & more a deep satisfaction at having begun again with you at having picked up broken pieces & being able to hold them together with some firmness. I hope it isn't imaginary; it seems quite solid, like something really won & *earned*, a real step forward in this horrific pilgrimage in which we're all engaged. I might so easily have come away feeling it had been merely a raking over of

15. Jacques Pierre Raverat (1885-1925), a Frenchman who had been educated at Bedales, the Sorbonne, and Emmanuel College, Cambridge, and was one of the group of friends called by VW the 'Neo-Pagans', another of whom, Gwen Darwin, he married in 1911. He became like her a painter, and they lived at Vence in the Alpes-Maritimes. Suffering increasingly from a form of disseminated sclerosis from which he was to die, his letters to VW were dictated to his wife; they are preserved in MHP Sussex—though not the one here alluded to. VW's reply, dated 25 August 1922, is in *II VW Letters*, no. 1280.

ashes; I was quite prepared for that; my mind was open. But on the contrary! I feel enriched & alive, delighted to think you are there & are you, & not even minding a bit if you think I'm a perfect ass.

Now for an excitement. I was just beginning to write this when the telephone rung. Bewildering noises, with shouts of 'I cant hear you' from me, a voice I seemed to know, & then I caught a name: 'Katherine?' 'Sydney, are you my enemy?' 'Good God, NO!' She's in Brett's house at Hampstead. Thats all I could make out. I'm going to see her on Wednesday. The plot thickens.[16]

Ever yours
S.W.

Friday 25 August

I have no time to comment. Indeed, it is a little stale, so I leave it to amuse a fresh eye. I think, still tentatively, that I have begun the story again— Brailsford writes to ask me to contribute stories &c to his new Leader. The Times (weekly) says my novels are by some thought among the finest of our time.[17] Yet, yet, I am not quite past the depression of hearing Sydney repeat what Murry said. Did I not mention a headache, though? Common sense informs me that, when the blood ebbs, any fly can settle. One can't brush them off. Oddly, though, sun shine, in these conditions, hardly illumines.

Saturday 26 August

Having done my morning's writing, at 11.20, & filled a whole page

16. Katherine Mansfield returned to London in August for six weeks in search of a new approach to her own tribulations of body and spirit; she attended the meetings being held by Ouspensky which led her ultimately to enter the Gurdjieff Institute at Fontainebleau where she was to die. She stayed alone in rooms in Brett's house in Pond Street, and saw very few of her friends at this time.

17. Brailsford's *New Leader*, the weekly journal of the Independent Labour Party, was to give Labour politics a cultural stimulus comparable to that of the *New Statesman*; but there is no record of any contribution by VW. In the Diary column of *The Times Weekly Edition* of 16 August 1922, after a reference to the recent death of Mrs Warre Cornish (Molly MacCarthy's mother and a sister-in-law of Anny Thackeray), a paragraph entitled 'Literary Descent' reads: 'Mention of Thackeray brings a reminder of a link with him not generally recognised. Few admirers of the work of Mrs Virginia Woolf, whose novels some consider among the finest of our time, are aware that she is the youngest daughter of Sir Leslie Stephen. Leslie Stephen's first wife was Thackeray's daughter. As she was not Mrs Woolf's mother, the literary succession is indirect so far as Thackeray is concerned.'

not so badly after all, I may as well let my brain finish its run on this more terrestrial soil. It is a fine day—one of the dozen this summer. I dont think I have said enough about the splintered disorder of June, July & August. A broken china closet it makes me think of—so many smashes & tergivasations. But today is fine, & yesterday we went to Charleston by the Bus, for the first time. After all, one must respect civilisation. This thought came to me standing in a Brighton street the other day from which one sees the downs. Mankind was fuming & fretting & shouldering each other about; the down was smoothly sublime. But I thought this street frenzy is really the better of the two—the more courageous. One must put up a fight against passive turf, with an occasional snail, & a swell in the ground which it takes 2,000 years to produce. But I daresay this thought was forced upon me: I much prefer the downs myself.

Charleston is as usual. One hears Clive shouting in the garden before one arrives. Nessa emerges from a great variegated quilt of asters & artichokes; not very cordial; a little absent minded. Clive bursts out of his shirt; sits square in his chair & bubbles. Then Duncan drifts in, also vague, absent minded, & incredibly wrapped round with yellow waist-coats, spotted ties, & old blue stained painting jackets. His trousers have to be hitched up constantly. He rumples his hair. However, I can't help thinking that we grow in cordiality, instead of drifting out of sight. And why not stand on one's own legs, & defy them, even in the matter of hats & chaircovers? Surely at the age of forty. . . . Nessa, who con-centrates upon one subject, & one only, with a kind of passive ferocity which I find alarming, took L. off primarily to discuss her attitude to Mary. Clive & I are much alike in our haphazard dealings with people. We do not concentrate; we are easily gulled & flattered; we expand & contract; we chatter & gossip; there is something much more fell, stable & determined in the characters of my sister & husband. Really, they can both determine a relationship & hold to it.

As for Duncan he requires, I think, peace for painting. He would like it all settled one way or the other. We saw a perfectly black rabbit, & a perfectly black cat, sitting on the road, with its tail laid out like a strap.

"What they call an example of melanism" said Clive—which amused me very much, & also made me like him. Why should this absurd trifle affect me when far more serious things make no impression whatever? And could one ever imagine this in the case of another person?[18]

I dislike Ulysses more & more—that is think it more & more

18. *Melanism*, the opposite to *albinism*; VW reverts to this 'absurd trifle' in a letter to Clive, *II VW Letters*, no. 1281, n.d.

unimportant; & dont even trouble conscientiously to make out its meanings. Thank God, I need not write about it. Yes, Murry actually goes out of his way to drag in my name with moderate praise today.[19] This must mean that he is coming to live in London; requires a dinner, anyhow people to get up & welcome him when he comes into a room.

Monday 28 August

I am beginning Greek again, & must really make out some plan: today 28th: Mrs Dalloway finished on Sat. 2nd Sept: Sunday 3rd to Friday 8th start Chaucer: Chaucer—that chapter, I mean, should be finished by Sept. 22nd. And then? Shall I write the next chapter of Mrs D.—if she is to have a next chapter; & shall it be The Prime Minister? which will last till the week after we get back—say Oct. 12th.[20] Then I must be ready to start my Greek chapter. So I have from today, 28th till 12th—which is just over 6 weeks—but I must allow for some interruptions. Now what have I to read? Some Homer: one Greek play; some Plato; Zimmern; Sheppard, as text book; Bentley's Life. If done thoroughly, this will be enough. But which Greek play? & how much Homer, & what Plato? Then there's the Anthology. All to end upon the Odyssey because of the Elizabethans. And I must read a little Ibsen to compare with Euripides—Racine with Sophocles—perhaps Marlowe with Aeschylus. Sounds very learned; but really might amuse me. & if it doesn't, no need to go on.[21]

Sunday 3 September

Perhaps the greatest revolution in my life is the change of nibs—no longer can I write legibly with my old blunt tree stump—people com-

19. In his review of *Georgian Stories*, 1922, in the *Nation & Athenaeum* of 26 August 1922, Murry wrote: 'A year ago [the *London Mercury*] contained a story by Mrs Virginia Woolf which was also superior to most of these.'
20. VW appears to have envisaged what was later to become the book *Mrs Dalloway* as a series of linked stories or episodes. 'The Prime Minister' was a guest at Mrs Dalloway's party (see *Mrs Dalloway*, p 181).
21. VW probably intended to read Alfred Zimmern's influential book *The Greek Commonwealth. Politics and Economics in 5th Century Athens* (1911); J. T. Sheppard's *Greek Tragedy* (1920); and J. H. Monk's *The Life of Richard Bentley* (1833), the two volumes of which, backed by her, were among the Woolfs' books at LW's death (see *Holleyman*, MH VII, p 4). Her comments on *The Odyssey*—'the story-telling of a sea-faring race'—do form the bridge between her consideration of Greek and of Elizabethan writing in *The Common Reader* as published.

plained— But then the usual difficulties begin—what is to take its place? At the present moment I'm using Blackie [*a fountain pen*] against his nature, dipping him, that is to say. I should be reading the last immortal chapter of Ulysses: but I'm hot with Badmington in the orchard; L. is stamping the distemper down on my head,[1] & we dine in 35 minutes; & I must change, & the Sangers are coming in afterwards, & .. & .. & .. I'm fretful with people. Every day will now be occupied till Tuesday week. So this is my last chance so far as diary goes, I daresay.

Walking in the church yard on Friday evening I made this remark— Its a very odd thing considering how impressive these country church-yards are, & how common. . . . when we saw Dora Sanger being escorted towards us by a stout country woman. On introduction we discovered this to be Daphne, aged 16: a nice, sleek headed, brown eyed girl; in a macintosh.[2] Now I had pictured her aged 6 or 10, still being given her bath by Charlie. We have met daily since; & as I say, they come round tonight, to sit up here & look at the view. Dora will look at the view. Charlie prefers spiritual scenery. And we never really show signs of running out of talk. I have only to say, what was a Greek bedroom like in the age of Pericles, & Charlie puts it before one.

Charlie, I was saying, puts it before one. And Daphne is very well informed, & how adorable the young are—like new brooms. I long to look over their shoulders, & see them sweeping clean. Indeed I much prefer them to the distinguished, wrapped soft in their reputations. She is at Bedales; goes to Newnham; then proposes to reform the world, by a moderate kind of revolution, so far as I understand her—for we only stood a second talking under the shadow of the tree outside the Rest, last night. She will write pamphlets, as a beginning. And the truth is that the world is reformed by Daphne Sanger's pamphlets—no doubt about it. At her age I was for knowing all that was to be known, & for writing a book—a book— But what book? That vision came to me more clearly at Manorbier aged 21, walking the down on the edge of the sea.[3] Never have I contrived so to wedge myself into my work as this summer—I cant endure interruptions. Maynard has asked us to Oare, where he keeps house with Lydia, & I should like to go, but we

1. VW wrote in a wood-built garden house near the churchyard wall; its loft, reached by an outside ladder, was used by LW for storing apples.
2. Daphne Theodora Sanger (b. November 1905) was the only child of C. P. and Dora Sanger; she was to go to Newnham in 1925.
3. Soon after the death of their father Sir Leslie in February 1904, the Stephen children spent about four weeks at Manorbier on the south Pembrokeshire coast; VW was in fact just twenty-two.

shan't.[4] The new plan of rotating my crops is working well so far: I am always in a fizz & a stew, either to get my views on Chaucer clear, or on the Odyssey, or to sketch my next chapter. A polite letter from Harcourt Brace informs me that my MS has not arrived—& they take great interest in my work.[5] This comes of not registering the parcel— L.'s fault, I'm glad to say. I am galloping on, astride a J pen now, not very compactly; but the whole day has been dissipated, & now I must tidy the room.

Yes, on looking at the pages, I think the balance is all in favour of a steel nib. Blackie too smooth; the old blunderbuses too elephantine. Look how neat this is.

Wednesday 6 September

Visitors leave one in tatters; yet with a relish for words. Phrases roll on my tongue—which, really, one can't produce for the delectation of my mother in law & Flora; who are now on their way back to Lewes; Carrington & Partridge being on their way to Chiddingley; the Sangers being on their way up Asheham Hill; & Lytton beginning to consider being on his way here.

We had our premeditated interview last night, with Ralph lying on the bed up here. Did his face show any change as Leonard went on— very forcible, measured, & impersonal. "Things have been unsatisfactory in my opinion" & so on. Ralph put up no more defence than a flock of sheep, which is disarming. So it is too to find him privately so enthusiastic about the H.P. that he could not contemplate any other career. I think it shapes itself into his becoming our printer; We take on Whitall as partner; & so start again—for ever. He is ready to face for ever, if we are, & money difficulties can be arranged. It is clear that he must live in London. Carrington is going to sit out his infidelities; which she does

4. Maynard Keynes had been lent Oare House, in the same Wiltshire village as the MacCarthys and the Waterlows, by Geoffrey Fry, who had worked under him in the Treasury.
5. Harcourt Brace and Company of New York had published *Monday or Tuesday* in November 1921, seven months after the Hogarth Press edition, and had presumably expressed interest in further books by VW. She refers (see above, 22 June and 3 August 1922) to *Jacob's Room* crossing the Atlantic, but this is the first reference to the firm which was now to become, and to remain, her American publishers. Negotiations with Donald Clifford Brace (1881-1955), the co-founder of the firm who took a very close personal interest in VW's work, were normally carried out by LW.

with her lips tight shut. She is going to paint. But she will never be a young woman again.

We had a great chatter party on Monday—Maynard, Nessa, Duncan, the Sangers. But how could I repeat the talk? It was a success though, save for the dim grey weather. Maynard is going to build a house: N. & D. are going to draw an income for 10 years from it. It is to be a hotel, perfectly appointed, in a field off Beanstalk Lane—8 suites of rooms, with 8 bathrooms, kitchens, waterclosets, surrounding a courtyard; in short a Peacock novel in stone; soon filled with the characters.[6] No doubt we have re-arranged life almost completely. Our parents were mere triflers at the game—went to the grave with all the secret ⟨drawers⟩ springs unpressed. Maynard, besides being our greatest living economist, has a dancer for mistress, & is now preparing to stage a Mozart ballet, with 13 nimble dancers; interviews the Coliseum Manager; is an expert at contracts; knows the points of dancers, & can tell you all about the amours at the Imperial academy at Petersburg.[7] Then Duncan is going to dance with Lydia. And Roger—but I need not go through the list; for my point is the same—we have all mastered the art of life, & very fascinating it is. Am I not about to manufacture coloured papers?

My proofs [of *Jacob's Room*] come every other day, & I could depress myself adequately if I went into that. The thing now reads thin & pointless; the words scarcely dint the paper; & I expect to be told that I've written a graceful fantasy, without much bearing upon real life. Can one tell? Anyhow, nature obligingly supplies me with the illusion that I am about to write something good: something rich, & deep, & fluent & hard as nails, while bright as diamonds.

I finished Ulysses, & think it a mis-fire. Genius it has I think; but of the inferior water. The book is diffuse. It is brackish. It is pretentious. It is underbred, not only in the obvious sense, but in the literary sense. A first rate writer, I mean, respects writing too much to be tricky; startling; doing stunts. I'm reminded all the time of some callow board school boy, say like Henry Lamb, full of wits & powers, but so self-conscious & egotistical that he loses his head, becomes extravagant, mannered, uproarious, ill at ease, makes kindly people feel sorry for him, & stern ones merely annoyed; & one hopes he'll grow out of it; but as Joyce is 40 this scarcely seems likely. I have not read it carefully;

6. Beanstalk Lane was a section of the old road from Firle which ran along the foot of the downs just to the south of Charleston; this building fantasy came to nothing.

7. Lydia Lopokova was trained at the Imperial Ballet School, St Petersburg; no Mozart ballet appears to have been staged in London until 1933.

& only once; & it is very obscure; so no doubt I have scamped the virtue of it more than is fair. I feel that myriads of tiny bullets pepper one & spatter one; but one does not get one deadly wound straight in the face —as from Tolstoy, for instance; but it is entirely absurd to compare him with Tolstoy.

Thursday 7 September

Having written this, L. put into my hands a very intelligent review of Ulysses, in the American Nation;[8] which, for the first time, analyses the meaning; & certainly makes it very much more impressive than I judged. Still I think there is virtue & some lasting truth in first impressions; so I don't cancell mine. I must read some of the chapters again. Probably the final beauty of writing is never felt by contemporaries; but they ought, I think, to be bowled over; & this I was not. Then again, I had my back up on purpose; then again I was over stimulated by Tom's praises.

We are having 3 fine days, & may even have 4 or 5. The garden is at its finest: the big bed spread with brilliant flowers, their petals almost touching. Henry Dedman has weeded the paths. At 7.30 on a fine night they have a phosp[h]orescent look, gleaming out. But it gets too cold for night wandering, & alas, I rather regret sharing my fire, & relinquishing my arm chair tonight, for the Sangers are coming. The three of them stalk in: Dora at least stumps. And though I like youth in the beginning, poor Daphne is a bit of a lump, & they fuss over her unnecessarily, & she shakes us all off, puzzled, exasperated, but not very good company, poor wretch.

Friday 8 September

When Mrs Woolf was here, she said she had been asked several times at Philip's wedding the meaning of the word honeymoon—Mr Sturgeon has now supplied it. What things people say at weddings! She said, Again I'm a wanderer on the earth. If I could find someone to go with me, I'd buy a caravan. Now having had 10 children I am to live in 2 rooms in South Kensington. Leonard cant drink milk with the skin on. None of his family can. "I could see it in Mrs Woolf's eyes" said Lottie —a wonderful piece of psychology. Flora told me that they eat funguses in Sweden; which grow there in great quantities. They eat all except the

8. The review by Gilbert Seldes appeared in the New York *Nation* of 30 August 1922. See *James Joyce, 1907-27* in the Critical Heritage Series, edited by Robert H. Deming, Routledge & Kegan Paul, 1970.

red funguses. She found a green one & threw it away. It was one of the best. Mrs W. said that Sweden is a great knife & fork country. They think too much about eating she said. Each of these sayings seemed to me very significant at the time; though I daresay I shant be able to see why.

The Sangers came last night. Charlie's views on literature are oddly cut & dry to me. He discoursed upon languages, Latin & German: I know not why it is that people who aren't writers always give one a dry bone in one's hand, however much they may know. He has a very low opinion of Proust, but thinks that you cant write a psychological novel in French. From French he hops to Latin, to German, to Russian: but the perches are dry.

Tuesday 12 September

Lytton drove off an hour ago; & I have been sitting here, unable to read or collect myself—such is the wreckage dealt by 4 days of conversation. We had the Sangers once, & Shanks last night, so we lashed our tongues lavishly. A bitter wind blew splinters of sunshine. On Sunday it poured—as it has now once more started to do.

I told Lytton I should try to write down his talk—which sprang from a conversation about Boswell. But said Lytton, I never do talk. But you are witty, so they say, I replied. Lytton had of course read Mrs Thrale.[9] And then we talked about Gibbon, whose method of dealing with the approach of the barbarian is quite magnificent. One night he gave us a complete account of the prison system, based on reports which he has been reading—thoroughly, with mastery, & a kind of political ability which impresses me.[10] He would have been an admirable ruler of an Indian province. However, as usual, there was one main theme to which we returned—Ralph & Carrington. There are two questions to be settled—R. & V[alentine]. D[obrée]. (who is settled in London) & R. & his livelihood. Both weigh upon poor old Lytton who feels himself in the position of a father, is slightly in love, yet sees, with his usual candour, all the faults & drawbacks. Ralph, too, lays the responsibility much on him—for the Hogarth Press that is—he refuses to discuss his

9. *Anecdotes of the late Samuel Johnson, LL.D. during the last twenty years of his life*, by Hesther Lynch Piozzi, London 1786; and perhaps *Autobiography Letters and Literary Remains of Mrs Piozzi (Thrale)* edited . . . by A. Hayward, London 1861.
10. *English Prisons Today. Being the Report of the Prison System Enquiry Committee* (established in January 1919 by the Executive of the Labour Research Department under the chairmanship of Sir Sydney Olivier), edited by Stephen Hobhouse and A. Fenner Brockway, 1922.

love affairs, & Lytton sees, apprehensive & cautious as he is, how easily one might take the wrong line, & break off all communications. And so we discussed possible plans—that they should buy Suffield; that we should move into 38 Brunswick Square;[11] that R. should be set up in a farm; that they should live in Boulogne, so that Lytton might write indecently. Perhaps Lytton was depressed. But we said scarcely anything of 'our writing'. Not a compliment passed. I daresay this is a healthier atmosphere than the other—it is not quite so pleasant.

Then Shanks came in last night—a snub nosed putty faced shapeless little man—entirely lacking in temperament, according to Lytton—who was very silent. We chattered reviewers shop; & could not leave those rails. He tells me that the Lit. Sup. is not paying any of its contributors. Jack Squire, he said, is becoming stiff with morality. "Thats a pretty girl," says someone in the street, whereupon Jack blushes scarlet. Indeed, Shanks says that he left the London M[ercury]. because Squire refused to review Ulysses (wh. I have lent Shanks).[12] No doubt Mrs Shanks & Miss Hawkesford somehow came in. But I gathered that Shanks does not take Squire quite so seriously as we had thought. However, I doubt that we shall get much further with a man with a boneless mind. He said he would give me mulberries. Nobody could feel sure what he thought of his evening.

Tuesday 26 September

A great many things have happened, unrecorded. This has been the most sociable summer we've ever had. Sometimes I feel as if, instead of sleeping through the months in a dark room, I'd been up in the light all night. Clive & Mary came; Mary in grey silk stockings; couldn't jump a ditch; was very affable; said she liked long walks; sat on the floor; praised Clive; & half invited me to Wittering. Morgan came on Friday; Tom on Saturday. My talk with Tom deserves writing down, but won't get it for the light is fading; & one cannot write talk down either, as was agreed at Charleston the other day.

There was a good deal of talk about Ulysses. Tom said "He is a purely literary writer. He is founded upon Walter Pater with a dash of Newman." I said he was virile—a he-goat; but didn't expect Tom to agree. Tom

11. The Woolfs had already sold Suffield House—the other half of Hogarth House, both of which they had bought in 1920; the idea of returning to the house in which they had lived with Adrian Stephen, Maynard Keynes and Duncan Grant before their marriage in 1912 more than once presented itself to them.

12. The last number of the *London Mercury* to bear Edward Shanks' name as assistant-editor was that of May 1922; but he continued to contribute.

did tho'; & said he left out many things that were important. The book would be a landmark, because it destroyed the whole of the 19th Century. It left Joyce himself with nothing to write another book on. It showed up the futility of all the English styles. He thought some of the writing beautiful. But there was no 'great conception': that was not Joyce's intention. He thought that Joyce did completely what he meant to do. But he did not think that he gave a new insight into human nature—said nothing new like Tolstoi. Bloom told one nothing. Indeed, he said, this new method of giving the psychology proves to my mind that it doesn't work. It doesn't tell as much as some casual glance from outside often tells. I said I had found [Thackeray's] Pendennis more illuminating in this way. (The horses are now cropping near my window; the little owl calling; & so I write nonsense.)

So we got on to S. Sitwell who merely explores his sensibility—one of the deadly crimes as Tom thinks: to Dostoevsky—the ruin of English literature, we agreed; Synge a fake:[13] present state disastrous, because the form don't fit; to his mind not even promising well; he said that one must now be a very first rate poet to be a poet at all: when there were great poets, the little ones caught some of the glow, & were not worthless. Now there's no great poet. When was the last? I asked; & he said none that interested him since the time of Johnson. Browning he said was lazy: they are all lazy he said. And Macaulay spoilt English prose. We agreed that people are now afraid of the English language. He said it came of being bookish, but not reading books enough. One should read all styles thoroughly. He thought D H Lawrence came off occasionally, especially in Aaron's Rod, the last book;[14] had great moments; but was a most incompetent writer. He could cling tight to his conviction though. (Light now fails—7.10. after a bad rainy day.)

Wednesday 27 September

An epoch making conversation is now going on within earshot. I think the Dedmans may be going, & Dedman saying so to L. But to return. While Tom & I talked in the drawing room, Morgan wrote an article up here; or flitted through; humble, deprecating, chubby like a child; but very observant. Tom's head is all breadth & bone compared

13. The youngest of the conspicuous Sitwell trio (see above, 17 July 1922, n 2), Sacheverell had at this time published only poetry; he later enlarged his field of interest as a writer. John Millington Synge (1871-1909), the dramatist who drew his themes from Irish peasant life.

14. *Aaron's Rod* had been published in June 1922.

with Morgan's. He still remains something of the schoolmaster, but I am not sure that he does not paint his lips. After Joyce, however, we came to ticklish matters—the Eliot fund; the upshot of it was (& we were elliptical, tactful, nervous) that Tom won't leave the Bank under £500, & must have securities—not pledges. So next morning, when Ott's letter & circular arrived, aiming at £300, on a 5 year basis of pledges, I had to wire her to stop, & then to draft a long letter giving my reasons; & another to Tom, asking him to confirm my information.[15] I shall be scalded in two separate baths of hot water no doubt. But this can wait.

For the rest the week end was chilly & stormy. We had one blow on the hills. Tom left before dinner. Then we snuggled in, & Morgan became very familiar; anecdotic; simple, gossiping about friends & humming his little tunes; Tom asked him to contribute to the Criterion. I was impressed by his complete modesty (founded perhaps on considerable self assurance). Compliments scarcely touch him. He is happy in his novel, but does not want to discuss it. There is something too simple about him—for a writer perhaps, mystic, silly, but with a childs insight: oh yes, & something manly & definite too. He had been staying with Hardy, who is given up to vanities & attends punctiliously to reviewers. He complained of the Spectator; which was hostile he said, because he knew Lytton; & the cousins had quarrelled. Then to his pets burial ground; & some story about cats killed on the railway line— Poor old Hardy is perfectly ordinary, nice, conventional, never says a clever thing; says commonplaces about his books; has tea at the rectory; is very healthy; objects to American visitors; & never mentions literature. How am I to dress this for the Obituary?[16]

Wednesday 4 October

Our last whole day. From the weather point of view, the summer has been altogether disappointing. It has promised & then withheld. We have not had 7 consecutive good days. There has been a scattering of good ones, but in the midst of rain, wind, & dark London looking skies. Often the Roman road was so muddy I could not walk along it. And

15. See *II VW Letters*, nos. 1289 (to T. S. Eliot) and 1290 (to Lady Ottoline Morrell).

16. VW retailed this gossip about Hardy to Janet Case in a letter written while Forster was in the house (see *II VW Letters*, no. 1288). The *Spectator* was owned and edited by Lytton's cousin John St Loe Strachey (1860-1927); he had employed both Lytton and James but disapproved strongly of their pacifism during the war; he had also made a very bitter attack upon *Eminent Victorians*.

often I heard the thunder murmuring as I walked. Grizzel was frightened & ran home—as if God would go out of his way to hurt a mongrel fox terrier walking on the flats at Rodmell! But there's no arguing about these things. I think the garden has never been better, & we have had good crops of apples & pears, & green peas only 2 days ago.

Spiritually speaking we have made some progress in Rodmell society. I was struck by the bloodlessness of philistines the other day at the Rectory. They seem far less alive than we intellectuals. Mr Shanks & the Hoggs [*unidentified*] are, after all, so pale, so watery, so mild. Mrs Hawkesford still discusses the country & London; says, for the 20th time, that she is so glad she kept the tennis court going, even though they turned the pony on it during the war. Boen sits lackadaisical, & helps me to Shanks' cigarettes. Then I don't like underbred young men —Hogg to wit. They seem to me a little peevish & conventional; & talk slang which covers any character they may have.

I am a little uppish, though, & self assertive, because Brace wrote to me yesterday "We think Jacob's Room an extraordinarily distinguished & beautiful work. You have, of course, your own method, & it is not easy to foretell how many readers it will have; surely it will have enthusiastic ones, & we delight in publishing it"—or words to that effect. As this is my first testimony from an impartial person I am pleased. For one thing it must make *some* impression, as a whole; & cannot be wholly frigid fireworks. We think of publishing on Oct. 27th. I daresay Duckworth is a little cross with me.[1] I snuff my freedom. It is I think true, soberly & not artificially for the public, that I shall go on unconcernedly whatever people say. At last, I like reading my own writing. It seems to me to fit me closer than it did before. I have done my task here better than I expected. Mrs Dalloway & the Chaucer chapter are finished; I have read 5 books of the Odyssey; Ulysses; & now begin Proust. I also read Chaucer & the Pastons. So evidently my plan of the two books running side by side is practicable, & certainly I enjoy my reading with a purpose. I am committed to only one Supt. article—on Essays—& that at my own time; so I am free.[2] I shall read Greek now steadily & begin 'The Prime Minister' on Friday morning. I shall read the Trilogy

1. The letter from Donald Brace was dated 20 September 1922; it has been very slightly paraphrased by VW. After publishing her first two novels, Gerald Duckworth had agreed to relinquish his option on her third, *Jacob's Room*, to enable the Woolfs to publish it themselves. 290 pages long, it was the Hogarth Press's largest undertaking so far; it was printed for them by R. & R. Clark of Edinburgh.

2. VW's review of *Modern English Essays*, edited by Ernest Rhys, appeared in the *TLS* of 30 November 1922 (Kp C229).

& some Sophocles & Euripides & a Plato dialogue: also the lives of Bentley & Jebb.[3] At forty I am beginning to learn the mechanism of my own brain—how to get the greatest amount of pleasure & work out of it. The secret is I think always so to contrive that work is pleasant.

Saturday 8 October

Back again, over the fire at Hogarth House, having read the first chapters of Bentley. Grizzel sits on L.'s knee. Boxall—the kitten, called after Nelly to ingratiate her, is happily off mine; temporarily, or I could not write.

But the day has been spoilt for me—so strangely—by Kitty Maxse's death; & now I think of her lying in her grave at Gunby, & Leo going home, & all the rest. I read it in the paper. I hadn't seen her since, I guess, 1908—save at old Davies' funeral, & then I cut her, which now troubles me—unreasonably I suppose.[4] I could not have kept up with her; she never tried to see me. Yet yet—these old friends dying without any notice on our part always—it begins to happen often—saddens me: makes me feel guilty. I wish I'd met her in the street. My mind has gone back all day to her; in the queer way it does. First thinking out how she died, suddenly at 33 Cromwell Road; she was always afraid of operations. Then visualising her—her white hair—pink cheeks—how she sat upright—her voice—with its characteristic tones—her green blue floor —which she painted with her own hands: her earrings, her gaiety, yet melancholy; her smartness: her tears, which stayed on her cheek. Not that I ever felt at my ease with her. But she was very charming—very humorous. She got engaged at St Ives, & Thoby thought it was Paddy talking to his boy. They sat on the seat by the greenhouse in the Love Corner.[5] However, I keep going over this very day in my mind.

3. The *Life and Letters* of Sir Richard Claverhouse Jebb (1841-1905), classical scholar renowned for his translations and critical editions of Sophocles in particular, was published by his wife Caroline in 1907. The Oresteian trilogy is by Aeschylus.
4. Kitty Maxse died on 4 October 1922 after a fall at her London home, and was buried beside her sister Margaret—whose widower Stephen Massingberd owned Gunby Hall—at Gunby Burgh in Lincolnshire on 7 October. Leopold James Maxse (1864-1932), whom she had married in 1890, was the owner and editor of the political monthly *National Review*. Old Davies was Margaret's father, the Rev. John Llewellyn Davies; his funeral took place at Hampstead on 22 May 1916.
5. This recollection recurs in VW's Memoir Club contribution '22 Hyde Park Gate' written in 1921, and in 'A Sketch of the Past,' 1940; see *Moments of Being*, p 143 and p 111.

Saturday 14 October

I was interrupted in this, & now Kitty is buried & mourned by half the grandees in London;[6] & here I am thinking of my book. Kitty fell, very mysteriously, over some bannisters. Shall I ever walk again? she said to Leo. And to the Dr "I shall never forgive myself for my carelessness". How did it happen? Some one presumably knows, & in time I shall hear. Nessa regrets her, but says that the breach came through Kitty. "It seems rather melancholy that it should come to an end like this" Nessa said; but she was putting Angelica to bed, & we could not dig in our past.

I have seen Nessa, Maynard, Lydia, Desmond, Saxon, Lytton, Frankie Birrell & Marjorie Fry, all within this week;[7] & had two letters, from Lytton & Carrington, about Jacob's Room, & written I don't know how many envelopes; & here we are on the verge of publication. I must sit for my portrait to John o'London's on Monday. Richmond writes to ask that date of publication may be put ahead, so that they may notice it on Thursday.[8] My sensations?—they remain calm. Yet how could Lytton have praised me more highly? prophecies immortality for it as poetry, is afraid of my romance; but the beauty of the writing &c. Lytton praises me too highly for it to give me exquisite pleasure; or perhaps that nerve grows dulled. I want to be through the splash & swimming in calm water again. I want to be writing unobserved. Mrs Dalloway has branched into a book; & I adumbrate here a study of insanity & suicide: the world seen by the sane & the insane side by side—something like that. Septimus Smith?—is that a good name?—& to be more close

6. The memorial service for Mrs Leo Maxse was held at Holy Trinity, Brompton, on 11 October, and was attended by a large number of socially prominent people, from the French Ambassador to George Duckworth.

7. Francis Frederick Locker Birrell (1889-1935), elder son of Augustine Birrell, educated at Eton and King's, was David ('Bunny') Garnett's partner in the bookshop they had started after the war and which had recently moved from 19 Taviton Street to 30 Gerrard Street. Margery Fry (1874-1958), Roger's youngest sister, had shared his home in Holloway for three years; she was now Principal of Somerville College, Oxford. She and Frankie Birrell dined with the Woolfs on Friday 13 October.

8. For Lytton's letter, see *Virginia Woolf & Lytton Strachey, Letters*, 1956, p 103; and for Carrington's, MHP Sussex: '... I suspect you would make an amazing painter. Your visions are so clear & well designed ...' *John O'London's Weekly* of 11 November 1922 reproduced a drawing ('from life ... by F. H. Warren') of VW; and the same issue contains a review of *Jacob's Room* entitled 'The Futurist Prose of Virginia Woolf' by Louis J. McQuilland. Until November 1935 (when it changed to Saturdays) the *TLS* appeared each Thursday; *Jacob's Room* was due to be—and was—published on Friday 27 October.

to the fact than Jacob: but I think Jacob was a necessary step, for me, in working free. And now I must use this benignant page for making out a scheme of work.

I must get on with my reading for the Greek chapter. I shall finish the *Prime Minister* in another week—say 21st. Then I must be ready to start my Essay article for the Times: say on the 23rd. That will take say till 2nd Nov. Therefore I must now concentrate on Essays: with some Aeschylus. & I think begin Zimmern, making rather a hasty end of Bentley, who is not really much to my purpose. I think that clears the matter up—though *how* to read Aeschylus, I don't quite know: quickly, is my desire, but that, I see, is an illusion.

Our great interview with Lytton as to Ralph came off on Thursday. Lytton was extremely adroit, & made points which Ralph prompt[l]y gave away. For Ralph will stay on any terms. Lytton proposes that we should give him complete business control; but this is coupled with his decision on no account to increase his hours of work. I'm rather in the mood to say that I won't give serious books to a manager who wont give up his chicken breeding to look after them. And then how far could L. stand & watch Ralph's howlers? And lunch & tea with Ralph for ever? And Whitall? This accumulates. We are to go to Tidmarsh after the rush is over & excogitate. As for my views about the success of Jacob, what are they? I think we shall sell 500: it will then go on slowly, & reach 800 by June. It will be highly praised in some places for 'beauty'; will be crabbed by people who want human character. The only review I am anxious about is the one in the Supt.: not that it will be the most intelligent, but it will be the most read & I cant bear people to see me downed in public. The W[estminster]. G[azette]. will be hostile; so, very likely, the Nation.[9] But I am perfectly serious in saying that nothing budges me from my determination to go on, or alters my pleasure, so whatever happens, though the surface may be agitated, the centre is secure.

Tuesday 17 October

As this is to be a chart of my progress I enter hastily here, one, a letter from Desmond who is halfway through: says "You have never written

---

9. The anonymous review of *Jacob's Room* in the *Weekly Westminster Gazette* of 15 November *was* essentially hostile. Forrest Reid, in the *Nation & Athenaeum* of 4 November, though puzzled by the form, recognised VW as an entirely original writer and, echoing the words of M. Bergeret, wrote "Si pourtant c'était un chef-d'oeuvre?"

so well ... I marvel & am puzzled"—or words to that effect:[10] (2) Bunny rings up enthusiastic, says it is superb, far my best, has great vitality & importance: also he takes 36 copies, & says people already 'clamour'. This is not confirmed by the bookshops, visited by Ralph. Those sold under 50 today; but the libraries remain, & Simpkin Marshall.

Sunday 29 October

Miss Mary Butts being gone, & my head too stupid for reading, I may as well write here, for my amusement later perhaps.[11] I mean I'm too riddled with talk & harassed with the usual worry of people who like & people who don't like J.R. to concentrate. There was the Times review on Thursday—long, a little tepid, I think; saying that one can't make characters in this way; flattering enough. Of course, I had a letter from Morgan in the opposite sense—the letter I've liked best of all.[12] We have sold 650, I think; & have ordered a second edition. My sensations?—as usual—mixed. I shall never write a book that is an entire success. This time the reviews are against me, & the private people enthusiastic. Either I am a great writer or a nincompoop. "An elderly sensualist" the Daily News calls me. Pall Mall passes me over as negligible.[13] I expect to be neglected & sneered at. And what will be the fate of our second thousand then? So far of course, the success is much more than we expected. I think I am better pleased so far than I have ever been. Morgan, Lytton, Bunny, Violet, Logan, Philip, have all written enthusiastically. But I want to be quit of all this. It hangs about me like Mary Butts' scent. I dont want to be totting up compliments, & comparing reviews. I want to think out Mrs Dalloway. I want to foresee this book better than the others, & get the utmost out of it. I expect I

10. See MHP Sussex, Desmond MacCarthy to VW: '*You have never written so well....* You are a marvel and a puzzle, as a writer.'
11. Mary Butts (c. 1893-1937), author and bohemian. It was probably at Carrington's suggestion that she had sent her novel to VW to read, and had been invited to tea (see *II VW Letters*, nos. 1278 and 1307).
12. *Jacob's Room* was reviewed in the *TLS* of 26 October 1922 (the day before publication); see *M & M*, p 95. A copy of E. M. Forster's letter, dated 24 October, is in MHP, Sussex. He had written: 'I am sure it is good' and had gone on to congratulate VW on maintaining the reader's interest in Jacob, in his 'character as a character ... I find this a tremendous achievement.'
13. *Daily News*, 27 October 1922: 'BOOKS AND AUTHORS. MR ARNOLD BENNETT'S NEW NOVEL. MIDDLE-AGED SENSUALISTS by Lewis Bettany' (see *M & M*, p 98). *Pall Mall Gazette*, same date: 'AN IMPRESSIONIST' (see *M & M*, p 99).

could have screwed Jacob up tighter if I had foreseen; but I had to make my path as I went.

One of the perquisities of Jacob seems to be society. I am going to Ly Colefax on Tuesday to hear Valery lecture: also to Miss Sands.[14] They are all now (momentarily, through Logan I daresay) on my side. And at the moment I feel inclined for a plunge, though it must be on my own terms: in my own clothes, & at my own hours. I can't go in to Whitall's visit at length. But our position becomes more & more complicated. Clearly we cannot go on publishing seriously with Ralph attached to us like a drone. Whitall is a greyhound looking nervous American, serious, matter of fact, forced to make money. How far do we want to make money with him? At anyrate the labour & worry of getting out a long book makes me decided not to do it again on the present system. We have to go to Tidmarsh next week to explain the position. Carrington says that Lytton is most anxious for some arrangement, & the uncertainty is trying Ralph's nerves. Yet this nervous man makes no attempt to do the most ordinary things for us. L. has to tie parcels every morning. Ralph catches no earlier or later trains. Thursday morning he spent at the tailor's. But there is the American element in Whitall to be distrusted—in short it bothers us, & the election is beginning to roar in the newspapers.[15] L. has a chance of getting in. We have bitten off a large piece of life—but why not? Did I not make out a philosophy some time ago which comes to this—that one must always be on the move?

Tuesday 7 November

I am, probably, through the splash, & must really try to settle in again. It has not been, publicly, much of a splash. The reviews have said more against me than for me—on the whole. Its so odd how little I mind—& odd how little I care much that Clive thinks it a masterpiece. Yet the private praise has been the most whole hearted I've yet had. They seem to agree that I have accomplished what in the other books

14. Paul Valéry (1871-1945), the French poet and critic, had recently published a new collection of poems, *Charmes* (1922). In her Memoir Club contribution ('Am I a Snob' (1936, see *Moments of Being*, pp 188-9), VW makes out that she refused Lady Colefax's invitation to meet him; but she did go (see *II VW Letters*, no. 1311). Ethel Sands (1873-1962), American-born painter, pupil and great friend of Sickert, was wealthy and sociable, and alternated between France and her house in The Vale, Chelsea, where she entertained freely.
15. The Coalition Government of Lloyd George had fallen on 19 October, and polling day for the new election was 17 November.

I only got near accomplishing. But we scarcely sell, though it has been out 10 days. Nor do I much mind that— What do I mind then? I want to grapple with the 10th of June, or whatever I call it. Meanwhile, to keep me unsettled I get invited out. We went to Logan's last week, & there met Percy Lubbock after 12 years. I sat next him at the Smiths the night Lytton proposed to me. I remember I saw a red azalea fountain in the middle of the dinner table; but not much else. Lady Grose [*unidentified*] was late; Percy pale.[1] Percy is still pale, but mild & elderly. I was re-assured by his shabby boots. He is a slow kind melancholy man; I run round him, & plant darts in his flanks, & we are to ask him to dinner. Then there was Mrs Hammersley remembering my father & the Duckworths, & I'm to go to her; & to Ethel Sands; & to the Oriental Club to lunch with Lytton.[2] We had a stormy week end at Tidmarsh, & I'm afraid I have concluded that Ralph must go. His jealousy, & irrationality, combined with his fixed determination to make a permanent hobby out of what's a profession to us, make the position less & less possible. Yet I am sorry, & like him, & the association. On the other hand what fun to spring off & make a good job of it! Suppose one could get a young man or woman of wits who would work violently & rashly.

Last night I dined for the first time with Clive in his rooms. Now I must make up my work account, for I have no time to say how strange that dinner was with Nessa & Clive again as we used to be so often; now a little formal superficially, & yet, miraculously, still intimate beneath: all 40 & over; all prosperous; & my book (that I felt somehow pleasing) acclaimed by Nessa "certainly a work of genius". Lytton came in later, which made it yet stranger; & there we sat, with H[arcourt]. Brace's catalogue talking of us all by name as the most brilliant group in Gordon Square! Fame, you see.

I shall polish off my Essay article tomorrow, Wed. 8th. Then I think I shall try to sketch out Mrs D. & consult L. & write the aeroplane chapter now, for I must write out of my head again. A fortnight's criticism is my stint. So if that takes a week, or 10 days, & brings me to 18th Nov. I must be ready to start the Greek chapter say on the 20th; only I have not read half or a 20th part, owing to interruptions. So I incline to writing that chapter in bits. First introduction & Bentley:

1. Percy Lubbock (1879-1965), man of letters and biographer. Lytton Strachey had proposed marriage to VW on 17 February 1909, but immediately disengaged himself. Reginald John Smith (1857-1916), editor of the *Cornhill Magazine* from 1897, had been a friend of Sir Leslie Stephen who had been a previous editor.
2. Violet Mary Hammersley (1878-1964), a celebrated hostess and patron of the arts. Both Lytton and Oliver Strachey were members of the Oriental Club, 18 Hanover Square.

then Odyssey: then on to Aeschylus, reading furiously the while. It is terribly easy to let the reading slip; so I must make an effort to get 2 hours either before dinner or after, & must now write to Will A.F. & refuse to go there, since I am out daily till Saturday. But oh the question of Ralph! & now I have a pressing appeal from Carrington.

Monday 13 November

And I lost my temper with Ralph, over Constable's offer.[3] For things are moving briskly this autumn, & Logan took me aside at Ethel Sands' (same setting, same company, same sayings, doings & feelings) in order to negotiate an arrangement between us & Constable, who has a room to let, & wants us to combine. Ralph is jealous as a sore bear; obstructs every proposal with trumped up arguments, designed to protect his own skin, & not English literature, as he rashly makes out, & thus requires correction at my hands. We have not advertised this week owing to [the] Election, & sell slowly. Reviews are now favourable & utterly contradictory, as usual. I am quite able to write away without bother from self-consciousness, now; which shows that my splash is over. On the whole, I am perfectly satisfied, though; more so, I think, than ever before. And now I have a multitude of pleasant jobs on hand, & am really very busy, & very happy, & only want to say Time, stand still here; which is not a thing that many women in Richmond could say I think. Nessa & I are collaborating over a paper for covers which she has designed, & I am to colour. We went to the Beggars Opera the other night, L. being at Liverpool. That is the only move he is to make. But his address seems to give satisfaction, & I doubt not he could get in if he chose—next time if not this. America wishes him to write a monthly article—New York Times that is; which increases our income, & proves him at the tree top. People write little articles about him, saying he is selfless in his work for the public, & the most brilliant of our writers, & leaders of the younger school. I like this, & forgive Massingham his abuse of me from this time forward. L. is now writing his weekly article, on Turkey, having been up to see Massingham, found a pea soup [*fog*] in London.[4] I walked in the Park, bought 2 wild duck & 6 snipe,

3. Constable & Co, of Orange Street, Haymarket, were Logan Pearsall Smith's own publishers.

4. In a paragraph of 'A Londoner's Diary' in the *Nation & Athenaeum* of 22 October 1922, 'A Wayfarer' (i.e. H. J. Massingham) extolled LW's virtues and exhorted his readers to return him to Parliament on 17 November as member for the Seven Universities seat. The disastrous end of the Greek adventure in Asia Minor and the advent of an aggressive nationalist government in Turkey had resulted in

all fresh & bleeding, just shot at Beaconsfield by 2 poachers I suspect. I paid 8/6, thus introducing a good deal of stir in Hogarth House kitchen. And now I must try to make out what Aeschylus wrote.

Monday 27 November

I need not say that my wild duck stank like old sea weed & had to be buried. But I cannot dally over this incident, which in tamer days might have provided some fun, because I have such a congeries of affairs to relate, & have to steal time from the Agamemnon. There is the Press to be chronicled. We had to meet Whitall at the Club, to discuss the Heinemann offer; & waiting there, we overheard one of those usual shabby, loose, cropheaded, small faced bright eyed young women, who was leaning negligently over the sofa side, & chatting with Scott as he drank tea, tell him that she was tired of teaching & meant to become a printer.[5] "They say there's never been a woman printer; but I mean to be one. No I know nothing whatever about it . . . &c." When she went into the writing room, I followed, plucked her out, & revealed us to her as proprietors of the Hogarth Press. Yesterday she & "a friend" came to tea. This friend we called mistakenly Jones; he being Joad, of the 1917 Club; a philosopher;[6] a sturdy short man, with very bright round eyes, hair touched with grey, cocksure, reposing much weight upon the sterling quality of his intellect, & thus dispensing with the graces & amenities, as usual with sterling young men. He tipped one of my chairs on two legs, & ate a large tea, keeping close watch over Marjorie's interests at every point. For it was evident that she was ready to bind herself hand & foot to us, & make fantastic promises. Still, she has been thoroughly educated, must earn her living, & has written, Joad says, a first rate novel. Well its not quite written, she said; being of course, far

---

British intervention, a show of force, and a crisis in which war seemed imminent. The paragraphs on this subject which appeared regularly under 'Events of the Week' in the *Nation & Athenaeum* were presumably written by LW; his unsigned article published on 18 November was headed: 'The Old Game with Turkey'.

5. James Whitall was employed as a reader by the publishers William Heinemann and had interested them in the future of the Hogarth Press. William Heinemann, the founder of the firm, was dead, and the managing director was now Charles Evans. See *IV LW*, p 79. Scott was probably Cyril Scott (1879-1970), the composer.

6. The young woman was Marjorie Thomson (*c.* 1900-1931), who had been a student at the London School of Economics. She was living with Cyril Edwin Mitchinson Joad (1891-1953), a civil servant in the Ministry of Labour, and a man of fertile brain and energy which was largely deployed in writing and teaching on philosophical and political subjects. He was married and the father of three children, but Marjorie Thomson used his name, and they were ostensibly married.

more modest & less self confident & more excitable than Cyril. "We are going to be married in February" she said, when we came up here from the scullery. And I mean to go on working after I'm married. She now teaches at a Girls School in Gordon Square.[7] And what does it all amount to? I should say she is 25 or 6: quick, impulsive, but with a steel thread in her from earning & learning, which is an invaluable property, & one that gives an edge to the rest. In short she might take us on & make a life work of it. Since heaven dropped the seed into her naturally, she will want no urging, & will cleave to it as to her own flesh & bone, I can see. Joad, who detests my books & adores the work of Beresford & sticks his little horns manfully into facts, may be an obstacle; since he may try to impose his literary views upon us; & I imagine him one of the steely intellectuals who treat literature as though it were an ingenious picture puzzle, to be fitted accurately together. But I dont know. Moreover, we both liked him, & her too (but she was less self assertive, passed the cake, praised the dog, & sensitively appraised the situation with antennae quivering, woman like). We all kept our heads very creditably, insisted upon strict business dealings, & are to meet again on Sunday week. But where then does Ralph come in? He looks a little glum, & says very little. I fancy our teas & lunches are a little strained. Tomorrow we interview Heinemann at his office, but I don't think much will come from that.

Jacob has now sold 850 copies, & the second edition wont come much before it is needed I hope. People—my friends I mean—seem agreed that it is *my* masterpiece, & the starting point for fresh adventures. Last night we dined with Roger & I was praised whole-heartedly by him, for the first time; only he wishes that a bronze body might somehow solidify beneath the gleams & lights—with which I agree. He has been cured, so he says, by Coué; but seemed old to me.[8] The approaching marriage of Pam, which drains upon his paternal feelings generally not shown, depresses him, & puts the stress on a side of him which is private & difficult, for, as he has always kept clear of fatherly responsibilities, he is now shy of them; cant deny his feelings for her; but cannot exercise

7. Marjorie Thomson taught at Miss Peters' private school for girls at 55 Gordon Square. (It also took younger children of both sexes, amongst others Julian and Quentin Bell.)

8. Early in November 1922 Roger Fry sought a cure for his continuing maladies by attending the clinic at Nancy of Dr Emile Coué (1857-1926). Dr Coué believed that the patient could cure many of his own diseases by means of auto-suggestion. Fry considered that the theory deserved a fair trial, he was attracted by Coué's personality, and for a time followed his methods; but tradition has it that he only succeeded in driving a severe cold out of his right eye and into his left eye.

his rights—to forbid the marriage. Oh how cold it was coming home in the train!

Sunday 3 December

I should be at Aeschylus, for I am making a complete edition, text, translation, & notes of my own—mostly copied from Verrall; but carefully gone into by me. But these are historic days. The Hogarth Press is in travail. Heinemanns made us a most flattering offer—to the effect that we should give us [sic] our brains & blood, & they would see to sales & ledgers. But we sniff patronage. If they gain, we lose. Our name has to be coupled with theirs. In the opinions of Desmond, Clive, Roger & I think Vanessa, the exchange would be capitulation. We are both very willing to come to this conclusion, & have decided for freedom & a fight with great private glee. This brought on an argument with Ralph last Friday. We must have a whole timer in January, or close down partially. After some demur, he brought forth a plan obviously concocted at Tidmarsh, by which we are to become a company, with Noel C[arrington]. for London manager, Lytton, L. & I for partners, with Ralph remaining as he is.[1] Lytton is said to hint a possibility that we should have all his work. At first tempting, this plan becomes to us less & less feasible; considering that we should have to keep N.C. in work, be ready to tackle an enormous commercial success, & fall more & more, so we suspect, into readers & advisers to the firm of Partridge & Carrington, who would become by force of circumstances, commercial mainly with only a dab of Hogarth gold left on top. At this moment we incline to Miss Tomson & freedom. Let P. & Carrington start their own press, & go ahead for ourselves, gradually branching as opportunity occurs. One is much attracted by the idea of a keen worker; & to tell the truth, Noel did not give either of us the desire to strive for him. Why, after all, should we conciliate Ralph? And is it not better to end this perpetual strain of friendship's burden—hurting Lytton's feelings that is, by failing to consider how fast poor R.'s heart beats after a conversation with us? Such, in short, are the reasons which come to the front; & we have to refuse to talk Hogarth matters, for the discussion is endless. Tomorrow, Ralph is going to lay before us a definite proposal on the part of Lytton.

1. Noel Lewis Carrington (b. 1894), Carrington's younger brother and an Oxford friend of Ralph Partridge, had been working for the Oxford University Press in India since 1919, and was thought, reasonably enough, to have good qualifications as a potential manager of the Hogarth Press.

But there is serious reason, & not mere restlessness, in our need for re-organisation. We are both giving all our spare time, & still there is far more work than we can do. Jacob has sold, I think, 850; with review copies 950; there is an ominous slackening of Simkin's orders this last week, which shows, perhaps, that the rush is over. But we shall broach our second edition, & shall not lose, even if we sell no more, more than £10; so I am satisfied. But the books press. There are now Miss Hobhouse's diary, & Stephen Reynolds' letters to be read & considered, & at this rate, we have work for not 3 people but 4 or 5 or 6.[2]

This autumn has been perhaps the busiest of my dilatory life. People & books—I sing that to the tune of Woman & Wine, which comes in the Beggars Opera. I dined with Mary on Friday, met Clive & Aldous; Aldous very long, rather puffy, fat faced, white, with very thick hair, & canary coloured socks, is the raconteur; the young man of letters who sees life. We all said we despised reviewers & told little stories to our own advantage. Both the gentlemen had been complimented by Max— but not the lady. At first one thinks the

Friday 15 December

I forget what I was to say, & only write this now as I have 15 minutes before my solitary dinner, L. dining with Sangers, after a terrific Hogarth Press discussion ending in the final parting with Ralph. It was a question of the terms upon which the Tidmarsh Press (he was to run one in conjunction with us) was to have. He stood out for one third. Finally we agreed; but the discussion raised our backs, & so—(Nell said that orange was bad—everything goes through—Lottie's conversation is running while I write). I am too muzzy headed to make out anything. This is partly the result of dining to meet the lovely gifted aristocratic Sackville West last night at Clive's. Not much to my severer taste— florid, moustached, parakeet coloured, with all the supple ease of the aristocracy, but not the wit of the artist. She writes 15 pages a day—

2. Stephen Reynolds (1881-1919); his *Letters*, edited by Harold Wright, were published by the Hogarth Press in May 1923 (*HP Checklist* 39). A man of middle-class background with a university education, he went to work in Sidmouth as a fisherman and boatman; he published several works dealing with the sea and with socio-political themes. Emily Hobhouse (1860-1926), herself the author of diaries which formed the basis of a memoir published in 1929, had translated from the Afrikaans *Tant' Alie of Transvaal: Her Diary, 1880-1902*, which was probably the diary offered to the Hogarth Press. It was published by Allen & Unwin in 1923.

has finished another book—publishes with Heinemanns—knows every-one— But could I ever know her? I am to dine there on Tuesday.

Waiting for L., I will continue. Half past ten just struck on one of these fine December nights, which come after sunny days, & I don't know why, keep sending through me such shocks from my childhood. Am I growing old & sentimental? I keep thinking of sounds I heard as a child—at St Ives mostly.

The aristocratic manner is something like the actresses—no false shyness or modesty: a bead dropped into her plate at dinner—given to Clive—asks for liqueur—has her hand on all the ropes—makes me feel virgin, shy, & schoolgirlish. Yet after dinner I rapped out opinions. She is a grenadier; hard; handsome, manly; inclined to double chin. Dear old Desmond moped like a tipsy owl in his corner, affectionate & glad to talk to me, I think. He said something about the French admiring Jacob, & wishing to translate it. I go on getting letters, & reap more praise than ever before. Sales sluggish though. Not yet 1000. But I don't mind.

As for Ralph—that question certainly cant be settled before L. comes in. Why did he make me, & L., so furious by saying, in his sulky school-boy voice, that if this crisis hadn't happened, he would have had a nice surprise to offer us at Easter?—something of Lytton's presumably? I think the kernel of our discontent lies in that sentence—the bully, the swagger, the bribe offered us by Lytton, through this gawkish boor, & his simple rustic faith that writing by Lytton must solve all difficulties instead of which it complicates things.

So far as I can see, Ralph's disappearance would leave us more freedom, but give us more work. We should have to make further arrangements. But the basis would be sound, which is the great thing. If we keep Ralph, there will be constant disease. He hinted that he wished to be able to break. Again, the question of borrowing money from Lytton always recurs: & the obvious pressure they make to consolidate their position. This would be perfect if Ralph were not Ralph. I see him rigid & ossified in middle age; repeating more & more accurately his lesson learnt from Lytton. And though I would give a good deal to combine with Lytton in producing literature, there is little to be got from him save his own works. I mean, I think by our own merits now we attract all the young.

1923

1923

Four days after her last diary entry, on Tuesday 19 December 1922, VW dined with Vita Sackville-West; Leonard dined at the Cock in Fleet Street. They went, with their servants, to Monks House for Christmas, but neither of them made any record of this period. They returned to London on Monday 1 January 1923, and VW went to Gordon Square to see Vanessa and her family, who had spent Christmas at Cleeve House in Wiltshire with Clive's parents. The following entry, mis-dated by VW 3 January, is written in in her 1922 diary, DIARY XI.

Tuesday 2 January

If I were a dissembler I should date this the last day of 1922. So it is to all intents. We came back from Rodmell yesterday, & I am in one of my moods, as the nurses used to call it, today. And what is it & why? A desire for children, I suppose; for Nessa's life; for the sense of flowers breaking all round me involuntarily. Here's Angelica—here's Quentin & Julian. Now children dont make yourself ill on plum pudding tonight. We have people dining. There's no hot water. The gas is escaping in Quentin's bedroom—I pluck what I call flowers at random. They make my life seem a little bare sometimes; & then my inveterate romanticism suggests an image of forging ahead, alone, through the night: of suffering inwardly, stoically; of blazing my way through to the end—& so forth. The truth is that the sails flap about me for a day or two on coming back; & not being at full stretch I ponder & loiter. And it is all temporary: yet let me be quite clear about that. Let me have one confessional where I need not boast. Years & years ago, after the Lytton affair, I said to myself, walking up the hill at Beireuth, never pretend that the things you haven't got are not worth having; good advice I think.[1] At least it often comes back to me. Never pretend that children, for instance, can be replaced by other things. And then I went on (the thought is always connected with Mrs Freshfield—why?) to say to myself that one must ⟨put all one's weight upon⟩ (how am I to convey it?) like things for themselves: or rather, rid them of their bearing upon one's personal life. One must throw that aside; & venture on to the things that exist independently of oneself. Now this is very hard for young women to do. Yet I got

[1]. In August 1909, six months after Lytton's proposal, VW went with Adrian Stephen and Saxon Sydney-Turner to the Wagner Festival at Bayreuth. See *I QB*, 149-50.

satisfaction from it. And now, married to L., I never *have* to make the effort. I do it, if I enjoy doing it. Perhaps I have been too happy for my soul's good? Perhaps I have become cowardly & self-indulgent? And does some of my discontent come from feeling that? I could not stay at 46 last night, because L. on the telephone expressed displeasure. Late again. Very foolish. Your heart bad—& so my self reliance being sapped, I had no courage to venture against his will. Then I react. Of course its a difficult question. For undoubtedly I get headaches or the jump in my heart; & then this spoils his pleasure, & if one lives with a person, has one the right— So it goes on. And I will try to make up my accounts on the spiritual side before attacking the temporal, only, as usual, jerkily, disconnectedly, & without more than the sort of tap a chemist might give to the jars in his shop, naming them shortly, because he knows what is in them. At fifty, when I re-read, perhaps I shall know what I meant.

Middle Age then. Let that be the text of my discourse. I'm afraid we're becoming elderly. We are busy & attach importance to hours. I have my correspondence to finish, says L. today. I don't laugh. I take it seriously. But we must not let our hobbies & pleasures become objects of fetish worship. L., I think, suffers from his extreme clarity. He sees things so clear that he can't swim float & speculate. And now we have such a train attached to us that we have to go on. It is easy, at least, to pretend that pressure is upon us. Nessa, though, who might so easily plead ties & circumstances, rides much more freely than we do. She will spend Easter travelling with the children, for instance. We have to make money —that is true. We have to have a house; 2 houses; 2 servants; a press; a Tomson; a Ralph. Yet most of this is for my sake; & am I honest in wishing it otherwise? Dont I feel (mainly) that I must ease the strain of circumstances in order to write?—that interruptions bore me: put gross matter in my fire?

I will leave it here, unfinished, a note of interrogation—signifying some mood that recurs, but is not often expressed. One's life is made up, superficially, of such moods; but they cross a solid substance, which too I am not going to hack my way into now.

So this is the end of 1922.

DIARY XII

Sunday 7 January

Let the scene open on the doorstep of number 50 Gordon Square. We went up last night, carrying our bags, & a Ceylonese sword. There was

Mary H. in lemon coloured trousers with green ribbons. & so we sat down to dinner; off cold chicken. In came Roger & Adrian & Karin; & very slowly we coloured our faces & made ready for number 46. It was the proudest moment of Clive's life when he led Mary on one arm, Virginia on the other, into the drawing room, which was full, miscellaneous; & oriental for the most part. Suppose one's normal pulse to be 70: in five minutes it was 120: & the blood, not the sticky whitish fluid of daytime, but brilliant & prickling like champagne. This was my state, & most peoples. We collided, when we met: went pop, used Christian names, flattered, praised, & thought (or I did) of Shakespeare. At any rate I thought of him when the singing was doing—Sh[akespear]e I thought would have liked us all tonight. Not that Bobo was other than a damp owl, with some private gloom which being too personal for my taste, she brought with her. Then there was a plain woodfaced Darwin —which? And Hussey, like a Victorian seamstress by a table covered in mohair checks. My luck was in though, & I found good quarters with Frankie & Sheppard & Bunny, & Lydia—all my friends in short. But what we talked about I hardly know. Bunny asked me to be his childs godmother.[2] And a Belgian wants to translate me. Arnold Bennett thinks me wonderful &—&—(these, no doubt were elements in my hilarity). Gumbo distorted nursery rhymes; Lydia danced; there were charades; Sickert acted Hamlet.[3] We were all easy & gifted & friendly & like good children rewarded by having the capacity for enjoying ourselves thus. Could our fathers? I, wearing my mothers laces, looked at Mary's little soft Jerboa face in the old looking glass—& wondered.

I daresay no one said anything very brilliant. I sat by Sickert, & liked him, talking in his very workmanlike, but not at all society manner, of painting, & Whistler; of an operation he saw at Dieppe. But can life be worth so much pain, he asked? "Pour respirer" said the Dr. That is enough. But for two years 'after my wife's death' I did not wish to live said Sickert. There is something indescribably congenial to me in this

2. Bunny Garnett had married Rachel Marshall in 1921; their elder son, Richard Duncan Carey Garnett, was born on 8 January, two days after this party. There was no real question either of the child being christened or of VW standing Godmother in the accepted sense.

3. Walter Richard Sickert (1860-1942), painter, had in his youth been an actor; pupil and studio assistant to Whistler, he later became a friend and follower of Degas. He lived and worked in Dieppe and Venice; returning to London in 1905, he became a leader of the avant-garde, very active and influential in the affairs of various associations of artists. His second wife, Christine Drummond Angus whom he had married in 1911, had died of cancer at their home near Dieppe in October 1920.

easy artists talk; the values the same as my own & therefore right; no impediments; life charming, good & interesting; no effort; art brooding calmly over it all; & none of this attachment to mundane things, which I find in Chelsea. For Sickert said, why should one be attached to one's own body & breakfast? Why not be satisfied to let others have the use of ones life, & live it over again, being dead oneself? No mysticism, & therefore a great relish for the actual things—whatever they may be— old plays, girls, boys, Proust, Handel sung by Oliver [Strachey]; the turn of a head & so on.

As parties do, this one began to dwindle, until a few persistent talkers were left by themselves sitting in such odd positions—Oliver full length by Barbara on the floor; Ralph astride a chair in the middle of the room; Lytton & I side by side on the sofa.

"And what do you think of the Tidmarsh Press", said Lytton.

And this was his craftly way of telling me that Ralph means to set up on his own, or rather on his own after the Hogarth model after easter. Lytton was anxious to sound me. Should we think it poaching? For it would be exactly the same as the Hogarth Press. I said I should say sharp things, but there was quite enough work for two. In the middle of the night of course I blazed up & abused Ralph for a pickpocket (myself to myself that is). But Lytton was not altogether urbane. He is possessive. His baby shall have his toy, & he shan't share it with anyone else this time. Well—so be it. The immediate effect is to make L. & me set to— wire in as Nelly would say—& bestir ourselves for the future. We wont be downed by the prestige & power & pomposity of all the Benson medallists in England.[4] In fact, the struggle is invigorating; though it does not improve our opinion of the ass. I especially dislike his effect upon Lytton. Lytton becomes jealous, & suspicious, & uses his wits to make the worse appear the better cause. Love is the devil. No character can stand up against it. But this passed in our trivial champagne pricking way. And so, at 3, I suppose, back to no. 50 to which Clive had gone previously.

I went up & found the light burning & so turned it out. I noticed a bluish glimmer under Clive's door. "Reading in bed," I thought, & hoped I should not be called in to talk. But the house was too noisy for me to sleep. People seemed to be walking. Then a woman cried, as if in anguish, in the street, & I thought of Mrs Thompson waiting to be ex-

4. Lytton Strachey had been awarded the Benson Silver Medal in respect of *Queen Victoria* in December 1922. The award, endowed in 1916 by A. C. Benson, was made by the Fellows of the Royal Society of Literature in recognition of 'meritorious work'.

ecuted.[5] I turned about. Footsteps sounded. A door opened. I heard voices. At this hour, I thought innocently, no one can be up without cause—illness or accident. So up I jumped, thrust in my upper teeth, & opened the door.

"Is something wrong?" I asked of Clive's shadow on his bedroom wall, for his door was open.

"I hope I've not waked you", he said.

Obviously nothing was wrong. The shriek was Mary's.

And so we breakfasted together this morning, with the church bells ringing, & all the houses full of Stracheys, Grants, Stephens & Bells & Partridges—a wet grey morning, in the heart of London, where I am so seldom at that hour.

Such is my frontispiece, which needless to say, I meant to make more brilliant, but as Nessa said this morning, I dont want brilliance. The only thing I care for is to be at my ease. (we were discussing Mary).

Now, briefly to make out my work list.

I shall write at Mrs Dalloway till, next Monday, perhaps, bringing her into full talk, I hope.

Shall I then dash off an article for Squire upon memoirs?[6] which will take till Monday 29th. Then do the Greek chapter, for which I shall have read Odyssey (6 books) Agamemnon: Oedipus Tyrannus, Zimmern, Jebb's Homer—Life of Jebb, & some dialogue of Plato's? This puts off writing till rather late in the day; but I want to make myself a certain amount of money regularly, if only for pocket money. Now, therefore, I must finish Pilkington;[7] read Greek regularly; & tackle, perhaps, another vol of Proust. First then, I must master the Agamemnon (this refers to the immediate moment). & before doing that I must write to the new apparition Vita, who gives me a book every other day.

Tuesday 16 January

Katherine has been dead a week, & how far am I obeying her "do

5. Mrs Edith Jessie Thompson was executed at 9 a.m. on Tuesday 9 January 1923 for the murder of her husband, Percy Thompson, stabbed to death in Ilford on 4 October 1922. Her lover and accomplice, Frederick Edward Francis Bywaters, was also executed. An appeal for their reprieve had been turned down by the Home Office on 5 January 1923.

6. This was VW's article 'Lives of the Obscure' (Kp C244), which was not published in the *London Mercury* until January 1924, after some dispute about the fee (see below, 17 March 1923).

7. VW's essay 'Laetitia Pilkington', based upon the memoirs of the Irish adventuress which were first published in 1748, appeared in the *Nation & Athenaeum* on 30 June 1923 (Kp C237). (The DNB gives Mrs Pilkington's dates as 1712-1750, whereas VW gives 1712-1759: perhaps a misprint?)

not quite forget Katherine" which I read in one of her old letters?[8] Am I already forgetting her? It is strange to trace the progress of one's feelings. Nelly said in her sensational way at breakfast on Friday "Mrs Murry's dead! It says so in the paper!" At that one feels—what? A shock of relief?—a rival the less? Then confusion at feeling so little—then, gradually, blankness & disappointment; then a depression which I could not rouse myself from all that day. When I began to write, it seemed to me there was no point in writing. Katherine wont read it. Katherine's my rival no longer. More generously I felt, But though I can do this better than she could, where is she, who could do what I can't! Then, as usual with me, visual impressions kept coming & coming before me—always of Katherine putting on a white wreath, & leaving us, called away; made dignified, chosen. And then one pitied her. And one felt her reluctant to wear that wreath, which was an ice cold one. And she was only 33. And I could see her before me so exactly, & the room at Portland Villas. I go up. She gets up, very slowly, from her writing table. A glass of milk & a medicine bottle stood there. There were also piles of novels. Everything was very tidy, bright, & somehow like a dolls house. At once, or almost, we got out of shyness. She (it was summer) half lay on the sofa by the window. She had her look of a Japanese doll, with the fringe combed quite straight across her forehead. Sometimes we looked very steadfastly at each other, as though we had reached some durable relationship, independent of the changes of the body, through the eyes. Hers were beautiful eyes—rather doglike, brown, very wide apart, with a steady slow rather faithful & sad expression. Her nose was sharp, & a little vulgar. Her lips thin & hard. She wore short skirts & liked "to have a line round her" she said. She looked very ill—very drawn, & moved languidly, drawing herself across the room, like some suffering animal. I suppose I have written down some of the things we said. Most days I think we reached that kind of certainty, in talk about books, or rather about our writings, which I thought had something durable about it. And then she was inscrutable. Did she care for me? Sometimes she would say so—would kiss me—would look at me as if (is this sentiment?) her eyes would like always to be faithful. She would promise never never

8. Katherine Mansfield died quickly on the night of 9 January 1923 following a haemorrhage; Murry was visiting her at the Gurdjieff Institute for the Harmonious Development of Man at Fontainebleau where she had been living since October. Copies of 30 of her letters to VW are in MHP, Sussex; the final sentence, omitted by Murry in his edition of his wife's letters (1928, vol. I, p 75), of one written in July 1917 reads: 'Do let us meet in the nearest future darling Virginia, and don't quite forget.'

to forget. That was what we said at the end of our last talk. She said she would send me her diary to read, & would write always.[9] For our friendship was a real thing we said, looking at each other quite straight. It would always go on whatever happened. What happened was, I suppose, faultfindings & perhaps gossip. She never answered my letter.[10] Yet I still feel, somehow that friendship persists. Still there are things about writing I think of & want to tell Katherine. If I had been in Paris & gone to her, she would have got up & in three minutes, we should have been talking again. Only I could not take the step. The surroundings—Murry & so on—& the small lies & treacheries, the perpetual playing & teasing, or whatever it was, cut away much of the substance of friendship. One was too uncertain. And so one let it all go. Yet I certainly expected that we should meet again next summer, & start fresh. And I was jealous of her writing—the only writing I have ever been jealous of. This made it harder to write to her; & I saw in it, perhaps from jealousy, all the qualities I disliked in her.

For two days I felt that I had grown middle aged, & lost some spur to write. That feeling is going. I no longer keep seeing her with her wreath. I dont pity her so much. Yet I have the feeling that I shall think of her at intervals all through life. Probably we had something in common which I shall never find in anyone else. (This I say in so many words in 1919 again & again.) Moreover I like speculating about her character. I think I never gave her credit for all her physical suffering & the effect it must have had in embittering her.

The Nation is probably sold over Massingham's head;[11] L. has a violent cold. I have been in bed, 101, again. Fergusson threatens to cut my tonsils.

Sunday 28 January

A certain melancholy has been brooding over me this fortnight. I date

9. See above 25 August 1920: '. . . we propose to write to each other—She will send me her diary. Shall we? Will she?'

10. See *II VW Letters*, footnote to no. 1156, referring to a letter to Katherine Mansfield dated 13 February 1921 'not yet available for publication'. This would appear to be the letter also referred to by VW in writing to Brett on 2 March 1923 (*III VW Letters*, no. 1365): 'I must have written to her sometime in March 1921. . . . perhaps she never did get my letter. . . . Murry . . . said she was lonely and asked me to write. . . . It hurt me that she never answered.' As VW sat next to Murry at his 'farewell dinner' on 11 February 1921, her letter was probably the one dated 13 February, and she was mistaken in thinking she had written in March.

11. See below 28 January 1923, and n 12.

it from Katherine's death. The feeling so often comes to me now—Yes. Go on writing of course: but into emptiness. There's no competitor. I'm cock—a lonely cock whose crowing nothing breaks—of my walk. For our friendship had so much that was writing in it. However then I had my fever, & violent cold, was in & out of bed for a week, & still am below normal, I think. In casting accounts, never forget to begin with the state of the body.

K., so Ralph reports via Brett, died in 10 minutes of haemorrhage, walking upstairs with Murry who happened to be there. Brett is 'very hard hit' Ralph says. I soon shant have Ralph's sayings to report. Does that make me melancholy? Like most of one's feelings mine on losing him are mixed. We now have had Joad twice—Margery I should & do call her, & she comes tomorrow full time. She has a little too much powder & scent for my taste, & drawls. In short she is not upper class. But she has honest intent eyes, & takes it seriously, which, as she is quite without training, is as well. My only fear is lest she should prove a flibbertigibbet. Her quickness of movement, keenness, & dependability are so far a great gain on Ralph. There he sits thick as an oak & as angular. We have heard no more of the Tidmarsh Press.

I have seen quantities of people—having them here, as my invalid ways induced, bright pictures, tunes on the gramophone—but I must not insult the human soul for which I have really so much respect. Bobo & Betty have nothing sharp or bright about them. Both seem to dissolve in a November cloud; depressed, emotional, with no target for emotion. Bobo is vaguely indulging in an affair—perhaps with a medical student called Stanley—(she does not confide names). He takes her out, makes love, which she enjoys but finds somehow inferior. She likes the surroundings. She had been out with him somewhere, the night before, & said the surroundings were glittering. She yielded to the unreality; then repented, & told him this was the last time. Then she repents of that, forages in her pocket for principles, forages in mine, & I, not knowing her case, advised her to fling herself into life, to reflect, but not to withdraw, which of course pointed the way she secretly wished, & yet privately feels impure. So do I in this case.

Betty had not even any case to put before me. Never was there a limper, less objective, creature. There she lounges in the arm chair opposite, never thinking she need speak, or invent, or comment or do any of the tricks which human beings have devised for keeping the water fresh. One stagnates kindly, gently. She is a nice girl, by which I mean gentle & affectionate, but also clinging & selfish & egotistical. She says dress is a great snare. She says she lives with rotten people. She says she means to go abroad & learn singing. Meanwhile she has taken a flat in the Queen's Road [? Richmond], so far from her haunts that she must lunch out, & spends hours daily wandering the streets, looking in at shop windows I suppose & coveting dresses.

Who else? Roger & Bob: Bob with his lid on, not talking but bubbling underneath. He had to be kept under or would have foamed all over us. Much talk of the Nation, wh, as I should have recorded, is sold to Maynard & a group, & our future once more quite uncertain.[12] Still I cant fabricate doubts, & hereby record my expectation that we shall emerge richer in 2 months time. Massingham will start a new paper: Maynard will retain Leonard at a handsome fee. And then? (I race, before dinner comes.) Roger's lecture, the last.[13] Before it I dined with Noel Olivier (Richards) at the Club. She looked at me with those strange eyes in which a drop seems to have been spilt—a pale blue drop, with a large deep centre— romantic eyes, that seem to behold still Rupert bathing in the river at Christow: eyes pure & wide, & profound it seems.[14] Or is there nothing behind them? I as good as asked her. Why didn't you marry any of those romantic young men? Why? Why? She didn't know, said she had moods; all Oliviers are mad she said. And Rupert had gone with Cathleen Nesbitt & she had been jealous, & he had spoken against women & gone among the Asquiths & changed.[15] But when she read his love letters—beautiful

12. H. W. Massingham had edited the *Nation* since it was founded in 1907 by the Rowntree family, who were Liberal in politics. Under his editorship the paper had, by 1923, become 'to all intents and purposes a Labour paper' (*IV LW*, p 96), a state of affairs the Rowntrees could no longer countenance. They decided to sell, giving Massingham first option to buy. He sought but failed to find financial backing. On Maynard Keynes and other Liberals coming forward with adequate resources, the Rowntrees agreed to their acquiring control of the paper, in which they then retained an interest. In April therefore Keynes became chairman of the new Board; Hubert Henderson took over the editorship, and, after some uncertainty, LW was appointed literary editor. See also below, 7 February 1923; and Roy Harrod, *The Life of John Maynard Keynes*, 1951, pp 335-7.

13. Beginning on 6 December, Roger Fry had given a series of four lantern lectures 'on Art' on Wednesday evenings at the Lower Hall, Mortimer Street, W.1.; the last was on 17 January.

14. In August 1911 VW had joined a party which included Rupert Brooke and Noel Olivier, whom he loved, who were camping at Clifford Bridge on the River Teign in Devonshire; Christow was a few miles downstream.

15. Before the war Edward Marsh, Winston Churchill's private secretary and a great patron of poets and painters, had taken up Rupert Brooke, who at the time was suffering a neurotic aversion to some of his former friends, and introduced him to a more worldly and sophisticated London society which included the Asquiths, and the actress Cathleen Nesbitt (b. 1888). She became a fresh and uncomplicated focus for his confused emotions.

beautiful love letters—real love letters, she said—she cries & cries. How direct & unyielding these young women are. But she is "over 30"—she would not say how much. & I am 41: which I confess. So we parted.

Then?— Morgan, buttoned like a hairdresser, cheerful, communicative, but come to talk business & soon gone.

Then Lilian [Harris], with her hands in her lap, facing old age, & horribly bored. The egotism—gentle & blood sucking—of these elderly women! She wanted work, advice, & the names of Inns. I was amused to detect her complete absorption in Margaret; her childlike record of every symptom meal & habit. But this is natural, indeed charming & pathetic too.

Wednesday 7 February

Nessa's wedding day.[1] Reflections suppressed. I must describe Cambridge. We walked from the station, past Rattee & Kett,[2] cold, starry; dismal; then familiar; King's College Chapel, hasty wash & dress, & dine with Sheppard. He was in evening dress. He carries a knobbed cane. Maynard, Norton, & Betty to dinner.[3] A good deal of raw time had to be manufactured. I had romanced so much about Cambridge that to find myself sitting there was an anti climax. No one else was excited. Then off in the motor to the A.D.C. I think I was genuinely excited, rather than moved by Oedipus Rex. The plot is so well tied; the storys[?] race so fast. Then the young men's faces; pink & plump under their wigs, moved me. I don't know whether memory poured a little mist. Among the audience were: Lytton, Irene Vanbrugh; Q; Faith; & so on.[4]

1. Vanessa Stephen and Clive Bell were married at St Pancras Registry Office on 7 February 1907.
2. The Woolfs went to Cambridge on Saturday 3 and returned to London on Monday 5 February. Rattee and Kett, Builders, whose premises were at the bottom of Station Road.
3. Jane Elizabeth Norton (1893-1962) was a younger sister of Harry Norton, with whom she shared a house in Cambridge; having graduated in 1917, she was doing research and teaching there. She later became Director of Birrell & Garnett's bookshop.
4. The Marlowe Society's production of Sophocles' *Oedipus Tyrannus*, in an English version by J. T. Sheppard, was performed at the Amateur Dramatic Club's theatre. Irene Vanbrugh (1872-1949), a leading comedy actress, distantly related to the Stracheys; 'Q' was Sir Arthur Thomas Quiller-Couch (1863-1944), since 1912 Professor of English Literature at Cambridge; Faith Marion Jane Henderson, *née* Bagenal (b. 1889), a Newnham graduate, sister of Nicholas Bagenal and old acquaintance of VW, wife of Hubert Henderson, presently lecturer in Economics at Cambridge, but soon to become editor of the *Nation & Athenaeum* (see above, 28 January 1923, n 12).

And so to bed; with King's bell saying very pompously all through the night the hour. We were happy & busy all Sunday, first Sheppard, then Pernel; sitting on the Backs, strolling up to Newnham the way I used to go; then lunching with the Shoves, & Fredegond is the image of Christina Rossetti. Her faith is charitable. She has nothing very definite to say. She attends mass.[5] She is happier & more full of vitality than before she says. Gerald, she says, took her to be confirmed, watched with interest &, coming out, wished he had a faith; wished to be a Quaker, but has taken no further steps. I think she makes the most of chance words he lets fall. So to the Moores, finding Moore smoking alone, who asked us directly whether we would come up or have the children brought down.[6] Stout Dorothy was bathing Timothy & smoking—a truncated woman, amiable, red, a little beery; anyhow cheery; & Moore said, very kindly, dearie to the baby, crying for food, like a wise old nurse. Rather they were like a couple of fat beavers with their young. Fine little cubs too, fat, hard, sturdy, likely to do us all credit when we are all dead. The elegiac note will creep in, & shall be justified if I have time. Then to Maynard's: I must say the pleasantest sitting room I have ever been in, owing to the colours & paintings, curtains & decorations of Bell & Grant. Here we dined well. Ramsay, the unknown guest, was something like a Darwin, broad, thick, powerful, & a great mathematician, & clumsy to boot. Honest I should say, a true Apostle.[7] The party began after a few brilliancies on my part about religion; emotional [?] capital which I did not know how to invest, I said. And Maynard kept the old ball smartly rolling. Indeed we were rather talk-dazed. And as people arrived, I suppose one's eyes tire; one's brain stales. Lucas is slightly deaf, & pure & sincere, needs that is rather an effort to talk to in the grand style, about literature. Besides, I rather wished to hear Sprott praise Jacob's Room. Never mind. Mrs Birch, honourable Mrs Birch of Firle, was introduced; like a white wild fox, body perfectly trained,

5. In her memoir *Gerald and Fredegond Shove* (1952, p 42), Fredegond wrote: 'I was longing to become a Catholic and . . . in 1927 this happened.'

6. The philosopher G. E. Moore with his wife (*née* Dorothy Ely, 1892-1977) and their two little boys, Nicholas and Timothy, lived at 86 Chesterton Road, Cambridge.

7. Vanessa Bell's and Duncan Grant's decorations for one of Keynes's rooms in Webb's Court of King's College included eight large wall panels, four by each artist, and appliqué curtains by Vanessa. See Richard Shone, *Bloomsbury Portraits*, 1976, pp 234-5. Frank P. Ramsey (1903-1930), still a student at Trinity, was already highly regarded as a mathematical logician and philosopher by Keynes, Bertrand Russell, and others. He was an Apostle and, later, a Fellow of King's; he died untimely. (His younger brother, who was of similar build but different beliefs, became Archbishop of Canterbury.)

intelligence wild.[8] not a bad combination. Like Vita she detests the scrolloping honours of the great, calls her family dull & stupid, complains of a girls life, Lowndes Square, Ascot, & Aunts who rail against what they call Bo-eemians. She should have married a Guardsman, & is now in Cambridge society, believing in Topsy as I could see, & in Mrs Dobree; humbly taking from our hands whatever we choose to give.

The depression which I mentioned comes partly from the uncertainty about the Nation. Leonard thinks himself a failure. And what use is there in denying a depression which is irrational? Can't I always think myself one too? It is inevitable. But there was Maynard arrived & trim, yet our junior. The absurd unreality of this as a standard strikes me, but it is not easy to make these truths effective. It is unpleasant waiting in a dependent kind of way to know what Massingham will do. The signs are favourable. Ramsay Muir, Maynard's editor, is on all hands a dull dog; Maynard is entreating Tomlinson to join him, & so support him against the Wee Frees, who are his co-directors.[9] My notion is, he will float the Nation, make a splash, then dive off, & leave it to its fate within the year. It will dwindle & die. Massingham is optimistic, but delays at Monte Carlo, & we only hear, vaguely, that he has a good chance of starting a threepenny weekly to coincide with the break on April 1st.[10]

And our depression comes too from the time of year, wet & wan, and from Joad's drawling voice, & Ralph's stubbornness, & from Lytton's hint that he means to start the Tidmarsh Press at once. Here, however, is some mystery, for Carrington professed to know nothing of it, & would only admit to a press for printing refined books, on commission— I think Joad & Ralph daily for lunch & tea, & the need for bright talk,

8. Walter John Herbert ('Sebastian') Sprott (1897-1971), a graduate of Clare College, recently appointed Demonstrator in the University Psychological Laboratory, was, like Frank Ramsey and Peter Lucas, one of a new generation of Apostles gathered round Maynard Keynes at Cambridge. He had been the companion of both Keynes and Lytton Strachey in their summer journeys abroad in the past two years. Mrs Birch was the Hon. Vera Benedicta (b. 1899), sister of Viscount Gage of Firle Place, Lewes; her husband Lt Cdr Frank Lyall Birch was a fellow of King's and a University lecturer in History.

9. It had been expected that Ramsay Muir (1872-1941), historian and active Liberal, would become editor of the reformed *Nation & Athenaeum*, but a divergence of outlook between him and Keynes resulted in the appointment of Hubert Henderson. Tomlinson had been literary editor of the paper under Massingham. By the 'Wee Frees' (an epithet derived from the Wee Free Kirk, a minority party in the Free Church of Scotland which in 1900 seceded from the main body) VW presumably meant Keynes's financial backers.

10. Massingham did not start a new weekly; he transferred his 'Wayfarer's Diary' from the *Nation* to the *New Statesman*.

depress also; & I shall be glad when the 15th March arrives. I suppose the Press must now lose something of its charm, & become more strenuous; acquiring let us hope a different charm. But I wish Joad were, somehow, a lady. Now to Wigmore Hall with Saxon to hear a severe Franck quintet, beyond me no doubt.[11]

Saturday 10 February

The omens are, I think, more favourable. Maynard has presented an ultimatum, to the effect I think, but this was gathered on the telephone, that he will not work with Ramsay Muir. For my own part, what with this & that, I think it fairly certain that Massingham's side will now prevail, in some form or other, since even if the Rowntrees are raging as red oxen, they must be open eyed enough to see that they can't safely deposit their trust in the Wee Frees minus Maynard. Then we have £40 from income tax return—I seem to see a feather floating favourably from that region where the Gods abide. So I said as we walked in the cemetery this afternoon. A charwoman was planting hyacinths on a wet grave. She was all wet grey wool; dull, drab, like a jackal; & I prowled too among the graves to look at names, & ascertain who could be deserving of several tons of granite crucifix—the Belgian soldiers, so it turned out. On we walk again. The spring the spring, I sing in imitation of Wagner, & saw a gorze bush set with soft yellow buds. Then we got into the Park, where the rain drove dogs & humans home, & so back, on the stroke of three. It is now our plan (a day old) to walk from 2 to 3; print from 3 to 5; delay our tea; & so make headway. In fact I set up a little of Read. Morgan is finished, save for one last printing off.[12] Ralph sticks on, defiant, argumentative, & gives one the lowest opinion of the manly virtues.

Is Mary an example of the womanly? She may be a good actress. She had a long talk with me two days ago, in the dusk, over the fire. The upshot of it is to my mind a little complex: does Vanessa misrepresent her? I don't accuse her of brilliance & wit. But I *think* I detect a humbler spirit than I expected; she is, she said, shy. And she never likes the people who like her, but attaches herself in spite of all snubs to those she likes. This refers to 46. She has a temper. She flies out. She would like to live with people in numbers—not merely see them. (I thought this sincere). She might be one of those impulsive, affectionate, rather unfortunately concocted natures who are to me interesting, perpetually

11. Played by Fanny Davies and the Bohemian String Quartet.
12. *Mutations of the Phoenix* by Herbert Read (*HP Checklist* 38), and *Pharos and Pharillon* by E. M. Forster (*HP Checklist* 29), were both published in May 1923.

venturing out, rashly importunate, & then snubbed back again; aspiring; fastidious, vain & so on, but impelled by a kind of passion, for Clive, I suppose, which is sincere. Then of course I rate a womans sensibility & sympathy very high, as pleasure givers that is. Nor is she uncritical: far from it. Didn't she tell me she could think me lovable if my desire for admiration about everything were not so insatiable? No, I said, I only want on most points to be assured that I'm of the average human stature. I have my astonishing twists & kinks, as you do. For I couldn't imagine you shy. Yet you say you can hardly brace yourself to enter the Ritz! —your triumphal path, I should have said. And is she really tremulous? a far more instinctive nature than mine or Nessa's & therefore one we are likely to misjudge. Nothing new, she said, would ever happen to her again. She loves pleasure, I note; & though she neither writes nor paints looks forward to the summer. One will get the blinds out, she said. But I suppose I talked most, & about myself. How I'd been depressed since Jan. 3rd. We ran it to earth, I think, by discovering that I began journalism on that day. Last Thursday, I think, I returned to fiction, to the instant nourishment & well being of my entire day. I wonder if this next lap will be influenced by Proust? I think his French language, tradition, &c, prevents that: yet his command of every resource is so extravagant that one can hardly fail to profit, & must not flinch, through cowardice.

Monday 19 February

How it would interest me if this diary were ever to become a real diary: something in which I could see changes, trace moods developing; but then I should have to speak of the soul, & did I not banish the soul when I began? What happens is, as usual, that I'm going to write about the soul, & life breaks in. Talking of diaries sets me thinking of old Kate, in the dining room at 4 Rosary Gardens; & how she opened the cabinet (wh. I remember) & there in a row on a shelf were her diaries from Jan 1 1877.[13] Some were brown; others red; all the same to a t. And I made her read an entry; one of many thousand days, like pebbles on a beach: morning, evening, afternoon, without accent. Oh how strangely unaccented she is, sitting there all of a piece, white, unjointed, level, sagacious, with the mute sagacity of elephant or grey mare! Only

13. VW's cousin Katherine Stephen (1856-1924), retired Principal of Newnham College, lived at 4 Rosary Gardens, South Kensington; Helen (1862-1908), was a younger sister; and 'Nun' was their and VW's aunt Caroline Emilia Stephen (1834-1909).

once or twice did I strike a spark in the one remaining pale blue eye, which is tenderer than the glass one. Orderly solidity marked every atom there. The vases stood on mats: each was supplied with a tuft of mimosa & maidenhair. The Xmas cards—6—were ranged on the mantelpiece. Helen, photo, in frame. Red tiles newly dusted. Green walls. Objects that came from India; bookcase that belonged to Nun. Did I remember it. And said Kate I intend to live to 1944 when I shall be 84. And on her last day she will say to the charwoman who attends her, Bring me the diaries which you will find in the cabinet; & now, put them on the fire. I scarcely tried to disturb what had the sculptured classic appearance of alabaster fruit beneath glass.

In scribbling this, I am led away from my soul, which interests me nevertheless. My soul peeped out. For it is the soul I fancy that comments on visitors & reports their comments, & sometimes sets up such a to-do in the central departments of my machinery that the whole globe of me dwindles to a button head. I think this dwindling is often the result of talking to second rate people. They make the world pinch beck. Now with my dear old Leo, such cheapening is unknown. Oh no, he may refuse to kindle, but he never detracts; & so, when he does kindle, the glow is of the purest fiery red—what I see in the fire now, verging on white.

Philip [Morrell] wished to be an actor, & suffers from dual personality. He sees himself, & seldom unifies—sees himself farmer, host, speaker, & so on. But talking to us he felt himself single, so he said, & there is something diluted in the quality of his emotion. He is an amorous man, a man of a different generation & tradition, in cross over waistcoat & jewels, half man of the world, half aesthete, appreciating furniture that is, but living my word! among what humbugs, & palming them off on us plausibly enough—Ottoline &c. Layers of shifting vapour trail over him perpetually, keep him restless, chattering uneasy. They have shut Julian in a convent school at Roehampton in order to break the stubborn materialism of her nature. She conflicts with Ott's vision of the universe. Philip says she runs after young men. And Philip has had his brat by the parlourmaid. It is all, at the foundations, a little obscene & pullulating, though on the surface so admirable, plausible—yes, plausible in the word that recurs, & uneasy.[14]

We had a surprise visit from the Nicolsons. She is a pronounced Sapphist, & may, thinks Ethel Sands, have an eye on me, old though I am. Nature might have sharpened her faculties. Snob as I am, I trace

14. Philip Morrell dined with the Woolfs on Sunday 18 February; the Nicolsons had been to tea that day.

her passions 500 years back, & they become romantic to me, like old yellow wine. I fancy the tang is gone. Harold is simple down right bluff; wears short black coat & check trousers; wishes to be a writer, but is not I'm told & can believe, adapted by nature. Soul, you see, is framing all these judgments, & saying as she sits by the fire, this is not to my liking, this is second rate, this vulgar; this nice, sincere, & so on. And how should my soul know? My soul diminished, alas, as the evening wore on; & the contraction is almost physically depressing. I reflect though that I'm the sink of 50 million pneumonia germs with a temperature well below normal.[15] And so these contractions are largely physical, I've no doubt. And we are still in suspense. Massingham is back; but Maynard is on the war path. Massm. says he is now going full speed ahead. He has to collect money. Strangely enough, I with my telephone, am acting as go between. I find out Maynard's plans from Nessa; L. telephones them on to Massm. And also I am trying to pull wires, to seat Tom at the Nation as literary editor, & unseat my foe Miss Royde Smith. Had I time I could detail my activities, & glory in my own importance. Yes, I am grown up. I give advice. I am taken seriously; & this no longer flurries me with excitement. I am a little bored indeed, & could wish that poor dear Tom had more spunk in him, less need to let drop by drop of his agonised perplexities fall ever so finely through pure cambric. One waits; sympathises, but it is dreary work. He is like a person about to break down—infinitely scrupulous, tautologous, & cautious.

Poor Snow can scarcely have her portrait drawn.[16] But how I pitied her! like an old woman forced to stare at a pitiless light. The flesh & juice of life have left her. She is brittle, airy, might blow along the gutter. Her old sparks & acidities have dissolved. She was nervous, had lost confidence, as if life had thrown her, but she must still ride on. I could feel her envying me. This I like, but still it depresses me. And then she wavers, apologises, says "Oh you would be bored if I came to stay!" & looks so searchingly at me, & wont be deceived. She amused me by saying that the streets of Cheltenham are notoriously unsafe. Foot passengers are perpetually killed by bicyclists. It is the rarest thing to motor through without being asked to take a corpse to the doctors.

15. During January and February VW suffered from persistent colds and temperatures; an attempt was made to cure this condition by the injection, on 15 February, of pneumonia germs.
16. Margery K. Snowden had been at the Royal Academy Schools with Vanessa at the beginning of the century, and had remained a faithful friend. She lived with a sister in Cheltenham.

And there was her story of the old lady of 94 poking the fire & almost breaking her own body with the coal. Sometimes she does fall down, & is light as a leaf to pick up. She sits in a room with a skylight, & sometimes can see a tree wave, but never goes out.

Tuesday 6 March

Undoubtedly this has been a very unpleasant quarter. I date our misery from Jan. 3rd. The main grievance has been this Nation affair, which hangs over us, lifting, then lowering, as it is at the present moment—low & black over our heads. Massm. goes on April 7th: our income ceases; Maynard has made us no definite offer—but that I think is assured so far as L. goes. But that is only £120 p.a. & we shall have to scrape up the rest rather dismally, doing journalism, I suppose. Msm. is now said to be waiting for the return of a gentleman in the East, who will he is certain finance him. The scheme is off till October anyhow. But its not the money trouble that worries us: but something psychological. The gloom is more on L.'s side than on mine. Mine is a gloom like a mist that comes & goes. One is unsettled. I dip into different circles—like Mary's, E. Sands', the Richmonds' concert, & come home either exalted or depressed. My chairs look dirty. Then the social question rises between L. & me. Are we becoming 'respectable'? Shall we dine with the Richmonds. L. says no. I regret it. Yes, some how I regret it seriously, this shutting of the door upon suburban studies. I love the chatter & excitement of other peoples houses. Have I not just said that it depresses me too? But then I wanted to meet Percy Lubbock & show myself off as a woman who can talk sense. & so on. I ask people here too often. In short I must take the social side into my own hands. I have, I think, got Reading on its feet, & hope to make way, & find my solace in that. But still I want to make life fuller & fuller.

Poor Katherine has taken to revisiting the earth; she has been seen at Brett's; by the charwoman.[1] I feel this somehow a kind of judgment on her for writing the kind of thing she did. Brett told me the story the other day & seemed so bare & rasped that I could not have taken this comfort from her had I wished. Nor do I wish, seriously, to obstruct any decent investigation of brains & nerves, seeing how much I've

1. On Katherine Mansfield's last visit to England in August 1922 she had stayed in Brett's house, 6 Pond Street, Hampstead; the 'sole domestic' there is mentioned in a letter of 29 September (see *The Letters of Katherine Mansfield*, vol. II, p 246). Dunning, whom the Murrys and presumably Brett had met at Garsington, was a practising Yogi; since the previous winter Murry had been his close friend and neighbour at Ditchling, Sussex.

suffered that way myself. But then Brett is not scientific; she at once takes the old fables seriously, & repeats some jargon learnt of Dunning, but no doubt diluted in transit, about day & night, birth, & *therefore* death, all being beautiful. She feels the 'contact' she says; & has had revelations; & there she sits deaf, injured, solitary, brooding over death, & hearing voices, which soon will become, I expect, entirely fabulous; & even now talking to her has a good deal robbed the image of K.M. of its distinctness. For it came distinctly back when I read her letters. And I saw her wink when poor Brett's note was handed in, & she said that little person can wait, or something like that. Now B. idolises her, & invests her with every quality of mind & soul. Do people always get what they deserve, & did K.M. do something to deserve this cheap posthumous life? & am I jealous even now?

No: I think one can be honest at my age.

Old Elena crossed the room to talk to me on Sunday. Oh how shy I was! How matronly & magnificent in a thick rich black way she was! & we couldn't look each other in the eyes—at least I couldn't; & she felt me shabby, self-conscious, suburban no doubt. I am putting down notes to use later in re-constructing this period. There is, I think, a sense of frustration & futility about just now. Partly the Nation again, I've no doubt. partly.... Never mind, I say; once get my claws into my writing & I'm safe. Eliot slightly disillusions me too; he is peevish, plaintive, egotistical; what it amounts to is that poverty is unbecoming. He nibbles at cherries. True, the offer, to co-operate with Royde Smith, is a wizened cherry. But he elaborates & complicates, makes one feel that he dreads life as a cat dreads water. But if I hint so much he is all claws. Now, considering my activity on his behalf no doubt I have some of the vile & patronising feelings of the benefactor. Its American, L. says; that & neurotic. I consulted Bruce Richmond—another proof of my importance. He said emphatically "He's not the man for the job." I can't help agreeing.

But life, life! How I long to take you in my arms & crush you out!

Saturday 17 March

Written, for a wonder at 10 o'clock at night, with L. doing Tolstoi at the white table; the fire rather hot, & my brain saturated with the Silent Woman.[2] I am reading her because we now read plays at 46. 46

2. *Tolstoi's Love Letters* (*HP Checklist* 40), and A. B. Goldenveizer's *Talks with Tolstoi* (*HP Checklist* 32), both translated by Koteliansky and (nominally) VW, were published in May and June 1923. *Epicœne, or the Silent Woman*, a comedy by Ben Jonson, was first acted in 1609.

is become a centre. For how long we don't know, as Maynard's marriage approaches. Nessa, astride her fine Arab, life I mean, takes further upheavals all in the days work. I daresay I shall feel it more. 46 has been very pleasant to me this winter. Two nights ago the Nicolsons dined there. Exposed to electric light eggs show dark patches. I mean we judged them both incurably stupid. He is bluff, but oh so obvious; she, Duncan thought, took the cue from him, & had nothing free to say. There was Lytton, supple & subtle as an old leather glove, to emphasise their stiffness. It was a rocky steep evening. We had the photographs out. Lytton said "I don't like your mother's character. Her mouth seems complaining" & a shaft of white light fell across my dusky rich red past.

And then? As to the soul, I've been snubbed by Squire. I sent him my memoir article, asking terms: he accepted, offering £13; £15 I said, or my ms back; & got it back by return. And now I accept £13—which perhaps I shan't get after all. Yet I dont much mind. & only think that poverty & the shifts it puts one to is unbecoming, as I've said. Poor Tom the other day actually couldn't speak for tears (thanking us) on the telephone. He is broken down, & yet must buckle to & decide: shall he take the Nation? can he defeat Maynard? I'm tired of writing the word guarantee—which is what he claims. To show his state, Richmond actually rang me up at 10 P.M. & asked me to intervene with Maynard. He seemed 'distraught' he said. Whether distraught people can edit the Nation lit. sup. I doubt. And it is more or less my doing. And I dont feel important. And after all we are happy. And Ralph is gone, casually, without good bye. I have seen Osbert Sitwell, Sebastian Sprot & Mr Mortimer.[3] As Nessa says, we are becoming fashionable. Sprot & I lunched at Mary's; then, tipsy with echoing brains, went to tea at Hill's in [Kensington] High Street. Infinitely old I felt & rich; he is very poor. His mother used to attend Barker's linen sales, so that he knew High Street. I dont know why his experience seemed to me so meagre. His father is a solicitor at Crowborough. He wished to meet Ottoline. He is hungry as a wolf, & snapping up delicacies in an alarming way. If at his age I had met Ottoline! —still, I wasn't much older. I have been reflecting about society again, & think one of its merits is that it needs courage. The going into rooms properly dressed is alarming. No one cares for one; that snubs vanity; one is on equal terms with one's

3. Ralph Partridge left the Hogarth Press on 14 March 1923. Raymond Mortimer (b. 1895), 'brought up on' (and reacting against) 'golf courses and racehorses and so on', had been at Balliol College, Oxford, had published one book (*The Oxford Circus*, 1921), and was beginning his distinguished career as a literary journalist and critic.

fellows. The privileges of the fireside no longer prevail. But Ethel [Sands] is off till October; & I don't know where next I shall alight. Indeed this is scribbled before a break.— Only for one month, but then physically, perhaps spiritually, the journey is long. How great writers write at night, I don't know. Its an age since I tried, & I find my head full of pillow stuffing: hot; inchoate. And tomorrow I must get on with How it Strikes a Contemporary.[4] Alas, for the break in my scheme of work—but we must make money, just when I don't want to; & so the novels get shelved, & Reading, which I had tackled afresh, must be put away, & I must accept Desmond's reviewing, & Maynard's too, if offered; still I haven't any good cause to complain.

Friday 23 March

No, not much reason to complain. L. has just come in with an offer from Maynard of the literary editorship of the Nation.[5] Well, thats unexpected! Here have I been toiling these 3 weeks to make Eliot take it; finally he shied; & this is the result. No doubt there are drawbacks, but it means safety for the moment, indeed luxury. And to me it opens interesting vistas—but here I am with the typhoid germs & cant write.

On Tuesday 27 March, by the Newhaven-Dieppe route, the Woolfs crossed the channel for the first time since 1912, and travelled via Paris to Madrid and Granada, and then to Yegen, where they stayed with Gerald Brenan from 5-13 April.[1] On the return journey Brenan accompanied them to Almeira, Murcia, and Alicante; they proceeded to Valencia, Perpignan, Montauban and thence back to Paris, which they reached on 22 April. LW returned to London on 24th, VW on 27 April. While they were away, Vanessa Bell and her family stayed at Monks House.

4. Published in the *TLS*, 5 April 1923 (Kp C231).
5. LW accepted the *Nation* post on conditions that were agreed by Keynes and Hubert Henderson (see *IV LW*, p 97).
1. Gerald Brenan (b. 1894), son of an army officer who intended him for an army career, escaped into a private world of books and poetry and set off to walk to China. He served, however, as an officer throughout the war, during which he became close friends with Ralph Partridge and hence with Carrington, by whom he was for many years obsessed. In 1920 he had gone to live by himself and write in a remote region of Spain; the Woolfs had met him at Tidmarsh in May 1922 on one of his visits to England. (See his autobiographical works *A Life of One's Own* (1962), and *Personal Record 1920-72* (1974); and for a description of the Woolfs' present visit, *South from Granada* (1957)).

Friday 11 May

The long break deserves a line, since I shall scarcely commemorate it otherwise. Have I not with infinite labour, written for the first number of the Nation To Spain?[2] Am I not sitting waiting for L. to 'come back from the office' like other wives. It annoys me to be like other wives. Ah there he is! No: damn it; only Nelly gone out. As I say, I cannot go into the journey, the Temples, Brenan, Spain, Paris, et cetera.[3] I stayed in Paris by way of facing life. Yes, I clap the spurs to my flanks & see myself taking fences gallantly. I 'took Jane [Harrison] & Hope [Mirrlees]; not much else, save the French language, at which I failed ignominiously, & now must learn to speak French if I am in future to respect myself. I meant to use this diary to pull myself up from a fortnights debauch of journalism, Nations affairs, & so on. I must make out a work scheme. But for a moment I will dally with description. Margery [Joad] is doing well, a sign of which is that we now scarcely notice her accent. If she were doing badly it would grate upon us intolerably. We are well up in our books.

Morgan dined here the other night. We tried to cajole him to write with £10 p. 1,000 for bait. "But I dont want £200 a year" he said. "I daresay I could spend it if I had it, but I don't want it." So what vice could we appeal to? Vanity was not much touched. Then he has an ascetic regard for principles. People he respects think that M[assingha]m. was badly treated. At any rate, Morgan wd. not like to write for us, & not for Desmond, who pays £4 instead of £10. He is detached as a saint. And we couldnt press him. So far, we don't feel the Nation blood of our blood. It may turn that way. We work very hard at it. It has temptations & attractions. How they balance the drawbacks I don't yet know. I like having the pick of new books. My own authority over the reviewing staff is not very exciting. I am a little malicious perhaps. People crowd & crush & press for work. It is mildly amusing to say, now don't worry, I'm not going to give you any. I have been so often in their position. But these delights are not very profound. I'm afraid it looks as though Reading must again be shelved. I can't afford not to make hay just now. One article a month paid at £15 or so. And that precisely uses the time I had to spend from writing my novel. Yet, to

2. 'To Spain' (Kp C233) appeared in the first number of the *Nation & Athenaeum* to appear under the new dispensation, i.e. on 5 May 1923.
3. On their way to his home in the remote Sierra Nevada, the Woolfs had been met by Gerald Brenan at Granada, where they spent two nights with his friends Charles Lindsay Temple (1871-1929), a former Governor of Nigeria, and his wife. See also *III VW Letters*, nos. 1376, 1380.

take up my work account, I think I must edge in a little time every now
& then at Reading. I am at the Greek chapter (in reading). Shall I read
a little Greek? My notion is that I can only sketch the chapter, & must
perpetually enrich it from time to time. Or shall I plunge into early
Elizabethans, of whom I am appallingly ignorant? What happened
between Chaucer & Shakespeare? I think that attracts me as a basis.
Make notes then; &, directly opportunity offers, dash in at the Pastons
& Chaucer. One might read Troilus & Cressida; but I dont feel inclined.

Sunday 12 May

It is a curious fact that I can write this diary when I am too much
distracted to read. Being Sunday, I am clearing off old letters, half formal;
& seven strikes; & 15 minutes can't be made much of for any purpose.
I might attempt a portrait. Karin was here yesterday with Ann. Adrian
is altogether broken up by psycho analysis.[4] (long interruption question
of printing Read) His soul rent in pieces with a view to reconstruction.
The doctor says he is a tragedy: & this tragedy consists in the fact that
he can't enjoy life with zest. I am probably responsible. I should have
paired with him, instead of hanging on to the elders. So he wilted, pale,
under a stone of vivacious brothers & sisters. Karin says we shall see a
great change in 3 months. But Noel [Olivier] would have done what none
of these doctors can do. The truth is that Karin, being deaf, & as she
honestly says, "Your sister-in-law lacks humanity, as perhaps you've
noticed", the truth is she does not fertilise the sunk places in Adrian.
Neither did I. Had mother lived, or father been screened off—well, it
puts it too high to call it a tragedy. Ann is like him, pale, lank, sensitive,
with the long cold fingers I know so well. For my part, I doubt if family
life has all the power of evil attributed to it, or psycho-analysis of good.
I liked Karin; pitied her too; & then felt come over me some mood of
depression, not worth entering upon here.
    Morgan told me that when he & Mortimer discussed novelists the
other day they agreed that Lawrence & I were the only two whose future
interested them. They think of my next book, which I think of calling
"The Hours", with excitement. This does encourage me. Oddly enough,
I get praise from my contemporaries, or youngers; never from old stagers,
who are said to step so generously from their platforms with words of
encouragment.

4. Adrian Stephen began his analysis under Dr James Glover and continued it,
   following the latter's death in 1926, under Ella Sharpe.

Monday 4 June

Nat. 1...	
N.S.	..3
Times	5
June Nat	10
July Nat.	10
Sept. Nat	10
	———
	2:18

But I cannot describe Garsington.[1] Thirty seven people to tea; a bunch of young men no bigger than asparagus; walking to & fro, round & round; compliments, attentions, & then this slippery mud —which is what interests me at the moment. A loathing overcomes me of human beings—their insincerity. their vanity—A wearisome & rather defiling talk with Ott. last night is the foundation of this complaint—& then the blend in one's own mind of suavity & sweetness with contempt & bitterness. Her egotism is so great. "I am much more sensitive than most people" she said to Julian: the first words she said that she meant. She returns to that subject again & again—to herself that is. And her lies have taken away all outlines. Yet on Saturday night I liked her. This was all clear to me a few minutes ago, but now I cannot write it.

Lyt[t]on & I talked all the way up in the train. He had seen a Greek Temple at Segestum.[2] And that's what I adore in him—his enthusiasm for beauty. He said it was like Sophocles. You saw the sea through the columns. Then we discussed Sh[akespea]re: he said he wanted to write about Shre as a dramatist; not as a philosopher or poet. He wanted to discuss his contrasts. The scene with Emilia in Othello for instance. And he may write on Lear from this point of view. And Sir Thomas Browne, & the letters of Phalaris;[3] I think he has written something that pleases him. He is absolutely happy. He is in love with Ralph. He has that extraordinary simplicity he said tenderly, tremulously, talking of Ralph & Othello. But why not let oneself be content in the thought of Lytton —so true, gentle, infinitely nimble, & humane? I seldom rest long in complete agreement with anyone. But here I think one's feelings should be unqualified.

Lord David is a pretty boy. Puffin Asquith an ugly one—wizened, unimpressive, sharp, like a street boy. Sackville West reminded me of

1. The Woolfs went to Garsington on the afternoon of Saturday 2 June. LW went home on Sunday evening and VW returned with Lytton on Monday.
2. In the spring Lytton, with Carrington and Ralph Partridge, had joined James and Alix Strachey for a two months' Mediterranean tour, visiting Algeria, Tunisia, Sicily and Italy. They had stayed a week at Palermo, which had enabled Lytton to see Segesta.
3. Lytton Strachey did not at least *publish* anything after this date specifically upon *King Lear*, Sir Thomas Browne (1605-1682), or the spurious *Epistles of Phalaris* edited by Charles Boyle in 1695.

a peevish shop girl. They have all the same clipped quick speech & politeness, & total insignificance. Yet we asked Ld David & Puff to write for the Nation, & also a dull fat man called Hartley.[4] What puts me on edge is that I'm writing like this here, & spoke so differently to Ott. I'm over peevish in private, partly in order to assert myself. I am a great deal interested suddenly in my book. I want to bring in the despicableness of people like Ott: I want to give the slipperiness of the soul. I have been too tolerant often. The truth is people scarcely care for each other. They have this insane instinct for life. But they never become attached to anything outside themselves. Puff said he loved his family, & had nothing whatever to knock over. He disliked cold indecency. So did Lord David. This must be a phrase in their set. Puff said—I dont quite know what. I walked round the vegetable garden with him, passing Lytton flirting with Byam Shaw on a green seat; & round the field with Sackville West, who said he was better & was writing a better novel, & round the lake with Menasseh (?) an Egyptian Jew, who said he liked his family, & they were mad & talked like books;[5] & he said that they quoted my writings (the Oxford youth) & wanted me to go & speak; & then there was Mrs Asquith. I was impressed. She is stone white: with the brown veiled eyes of an aged falcon; & in them more depth & scrutiny than I expected; a character, with her friendliness, & ease, & decision. Oh if we could have had Shelley's poems, & not Shelley the man! she said. Shelley was quite intolerable, she pronounced; she is a rigid frigid puritan; & in spite of spending thousands on dress. She rides life, if you like; & has picked up a thing or two, which I should like to plunder & never shall. She led Lytton off, & plucked his arm, & hurried, & thought 'people' pursued her; yet was very affable with 'people' when she had to be; sat on the window

4. Lord (Edward Christian) David Gascoyne-Cecil (b. 1902), younger son of the 4th Marquess of Salisbury and a nephew of VW's friends Lord Robert and Lady Eleanor Cecil; he was still an undergraduate at Christ Church. Anthony ('Puffin') Asquith (1902-68), only son of Mr Asquith the former Liberal Prime Minister and his second wife Margot; he was at Balliol. The Hon. Edward Charles Sackville-West (1901-65), only son and heir of 4th Baron Sackville, and a cousin of Vita's; he was at Christ Church. Leslie Poles Hartley (1895-1972), had returned to Balliol after war service. Asquith was to become a notable film director; the other three, writers of some reputation.

5. James Byam Shaw (b. 1903), scholar of Westminster and Christ Church, later to become a distinguished authority on Old Master drawings; Jean André Moise de Menasce (b. 1902), son of Baron Felix de Menasce of Alexandria, was at Balliol from 1921-24; he was later to join the Dominican order and became the Rev. Father Pierre de Menasce.

sill talking to a black shabby embroideress, to whom Ott. is being kind. Thats one of her horrors—she's always being kind in order to say to herself at night & then Ottoline invites the poor little embroideress to her party, & so to round off her own picture of herself. To sneer like this has a physical discomfort in it. She told me I looked wonderfully well, wh. I disliked. Why? I wonder. Because I had had a headache perhaps, partly. But to be well & use strength to get more out of life is, surely, the greatest fun in the world. What I dislike is feeling that I'm always taking care, or being taken care of. Never mind—work, work. Lytton says we have still 20 years before us. Mrs Asquith said she loved Scott. If I had time I would describe my surprise visit from Sydney, & my revelations about Murry's duplicity.[6] This is a very great shock, Sydney said. Sydney said that Murry has an angel & a devil in him. That is melodramatic said Sydney; but I do believe it. Dunning believes it. I cant help liking Sydney—fundamentally honest; fundamentally weak; gullible; & now settling down to 'repose', which is very delightful. And he's a vegetarian. Such a simplification, he said. But if I saw you every day for a week I could tell you what has been happening to me. Vegetarianism is part of a whole revolution— Don't I know it without being told it. And the Adelphi would inform me, were I ignorant.[7] Now for Urn Burial for the Times.[8]

Wednesday 13 June

Nessa is back & the London season of course in full swing.[9] So I judged yesterday in the Aeolian Hall, listening, in a dazed way, to Edith

6. 'Murry's duplicity' probably refers to VW's misapprehension that J. M. Murry had offered to serve as literary editor of the *Nation* until a permanent appointment might be made. VW certainly told Sydney Waterlow something of the sort at some point, as she writes to correct her inaccuracy later in the month; see *III VW Letters*, no. 1402. She also it seems told Ottoline Morrell, *ibid* no. 1400. Murry had apparently offered only to write for the paper and to help out generally during the transitional period after the overall editorship had passed from H. W. Massingham to Hubert Henderson.

7. Since Katherine's death, Murry had experienced a mystical sense of re-birth. With the support of Tomlinson and Sullivan and with Koteliansky as business manager, he had just launched a new monthly, *The Adelphi*; its contents were selected in accordance with the criterion 'significance for life'. The introductory editorial was personal and intense, and the first number was a sell-out.

8. VW's article *Sir Thomas Browne*, *TLS*, 28 June 1923 (Kp C235), dealt not only with that writer's *Urn Burial* but also with *The Garden of Cyrus* and *Religio Medici*.

9. Vanessa Bell and Duncan Grant had been in Spain, where they had been joined for a while by Roger Fry.

Sitwell vociferating through the megaphone.[10] There was Lady Colefax
in her hat with the green ribbons. Did I say that I lunched with her
last week? That was Derby Day & it rained, & all the light was brown
& cold, & she went on talking talking, in consecutive sentences like
the shavings that come from planes, artificial, but unbroken. It was not
a successful party, Clive & Lytton & me. For Clive's back; & he dined
here with Leo Myers the other night; & then I went to Golders Green
& sat with Mary Sheepshanks in her garden, & beat up the waters of
talk, as I do so courageously, so that life mayn't be wasted. The fresh
breeze went brushing all the thick hedges which divide the gardens.[11]
Somehow, extraordinary emotions possessed me. I forget now what.
Often now I have to control my excitement—as if I were pushing
through a screen; or as if something beat fiercely close to me. What this
portends I don't know. It is a general sense of the poetry of existence
that overcomes me. Often it is connected with the sea & St Ives. Going
to 46 continues to excite. Dear old Nessa returned shabby, loose, easy;
& 44, so she said. The sight of 2 coffins in the Underground luggage
office I daresay constricts [?] all my feelings. I have the sense of the
flight of time; & this shores up my emotions. N. & I sat talking, both
now well known women, if it comes to that. At dinner we discussed
what school Quentin should go to. "He means to be a painter", said
Nessa. "Yes" said Quentin, as if he were saying "yes, I am in love."
At least it made me feel queer.

Nothing else of great importance has happened. I should be describing
Edith Sitwell's poems, but I kept saying to myself "I dont really understand . . . I dont really admire." The only view, presentable view that I
framed, was to the effect that she was monotonous. She has one tune
only on her merry go round. And she makes her verse keep step
accurately to the Hornpipe. This seems to be wrong; but I'm all sandy
with writing criticism, & must be off to my book again. Leo Myers,
who is glazed with disillusionment & middle age, as tongues are glazed,

10. The occasion was the first public performance of *Façade*, a collaborative effort
by the Sitwells and the composer William Walton, in which the words and
voice (both Edith Sitwell's) were intended to play an equal and interdependent
part with the instrumental music. The poems were recited through a 'Senger-
phone' which protruded through the mouth of a grotesque head in the centre
of a drop-curtain painted by Frank Dobson. The performance called forth almost
universal obloquy from the press.
11. Mary Sheepshanks (*c.* 1870-1958), campaigner for women's suffrage, from 1899
to 1913 effective principal of Morley College where, in 1905, VW had taught
working men and women. She lived in the 'Garden Suburb' of Golders Green,
at Middle Way, NW11.

said that my turn & turn about method is wrong.[12] The Drs say so. He goes in for this kind of frigid examination of things. He has no impulses, nothing to do. He goes out every night everywhere. Clive & he capped stories of the demi-monde. Next day Clive rang up & said he had been ashamed. I fancy Clive is trying to take in a reef or two in his white waistcoat of dissipation. And as usual I want—I want— But what do I want? Whatever I had, I should always say I want, I want. Yet it comes over me that to sit on the grass at the Horse Show tomorrow with L. will be very contenting. But then I want to go to the Opera. Leo Myers said we all feel excluded. Yet he has 8,000 a year, tax free, 2 houses, 2 children, 1 motor car. We try to impress each other, he said; & had told me of a journey to Cherbourg for this purpose. True, I was deeply impressed. I said to myself he crossed in the Aquitania:[13] then he was quite free to go anywhere he liked. His life was full of romance. And it was I who got the romance by thinking this, not poor Leo, who is glazed like a tongue.

For the rest, I should be writing to Mrs Eliot. & will, now, directly, on the instant.[14] I say nothing about Duncan's show: about Mollie Hamilton or Henderson who dined last night, or Bob.[15]

Tuesday 19 June

I took up this book with a kind of idea that I might say something about my writing—which was prompted by glancing at what K.M. said

12. Leopold Hamilton Myers (1881-1944), educated at Eton and Trinity College, Cambridge, where he was contemporary with Clive Bell and LW; his delicate health and ample means allowed him to lead a leisured and uneventful life, pursuing his philosophical and literary interests. His novel *The Orissers* had been published earlier in 1923. His wife was American.

13. The Cunard transatlantic liner *Aquitania*, launched in 1914 and refitted after war service, was known as the 'Aristocrat of the Atlantic'.

14. Vivienne Eliot, *née* Haigh-Wood (1888-1947), had married T. S. Eliot in 1915; since then her perpetual ill-health, apparently neurotic in origin and which had recently brought her close to death, had formed the background to his life. No letter to her from VW at this time is known, though in a later letter (*III VW Letters*, no. 1416) VW says 'poor Mrs Eliot had a relapse' as a result of her reckless habit of letter-writing.

15. 'Recent Paintings and Drawings by Duncan Grant' were shown at the Independent Gallery, 7a Grafton Street, W1, in June; the exhibition comprised 27 paintings (including a portrait of Lydia Lopokova) and 13 drawings. Hubert Douglas Henderson (1890-1952), recently appointed editor of the reconstituted *Nation & Athenaeum*, had been a Fellow of Clare College and Lecturer in Economics at Cambridge University, 1919-23; he had married Faith Bagenal in 1915.

about *her* writing in the Dove's Nest. But I only glanced. She said a good deal about feeling things deeply: also about being pure, which I wont criticise, though of course I very well could.[16] But now what do I feel about *my* writing?—this book, that is, The Hours, if thats its name? One must write from deep feeling, said Dostoevsky. And do I? Or do I fabricate with words, loving them as I do? No I think not. In this book I have almost too many ideas. I want to give life & death, sanity & insanity; I want to criticise the social system, & to show it at work, at its most intense— But here I may be posing. I heard from Ka this morning that she doesn't like In the Orchard.[17] At once I feel refreshed. I become anonymous, a person who writes for the love of it. She takes away the motive of praise, & lets me feel that without any praise, I should be content to go on. This is what Duncan said of his painting the other night. I feel as if I slipped off all my ball dresses & stood naked—which as I remember was a very pleasant thing to do. But to go on. Am I writing The Hours from deep emotion? Of course the mad part tries me so much, makes my mind squint so badly that I can hardly face spending the next weeks at it. Its a question though of these characters. People, like Arnold Bennett, say I cant create, or didn't in J's R, characters that survive.[18] My answer is—but I leave that to the Nation: its only the old argument that character is dissipated into shreds now: the old post-Dostoevsky argument. I daresay its true, however, that I haven't that 'reality' gift. I insubstantise, wilfully to some extent, distrusting reality—its cheapness. But to get further. Have I the power of conveying the true reality? Or do I write essays about myself? Answer these questions as I may, in the uncomplimentary sense, & still there remains this excitement. To get to the bones, now I'm writing fiction again I feel my force flow straight from me at its fullest. After a dose of criticism I feel that I'm writing sideways, using only an angle of my

16. J. M. Murry's introductory note to *The Doves' Nest and Other Stories* (1923) by Katherine Mansfield contains several extracts from the author's *Journal*. In these she talks of the need for her writing to be '*deeply felt*' and of her feeling not 'pure in heart, not humble, not good'. See also below, 28 June 1923, n 22.

17. 'In the Orchard' was published in the *Criterion* in April 1923 (Kp C232). Ka Arnold-Forster wrote from Cornwall on 17 June 1923 (MHP, Sussex): 'No, I don't think I really liked in the Orchard—but then I'm a jealous critic—& I love you very much.'

18. Arnold Bennett's article 'Is the Novel Decaying?' appeared in *Cassell's Weekly* on 28 March 1923 (see *M & M*, p 112). 'I have seldom read a cleverer book than Virginia Woolf's *Jacob's Room*. . . . But the characters do not vitally survive in the mind because the author has been obsessed by details of originality and cleverness.'

mind. This is justification; for free use of the faculties means happiness. I'm better company, more of a human being. Nevertheless, I think it most important in this book to go for the central things, even though they dont submit, as they should however, to beautification in language. No, I don't nail my crest to the Murrys, who work in my flesh after the manner of the jigger insect.[19] Its annoying, indeed degrading, to have these bitternesses. Still, think of the 18th Century. But then they were overt, not covert, as now.

I foresee, to return to The Hours, that this is going to be the devil of a struggle. The design is so queer & so masterful. I'm always having to wrench my substance to fit it. The design is certainly original, & interests me hugely. I should like to write away & away at it, very quick and fierce. Needless to say, I cant. In three weeks from today I shall be dried up.

Having made this very inadequate confession about the soul, I may turn now to the body—which is money & America & Mr Crowninshield.[20] I'm asked to write for Vanity Fair & shall be paid says Clive £25 for 1500 words: & get £15 from the Nation; & two months ago I was hawking articles of 5,000 words to Jack Squire for £13.

Do you like becoming famous? Marjorie [Joad] asked me yesterday. The truth is I'm being pushed up, but many people are saying that I shant last, & perhaps I shant. So I return to my old feeling of nakedness as the backbone of my existence, which indeed it is.

For the rest, it is observed in Cornwall & the remoter parts of Weybridge[21] that we are living through a storm of obloquy & must be entirely engrossed in the Nation's affairs. It is not so at Hogarth House: I'm no longer so excited about the contents of L.'s dispatch box. But one thing I do feel pretty certain about & here confide it to my diary—we must leave Richmond & set up in London. The arguments are so well known to me that I cant bother to write them down. But when things come upon me in a clap I generally achieve them, because they are then things that matter to me. Leonard remains to be converted, & my God, the move—the horror—the servants. Still this is life—never to be sitting down for longer than one feels inclined.

19. The jigger insect: an americanism—harvester, harvest bug or tick, a very small but troublesome mite.
20. Francis (Frank) Welch Crowninshield (1872-1947), editor of the New York Vanity Fair from 1914-35.
21. A further reference to the letter from Ka mentioned above (footnote 17). E. M. Forster lived with his mother at Weybridge; LW no doubt had some talk with him at the Society (Apostles') dinner which was on 15 June.

Thursday 28 June

This may be life; but I doubt that I shall ever convert L. & now sit down baffled & depressed to face a life spent, mute & mitigated, in the suburbs, just as I had it in mind that I could at last go full speed ahead. For the capacities in me will never after 40, accumulate again. And I mind missing life far more than he does, for it isn't life to him in the sense that it is life to me. Oh to be able to slip in & out of things easily, to be in them, not on the verge of them—I resent this effort & waste. My evening is now wasted because I'm dining with the Myers. But what should be my course now? Really, I think, to find out exactly how much I mean by this. But half the horror is that L. instead of being, as I gathered, sympathetic has the old rigid obstacle—my health. And I cant sacrifice his peace of mind, yet the obstacle is surely now a dead hand, which one should no longer let dominate our short years of life— oh to dwindle them out here, with all these gaps, & abbreviations! Always to catch trains, always to waste time, to sit here & wait for Leonard to come in, to spend hours standing at the box of type with Margery, to wonder what its all for—when, alternatively, I might go & hear a tune, or have a look at a picture, or find out something at the British Museum, or go adventuring among human beings. Sometimes I should merely walk down Cheapside. But now I'm tied, imprisoned, inhibited. All I can do is to pretend I'm writing something very important, or reading with a view to a book I shall never write. (I'm letting my pen fling itself on paper like a leopard starved for blood—& I must wash & dress—so do not, in years to come, look too harshly upon this first outcry, the expression of many yet unheard). This is the pith of my complaint. For ever to be suburban. L. I don't think minds any of this as much as I do. But then, Lord! (not Lord in K.M.'s serious sense[22]) what I owe to him! What he gives me! Still, I say, surely we could get more from life than we do—isn't he too much of a Puritan, of a disciplinarian, doesn't he through birth & training accept a drastic discipline too tamely, or rather, with too Spartan a self control? There is, I suppose, a very different element in us; my social side, his intellectual side. This social side is very genuine in me. Nor do I think it reprehensible. It is a piece of jewellery I inherit from my mother—a joy in laughter, something that is stimulated, not selfishly wholly or vainly, by contact with my friends. And then ideas leap in me. Moreover, for my work now,

22. 'Lord, make me crystal clear for thy light to shine through.' Quoted from Katherine Mansfield's journal by Murry in his introductory note to *The Doves' Nest and Other Stories*, 1923.

I want freer intercourse, wider intercourse—& now, at 41, having done a little work, I get my wages partly in invitations. I might know people. In Richmond this is impossible. Either we have arduous parties at long intervals, or I make my frenzied dashes up to London, & leave, guiltily, as the clock strikes 11.

But let me bethink me that L. is very hard worked: the present state must go on till next Christmas, & to be forever worrying is fatal & cruel & only makes the question harder to settle amicably. Still I own I am depressed & baffled.

Saturday 8 July

So we went to dine with the Myers; & it is now the hottest day of the year. & I don't want to grumble; having seen many people—Anyhow, if a move is to be made, it can't be till the autumn, or new year. Anyhow I am content at present, or moderately so. I am alive; rather energetic; asked to write for 2 American papers, & so on & so on. I never said that Vanity Fair has invited me & the Dial & new Broom as well as the Nation & the Times, so that I can't help thinking myself about as successful journalistically as any woman of my day.[1] But that is not saying much. I wish I could write The Hours as freely & vigorously as I scribble Freshwater, a Comedy.[2] Its a strange thing how arduous I find my novels; & yet Freshwater is only spirited fun; & The Hours has some serious merit. I should like though to get speed & life into it. I got tempted, a week ago, into comedy writing, & have scribb[l]ed daily, & trust it will be done tomorrow. Yet I feel some reluctance to screw myself to The Hours again. Never mind. Should it bore me, into the fire with it!

The very thought of a fire is uncomfortable. I have said nothing about the weather for ages. How May & June melted into thin cold cloud. They were plucked from the year. By the way, on re-reading this book I resolved to write rather more carefully, & to record conversations verbatim. It is difficult to write carefully, as I am always

1. There is no record that VW ever did contribute to Frank Crowninshield's *Vanity Fair*, but this year her work was published in *Broom* (the New York successor to the international magazine of the arts edited by Harold Loeb and previously published in Italy); in the *New Republic*; and in the *Dial* (see Kp C232, C233, and C238).

2. Four years earlier VW had noted 'the superb possibilities of Freshwater, for a comedy'. (See *I VW Diary*, 30 January 1919); it was not in fact to be completed or performed until January 1935; it was published in 1976 with a preface by Lucio P. Ruotolo.

having at this book by way of killing time, filling time, or writing out the fidgets. As for recording conversations, nothing is harder. Let me try.

Desmond ⎫
Janet ⎪
Leonard ⎬ Scene tea-time Friday, 6th.
Virginia ⎭

Desmond I can't stay to dinner. No I must get back to my mother. She's become quite an old woman. She was thrown 10 yards by the cab, & though no bones were broken, she has lost her memory. She tells the same story over again. She never stops talking about her accident. I am taking her down to the Isle of Wight.

Enter Janet I was determined to come—

Virginia And is the Forest very lovely?

Desmond All the oaks are being devoured by caterpillars. Yes, you can hear a pattering sound beneath the trees. That is the caterpillars munching. And if they eat a tree for 3 years, it is dead.

Janet O how dreadful! I do hope that hasn't happened to our oak trees.

Leonard Well, Desmond have we settled our quarrel.

V. (explaining to Janet)
Theyre rival's you see. Desmond edits the New Statesman. They steal each others reviewers.

Leonard Desmond steals my reviewers.

Desmond Oh, the quarrel's all made up—I say who have you got this week:

L. Bertie & Graves.[3]

Desmond Oh thats all right. My Bertie comes next week.

So some gossip about the Nation.

Desmond Have you read the second number of the Adelphi? Have you read Murry "I have been a miserable sinner (acting & striking his breast). I have lied, I have swindled. I have laughed at what I love; but *now* I am speaking the truth." He's like a revivalist preacher. I saw Sullivan last week end. He says he doesn't agree with Murry. Hes not one of the push. He says you couldn't think him sincere if you only judged him by this evidence. But he says he is sincere.

3. i.e. Bertrand Russell and Robert Ranke Graves (b. 1895), poet, who went straight from school into the army in 1914, and after the war to Oxford, and was now on the literary treadmill. His long poem *The Feather Bed* was about to be published by the Hogarth Press (*HP Checklist* 33).

Le.   Its John Bull over again.[4] "If every reader will get another reader"—& that on top of his revelations about Katherine's death!

V.   I dont object to opening the heart, but I do object to finding it empty. Murry has nothing whatever to reveal. Yet he has sold his reticence.

Janet   Dear dear, dear dear! He talks about his wife's death? Dear, dear.

Desmond   Mortimer has done Katherine this week.[5] But he's not got to the bottom of her. Nor did I.

V.   I say Desmond, whatever the reason may be, the Hawk gets daily better & better. Its never been so good. People talk about the Hawk: about reading the paper for the Hawk.[6]

Des   Oh come Virginia, it wasn't as bad as all that before!

more gossip between Desmond & Leonard.

Janet (to me)

[*Tuesday 17 July*]

I forget now, it being Tuesday 17th July what Janet said. It was a hot day, I remember. Let me try another conversation. But there have been so many. Shall we attempt old Birrell the other night?

Persons: Aug. Birrell: Francis B. Tony B. L. & V.

Scene 70 Elm Park Road: first dark pannelled dining room; later the library, a room just beneath the grass of a large garden. Books all round; regular, back to back books in series & editions. Framed autographs on walls. One from Lamb. "Mary has got to leave me—She is going to be ill. Tell Forster."[7]

4. A reference to the promotional methods of the financial swindler Horatio Bottomley who had founded the popular weekly *John Bull* in 1906. For over two years, Murry introduced his selections from Katherine Mansfield's literary remains into every issue of his *Adelphi*.

5. In his review 'New Novels' in the *New Statesman* of 7 July 1923, Raymond Mortimer devoted the greater part of his page to a consideration of Katherine Mansfield's gift, arising from the posthumous publication of her stories *The Doves' Nest*.

6. 'Affable Hawk' was how Desmond signed his weekly 'Books in General' column in the *New Statesman*.

7. This must have been the letter written in April 1833 by Charles Lamb to Edward Moxon (see *Letters of Charles Lamb* ... edited by E. V. Lucas, 1935, vol. III, p 336): 'Mary is going off to be ill again. . . . Pray convey this to Forster as soon as you can. He was to come on Sunday. C. Lamb. Pray let Forster know.' (John Forster became Charles Dickens's biographer.)

A. Birrell Oh, thats dreadful.

He is a large fine untidy old man, in blue shirt, grey hair, no tie. Very vigorous & manly in the Victorian style.

I went to hear Dickens read at Liverpool (he gave away prizes). He had to name a girl called Weller—Miss Weller, he said: & I assure you there were Bishops, Mayors, Judges—every sort of person—& they roared with laughter. No other human being could have done that by just mentioning one of his own characters. You would have taken him for an actor—or a seafaring man. He had a blue coat; & a great necktie.—a wonderful looking man.

V.   (obediently, filially) And Thackeray, did you know?

A.B. No, never saw him.

V.   (‖   ‖   ) You should write your memoirs.

A.B. Good gracious no.

F.B. I can read all biographies—all childhoods anyhow.

A.B. (somehow got on to the Harmsworths). I knew Alfred, the father —an old Bailey Barrister—a nice chap, who *may* have drunk a little too much—may have. Well he was Vice President of a Club wh. met up at St Johns Wood, the Eyre Arms, I think, called what was it? The Sylvan, because they met in a wood—& I went sometimes & we debated—all young fellows. One night walking on the Embankment I met Alfred, very down on his luck he was. I'm going to die he said, & I've done nothing. I'm leaving my wife, & six children (I think he said) & I've done nothing. Well, I had an inspiration. My dear chap, I said, you've done the only thing you could do, & dont you worry, I said. Take my word for it, one of those boys'll do well. They'll look after their mother, I said; & so we parted. He died in a fortnight. And sure enough, the great Alfred got going, & made a fortune ever so soon, & every penny went to the old lady. One night I was splashed with mud from head to foot in Piccadilly, & there was the old lady, sitting in her barouche, furs on her knee, two horses, driving off to Berkely Street. Always his mother came first. When I knew them there was a smell of cold mutton & boots all over the house. But I saw what a remarkable woman she was. She controlled everything. And now she's still alive, & Lady Nth. has married my old friend Hudson.[8]

8. Alfred Harmsworth, a Dublin barrister, exchanged the Irish for the English bar in 1867; he had three daughters and seven sons, of whom the eldest, Alfred Charles William Harmsworth (1865-1922) became the great press lord and, in 1905, 1st Viscount Northcliffe. The latter was conspicuously devoted to his mother, born Geraldine Mary Maffett of county Down (who lived until 1925). His own widow,

(Somehow we got on to Hardy's novels; how he makes a woman confess she's had a bastard on her wedding night; upon wh. the husband packs his bag & goes to the South Seas[9]).

A.B. vehemently— You're all children. You dont know what your talking about. I'd have done the same. I'd have packed my bag anyhow. Silly woman! She should have told him in the cornfield— It was a silly disgusting thing to do. Its not a question of morality. Morality dont change. Its human nature.

F.B. My dear old Pater you're talking nonsense.

(They were very affectionate: Francis helping him to address Lady Wimborne's telegram correctly, which I don't think he could have done without).

V. Tennyson is a great poet.

A.B. Certainly he's a poet, not a great poet. Hallam was a donkey. Shall never forget his telegram to Eleanor: Passed away peacefully at 3.45. Liked Austin's book. Hallam carried his mother on his back. It was thought so beautiful. So he never had a profession & didn't want one. He was a lazy man. Tennyson was a very direct creature—didn't like second marriages. didn't like Lionel's dying at sea—no sod to visit—very old fashioned, conventional views.[10]

(Told the story of Ellen Terry running round the bedroom naked, & Watts going to Harcourt & saying "It frightened me." "It wouldn't have frightened me" said Harcourt, very loud & bluff.)[11]

Tony Birrell in a high shrill falling voice, he squints rather, is pale, wears spectacles, & suddenly disappears to range about the garden alone.

I had a letter from Hester the other day. She was coming here, but

---

Viscountess Northcliffe, *née* Mary Elizabeth Milner, married Sir Robert Arundell Hudson (1864-1927) in 1923.

9. The husband was Angel Clare in *Tess of the D'Urbervilles*, and it was Brazil that he went to.

10. Tennyson's elder son Hallam (1852-1928), the second Lord Tennyson, lived with his parents; according to the DNB, the Poet Laureate 'passed away' at 1.35 am on 6 October 1892. This news was telegraphed to Eleanor (*née* Locker) widow of Tennyson's second son Lionel (1854-1886), who died of jungle fever aboard ship in the Red Sea on his way home from India. In 1888 she had married Augustine Birrell, himself a widower, bore him two sons (Francis and Anthony), and died in 1915. Austin's book, unexplained.

11. In 1864 the painter G. F. Watts (1817-1904) married Ellen Terry (1847-1928), later the celebrated actress. As may be guessed from the above anecdote, the marriage was a failure. Sir William Harcourt (1827-1904), the Liberal statesman, was painted by Watts.

the motor car broke down!! (as if this were a surprising piece of news).

F.B. Tony, you look after the drinks don't you.

Tony goes & fidgets at the sideboard.

In the end A.B. gave me Boswell's Corsica, & wrote "to Victoria Woolf . . ." then wrote to apologise.[12] An interesting evening, highly Victorian, well furnished with drink & cigars & carpets & leather chairs. Old B. is a storyteller, & has had his day: been a figure in society, yet remains non conformist; not, I think, a very serious writer, but a good Victorian all round humane literary type, sunned by various kinds of life, as we aren't now—barrister, politician, essayist. He is anxious to write for L.

Persons: *Vivien Eliot, Tom; Sunday tea.*

Tom.   Put brandy in your tea, Vivien.

          No, no, Tom.

          Yes. You must. Put a tea spoonful of brandy in your tea.

Vivien. Oh all right—I don't want it.

V.   One doesn't like taking medicine before one's friends.

L.   What about the great question—the Adelphi? Whats to be said?

Vvn   What indeed? (she's very nervous, very spotty, much powdered, her first drive, overdressed, perhaps.)

Tom   I have put a note in the Criterion. I don't understand this business about Wells & life—this confusion that literature is not life.[13]

V.   Shall you write.

Tom.   Oh dear no. Murry is now comfortable for the first time. He's in the society he likes.

Vivien I'm living between him & Mr Joyce. Mr Joyce is very nice.

Tom   His wife is very nice too—& the children. Giorgio is away in la Banque Generale (he pronounces French always with great care & pride).[14]

V.   I've been setting up your poem. Its a good poem.

Vivien a damned good poem, did you say?

12. *An Account of Corsica. The Journal of a Tour to that Island; and Memoirs of Pascal Paoli.* By James Boswell Esq. A reprint, edited by S. C. Roberts, of the original edition of 1768 had just been issued by the Cambridge University Press.

13. Eliot's 'note' appears in the *Criterion* for July 1923; he maintained that those who 'affirm an antimony between 'life' and 'literature' are not only 'flattering the complacency of the half educated', but 'asserting a principle of disorder'. He does not refer to Wells.

14. James Joyce and his wife Nora, *née* Barnacle, spent the summer (mid-June to August) in England, staying for the greater part of their visit at Bognor in Sussex where they were visited by T. S. Eliot. Giorgio Joyce (b. 1905) worked in the Banque Nationale du Crédit in Paris.

V.   Well, you've improved what I said. But it is a d——d good
poem.[15]

Cetera disunt.

My impression being that they were nervous, contrasted us with them,
& liked us & our surroundings. And on the drive home, I daresay
Vivien said "Why can't we get on as the Woolves do?" I think they
meant us to feel them in sympathy together. Certainly they were lighter,
more affectionate.

Sunday 22 July

A great many conversations to record: dined with Mortimer &
Schofield Thayer the other night & went on with them to Mary's.[16]

Mortimer is Oxford, & thus not nearly so easy to come to terms with
as Sebastian [Sprott] for instance. He is all angle & polish. Wears a
swallow tail white waistcoat; wants brilliancy not intimacy, is half a
dandy.

M.   Its far better to write reviews than secondrate novels.
L.   I dont agree.
V.   I should like good criticism.
S.T.   Surely it would be much better if Rebecca West wrote criticism.[17]

He was a cautious hardheaded American, edited the Dial. Like
Mortimer he buys modern pictures; had met Roger outside the Nat. Gal.
& said "Surely, Mr Fry? I have the advantage of you Mr Fry: I know
you through your caricatures." & so on.

But the talk was too formal & too conventional to bear writing out;
or I cant do it; let me see, how did it go:

Adelphi abused.

Murry's writing abused. We tried to explain our dislike of K.'s stories.
M.   I used to have a boy to wait, & now only have an old woman
V.   But this is delicious (chicken in sauce) These are exquisite—china
fruit from Venice.

A good account of flying from T[hayer].

15. *The Waste Land*, which the Hogarth Press published in September 1923 (*HP
    Checklist* 28).
16. Scofield Thayer (1889-19), an American who had been a friend of T. S.
    Eliot's at Milton Academy, Massachusetts, at Harvard, and at Oxford, had in
    1919 become editor of the New York *Dial*, to which Eliot contributed a 'London
    Letter'.
17. Rebecca West (b. 1892), novelist, literary critic and political writer, had published
    Henry James (1916), and two novels, *The Return of the Soldier* (1918) and *The
    Judge* (1922).

S.T. The pilot sayd he wdn't start. The company had sold three seats instead of two. But I had taken my passage 10 days before. I wouldnt budge. Some luggage was left. One man took his dachs. But we felt overweighted. Then we got above a storm. One leant over & saw the lightning dashing up at one's face. It was terrible. I looked at my feet. One man kept going to the side & being sick. The other kept saying It is bad It is bad. And we all knew we were over weighted. Suddenly the engines stopped. We pitched up & down. We expected the whole thing to crash. The dog sat quite calm. Then after 10 minutes the engine began again. Towns looked like the handle of that salt cellar. Never again, no. And the pilot said he'd been guiding with one hand & fumbling with the other & suddenly touched the right spring by chance, & the engine started. But we might just as well have dashed to the ground.

Friday 28 July

These days before going, as we do on Wednesday are too dissipated for serious reading writing living or thinking. Variable as a barometer to phychical [sic] changes, my wits flutter & frizzle & I can get no work out of them because, somehow, they've picked up the rumour of a move to Sussex. Indeed, I've been gadding (to parody I've been roaming which we heard at Tancred, Mrs Lyttelton's intolerably tedious play the other night[18]) gadding too much for the health of my five wits. They soon jangle. Very soon I find myself out of talk, a disillusioned spectator, for instance, of Clive, Mary & Mortimer, of Mary's great evening party, of old Roger & old Margery [Fry], of Tidmarsh with young kitten Rylands verging on the albino.[19] However, I've enjoyed it too, in its rather agitating way, this half year has kept me on the hop. I like that; agitating though it is. I've taken my fences, as I say, & got some good gallops for my trouble. I have also to remind myself that risks imply

18. *Tancred*, adapted as a play from Disraeli's novel by Edith Millbank (the pseudonym of the second Hon. Mrs Alfred Lyttelton), opened at the Kingsway Theatre on 16 July and was withdrawn on 28 July. *The Times* judged it 'an indifferent attempt to represent that great novel' and 'unhappily tedious', and referred to 'a little song by Katherine', which was possibly that parodied by VW. The play was reviewed by LW in the *Nation & Athenaeum* of 28 July 1923.

19. George Humphrey Wolferstan ('Dadie') Rylands (b. 1902), Scholar of Eton and of King's College, Cambridge; in his first year he had appeared as Electra in Sheppard's production of the Oresteian Trilogy; he was an eager and talented participant in University theatrical ventures. Elected to the Society (Apostles), he was both an acute and personable recruit to the fraternity and had, inevitably, engaged the interest of both Maynard Keynes and Lytton Strachey.

falls. There are incidents that disquiet me. I have been peevish, exacting, excited, & moody. In these general terms I refer to a certain degree of society: to something stirring us to live more stormily than last year I think. Never settle, is my principle in life: & I try to put it in practice, but in talk more than in action I daresay. My theory is that at 40 one either increases the pace or slows down. Needless to say which I desire. But, to be just, my activity is also mental. I'm working variously & with intention. I've pulled through my Chaucer chapter; & written ahead at The Hours, & fill in spare space with 'serious' reading for my book, reading with pen & notebook. It encourages me to feel that all this reading has an end in view. In five years, I shall have fagged out a good book from it, I hope; a rough, but vigorous statue testifying before I die to the great fun & pleasure my habit of reading has given me. And I'm going to work hard, hard, hard, in every sense at Rodmell. I am going to tackle those old essays of mine, & see whether by drastic & spirited treatment they can be made worth reprinting. Courage & decision are my need, I think—to speak out, without mincing. At the moment I feel myself farely free of foreign influence: Eliot, or whoever it might be: & this I must prize, for unless I am myself, I am nobody.

As for the press, we have finished Tom, much to our relief. He will be published this August by Marjorie; & altogether we have worked at full speed since May. & that is I'm persuaded the root & source & origin of all health & happiness, provided of course that one rides work as a man rides a great horse, in a spirited & independent way; not a drudge, but a man with spurs in his heels. So I don't force myself any more to read against my will. I'm grown epicure in my middle age. Nevertheless, some compulsion is needed for the Greek chapter, which I must investigate at Rodmell. Also I shall explore—take a motor bus ride along the downs one day—see Steyning, & Arundel & so on. I much regret not having seen Windsor this spring. But I have at least ordered my French grammar. For plans, I have immediately to write a dialogue on Conrad: so must read for that too.[20] Fame? Is not Clive writing an article on me? Has not Bunny praised me in the Dial? Does not Madame Logé propose to translate The Voyage Out?— But fame "comes slowly up this way".[21]

20. 'Mr Conrad: a Conversation' was published in the *Nation*, 1 September 1923 (Kp C239).
21. Clive Bell's article 'Virginia Woolf' appeared in the *Dial* in December 1924; David Garnett's review of *Jacob's Room*, praising VW's originality and inimitability, was published in the *Dial* in July 1923; Mme Logé did not translate *The Voyage Out*. VW's quotation is from S. T. Coleridge: 'And the Spring comes slowly up this way.' *Christabel*, pt. i.

I am never praised except by my contemporaries or youngers. When Wells picks young writers, he neglects me. There are many other matters of importance to discuss at Rodmell though: the Nation; L.'s work; Hogarth House. Nessa last night, sitting in the Square, recommended Haverstock Hill.

Monday 6 August   [*Rodmell*]

I have ruined my mornings work by making bread & buns, which require constant voyages to the kitchen. The demon then always suggests that I shall read The Hours. Sheer weak dribble it seems to me (read in these circumstances). My comfort is that I can have at it in any way I like; & if it still goes wrong, to the fire with it. Nor do I think it wrong altogether. Whenever there is a breach in my content, all disparaging criticisms creep in; meanly enough, the good ones keep off.

We went over to Charleston yesterday. Although thinking quite well of ourselves, we were not well received by the painters. There they sat like assid[u]ous children at a task in a bedroom—Roger, Nessa, & Duncan; Roger on chair in foreground; Nessa on sofa, Duncan on bed. In front of them was one jar of flowers, & one arrangement of still live. Roger was picking out his blue flower very brightly. For some reason, the talk was not entirely congenial. I suspect myself of pertness & so on. Clive was sitting in the drawing room window reading Dryden.

A very good edition—I want to ask your husband some questions— Will he take an article. . . . V. O I thought your Lytton article very good. . . .[1] Van. Tea's ready— V. What am I to do with my cigarette?

Hollyhocks, decapitated, swam in a bowl; there was a loaf for tea, & a long slab of cake. Roger, I cant help thinking has become a little querulous with years. His grievances torment him; he talks of them too much. After tea, Angelica had her dolls' tea party in the window, & beat Clive, & when he cried, ran of her own accord & picked him a flower—which was a sensitive womanly act. She is sensitive—minds being laughed at (as I do). She said she wanted a 'slide' in her hair. "Dont laugh at me" she said, petulantly, to Roger.

I should say that the weather is perfect, soft as a cushion, blue to the heart. A gospel caravan has just pitched its tent near, & the other night 10 young men bawled hymns. . . . But I am laying [sic] my mind wander to The Hours. Now its a strange thing that if I have no gift for novel

1. Clive Bell's edition of Dryden was that prepared by Sir Walter Scott, revised and corrected by George Saintsbury, 18 volumes, 1882-93, of which he owned six. His article 'Lytton Strachey' had appeared in the *New Statesman* on 4 August 1923.

writing, yet it should so absorb me—I cant diagnose my own case—
which reminds me that I've started upon the revision of my old articles;
& feel rather charitable to that side of my faculty. Leonard is at this
moment beginning again his book, which I daresay he has not touched
since last Christmas.[2]

Friday 17 August

The question I want to debate here is the question of my essays; &
how to make them into a book. The brilliant idea has just come to me of
embedding them in Otway conversation. The main advantage would be
that I could then comment, & add what I had had to leave out, or failed to
get in e.g. the one on George Eliot certainly needs an epilogue.[3] Also
to have a setting for each would 'make a book'; & the collection of
articles is in my view an inartistic method. But then this might be too
artistic: it might run away with me; it will take time. Nevertheless I
should very much enjoy it. I should graze nearer my own individuality.
I should mitigate the pomposity & sweep in all sorts of trifles. I think I
should feel more at my ease. So I think a trial should be made. The first
thing to do is to get ready a certain number of essays;— There could
be an introductory chapter. A family which reads the papers. The thing
to do wd. be to envelop each essay in its own atmosphere. To get them
into a current of life, & so to shape the book; to get a stress upon some
main line—but what the line is to be, I can only see by reading them
through. No doubt fiction is the prevailing theme. Anyhow the book
shd end with modern lit:

		In order of time
6	Jane Austen	
5	Addison	
14	Conrad	Montaigne.
15	How it strikes a Contemporary	Evelyn.
11	The Russians	Defoe
4	Evelyn 1620	Sheridan
7	George Eliot	Sterne
13	Modern Essays	Addison

2. After 1921, when he published *Socialism and Co-operation*, LW was too heavily
committed to his journalistic and political work and to the Hogarth Press to
find much time for his own writing, but he was 'ruminating and slowly writing'
After the Deluge, volume I of which was published in 1931. See *IV LW*, p 88.

3. VW's recently published essay 'Mr Conrad: a Conversation' (see above, 28 July
1923, n 20) had taken the form of a conversation between the book-loving Penelope
Otway and an old friend. The essay on George Eliot had appeared in the *TLS* in
1919 (Kp C175).

10	Henry James	Jane Austen
	Re-reading novels	Ch. B.
8	Charlotte Brontë	George Eliot
2	Defoe 1661	The Russians
12	Modern Novels	The Americans
	Greeks	Thoreau
9	Thoreau	Emerson
	Emerson	Henry James
3	Sheridan?	Modern Fiction.
2	Sterne?	On re-reading novels
		Essays
1a	Old Memoirs	How it strikes a contemp.

These are, roughly, the headings.

Suppose one begins with old memoirs. I have materials on House of Lyme; Fanshawe. Boswells letters.[4]

1   Old Memoirs

Saturday 29 August

I've been battling for ever so long with 'The Hours', which is proving one of my most tantalising & refractory of books. Parts are so bad, parts so good; I'm much interested; can't stop making it up yet—yet. What is the matter with it? But I want to freshen myself, not deaden myself, so will say no more. Only I must note this odd symptom; a conviction that I shall go on, see it through, because it interests me to write it.

Clive & Mary came. So did Nick [Bagenal]; so did Mrs Jones; & we went to Seaford too. An odd instinct informed me that Mr Jones was non-existent. Who then could Hugh be? He is the child of Philip Morrell![5] So that puzzle has fitted itself together oddly enough. Mrs J. is too self-conscious to be a widow. She has no past to deplore—an uneasy future, under my eye. The little boy has strange blue eyes—but no look of the old ram. Nick's attachment to Barbara is very marked. By virtue of her astounding merits he is admitted among the great, in whom he still believes. He brought several pears & a melon. This melon, Molly Hamilton ate. She was windblown & breathless. She is tart, not em-bittered. She is brave; has herself in hand. Faces more facts every night

4. These are all old contributions to the *TLS*, namely 'The House of Lyme', 1917 (Kp C70); 'Lady Fanshawe's Memoirs', 1907 (Kp C6); and 'The Genius of Boswell', 1909 (Kp C29).

5. Alice Louisa Jones (1878-1970) had been Philip Morrell's secretary during the war; their son, Philip Hugh Jones, was born in 1917. She was now on the staff of the *Nation*.

than I do in a year. Of course her touch is not sensitive; vigorous rather, &, as I say, she licks the gilt off any scrap of gingerbread. I notice this in her descriptions. She never seems to enjoy people completely. But she admires me. I was 'nice' to her indeed; quite simple, quite unaffected, made no attempt to impose myself. But then, I thought, perhaps it is more amusing to be brilliant. One cannot condemn it utterly. It carries further.

Clive has an egg—a turkeys egg—for a head now—quite bald, unashamedly bald; never a hair will grow any more. Mary was shrinking, childlike, not brilliant, not attending when I read my play, but very anxious to say the right thing. She worships her canary. She pressed me to write about him. What view would I take—about this last phase, for instance, the Byronic? Chocolates she brought; she wore tight grey Alpaca, with large buttons, & she powdered & re-powdered in the drawing room. I cannot write out any verbatim talk; but will try again. Going to the dogs was discussed:

Thursday 30 August

I was called, I think to cut wood; we have to shape logs for the stove, for we sit in the lodge every night, & my goodness, the wind! Last night we looked at the meadow trees, flinging about, & such a weight of leaves that every brandish seems the end. Only a strewing of leaves from the lime tree, though, this morning. I read such a white dimity rice puddingy chapter of Mrs Gaskell at midnight in the gale "Wives & Daughters"— I think it must be better than Old Wives Tale all the same. You see, I'm thinking furiously about Reading & Writing. I have no time to describe my plans. I should say a good deal about The Hours, & my discovery; how I dig out beautiful caves behind my characters; I think that gives exactly what I want; humanity, humour, depth. The idea is that the caves shall connect, & each comes to daylight at the present moment — Dinner!

Wednesday 5 September

Here is the usual half hour to be filled before dinner, & such a mass to stuff it with as would burst a whole day. K.M. used to write all day, she told me; poor Katherine, I'm always inclined to say unpleasant things about her, for some reason: The Adelphi I suppose. Our week end was Francis Birrell & Raymond Mortimer. Leonard says that F. is 3 quarters grown up, Tony $\frac{1}{2}$. F. spills out the whole contents of his head like a nice little boy; never stops talking— And what was it about? About the Tennysons & his mother; my mother (The B[irrell]'s

didn't much like her: they had a culte for Minny) his father; aunts &
so on.[1]

"I wish I had distinguished Aunts" said Mortimer.

Rather obviously he hasnt. He is a curious half breed. An Oxford
young man, inclined to smartness, dress & culture. His soul is uneasy
in Cambridge company. He squirms a little visibly. One is not sure
how far one likes him. He flatters. He is not very simple, candid, or
talkative, like chatterbox F. who is as open as daylight.

My father is a solicitor—lives at Exmouth, & has really been a bachelor
since the death of my mother. She died when I was quite small. No I
dont mind being an only child at all. I am quite happy. I never look
ahead. If I had two thousand a year, I should never write. I should buy
pictures & travel.

We discussed writing novels on Asheham Hill. He had read the
V[oyage]. O[ut]. when it came out; & thought it frightfully good.
N[ight]. & D[ay]. he couldn't get through at first, but has now. J[acob']s
R[oom] the contemporary novel most to his liking. But he cant write
novels himself. Doesnt see why he should; has no originality. Likes
pictures perhaps best, because theres Picasso in painting & no one to
match him in writing.

"Palaeolithic men must have lived here. They lived an extraordinary
kind of life" we agreed in Asheham Hollow. "Now & then the clever
ones realised that they were human." At the same time we were talking
about Clive Bell who had been to luncheon, talking a great deal. I have
a culte for Bloomsbury, said Raymond (we have had to drop titles)
"He seems to me a perfectly happy & developed man. He is clever, &
he enjoys life too." I said "He has renounced a good deal all the same
—his great book for instance. And his happiness is partly pose". Still,
I admitted, he's a good fellow—he's done very well. Then Vanessa. "She
has such a lovely voice, & then shes very lovely to look at. Her personality
too is very impressive," he said. In short "You can't imagine what it
has been to me getting to know Bloomsbury. Theyre different human
beings from any I thought possible." Today I have a nice, I think, letter
from him. "I'd seem gushing if I told you how much I enjoyed my
visit. . . . I'm frightfully flattered, & something more than flattered by
your friendship, & only hope that when you see through my cleverness,
& are thoroughly bored with it, you won't be bored with me as well. . . .
Anyhow Floreat Bloomsburga!"

1. Frankie Birrell's mother was the widow of Lionel Tennyson; the Tennysons
were friends of the Thackerays; Minny Thackeray was Leslie Stephen's first wife.

This hits it off very well; my reserves & doubts, his self-consciousness & flattery is it?—let us call it "enthusiasm."

A great deal of time was spent in discussing Nation affairs—the Desmond row; & their position as reviewers. L. is trying to get Bertie & Clive to join in & make the position clear. Undoubtedly the Nation breeds a good many mosquitoes for us. There's Molly this week, refusing to sign her article.[2] And I'm slightly dashed by the reception of my Conrad conversation, which has been purely negative— No one has mentioned it. I dont think M[ortimer]. or B[irrell]. quite approved. Never mind; to be dashed is always the most bracing treatment for me. A cold douche should be taken (& generally is) before beginning a book. It invigorates; makes one say "Oh all right. I write to please myself," & so go ahead. It also has the effect of making me more definite & outspoken in my style, which I imagine all to the good. At any rate, I began for the 5th but last time, I swear, what is now to be called The Common Reader; & did the first page quite moderately well this morning. After all this stew, its odd how, as soon as I begin, a new aspect, never all this 2 or 3 years thought of, at once becomes clear; & gives the whole bundle a new proportion. To curtail, I shall really investigate literature with a view to answering certain questions about ourselves— Characters are to be merely views: personality must be avoided at all costs. I'm sure my Conrad adventure taught me this. Directly you specify hair, age, &c something frivolous, or irrelevant, gets into the book— Dinner!

Tuesday 11 September

Here we are back from The Knoll, Studland.[3] It was reckoned that we could have got to France in less time, reckoned at Charleston last week (on a hot September afternoon, with the children putting the kitten in a dead tree, which Duncan carried about as if it had been a Christmas tree; & then I read my play, & then I got excited, & then we bicycled home—all these things I should like to remember). I wanted to observe Lydia as a type for Rezia; & did observe one or two facts.[4]

2. The first of an eight-part series entitled 'A Nineteenth-Century Childhood' which appeared in the *Nation & Athenaeum* at intervals between 1 September 1923 and 14 June 1924 was signed M.M.; subsequent parts were signed Mary MacCarthy. (They were published as a book in 1924).
3. Maynard Keynes had rented this house in Dorset, and the Woolfs were invited for Friday to Monday, 7-10 September; their other companions were Lydia Lopokova, Raymond Mortimer, and George Rylands. They returned to Rodmell *via* London.
4. Rezia, Lucrezia Warren Smith, wife of Septimus in *Mrs Dalloway*.

It was very hot at Lulworth, & we sat with the sun in our eyes on a
verandah having tea. Suddenly she got cross, frowned, complained of
the heat, seemed about to cry, precisely like a child of six. She was concerned to know what Leonard meant by coupling her with me among
the "sillies".[5] It means that you can both be beaten, Maynard said.
Maynard is grown very gross & stout, especially when he wraps his
leopard spotted dressing gown tight round his knees & stands in front
of the fire. I was looking at him censoriously, through the eyes of good
M. Murry (4th no. of the Adelphi devoted to abuse of Mortimer &
Bunny[6]). He has a queer swollen eel like look, not very pleasant. But
his eyes are remarkable, & as I truly said when he gave me some pages
of his new book to read, the process of mind there displayed is as far
ahead of me as Shakespeare's.[7] True, I don't respect it so much. But to
continue. The poet Rylands was there & Mortimer. Dady's hair (he
became Dady at 10 A.M. Monday at Poole station) is precisely the colour
& consistency of the husk of straw—that thin glistening fabric which
one splits off the stalk of straw. Add to this a blue cornflower coloured
tweed suit, his apple red face, & blue eyes & you have—well, merely a
corn flower to me, but to Raymond the most intoxicatingly beautiful
young man that it is possible to imagine. Unfortunately (for R.) Dady
did not share these views. He, being honest Cambridge, puts R. down
for "a very clever Oxford man". L. is inclined to agree; indeed he calls
R. "slimy". He patted Dady, enclosed him, as he sat on the floor in his
arms, praised his beauty to his face; & one must agree, I think, that all
exhibitions of s—— feeling have something silly, mawkish, about them,
though why I can't say. Anyhow, R. had a cold in his nose, & his nose
is his worst feature, square at the tip, like something that has to stand
on a table. His features are not good; his hair dark; & his manners either
a little too clever or too flattering. Yet, I liked him better this week end

5. LW was greatly interested by what he called 'the strange psychology of the
"silly" ', a type described by Tolstoy in his autobiography and portrayed by
Dostoievsky in *The Idiot*. According to LW "sillies" are 'absurd in ordinary
life and by the standards of practical men'; they are 'terribly simple and at the
same time tragically complicated.' See *I LW*, p 137; *III LW*, p 174 & n.
6. Murry's editorial 'On Romanticism' in the September issue of the *Adelphi* was
concerned to castigate 'A clever young man called Mr Mortimer' who had lately
asserted in the *New Statesman*, on the sole evidence of the award of the Hawthornden Prize to *Lady into Fox*, that a great victory of classicism had overtaken modern
English literature; David Garnett's book, he wrote, was 'about as classical as a
carved cocoanut, with much the same . . . intrinsic importance.'
7. *A Tract on Monetary Reform* by J. M. Keynes, to be published in November
1923.

than last. Such are the elements of our party. I was interested to observe, & not much caring, as indeed happens oftener than not nowadays, to make a splash of my own. For one thing, we are grown so old now; & the young are so literal in their respect. We motored to Lulworth on Sunday, or rather to Warbarrow, which we climbed & walked 5 miles over the down. My shoes interfered with my pleasure rather. But I thought of the year 1830, & how most of England then looked as this coast looked, bays with their sweep untenanted, only coastguards & gray cottages, & rowing boats making off to little ships— And then I caught a view or two which I've no doubt will keep for some years & then be used: the red heather & water; the mediterranean aspect—but by the bye I must remember how curiously my week end transitory feeling conditioned all this: as if I were seeing something isolated, from a train. The clear water was very moving to me, with the pale stones showing under it like jelly fish. Lulworth of course was all skittles, & men playing in a yard; & people parading in front of a wall which, like an Italian wall, encloses the headland. An odd haze came down, so that we saw nothing distinctly: only outlines. Then we stopped, Maynard liking I think to be showman, at Bindon Abbey, having just before seen the old Manor house where Tess slept, or lived. At Bindon Lydia lay in her pink jacket with the white fur in a Bishops tomb—a kind of shaped tank sunk in the earth on the way up to the Calvary, & got up with leaves sticking to her cloak. She lay quite still, acting death, her muscular dancers legs in white silk stockings lying with the soles of the feet touching, & Maynard & I standing by.[8] What did she think about? About Maynard, & her death, & what would happen before? Heaven knows. Bindon is all grass & trees & long stretches of water, like those at Hampton Court. We sat on the mound of the Calvary, the cross being gone, & Maynard talked about palaeolithic man & an interesting theory about the age of man—how the beginning of history about 5,000 B.C. is only the beginning of another lap in the race; others, many others, having been run previously & obliterated by ice ages. Meanwhile Raymond took his Dady along the side walks by the fish ponds. It is

8. The ruins of Bindon Abbey stand near the village of Wool in Dorset, close to the River Frome. Woolbridge Manor, formerly the home of the Turberville family, is the 'Wellbridge Manor-house' of Thomas Hardy's novel *Tess of the D'Urbervilles*. There Tess and Angel Clare spent their wedding night, and in the Abbey ruins is the stone coffin in which Angel, walking in his sleep, put Tess. Of this coffin Hardy wrote: 'Against the north wall was the empty stone coffin of an abbot, in which every tourist with a turn for grim humour was accustomed to stretch himself.'

a damp romantic place; & one wh. perhaps I shall never see again, as I told L. I had an odd feeling that it is queer to find such places lying unknown in the country, inland. I can't get hold of it now. I am perhaps encouraged by Proust to search out & identify my feelings, but I have always felt this kind of thing in great profusion, only not tried to capture it, or perhaps lacked skill & confidence. To return: —Dady has an ingratiating manner of pawing ladies old enough to be his mother. He threw out an idea that he might join the Press. The printing mania has come upon him & Sebastian, & it looks as if we might now start a Cambridge branch; —he asked, lightly, for he is not emphatic & very happy I should think, with all his interests & successes, & no inhibitions & good health, & money in prospect, & an editor to print his poems, & a year more at Cambridge, & a possible fellowship & so forth—he asked lightly whether he might lodge with us in the holidays, & pay his way by working the press. So you see how the future branches & extends: I mean there are ways down the forest; roads leading to right & left hitherto unseen.

It was hot & prosy in London. I bought China at Heal's, & we lunched with Hubert H[enderson].—a small, testy, unheroic man, vaguely on the look out for offence, & suspecting I think our superior vitality, & longing for a compliment, which being honest at the moment, I could not give him. He ought to have stuck to Cambridge, as, I suspect, he begins to think. He is less of a personage than I thought. Once the flush of the adventure is past, he finds himself hard put to it to keep his end up. Maynard is his standby. Bloomsbury his pest. He wants safe, charming articles, like Molly's childhood series.

Any really good article, said L., is bound to be disliked intensely & liked intensely.

H.H. didn't much agree to this. He thought they could be liked by everyone. He was disappointed by Lytton, who gets £40 for 15,00 words, & I think by me. Left to himself, he would soon make The Nation into the Westminster Gazette. But I don't pretend to care very profoundly. Unfortunately, Desmond has cut up crusty, & L. is landed with F. B[irrell]. for whom he must provide £150 p.A. Mortimer I think, descends safely but a little ingloriously on the New Statesman side of the fence. And Bertie [Russell] says he will resign.

Tuesday 18 September

Leonard's day in London, & left with 30 minutes before I walk off to meet him I may as well write here. We have had visitors—Lytton &

the Partridges, unexpectedly; then Nessa & Duncan; then Morgan for the week end. There are times when I want no one, times when I relish the commonest animated slug. I am worn smooth with talk at the moment, & so did not come to grips with my friends, as I should have done. Yet how good, kind, tender, & clever we all are! Chiefly I remember sitting on the wall of the public house with Duncan & discussing his painting. He said he was trying to simplify; he wants I think, to express something very abstract simply. His own loveliness seems to him now negligible. "Nessa is a happy artist" he said in the bus (I went in to Lewes). I am a stupid artist she said. She has none of these changes. She does not think things out. Sometimes I am quite ready not to paint for a long time. I suppose he is intellectual, as I suppose I am; & she more instinctive. Yet she changes too. They notice old women & babies all the time. We stood in the High Street, & saw a man drive out of the White Hart, close clipped as a convict, wearing a hard grey bowler, & driving a high stepping piebald. Duncan could not imagine what his life was. So I walked home. Not much talk of interest with Lytton. He pounced on our books. Oh books, books! he cried, & carried off Mortimer's Oxford Circus.[9] Fame has made him confident, taken from him I suppose, some charm, turned it to strength of some kind. I always feel a kind of mass now behind his view of his own writing. The French at the Monastery had been so enthusiastic about Racine. That set him up, & made it needless to praise his articles in the Nation, which are not, so we think, good.[10]

Very well. We all grow old; grow stocky; lose our pliancy & impressionability. Even Morgan seems to me to be based on some hidden rock. Talking of Proust & Lawrence he said he'd prefer to be Lawrence; but much rather would be himself. We discussed his novels. I don't think I am a novelist, he said. Suddenly I said "No, I don't think you are" Ah! he exclaimed, eagerly, interested, not dashed. But L. denied this. "I'm not at all downcast about my literary career", he said. I think he has made up his mind that he has much to fall back on. He is aloof, serene, a snob, he says, reading masterpieces only. We had a long gossip

9. *The Oxford Circus.* 'A novel of Oxford and youth by the late Alfred Budd. Edited with a Memoir but no Portrait by Hamish Miles and Raymond Mortimer. Illustrated by John Kettelwell.' Published in 1922 by John Lane.

10. During the summer of 1923 Lytton Strachey attended the annual 'Entretiens d'été', a conference of writers and professors held at the Cistercian Abbaye de Pontigny (*Holroyd*, pp 859-62): his *Books and Characters* (1922) includes a study of Racine. Strachey's *Nation* articles since May had been on Sarah Bernhardt, Charles Greville, and John Aubrey.

about servants. He found wasps in the mint sauce. This made Agnes drop the dish & go off leaving the dining room door open. Mrs Forster was cold to her for some days. "She will begin to scream & die of appendicitis" he said. And so to Miss Grant Duff & his quarrel in Alexandria.[11] But it grows cold & dark; I shall walk off to meet L.

Monday 15 October   *Hogarth*

This last entry seems long ago. And I meant to record for psychological purposes that strange night when I went to meet Leonard & did not meet him. What an intensity of feeling was pressed into those hours! It was a wet windy night; & as I walked back across the field I said Now I am meeting it; now the old devil has once more got his spine through the waves. (but I cannot re-capture really). And such was the strength of my feeling that I became physically rigid. Reality, so I thought, was unveiled. And there was something noble in feeling like this; tragic, not at all petty. Then cold white lights went over the fields; & went out; & I stood under the great trees at Iford waiting for the lights of the bus. And that went by; & I felt lonelier. There was a man with a barrow walking into Lewes, who looked at me. But I could toy with, at least control all this, until suddenly, after the last likely train had come in I felt it was intolerable to sit about, & must do the final thing, which was to go to London. Off I rode, without much time, against such a wind; & again I had a satisfaction in being matched with powerful things, like wind & dark. I battled, had to walk; got on; drove ahead; dropped the torch; picked it up, & so on again without any lights. Saw men & women walking together; thought, you're safe & happy I'm an outcast; took my ticket; had 3 minutes to spare, & then, turning the corner of the station stairs, saw Leonard, coming along, bending rather, like a person walking very quick, in his mackintosh. He was rather cold & angry (as, perhaps was natural). And then, not to show my feelings, I went outside & did something to my bicycle. Also, I went back to the ticket office, & said to the humane man there, "Its all right. My husband

11. Agnes Dowland was engaged as parlourmaid by Forster's mother in 1904 and, though the two women never got on, she stayed for forty years. Miss Victoria Grant Duff (daughter of a Governor of Madras) was E. M. Forster's superior in the Red Cross in Alexandria during the period 1915-17 and, after being very friendly, suddenly became hostile to him when she thought the authorities had slighted her in his favour. In 1917 there was a long quarrel, in which the Red Cross supported him, and she finally resigned.

caught the last train. Give me back my fare" which he did. And I got the money more to set myself right with Leonard than because I wanted it. All the way back we talked about a row (about reviewers) at the office; & all the time I was feeling My God, thats over. I'm out of that. Its over. Really, it was a physical feeling, of lightness & relief & safety. & yet there was too something terrible behind it—the fact of this pain, I suppose; which continued for several days—I think I should feel it again if I went over that road at night; & it became connected with the deaths of the miners, & with Aubrey Herbert's death next day.[1] But I have not got it all in, by any means.

We have been dealing with domestic rows; a triumphant solution for us; since Lottie is declared fit for all work by her doctor; but the expense of spirit is too great to be worth while. We lunch on trays. Marjorie [Joad] does not much like it, but submits. Marjorie has her Champagne love affair with Ralph, now developed into an attack of influenza, as I thought likely. She is a cold honest woman; prepared for the worst. I like her literal good sense, though her spirit does not bounce & spring as one could like. Its her drawl thats the worst of her. And then? My first activity has been to see houses. So far I have seen the outsides of two. And the problem is a difficult one. Its my wish to live in London, no one elses. How far can this wish bear the weight of the removal, the expense, the less pleasant surroundings, & so on? But I shall go on steadily, looking, & I hope, working. Here we are tight wedged in printing & editing. People come (Madge & Janet yesterday for 4 hours, leaving me with a brain like a wrung dish cloth) And we have Dadie in prospect.[2]

This young man with hair like the husk of corn, says he wishes to devote his life to the Hogarth Press, & is writing a letter to that effect to Leonard. This will begin in June. He shall be a partner, & take over the work; & we shall supervise, & by degrees it will become more & more important, & we shall be the benefactors of our age; & have a shop, & enjoy the society of the young, & rummage & splash in the great bran pie, & so never, never stop working with brains or fingers or toes till our limbs fly asunder & the heart sprays off into dust. Such

---

1. On 25 September 1923 the No. 23 Redding Pit near Falkirk was flooded and 41 men lost their lives. Lt.-Col. Aubrey Herbert MP (b. 1880), died on 26 September 1923; he was a half-brother of Lady Margaret Duckworth.
2. Janet Maria Vaughan (b. 1899), daughter of VW's cousin William Wyamar Vaughan and his wife Madge, née Symonds. At this time she was beginning her medical career. LW's diary for 6 October 1923 notes: 'Rylands came lunch & stayed week end.'

is my fancy picture— But I must write a careful letter to Frances Cornford & so have no time.[3]

I am now in the thick of the mad scene in Regents Park. I find I write it by clinging as tight to fact as I can, & write perhaps 50 words a morning. This I must re-write some day. I think the design is more remarkable than in any of my books. I daresay I shan't be able to carry it out. I am stuffed with ideas for it. I feel I can use up everything I've ever thought. Certainly, I'm less coerced than I've yet been. The doubtful point is I think the character of Mrs Dalloway. It may be too stiff, too glittering & tinsely— But then I can bring innumerable other characters to her support. I wrote the 100th page today. Of course, I've only been feeling my way into it—up till last August anyhow. It took me a year's groping to discover what I call my tunnelling process, by which I tell the past by instalments, as I have need of it. This is my prime discovery so far; & the fact that I've been so long finding it, proves, I think, how false Percy Lubbock's doctrine is—that you can do this sort of thing consciously.[4] One feels about in a state of misery—indeed I made up my mind one night to abandon the book—& then one touches the hidden spring. But lor' love me! I've not re-read my great discovery, & it may be nothing important whatsoever. Never mind. I own I have my hopes for this book. I am going on writing it now till, honestly, I cant write another line—Journalism, everything, is to give way to it.

Saturday 3 November

And now I've found a house 35 Woburn Square.[1] Yes, shall I write that address often? Certainly I hope to. For me it would be worth £500 a year in pleasure. Think of the music I could hear, the people I could see, easily, unthinkingly. And then comes before me the prospect of walking through the city streets; starting off early, some day L.'s at the

3. Frances Crofts Cornford, *née* Darwin (1886-1960), poet, daughter of Sir Francis Darwin by his second wife; half-sister of Bernard Darwin and first cousin of Gwen Raverat (see above, 8 August 1922, n 15). She was the wife of Francis Cornford, Fellow of Trinity College, Cambridge, and a central figure in the group of friends, somewhat junior to VW, which the latter referred to as the Neo-Pagans. VW's letter, if written, does not survive.

4. VW had discussed Percy Lubbock's *The Craft of Fiction* in her article 'On Re-Reading Novels', *TLS* 20 July 1922 (Kp C228). She continued to measure her own critical views against those of Lubbock for some time. See *III VW Letters*, no. 1498 to Roger Fry; *ibid*, no. 1832, to E. M. Forster; also 'Modern Fiction' in *The Common Reader*, 1925.

1. There is a rough sketch plan of the rooms of this house on the opposite page.

office, & walking say to Wapping; & then to tea at the office. Why this so obsesses my mind I don't know. It was a beautiful clear November day, yesterday, when I went up & past our house (with green doors opposite the mews) & the squares with their regular houses, & their leafless trees, & people very clearly outlined filled me with joy. Indeed, it was so lovely in the Waterloo Road that it struck me that we were writing Shakespeare; by which I mean that when live people, seeming happy, produce an effect of beauty, & you dont have it offered as a work of art, but it seems a natural gift of theirs, then—what was I meaning?—somehow it affected me as I am affected by reading Shakespeare. No: its life; going on in these very beautiful surroundings. As for the house question I am solving it tonight in this fashion. We will take the house, live in our own flat upstairs—a most lovable & delightful little place; have Nelly to cook; let out the next floor to Saxon; Lottie shall do for him. Then Dady (I think, but am not sure) shall be lodged on the ground floor, entirely apart, with his own servant in the basement, & control of the press which is also lodged there. This seems to me a perfectly feasible solution of innumerable difficulties. Of course Marjorie remains. We broke Dadie to her two days ago. Leonard did it in so many words.

M. But I dont think I shall like that.

V. Did you dislike him?

M. I shant like being under him. He'd make me typewrite all day. And I suppose I should have to do what he told me?

L. He would be in the same position to you that we are.

M. I've never minded working under you. But this is the first time it happened. I've never been able to work with other people. I quarrelled with the headmistress, where I was before this.

(here is an example of the resolute, uncoloured honesty with which she behaves. But she did not show up otherwise in an attractive light— except that one can't blame these unimaginative people for anything. She fears the loss of prestige. She is jealous, rather grasping, wants her way; but of course knows all this. That is the modern advantage.

But I have wasted my time drawing a plan of 35 on the opposite page. Nothing runs away with time like these house dreams. I must read Sophocles. After 20 years, I now know how to read Greek quick (with a crib in one hand) & with pleasure. This is for the eternal book. And my mind whips off to rents—how much can we ask for this house? I'm heartless about poor old Hogarth, where for 9 years we have been so secure. My mind whips away from Ka, & Altounyan, except that Ka was more like a sack of some of the commoner garden vegetables than ever.[2] She has some worm gnawing at her, some persistent desire to impress us, with her romantic life, with Will's romantic nature. Now there's nothing human beings so quickly see as this motive, & none they more resent. For one thing, it implies some divergence of interest. She's thinking not of you, but of how to impress you. More serious, though, is the dilution of her own interest, since she does not put her full weight on it, but only on half of it, thinking as she must, of making it impress. Her condescension is very curious. She is, or seems to be, one of the county; this she enjoys. But she is aware that being county doesn't carry far in London, or even Richmond. Anyhow she tells too many stories about the strange figures who drive up to the Eagles Nest. Gordon Bottomley, the Ranee of Sarawak. She dwells too much upon good Will's passion for the conscription of natives by the French.[3] All this protesting—thats whats at the bottom of it. But she was in some way very pathetic about Rupert. How Mrs Brooke had suddenly smiled at Mark as Ka had never seen her smile, exactly like Rupert. But if I hadn't driven her off rather arbitrarily to the past, I don't know how we should have got through the evening. I was glad to hear Leonard & Altounyan coming down. But I must descend to the basement, & see whats doing with Clive's cover; which Leonard does for 8 hours daily.[4]

Friday 16 November

No we didn't take 35 Woburn Square, & the colour has gone out of it, & I dont want to write about it at the moment. I'm back from lunch Lady Colefax, meet Anrep at the Tate,[5] tea Marjorie, discuss Ralph;

2. Ka Arnold-Forster and Ernest Altounyan (1889-1962) dined with the Woolfs on 2 November. He was a half-Armenian doctor educated in England, who had been introduced to LW by E. M. Forster in 1915 (see *I VW Diary*, 22 May 1919, n 13.) He aspired to be a writer, but since 1919 had had to assist his father in the latter's private hospital in Aleppo.

3. Gordon Bottomley (1874-1948), prolific poet and dramatist, and the 1923 winner of the Femina Vie Heureuse prize. Brett's younger sister Sylvia Leonora (1885-1971) had in 1911 married Charles Vyner Brooke, the Rajah of Sarawak—but is not to be confused with Mrs Brooke, Rupert's mother. Since the war Will Arnold-Forster had been increasingly concerned with League of Nations' matters.

4. Clive Bell's narrative poem *The Legend of Monte Sibilla*, with decorations by Vanessa Bell and Duncan Grant, was published by the Hogarth Press in December 1923 (*HP Checklist* 27).

5. Boris von Anrep (1883-1969), Russian mosaicist, who had studied in Paris and Edinburgh before the war, and contributed to Roger Fry's Second Post-Impressionist Exhibition in 1912. In 1918 he had married Helen Maitland; they

Leonard back from Rodmell: & in rather a fritter, too much so to read Euripides. Indeed, I've been talking to Hugh Walpole—not an impressive man—a man who protests too much; an uneasy, prosperous vain man, who harbours some grudge against clever intellectuals & yet respects them, would like to be one. He has the look of a kindly solicitor or banker; red cheeks; very small bright eyes; a genial, but not profound or cordial manner. We talked of contemporary fame. He dwelt a good deal upon the different sets & critics, & how no book was good in the same parish. Somehow it all referred to him. An uninteresting mind, & really not able to cast a shadow even upon me. I did not feel knocked over, dashed to pieces, or anything very vividly, except that he was slightly in awe of me.[6] There was old Lady Horner, with her grey big eyes very far apart in a face creased & crumpled like some old faded glove—an interesting subtle face; a mind worn down by society, into that kind of simple ease which enhances even small talk. I mean what she said was so freely & easily said that it had a manner with it. Spacious gardens & money have gone to it. Poor unhappy old woman— Am I sentimental to think so often of peoples unhappiness, or is it indirectly some tribute to myself? Lytton is very suave in such society[;] sits in the shadow & now & then draws his sword effectively. Desmond of course does his jolly delightful tricks—eating & drinking meanwhile—acting an actress who cleans her arms like a fly in Nassau. As for Ly Colefax, there she sits painted & emphatic at the head of her table, broadcheeked, a little coarse, kindly glass eyed, affectionate to me almost, capable, apparently disinterested—I mean if she likes to listen to clever talk & to buy it with a lunch of four courses & good wine; I see no harm in it. Its a taste; not a vice. Off we streamed at 3. It amuses me to hear Ly Horner asking the servants to find out Lady Lovat's telephone number. These free & easy ways remind me of Ly Bath, the Herberts—little

---

had a house in Pond Street, Hampstead (where Murry rented two of their rooms). Ethel Sands was one of his most enthusiastic patrons and promoters, and had contributed to a fund enabling the Tate Gallery to commission the mosaic floor in the Blake Room on which he was now working.

6. Hugh (Seymour) Walpole (1884-1941), popular novelist and man of letters. He was to become devoted to VW and to make her his confidant even in the most intimate matters; she was less candid. (See *II QB*, pp 137-8.) VW presumably met him at luncheon with Lady Colefax, together with Lady Horner, of Mells in Somerset, who was an old friend and neighbour of Violet Dickinson. Born Frances Jane Graham, she had been the object of Burne-Jones's devotion. Both her son and her son-in-law had been killed in the war, and her younger son died in 1908.

accidents that impressed me years ago.[7] Yet all it amounts to is that Ly Horner drives about London in a motor car, & has a sort of airiness instead of stuffiness about her. So to the Tate with Lytton. Lytton & I don't need much preliminary.

Heres my book—Q.V. in French.[8]

I daresay it reads better in French

He has almost bought a house near Hungerford, in the downs, but hesitates over the last £500. There are no drains & no water. Still I advised the leap, as I always advise leaps. And then there was Anrep, & his tinted floor, all raying out in greens & browns, like the waves of a sea; not a good metaphor, for it is really very compact, strong, & contained. Droves of schoolchildren kept sweeping over it. He explained it to me, smelling rather too much of whisky. Then he drove me to Waterloo. Now I lose interest in these facts, much as I do in writing my novels, & thus have to find a way out of saying them. Hugh Walpole wd. not be bored I suppose; therefore he is convincing. I'm now writing my Greek chapter in alternate bursts of hot & cold. It seems so superficial, & not worth foisting off upon a world provided with so much knowledge already. Yet I really must write a book about facts once in a way. And I cant keep grinding at fiction, which however goes easier this last lap than before. Here though I come lamely & softly & comfortably to a full stop. I must add that "I've broken off with Ralph. We had nowhere to meet. And its true—he ought to be in a park; not in restaurants. And I had two dreadful scenes with Cyril [Joad]. He wont let him come home, or let me stay away with him. I dont want to lie about it. So we've broken off". Rather to her credit, I think, & certainly to our relief.

Monday 3 December

Back from Rodmell; unable to settle in; therefore I write diary. How often I have said this! An odd psychological fact—that I can write when I'm too jangled to read. Moreover, I want to leave as few pages blank as possible; & the end of the year is only some three weeks off.

I meant to write about the change which I discovered last May (about) from seclusion & obscurity to some degree of prosperity & society. My

7. Lady Lovat, *née* the Hon. Laura Lister, daughter of the 4th Baron Ribblesdale, married Simon Fraser, Baron Lovat, in 1910. Lady Bath was the mother of VW's friends from early days, Lady Beatrice and Lady Katherine Thynne (Countess of Cromer); the Herberts were the family of George Duckworth's wife, Lady Margaret.

8. Published in a translation by F. Roger-Cornaz as *La Reine Victoria* by Editions Payot of Paris in 1923.

prediction was that we [were] on the verge of something of the kind. And I see now I shall get my Saxon & my house. Oh there's Adrian's catastrophe to record—now 2 weeks old. Nessa rang me up in the middle of dinner with Tom here. "Adrian & Karin are going to separate." You could have knocked me down with a feather, & Clive too, so he says. The devoted & inseparable couple! And it seemed (then—this is no longer so) tragic to me; & I was overcome, at hearing they'd been unhappy for years; & then went & told Tom & Leonard; & then 2 days later, met Adrian in the bathroom at 46; kissed his hand, & he burst into tears. Its an agony! he cried. So we went upstairs holding hands, (I to get ready for my speech at the School of Economics[1]) & he walked to the bus, & told me how it had never been right—almost, but never quite right. They hadn't quarrelled. I am too shaky to write. But then he stayed here & I felt come over me the old despair; the crouching servile feeling which is my lowest & worst; the desire for praise, which he never gets; & the old futile comparisons between his respect for Nessa & his disrespect for me came over me, that made me so wretched at Fitzroy Sqre. To my amusement, I found that Nessa, who had been cordial & sanguine about him had changed her view, owing to his visiting her, & now only foretells with despair several long silent sittings. She says, & Clive says, that Karin did it; Karin felt it more than he did. She felt all I used to feel: the snub; the check; the rebuke; the fastidiousness; the lethargy. Poor old Adrian!—he now subsides into a flat in Mecklenburgh Sqre; & drifts phantomlike forever. Undoubtedly Haynes was right: the D.N.B. crushed his life out before he was born.[2] It gave me a twist of the head too. I shouldn't have been so clever, but I should have been more stable, without that contribution to the history of England. Now for a hot bath.

Wednesday 19 December

I dont know if this is my last chance of writing, or if I shall take the black book to Rodmell & fill its last pages there. I am so stifled with work of all sorts, society of all sorts, & plans of all sorts, that I can't pour a pure stream from my tap. In an hour Sprott & Mary are coming. Merely to count my company since I wrote would take my time & waste

1. No other record of this occasion has been found; Eliot had dined with the Woolfs on 19 November, so it would have been on Wednesday 21 November.
2. Edmund Sidney Pollock Haynes (1877-1949), solicitor, writer, wit and bon-viveur; he was a cousin of Sir Frederick Pollock and had participated in the 'Sunday Tramps' organised by him and Leslie Stephen, whom he venerated.

it. How elliptical this book becomes! I dont respect events any more: I'd like to record poor Tom's getting drunk, all the same. We went to a flat in an arcade, & asked for Captain Eliot.[3] I noticed that his eyes were blurred. He cut the cake meticulously. He helped us to coffee— or was it tea? Then to liqueurs. He repeated, L. noticed, "Mrs Ricardo", as L. told his story; he got things a little wrong. There was a long pale squint eyed Oxford youth on the floor. We discussed the personal element in literature. Tom then quietly left the room. L. heard sounds of sickness. After a long time, he came back, sank into the corner, & I saw him, ghastly pale, with his eyes shut, apparently in a stupor. When we left he was only just able to stand on his legs. We heard a shuffling as we went, & Clive went back. Next day, I spent 10 minutes at the telephone receiving apologies—how distressing, what could we all think? Could we forgive him—the first time—would we ever come again? no dinner, no lunch—then sudden collapse—how dreadful—what a miserable end to the evening—apologise please to Leonard, to your sister— & so on. One of those comedies which life sometimes does to perfection.

I must briefly touch on Dadie; house problem not settled; Maynard threatening to cut down reviews; Leonard at this moment threatening to resign; Mary & Sprott; Clive & Braithwait,[4] publishing, writing; doing Hardy, & Montaigne & the Greeks & the Elizabethans & the Hours; accepted in America, neglected by all prize givers, very happy, very much on the go—thats my state, at the moment of writing 6.14 P.M. on Wednesday aforesaid.

The Woolfs went to Monks House for Christmas on Friday 21 December; on the 28th they went to dine and spend the night at Charleston with Clive and Vanessa Bell and her three children. VW had dictated to Quentin the text of a squib entitled 'Scenes in the Life of Mrs Bell' for inclusion in the Christmas number of the Charleston Bulletin, *the Bell children's family newspaper.*

3. On 10 December 1923 Eliot had invited Lytton Strachey to a small party at 38 Burleigh Mansions (see *Holroyd*, p 777 fn); perhaps that which the Woolfs went to on 17 December, after dining with Clive and Vanessa Bell and Mary Hutchinson at the Commercio. LW's story has not been retrieved.
4. Richard Bevan Braithwaite (b. 1900), moral philosopher, Scholar of King's College, an Apostle, and a member of Maynard Keynes's inner intellectual circle at Cambridge.

1924

1924

The Woolfs were back at Hogarth House from Rodmell on New Year's Day 1924. VW began a new book—DIARY XIII—on the first page of which she wrote:

Hogarth House
Paradise Road
Richmond
Jan. 3rd 1924

On the following page she has written out the calendar for the first three months of 1924 (see 12 January below).

Thursday 3 January

This year is almost certainly bound to be the most eventful in the whole of our (recorded) career. Tomorrow I go up to London to look for houses; on Saturday I deliver sentence of death upon Nellie & Lottie; at Easter we leave Hogarth; in June Dadie comes to live with us; & our domestic establishment is entirely controlled by one woman, a vacuum cleaner, & electric stoves. Now how much of this is dream, & how much reality? I should like, very much, to turn to the last page of this virgin volume & there find my dreams true. It rests with me to substantiate them between now & then. I need not burden my entirely frivolous page with whys & wherefores, how we reached these decisions, so quick. It was partly a question of coal at Rodmell. Then Nelly presented her ultimatum—poor creature, she'll withdraw it, I know,—about the kitchen. "And I must have a new stove; & it must be on the floor so that we can warm our feet; & I must have a window in that wall. . . ." Must? Is must a word to be used to Princes? Such was our silent reflection as we received these commands, with Lottie skirmishing around with her own very unwise provisoes & excursions. "You won't get two girls to sleep in one room as we do" &c. "Mrs Bell says you can't get a drop of hot water in this house. . . ." "So you wont come here again, Nelly?" I asked. "No, ma'am, I wont come here again" in saying which she spoke, I think, the truth. Meanwhile, they are happy as turtles, in front of a roaring fire in their own clean kitchen, having attended the sales, & enjoyed all the cheap diversions of Richmond, which begin to pall on me. Already I feel ten years younger. Life settles round one, living here for 9 years as we've done; merely to think of a change lets in the air. Youth is a matter of forging ahead. I see my contemporaries satisfied, outwardly; inwardly conscious of emptiness. Whats it for? they ask themselves now & then, when the new year comes, & can't possibly upset their comfort for a moment. I think of the innumerable tribe of Booth, for example; all lodged, nested, querulous, & believing firmly that they've been enjoined so to live by our father which is in heaven. Now my state is infinitely better. Here am I launching forth into vacancy. We've two young people depending on us.[1] We've no house in prospect. All is possibility & doubt. How far can we make publishing pay? And can we give up the Nation? & could we find a house better than Monks House? Yes, thats cropped up, partly owing to the heaven sent address of Nelly. I turned into Thornton's waiting for my train,[2] & was told of an old house at Wilmington—I'm pleased to find [how] volatile our temperaments still are—& L. is steady as well, a triumph I can't say I achieve—at the ages of 42 & 43—for 42 comes tripping towards me, the momentous year.

Now it is six, my boundary, & I must read Montaigne,[3] & cut short those other reflections about, I think, reading & writing which were to fill up the page. I ought to describe the walk from Charleston too; but can't defraud Montaigne any longer. He gets better & better, & so I cant scamp him, & rush into writing, & earn my 20 guineas as I hope. Did I record a tribute from Gosse: that I'm a nonentity, a scratch from Hudson, that the V.O. is rotten; & a compliment all the way from America from Rebecca West?[4] Oh dear, oh dear, no boasting, aloud, in 1924. I didn't boast at Charleston.

Wednesday 9 January

At this very moment, or fifteen minutes ago, to be precise, I bought the ten years lease of 52 Tavistock Sqre London W.C.1—I like writing Tavistock. Subject of course to the lease, & to Providence, & to the unforeseen vagaries on the part of old Mrs Simons, the house is ours: & the basement, & the billiard room, with the rock garden on top, &

1. i.e. Marjorie Joad and Dadie Rylands.
2. J. R. Thornton & Co, Auctioneers and Estate Agents, of 66 High Street, Lewes.
3. VW's review of Essays of Montaigne, translated by Charles Cotton, appeared in the *TLS* of 31 January 1924 (Kp C243).
4. Neither Gosse's 'tribute' nor Rebecca West's compliment have been traced; Hudson had in 1915 written to Edward Garnett pouring cold water on his enthusiasm for *The Voyage Out* (see *M & M*, p 61). This letter was published in *Letters from W. H. Hudson to Edward Garnett* in 1925, but conceivably its general drift had been conveyed to VW orally.

the view of the square in front & the desolated buildings behind, & Southampton Row, & the whole of London—London thou art a jewel of jewels, & jasper of jocunditie⁵—music, talk, friendship, city views, books, publishing, something central & inexplicable, all this is now within my reach, as it hasn't been since August 1913, when we left Cliffords Inn, for a series of catastrophes which very nearly ended my life, & would, I'm vain enough to think, have ruined Leonard's.⁶ So I ought to be grateful to Richmond & Hogarth, & indeed, whether its my invincible optimism or not, I am grateful. Nothing could have suited better all through those years when I was creeping about, like a rat struck on the head, & the aeroplanes were over London at night, & the streets dark, & no penny buns in the window. Moreover, nowhere else could we have started the Hogarth Press, whose very awkward beginning had rise in this very room, on this very green carpet. Here that strange offspring grew & throve; it ousted us from the dining room, which is now a dusty coffin; & crept all over the house.

And people have been here, thousands of them it seems to me. I've sat over this fire many an evening talking, & save for one fit of the glooms last summer, have never complained of Richmond, till I shed it, like a loose skin.

[*Postscript by VW:*] I've had some very curious visions in this room too, lying in bed, mad, & seeing the sunlight quivering like gold water, on the wall. I've heard the voices of the dead here. And felt, through it all, exquisitely happy.

Saxon is dining here tonight, & will be invited to move in with his troupe of lunatics at Easter.⁷ Our move can take place any time between Feb. 1st & then. Really, since I dont want to give auctioneers particulars, I may as well say briefly that my good genius for houses whispered in my ear on Monday, when, as I was leaving Mr Coade, the flushed young lady said "Mrs Woolf, are you still looking for a house?" "Thats what

5.   'London, thou art the flour of cities all.
        Gemme of all joy, jaspre of jocunditie,
        Most myghty carbuncle of vertue and valour;'
            In Honour of the City of London by William Dunbar (1465?-1530?)
6. VW refers to her breakdown and madness of the late summer, autumn and winter of 1913 in the course of which, on the evening of 9 September, she had tried to kill herself. See *II QB*, pp 11-19. The Woolfs had taken rooms in Clifford's Inn, off the Strand, shortly after returning to London in October 1912 from their honeymoon.
7. Saxon wished to remove his widowed mother from Hove, where his father had kept a private nursing home, and was negotiating with the Woolfs to rent Hogarth House and instal her there.

I'm here for" I said. "But I'd begun to think I'd better take a flat."
"Oh well, 52 Tavistock Sqre might suit you. It has a large studio."
The perverse young man made me come to Gordon Sqre next, then
misdirected me; & then I ran into Adrian; & then both together we
went into Messrs Dollman & Pritchard's, through great green baize
swing doors, up stairs, into a flat, now semi-dark; & then, down into
the basement where I very rapidly lost count of rooms, & out into the
old gentleman's billiard room; & so decided this is our place if ever there
was one.[8]

Well, we had a long cold busy day yesterday—going, I did, twice
to London, & ending with The Flame, a play which invented emotions
which nobody has felt these 100 years; nobody felt even in 1824.[9] But by
a process of hypnotism, half Bayswater last night made themselves
believe that other people felt like this & therefore that they ought to.

I may say that coincident with the purchase of 52 Tavistock Sqre
(how I like writing that!) is the purchase of a nine penny pen, a fountain
pen, which has an ordinary nib, & writes—sometimes very well. Am I
more excited by buying Tavistock Sqre, or by buying my new fountain
pen?—which reflection reminds me that I have volume 7 of Montaigne
to polish off, & Saxon dining here. So in spite of a clouded brain, upstairs,
fetch the books, & begin. First, though, one gaze into the fire—& oh
dear, I've forgotten my ultimatum to the poor domestics. Both to go;
& both very game, & also affectionate—a trying combination.

Saturday 12 January[10]

I have just introduced a great improvement in the cover of this book
—a calendar. But to revert to those other improvements—shall I survive
the process? There's a snag in the lease: some drastic clause saying that
Bedford can refuse permission to sublet.[11] If exercised, this would throw

8. J. W. Coade Son & Budgen were auctioneers and estate agents of 118 Southampton
   Row, WC1; Dollman and Pritchard was a firm of solicitors in occupation of the
   ground and first floors of 52 Tavistock Square, which they rented from the departing
   leaseholders, old Mr and Mrs Simon.
9. *The Flame*, a play adapted from the French of Charles Méré by James Bernard
   Fagan, opened with Violet Vanbrugh at Wyndham's Theatre on 7 January. LW
   no doubt had Press seats: in the *Nation & Athenaeum* of 19 January 1924, the play
   was described as 'the last word in sentimental unreality.'
10. On the page facing the entry for 12 January VW has noted: *Goossens. Wed. Jan.*
    16th. 5.15. Aeolian Hall. Queens Hall. 8.30. Wed. Jan. 30th. Monvel.
11. Tavistock Square was part of the Bloomsbury estates laid out by the Dukes of
    Bedford from the late eighteenth century onwards; the Bedford Estate reserved
    certain rights over its leasehold properties.

the offices, now let at £250, on our hands. But they offer us the flat & basement separate. All this involves calculation; & what is worse, a good deal of depression on L.'s side. Then I ask myself, why do I do it? Is it worth it? Aren't the risks too great? And I reply according to the mood I'm in. My heart turned like a wounded eel in my breast on Thursday night: it was serene as a summers day yesterday; now its sore and choppy. But I like myself for taking my fences. So long as rashness don't become silliness. Suppose it all fails, anyhow I shall have tried to bring it off. Then Nelly has agreed to stay on alone as a general; & I am to find Lottie a place in Gordon Square. I see difficulty upon difficulty ahead. None of this would much matter if L. were happy; but with him despondent or grim, the wind is taken out of my sails, & I say what's it all for?

But the truth is—no, I dont think I know the truth. Undoubtedly my chief prop is my writing, which cant fail me here or in London. But according to Montaigne, one is various. I cant lay down a law for my own feelings.

Its odd how entirely this house question absorbs one. It is a radical change, though. It means a revision of 4 lives. As for Lottie, I have my doubts, for her temper will always be unseating her, & I feel, after 7 years, or is it 8?, some responsibility for her. If by my doing she got into difficulty, I suppose I should blame myself. Yet for people of our age, which is in full summer, to dread risk & responsibility seems pusillanimous. We have no children to consider. My health is as good as it will be in this world, & a great deal better than it ever has been. The next ten years must see the press into fame or bankruptcy; to loiter on here is a handicap. But I've gone through all these matters time & time again, & wish I could think of something else. I've so much work on hand. Its odd how unimportant my work seems, suddenly, when a practical matter like this blocks the way. I see it as it appears to the world, from outside, not all cavernous & lit up as it appears from within.

Who have I seen? Saxon chiefly, & the Grants. They have a good deal of solid comfort at Grosvenor House Twickenham: chairs & tables & little mats on the dressing tables. There was a tight mute woman by the fire & Jim Rendel, playing chess with the old fluffy haired Major[12]—that failure, that vivacious irresponsible old man, who lies on his sofa, a perfect gentleman, a man of the world, humorous, shrewd, practical, but

12. James Meadows (Jim) Rendel (1854-1937) was the husband of Major Grant's niece Elinor, the eldest of his sister Lady Strachey's ten children; he had been Chairman of the Assam Bengal Railway, and was in fact two years older than his old uncle. The Woolfs' visit was on Sunday 6 January.

ineffective utterly. In comes Ethel, & I perceive how lovely she was, & something charming still in their relationship, which is all worn away & staled; & she knows him, I suppose to be dying, & has her mind so set on practical affairs (they're very poor) that she can't feel anything. She is a stately kind, unimaginative woman, who pities me a little, I think. (Now dont think of the house problem!)

Seeing Saxon dont amount to much, though I see him now a distinguished man. If I met him in a room full, I should say who's that? I think. Its partly that he's become more sure of himself. And then, I fancy, reading Plato all through tells. I like his absence of detail—in discussing plans, for instance; though when it comes to practice, he's a meticulous man, can't order a taxi for himself without endless deliberations.

I saw Adrian & Karin too. There's an unhappy woman if you like. But what is happiness? I define it to be a glow in the eye. Her eyes are like polished pavements—wet pavements. There's no firelit cavern within. Molly's eyes are a different matter. For I went to tea with her, in a very clean house in Oakley Street. There was Michael, a young man, blushing, nervous, in trousers.[13] He had been out to tea, but didn't like the people; they discuss such details, he said. "Which part of Devonshire do you like best?" Its amusing to see how that sort of question appears in reality, before one's used to it. Molly is very pale, very shapeless, like a walrus, rather; has cut a fringe, which is pure grey; & manages to dress much better than I do. I love the distracted busy ways of these mothers —no parsimony of life, as there is with the childless—always something that must be decided, or done. Old Mrs MacCarthy is, I think, the most arrant & pernicious bore in the world; like a child, but not to be put down; insisting on her story being heard; utterly unable to see beyond her own plate of bread & butter; must know what kind of jam it is. Really I fancy these old ladies, without occupation, the most trying in the world. Two days ago she became a Roman Catholic. Charlie Sanger came in; patted Molly's hand. He too respects maternal warmth. He has a great respect for the worth of human nature, it always strikes me; respects the upstanding qualities; knows how hard life is—not, perhaps, how pleasant. One of these days I mean to write a story about life turning all the faces in a tube carriage grey, sodden, brave, disillusioned. But why doesn't it make any one of them look contented, happy, as if they'd got what they wanted? It gives a vivacity to the young, content to the elderly, very little intense pleasure, I shd. say, looking at them.

13. The MacCarthy's eldest child Michael had been born in 1907.

Sunday 20 January

————the clock striking six, & Lord Berners, Siegfried Sassoon & William the chauffeur just gone.[14] Yes, we have got into the peerage. Do I altogether like the peerage? The trouble is that there's something a little opaque; they tell good stories; & I've rather lost the art of listening to their points. This Lord is as Siegfried says, a Kilburn Jew; round, fat, pale—no fairly chubby, a determined little man, whose rank, I fancy, gives him some consistency not otherwise his. Still, rank, nowadays, at my age, is slightly vulgar, like a fringe to the mantelpiece. Vita dined here with him; & with her too rank is a velvet fringe; theres something dense instead of vibrant. Old S.S. is a nice dear kind sensitive warm-hearted good fellow. He came back, with William waiting, half shut the door, & asked me to get reviewing for [W. J.] Turner—"he hasn't asked this himself mind you". (I dont like being in any way deflected from my comfortable ways, when it comes to writing. That's the worst of exciting society: it somehow makes one, momentarily, meretricious, in that department.) But to return. Siegfried is all right. Then what else has happened? No final news of Tavistock Square yet, but Saxon's cook has apparently taken Hogarth; & says the garden will be very nice for her little girl, & if Mrs Turner may bring the gas stove which was the Drs present, they'll come in March. (The thing about aristocrats is that they veil all pretence very humbly; & let one ride on their backs; & then suddenly turn seignurial). Here we are, though, going through a time of waiting. I shall be happy so soon as my claws are into the move. At present, I feel Oh God another journey? Must I go up by train? Where am I to change before dinner tomorrow, & so on. Lottie vacillates. First she says she's going to get £60 & be maid housekeeper to Kid Lewis;[15] then she'll stay with Saxon—God knows what'll be the end; & I shall be sorry to miss her— Now, I must tackle my Montaigne quotations, since thats demanded by some Cockney in charge of the Supt.

14. Gerald Hugh Tyrwhitt-Wilson, 14th Baron Berners (1883-1950), musician, artist and author, inherited the ancient barony of Berners from his uncle in 1918. Siegfried Sassoon (1886-1967), poet, educated at Marlborough and Cambridge, served as an officer throughout the war, which experience moved him to protest publicly against its political mismanagement and the consequent prolongation of the slaughter. He had published two books of verse, and had become literary editor of the Socialist *Daily Herald*.

15. Ted ('Kid') Lewis (1894-1970), world welter-weight champion in 1915 and from 1917-19.

Wednesday 23 January

And on Monday if I'd written here I should have had to say "We have lost Tavistock Square"—lost it through the sharp practice of Mr Simon, & the easy going indolence of Mr Guy Hemsley.[16] It was a very unpleasant shock, & for my part I don't think we could easily have got over it—found as good a house that is, let alone the infinite dreariness of the hunt. Anyhow, after sitting fidgetting at the play (Munro's Progress[17]) & damning it considerably I went off to Coade, found myself expected, heard a very queer story—how Simon would let the Woolves have it if Coade would take £30 instead of £40: which Coade wouldnt; so I offered the extra £10; communicated with my solicitors by phone, across the office table (oh yes I'm grown up now) & had the matter arranged in 15 minutes, & went on to tea with Nessa swelling with pride & excitement—all great nonsense, L. would say. But my house finding genius was outraged; whats the good of me, it asked, if you let these sharpers trick you? And I warn you, 52 is your house. So, practically not only spiritually speaking it now is; for in spite of Hemsley & the strike & the failure of the draft contract to arrive, &c &c; I visited the office with cheque & signature before one today; & then spent a shilling on a plate of beef. Ah well! Now I can sigh contented over my fire, in spite of the rain, & the strike,[18] & Lady Colefax & Ethel Sands, & all cares & sorrows & perplexities. They aren't very grievous at the moment. The New Republic has taken my article on Jane Austen; £22 from the Dial for Lives of Obscure; &c &c.[19] This time last year we were in a very different pair of shoes. Not that even then I was more than surface ruffled. No: I remember some very black, stagnant days about this time of year.

16. A partner in Messrs Halsey, Lightly and Hemsley, the family solicitors acting for the Woolfs.

17. *Progress* by C. K. Munro was performed by the Stage Society at the New Theatre; it took four and a half hours. The review published in the *Nation & Athenaeum* on 26 January referred to stretches of prolonged tediousness, and said that the author had failed to master the immense material of his project—a gigantic tragi-comedy 'in which the actors are races, nations, movements, tendencies, ideals'; but that even so his experiment was of interest.

18. The strike by members of the Associated Society of Locomotive Engineers and Firemen lasted from 21 to 29 January. The National Union of Railwaymen did not give their support and railway services were only partially disrupted.

19. 'Jane Austen at Sixty' was first published in the *Nation & Athenaeum*, 15 December 1923, and reprinted in the *New Republic*, 30 January 1924 (Kp C241); 'The Lives of the Obscure', for which VW had had to accept £13 from Squire (see above, 17 March 1923), appeared in the *Dial* in May 1925 (Kp C244).

I have seen Roger; seen his pictures, which with the irrepressible vanity of the artist, he makes even the blind like me report on, by electric light, in a hurry. But enough of that; in every other way he abounds: cut him, wherever you like, & the juice wells up. Pamela is about to bear; so was his cat. Lytton has bought his house.[20] Nessa is convicted by the law of not owning her flat at 50. I've said nothing of this great affair—the battle of Bells & Stephens. Clive will be turned out & the Americans will triumph.[21] And this reminds me that I'm resolved to draw in my horns with Mary H. I was absurdly exacerbated by a laughing report of Roger's that Clive is circulating an account of me, wishing to dress like Lady Diana &c.[22] Mary will cheerfully roast me to make Clive smile; & I think she relishes a little vinegar in my wounds. But I'm not proud of my own behaviour either—except that I like being natural, & talking nonsense if I've a mind. This one cant do safely with her, & the excitability of my temper is such that when a light flick of the whip, like Roger's is given me, I lose more—much more—than all the pleasure I get from talking like a genius over my fire to poor dear Mary—whom I like too. But it can't be helped. And in London I shall have too many Mary's, & can't face the fritter to my nerves of the old intriguing ways.

Now I'm sending off Montaigne, & back again tomorrow to The Hours, which I was looking at disconsolately—oh the cold raw edges of one's relinquished pages—when the House business started this morning. But now I am going to write till we move—6 weeks straight ahead. I think its the design that's good this time—God knows.

A letter from Morgan today saying "To whom first but you & Virginia should I tell the fact that I've put the last words to my novel?" He is moved, as I am always on these occasions.[23]

20. Lytton Strachey wrote to his brother James on 4 January that he believed he had bought the lease of Ham Spray House, near Hungerford in Wiltshire, for £2,300 but, he added, 'it still totters'. The purchase was completed by the end of the month. See *Holroyd*, p 864.

21. This now rather obscure affair arose from the question whether the Stephens were legally entitled to sub-let the upper part of 50 Gordon Square to the Bells; in the event Clive was not turned out. 'Americans' was probably a pleasantry at Karin Stephen's expense.

22. Lady Diana (b. 1892), daughter of the 8th Duke of Rutland and wife of Alfred Duff Cooper, a famous beauty and social success.

23. E. M. Forster wrote to LW (undated): 'I have this moment written the last words of my novel and who but Virginia and yourself should be told about it first?' MHP, Sussex (copy).

Sunday 3 February

I didn't write however, because L. started the flu, the very next day, & gave me an unpleasant day; but there's an odd pleasure too, purely feminine I suppose, in 'looking after' being wanted; giving up my pen, & sitting with an invalid. But he was up in 4 days or less; & here we are, on the rails again, a very lovely spring day, which, by Heaven's grace, we have spent alone. No servants at the moment; no callers. The sun laid gold leaf over the trees & chimneys today. The willows on the bank were—what word is it?—soft yellow plumy, like a cloud; like an infinitely fine spray; something showery in it; & also grains of gold. I can't find the exact word; but reflect that I shant be walking here again next spring. I am not sentimental about it: Tavistock Square with the pale tower is more beautiful I think, let alone the adorable omnibuses.[1]

Owing to the influenza, I don't think I have seen more than a handful; went to Ethel [Sands]'s, was congratulated on Montaigne by Logan; Roger had stuck in it, though; talked to Arnold Bennett, a lovable sea lion, with chocolate eyes, drooping lids, & a protruding tusk.[2] He has an odd accent; a queer manner; is provincial; very much a character; "I dont understand women—" This said as a schoolboy might say it. Everyone laughs. Then "No woman is as sensitive as I am—no woman could be...." I suspect he minds things, even my pinpricks. He is slow, kind, affectionate, hauls himself along a sofa. But there was Logan, launching questions at my head; balls one had to return. Roger came in, rather wild eyed & staring. Prince Bibesco, & a Princess, who, said Roger, made the rest of us appear provincial. What a cosmopolitan he is—how he dreads the British Parish; how he adores Paris. "She had lived in Paris" he said of this Princess: "So of course she cd. talk at once about interesting things."[3] But I did not stay to hear them.

1. No. 52 Tavistock Square faced north towards the neo-classical St Pancras Church standing at the intersection of Upper Woburn Place and Euston Road; built in 1818-22 by the Inwoods, father and son, the three-tier steeple is adapted from the Tower of the Winds in Athens.

2. This is the first record of VW's meeting Arnold Bennett (1867-1921), at this time acknowledged as one of the great men of English letters, rich and successful as a novelist, and an influential journalist. The first twenty years of his life had been spent in the Potteries.

3. Prince Antoine Bibesco's cousin Princess Marthe Bibesco, *née* Lahovary (1888-1973), Roumanian-born writer and beauty; long resident in Paris and of Proust's intimate circle, she was a frequent visitor to London. See *II RF Letters*, no. 561 (Paris, May 1925): 'Ah! but the Princess Bibesco—alas another illusion gone.... I've only seen her twice before; once at Ethel Sands's where she shone brilliantly ... but today ... just the old silly aristocratic gabble.'

Yesterday, the parochial Turners came to measure the alcoves, & ask me whether Mrs Turner's father's bureau could stand in the study— You must remember the piano, & the pianola case, said Edith, one of those worrying vague 'bodies', who compose the middle classes; wearisome women, machine made, but all bristling with their views; they get hot & cold, peevish & fluttered, like other people; more so indeed; but I can't see why nature provides them, unless to supply Dartmouth with cadets, & colonels with wives.[4] Nelly went to the flat with me, & next day wrote out a time table, to show that by 3 P.M. she would still have to wash up luncheon & do Leonard's boots. Very well, I said, find a place with Lottie. But the end of a weeks consideration is, apparently, that Lottie goes with the Turners, & Nelly clings to us. The money is paid over, & the house presumably ours tomorrow. So I shall have a room of my own to sit down in, after almost 10 years, in London. I must now write to Logan, to ask for a book for the press,[5] & then read Elizabethan for my next chapter. At any rate the reading for this blessed book is a great source of delight to me.

Saturday 9 February

We have been measuring the flat. Now the question arises Is it noisy? No need to go into my broodings over that point. Fitzroy Sqre rubbed a nerve bare which will never sleep again while an omnibus is in the neighbourhood. My feeling about this move is that we're doing the courageous thing; facing the facts, which for ten years, it will be good to do. Yes, this little achievement has been good I think.

Morgan was here last night; A Passage to India done; & he is much excited, on the boil with it, consulting L. about terms; has been offered £750. So he's all right. And Heinemann this morning wants to publish my essays. Hendersons to dine, & Janet [Vaughan]. I boasted of L. (he says). One cant joke with people one doesn't know. They don't even take dinner in the basement naturally. Desmond pitched down Mary's stairs two nights ago, & broke his knee cap. Clive couldn't stay with him. He was in great pain, but Ethel Sands said, very brave. Now he's very irritable. So our feelings for our friends change. Cut me anywhere, & I bleed too profusely. Life has bred too much 'feeling' of a kind in me. Then (I'm so tired with parcels &c I cant concentrate) Marjorie has put earrings in her ears & left Joad. Poor chit! at 24. I was at Fitzroy then, & devilish

4. Edith was possibly old Mrs Turner's only daughter-in-law; Dartmouth, the Royal Naval College.
5. See III VW Letters, no. 1442: 'the letter of a grasping publisher'.

unhappy too. She found a letter, left the house,—lives in a basement. Its melodrama, but forced on her by Cyril I expect. I'm working at The Hours, & think it a very interesting attempt; I may have found my mine this time I think. I may get all my gold out. The great thing is never to feel bored with one's own writing. That is the signal for a change— never mind what, so long as it brings interest. And my vein of gold lies so deep, in such bent channels. To get it I must forge ahead, stoop & grope. But it is gold of a kind I think. Morgan said I had got further into the soul in Jacob's Room than any other novelist. He was taking piano lessons from Hilda Saxe—spun his fingers very nimbly on the score. (And it's just as noisy here, if one listens, as it can possibly be in T[avistock]. S[quare]. One gets into a habit of not listening. Remember this sage advice). Tom, the incredible Tom, writes "I do not take any prevision of antagonism" saluting some new review. Meredith white & laurel crowned could not be more magisterial.[6]

Karin has been confiding. Adrian wants to come back. She wants life. I dont altogether like her, kicking up her heels, yet see her point, & respect her conscience, for she has A. on her mind. He sits alone in Mecklenburgh Sqre. 'Its the quality you Stephens have she said. Its the real thing' like an American with a Sheraton table. Faith Henderson says she flirted with Ralph, wants moonlight, big men, diamonds, kisses; but is too old; & not good enough. Hubert takes his views from her. Janet has the Vaughan rattle in her throat; a lady; large, gawky, will marry & breed.

Saturday 23 February

Really I've a thousand things to do. I've just said to L. I'm so busy I can't begin, which unfortunately is too true of me. My mind sits in front of a fence & pours out clouds of ideas; I have to stick spurs in sharp to make it jump. I should be reading Miss Mayor's first chapters; Miss Bosanquet on Henry James & the Birds.[7] Then I bethink me that

6. Cf *Nation & Athenaeum*, 9 February 1924, p 678: 'The "Trans-Atlantic Review"— the miscellany sent forth from Paris by Mr F. M. Ford . . . sets out with authoritative blessings. Mr T. S. Eliot writes "From the prospectus which you have sent me I take no prescience of antagonism".'

7. Flora MacDonald Mayor (1872-1932), sister of Robin Mayor; the Hogarth Press published her *The Rector's Daughter* in May 1924 (*HP Checklist* 49); Theodora Bosanquet was Henry James's amanuensis from 1907 until his death in 1916; her *Henry James at Work* was published as a Hogarth Essay in November 1924 (*HP Checklist* 42); *The Birds*, a political satire by Aristophanes.

with life in its present rush, I may never again write a word of this book at Hogarth House. & so should take a few minutes to lay the sod, or whatever the expression is. Its very cold, barbarous weather. Twice we have meant to go to Rodmell & failed. L. says Wells says there comes a stage when one can't face an uncomfortable week end. Warmth is the one need I have. May's Man, a great giant in gaiters who shook L. by the hand because we are real people & own a press, came today, & will move us on March 13th for £15.[8] Nessa gets busy at 52 Tavy on Monday. I am going to force L. into the outrageous extravagance of spending £25 on painted panels, by Bell & Grant. We are trying to hook together all the resources of civilisation—telephone, gas, electric light, &, at this distance, naturally find it arduous. The electric light man doesn't turn up. Lottie is going to Karin—I fancy I have forgotten that item. Really, if providence had tried, or I had set my wits to work at their most optimistic, I don't think I could have arranged things better. First number 52 & its studio (wh. we think to make £75 on[9]) then Saxon coming here; then Lottie next door, & so keeping Nelly in society. All could not have fallen out better, so far, I say, being by no means ready to bait the deity, who can always show his claws. That reminds me of the celebrated Mr [Bertrand] Russell the other night at Karin's. (She gives her weekly party in the great gay drawingroom which is nevertheless a little echoing & lofty & very very chill). He said "Just as I saw a chance of happiness, the doctors said I had got cancer. My first thought was that that was one up to God. He had brought it off—just as I thought I saw a chance of happiness. When I was just getting better—I had very nearly died—my temperature was 107 twice over—the thing I liked was the sun: I thought how nice to feel the sun & the rain still. People came a long way after that. I wanted people very much, but not so much as the sun. The old poets were right. They made people think of death as going where they could not see the sun. I have become an optimist. I realise now that I like life—I want to live. Before that illness, I thought life was bad. Its an odd thing—both my pessimism & my optimism are instinctive" (I forget which he said was the deeper of the two.) So to Charlie Sanger, who is good all through; & then on to Moore. "When he first came up to Cambridge, he was the most wonderful creature in

8. Joseph May was a large firm of furniture removers in Howland Street, Tottenham Court Road. The decorations by Bell and Grant were destroyed by bombs in 1940: some photographic evidence remains, notably in the photographs taken of the Woolfs in the late 1930's by Gisèle Freund.
9. The 'studio' (built as a billiard room) was not let, but was used by VW as her workroom and by the Hogarth Press as a store.

the whole world. His smile was the most beautiful thing I have ever seen. We believed in Berkeley" (perhaps). "Suddenly, something went wrong with him; something happened to him and his work. Principia Ethica was nothing like so good as his Essay on Judgment (?). He was very fond of Ainsworth.[10] I don't know what happened— It ruined him. He took to putting out his tongue after that. You (I, that is) said he had no complexes. But he's full of them. Watch him putting his tongue round his mouth. I said to him once, Moore, have you ever told a lie? "YES" he said—which was the only lie he ever told. He always speaks the truth at the Aristotelian. An old gentleman met me on my way here, & asked if I were going. No; I said ⟨not such a fool⟩. Joad is speaking tonight. Haldane made a speech once, & old Shad Hodgson had to pass a vote of thanks. He had had an epileptic fit that afternoon. He got up & talked nonsense—utter nonsense. So they asked me. And *I* had to thank Haldane, though I'd got ready to criticise every argument he used. Never mind: I put them all into an article, & that stung much sharper."[11] I asked him, as I ask everyone, to write his life for the press. But my mind is absolutely relevant. I cant ramble. I stick to facts. "Facts are what we want. Now the colour of your mother's hair'?' "She died when I was two—there you are—relevant facts. I remember my grandfather's death, & crying, & then thinking it was over. I saw my brother drive up in the afternoon. Hooray! I cried. They told me I must not say hooray at all that day. I remember the servants all looking very attentively at me when I was brought to Pembroke Lodge after my father died. Whitehead's father, who was the local parson, was sent for to persuade me that the earth was round. I said it was flat. And I remember —some seaside place, now destroyed—remembered the sands, I think."[12]

10. G. E. Moore's 'The Nature of Judgment' was published in *Mind*, vol. viii, 1899; his *Principia Ethica* in 1903. Alfred Richard Ainsworth (1897-1959), Scholar of King's, an Apostle, was a close friend of Moore's; in 1894 the two went to Edinburgh together, where from 1903-07 Ainsworth was a lecturer in Greek. In 1908 he married Moore's youngest sister Sarah (an unhappy union which ended in divorce) and joined the Board of Education which he was to serve until 1940.
11. The Aristotelian Society, with lay as well as academic membership, was founded in 1880; the presidential address by Richard Burdon Haldane, 1st Viscount Haldane (1856-1928), statesman and sometime Lord Chancellor, criticised by Russell (see *Mind*, vol. xvii, 1908), was on 'The Methods of Modern Logic and the Conception of Infinity'. Shadsworthy Hollway Hodgson (1832-1912) was the first president, 1880-1894, and a leading spirit of the Aristotelian Society.
12. Both Bertrand Russell's parents—John Russell, Viscount Amberley (1842-1876) and Katherine Louisa, *née* Stanley (d. 1874), had died before he was four years old, and he and his brother were taken to Pembroke Lodge, Richmond Park,

He had no one to play with. One does not like him. Yet he is brilliant of course; perfectly outspoken; familiar; talks of his bowels; likes people; & yet & yet— He disapproves of me perhaps? He has not much body of character. This luminous vigorous mind seems attached to a flimsy little car, like that on a large glinting balloon. His adventures with his wives diminish his importance.[13] And he has no chin, & he is dapper. Nevertheless, I should like the run of his headpiece. We parted at the corner of the Square; no attempt to meet again.

Tuesday 4 March

Really I'm writing too much here. The twelve months at this rate will overflow. This is another, provisional farewell, for I may have no time—(& Thank God here's L. Grizzle knows the way he shuts the door & jumps down & runs out:)

Wednesday 12 March

And I'm now going to write the very last pages ever to be written at Hogarth House. First; the state of the weather. Its as if a fine veil had descended & lay, clear, over the chimneys; which are a pale yellow, & brick red. The veil clouds to the horizon, & I do not see the pagoda or the trees of Kew.[1] My head is stuffy & heavy. Last night we dined at Blunden's farewell party, 35 covers laid, 6 or 7 speeches made, I between honest claret coloured soapy Wright, & the nice, but melo-

---

the home of his grandfather Lord John Russell, 1st Earl Russell; the elder boy Frank (John Francis, 2nd Earl Russell, 1865-1931) was sent to Winchester, but Bertie was brought up by his grandmother in rigorously disciplined, isolated, spartan conditions. The summer of 1877 he spent with his grandparents in the Isle of Thanet, in the parish of St Peter's, of which the Rev. Alfred Whitehead was vicar; his son Alfred North Whitehead (1861-1947), FRS, mathematician and philosopher, was co-author with Russell of the commanding *Principia Mathematica* (1910-13). See *The Autobiography of Bertrand Russell, 1872-1914*, 1967.

13. Bertrand Russell's first, and for almost two decades loveless, marriage to Karin's aunt Alys Pearsall Smith finally ended in divorce in 1921, when he married Dora Black; but he had had in the interim several manifest affairs with married women. See Russell's autobiographical volumes and *The Life of Bertrand Russell* by Ronald W. Clark, 1975.

1. Sir William Chambers' ten storey, 163 ft, octagonal Pagoda, erected at Kew Gardens in 1761, was normally visible from the rear windows of Hogarth House.

dramatic looking Lynd.[2] My little drama however was provided by Murry—Lynd's neighbour—who shook hands, about the fish course, warmly. Then, as people were going, came & sat beside me. This he volunteered: I asked him to come & lay his case before me at Tavistock. "We're enemies" "Not enemies. We're in different camps. But I've never said a word against you, Virginia." "Nor I against you. But what is wrong with us?" "You begin out there—" spreading his hands. "We make patterns of pretty words?" "No. But you won't begin with your instincts. You won't own them. With all your exquisite sensibilities— you're content to stay at that." Here we came into a swift confused wrangle about "writing well". I said one must throw every ounce of oneself into expression; & that the instinctive writers scamped their work. "I *don't* scamp my work" said Murry. "You say that only men who write well can say what they mean. My God Virginia—" but here L. came up, & Murry who was beginning on Jacob's Room switched off to L.'s article on Moore.[3] Thats typical: you dont go down to the root of things. Moore ought to have [been] smacked on the bottom for talking about Hardy as he did. That disgraceful sentence about Hardy wanting a place by Aeschylus—as if Hardy thought of any place except one by Rhoda Broughton[4]— L. defended: said we must go. But I shant meet Murry for 10 years, & I want to finish the argument— Shall I come to the Adelphi? "Do." "Not unless you'll come to see me—I shall stand on my rights—" If you put it like that I will, he said, ferociously (yet so oleaginously, with a rolling lustful, or somehow leering, eye, so

2. Edmund Charles Blunden (1896-1974), poet, writer, and critic; educated at Christ's Hospital and Queen's College, Oxford, he served in the army in France and Belgium 1916-19; for his collection of poems *The Shepherd* he was awarded the Hawthornden Prize in 1922; in 1924 he was appointed Professor of English at the University of Tokyo. The farewell dinner at the Florence Restaurant, Rupert Street, on 11 March was presided over by Hubert Henderson, editor of the *Nation & Athenaeum* on which Blunden had been employed, and speeches were made by H. M. Tomlinson, H. W. Nevinson and A. G. Gardiner among others. Harold Wright (1883-1934) was assistant editor of the *Nation* at this time.

3. LW's weekly page 'The World of Books' in the *Nation & Athenaeum* was on 16 February 1924 devoted to 'Mr Moore and the Critics', and arose from George Moore's recently published *Conversations in Ebury Street*. LW's view was that Moore's 'naughtiness'—his dismissal for example of Hardy as a writer of "ill-constructed melodramas feebly written in bad grammar"—was a logical expression of his own literary taste which need surprise or upset no one. Murry himself smacked Moore on the bottom in the subsequent number of his *Adelphi*.

4. Rhoda Broughton (1840-1920), a prolific and popular novelist (author of *Not Wisely but too Well*, 1867), whose early reputation for audacity diminished as literary fashion overtook her.

that I kept thinking how he'd come down in the world, spiritually, what tenthrate shillyshallying humbugs he must live among.) And we said goodbye for ten years. He liked me, he said; he had always liked me, & enjoyed meeting me like this. Off we went. How honest [?] & trusty & sterling Francis Birrell was in comparison!

So home that long cold exhausting journey for the last time. Some odds & ends of ideas came to me at the dinner. For one thing, how pungent people's writing is compared with people's flesh. We were all toothless insignificant amiable nonentities—we distinguished writers— Not a fig would I give for anyone's praise or curse. Jack Squire, fat, & consequential; Eddie [Marsh] grown grey & fatherly; Nevinson beetroot coloured, & a little praising blood, & by inference himself;[5] Tomlinson like the hard knob of a walking stick carved by a boy of 8; Blunden, despairing, drooping, crow-like, rather than Keats' like. And did we really all believe in Blunden's 'genius' Had we read his poems? How much sincerity was there in the whole thing? The truth is these collective gatherings must be floated by some conventional song, in which all can join, like He's a jolly good fellow, which Squire started. Subtler impressions did occur to me, but I cant place them at the moment. Nor at the moment can I think of any farewell for this beautiful & lovable house, which has done us such a good turn for almost precisely nine years, so that, as I lay in bed last night, I nearly humanised it, & offered it my thanks. Old Mrs Turner will lie in my room now, & die there, it is predicted in two years time, among her china, her linen, & her great flowering wall papers, her father's bureau, & several enormous wardrobes.[6]

The Woolfs' move from Hogarth House to 52 Tavistock Square, Blooms-bury, took place on 13 and 14 March; on the latter date they stayed the night at Clive Bell's in Gordon Square, and first slept in their new home on Saturday 15 March. They were to inhabit the two top floors of the large four-storey house, one of those forming the block on the southern side of the square; the sitting tenants, Messrs Dollman & Pritchard, Solicitors, con-tinued their tenure of the ground and first floors; the extensive basement was given over to the Hogarth Press; and a large billiard room built in

5. Henry Woodd Nevinson (1856-1941), author, war correspondent, crusading journalist and socialist, was a member of the *Nation* staff, 1907-23, and also wrote for the *Daily Herald* and *Manchester Guardian*.
6. Mrs Moxon Turner did die at Hogarth House, probably within two years; Saxon exercised his option to terminate his lease at the end of three, rather than seven, years, and in 1927 Hogarth House was sold to a Mrs Hazle.

place of a back garden became both VW's study and the storeroom for Hogarth Press books.

52 Tavistock Sqre

Saturday 5 April

Well, I will make a brief beginning—after 3 weeks silence. But it has not been silence at all. The noise of bus & taxi has worried me, & the noise of the human tongue has disturbed me, pleasantly & otherwise, & now I'm half asleep. Leonard working as usual.

Tonight, & one other, are the only nights I've been in this week; & all this afternoon went in talking to Mr Littell of the New Republic.[1] But can I collect any first impressions? how Marchmont Street[2] was like Paris; how my first night in the basement I saw the moon, with drifting clouds, & it was a terrifying & new [?] London moon; dreadful & exciting; as if the Richmond moon had been veiled. Oh the convenience of this place! & the loveliness too. We walk home from theatres, through the entrails of London. Why do I love it so much? . . . for it is stony hearted, & callous. The tradespeople don't know one—but these disparaging remarks about the shopkeepers of Marchmont Street were interrupted & it is now *Tuesday, April 15th*, & L. & I have been having one of those melancholy middle aged summings up of a situation which occur from time to time, but are seldom recorded. Indeed most of life escapes, now I come to think of it: the texture of the ordinary day. We were to have had a quiet week, & I brought in Mortimer after Gerhardt last night,[3] & he stayed & talked, aimlessly enough, about his money & his uncles; & so L. was desperately gloomy. Not a stroke of work done he says, since we came to London. This is largely imagination anticipating what people say must happen I think, though its true fish keep drifting into the net. Gerald Brenan back; Roger rampant to paint us; Morgan, elflike, mocking, aloof; Nessa & Duncan. Then there was Angelica's accident which, for the psychology of it I should have described. Here was Nessa painting, & I answering the telephone. Positively bad news has to batter down optimism before it reaches one's ears. Louie & Angelica have

1. Philip Littell (1868-1943) was the retiring editor of the *New Republic* which he had edited since 1914; it was to become the main American recipient of VW's articles.
2. The local provision centre, full of small shops and bustle.
3. The great German singer Elena Gerhardt (1883-1961) gave a series of song recitals at the Queen's Hall in April 1924; that on the 14th was devoted to Brahms.

been knocked down by a motor & are in the Middlesex hospital.[4] Having
got that into my head, I had to repeat it to Nessa: to destroy all that
simmering everyday comfort, with the smell of paint in the room, &
Tom just coming up stairs to tea. She ran out & away from the telephone
instinctively, ran round in an aimless way for a second. Then off they
dashed & I after them, & so to the hospital, holding hands in the cab;
& then sheer agony, for there was Louie, with her foot bandaged, &
no Angelica; only an evasive nurse, parrying enquiries & taking us
behind a screen where Angelica lay in bed, still, her face turned away.
At last she moved. "She's not dead" Duncan said. They both thought
her dead. Then the young Dr came, & seemed silently & considerately
but firmly to wish the mother to know that the case was hopeless: very
grave; run over across the stomach. Yes there may have to be an operation. The surgeon had been sent for, & was now on the train. So Nessa
went back to sit there, & I saw again that extraordinary look of anguish,
dumb, not complaining, which I saw in Greece, I think, when she was
ill. The feelings of the people who don't talk express themselves thus.
My feeling was "a pane of glass shelters me. I'm only allowed to look
on at this." at which I was half envious, half grieved. Moreover, I was
sent off to find Clive, & so spared, or not allowed, the long wait there,
in the chattering ward. Its a queer thing to come so close to agony as
this, & just to be saved oneself. What I felt was, not sorrow or pity for
Angelica, but that now Nessa would be an old woman; & this would
be an indelible mark; & that death & tragedy had once more put down
his paw, after letting us run a few paces. People never get over their
early impressions of death I think. I always feel pursued. But theres an
end of this. Nothing was wrong with Angelica—it was only a joke this
time.

It takes a long time to form a habit—the habit of living at 52 Tavistock
Sqre is not quite formed, but doing well. Already I have spent a week
without being bothered by noise. One ceases to hear or to see. The
dominant interests, I suppose assert themselves, make order by triumphing
over the lesser. I notice things much less than I did 10 days ago. Soon I
shall be making a habit of life in this room.

As for work, I have done the Dr chapter in my novel: & am furbishing
up the Greeks; the usual depressions assail me. My criticism seems to
me pretty flimsy sometimes. But there is no principle, except to follow
this whimsical brain implicitly, pare away the ill fitting, till I have the
shape exact, & if thats no good, it is the fault of God, after all. It is He

4. Louie Dunnet was Angelica's nurse; the Middlesex Hospital in Mortimer Street is
one of London's larger teaching hospitals.

that has made us, not we ourselves. I like that text.[5] I don't at all regret
Richmond. Ethel Sands &c think I ought to mourn my beautiful room.
But I now behold what is more beautiful—the ⟨Russell⟩ Imperial Hotel
in the evening sunshine; pink & yellow like the Brighton front.[6] I regret
saturday afternoons a little— How I meander & drivel!

Marjorie [Joad] is on her holiday. I keep shop of a morning. Dadie
has been—a sensitive vain youth, with considerable grit in him, I judge.
Sometimes the future appears perilous; problematical rather, the press
that is, but always fruitful & interesting. I have said nothing of my
speech at the London Group, which drew tears;[7] or of a host of matters.
On Thursday we go to Rodmell, the test of poor Nelly's endurance.
And now for the Elizabethans.

Grosvenor Sqre houses are precisely like saloons in Victorian Inns,
or glorified boarding houses: handsome ill-proportioned rooms; gilt
chairs, fretted tables; urns & vases depicted in pale mauve on the watered
silk walls. Each wall has a piece—smugglers, coaching & so on; a little
fire burns in a large grate; a glass screen fends it off, & there Nelly &
Lord Bob perch, very chilly & formal, a dragoon bringing in little cakes.[8]

Monday 5 May

This is the 29th anniversary of mothers death. I think it happened
early on a Sunday morning, & I looked out of the nursery window &
saw old Dr Seton walking away with his hands behind his back, as if
to say It is finished, & then the doves descending, to peck in the road, I
suppose, with a fall & descent of infinite peace. I was 13, & could fill a
whole page & more with my impressions of that day, many of them ill
received by me, & hidden from the grown ups, but very memorable

5. From Psalm 100, verse 3.
6. Two hotels face towards Russell Square on its north-eastern side, the huge late-
   Victorian Hotel Russell, in pale terracotta, and the more exuberant dark brick
   Imperial Hotel, dating from Edwardian times (now demolished). They were both
   presumably visible from the back windows of 52 Tavistock Square as one side of
   Woburn Place was demolished at this time.
7. A London Group dinner, presided over by Roger Fry, was held in honour of
   Bernard Adeney, its retiring president, at Pinoli's Restaurant, Wardour Street, on
   31 March 1924. A sympathetic account of VW's terror and triumph as a speaker
   on this occasion is given by Osbert Sitwell (whose speech preceded hers) in
   Laughter in the Next Room, 1949, vol. 4 of his autobiography *Left Hand, Right
   Hand*. Her theme was the unity of the arts.
8. Lord and Lady Robert Cecil, with whom the Woolfs went to tea on 10 April,
   were living in the town house of her brother the Earl of Durham at 39 Grosvenor
   Square, W1.

on that account: how I laughed, for instance, behind the hand which was meant to hide my tears; & through the fingers saw the nurses sobbing.[1]

But enough of death—its life that matters. We came back from Rodmell 7 days ago, after a royal Easter which Nelly survived heroically. After weeding I had to go in out of the sun; & how the quiet lapped me round! & then how dull I got, to be quite just: & how the beauty brimmed over me & steeped my nerves till they quivered, as I have seen a water plant quiver when the water overflowed it. (This is not right, but I must one day express that sensation). Then my troubles with the noise here—did I have a headache, or what? I quite forget, being now come back again from Rodmell for the 2nd time, & using up my fidgets in the old way. For it seems to me that this diary may die of London, if I'm not careful.[2]

Monday
May 26th

London is enchanting. I step out upon a tawny coloured magic carpet, it seems, & get carried into beauty without raising a finger. The nights are amazing, with all the white porticoes & broad silent avenues. And people pop in & out, lightly, divertingly like rabbits; & I look down Southampton Row, wet as a seal's back or red & yellow with sunshine, & watch the omnibus going & coming, & hear the old crazy organs. One of these days I will write about London, & how it takes up the private life & carries it on, without any effort. Faces passing lift up my mind; prevent it from settling, as it does in the stillness at Rodmell.

But my mind is full of The Hours. I am now saying that I will write at it for 4 months, June, July, August & September, & then it will be done, & I shall put it away for three months, during which I shall finish my essays; & then that will be—October, November, December— January: & I shall revise it January February March April; & in April my essays will come out; & in May my novel. Such is my programme.[3]

1. Cf 'A Sketch of the Past' written fifteen years later (see *Moments of Being*, p 84). Dr David Elphinstone Seton (c. 1827-1917) MD Edin 1856, of Emperor's Gate, South Kensington, was the Stephens' family doctor until the death of Sir Leslie.
2. The Woolfs were at Monks House from 17-28 April, and again from 23-26 May; between these visits they had stayed the night of 9 May at Tidmarsh with Lytton Strachey; and from 17-19 May were in Cambridge, where VW read a paper to the Society of Heretics on 'Character in Fiction', an expansion of ideas adumbrated in an article entitled 'Mr Bennett and Mrs Brown' (Kp C240) published the previous winter, which was to be revised and published as 'Character in Fiction' in the *Criterion* (KP C251), and then again as *Mr Bennett and Mrs Brown* in a Hogarth Press pamphlet (Kp A7).
3. To which she adhered: *The Common Reader* was published on 23 April 1925; *Mrs Dalloway* on 14 May 1925.

It is reeling off my mind fast & free now; as ever since the crisis of August last, which I count the beginning of it, it has gone quick, being much interrupted though. It is becoming more analytical & human I think; less lyrical; but I feel as if I had loosed the bonds pretty completely & could pour everything in. If so—good. Reading it remains. I aim at 80,000 words this time. And I like London for writing it, partly because, as I say, life upholds one; & with my squirrel cage mind, its a great thing to be stopped circling. Then to see human beings freely & quickly is an infinite gain to me. And I can dart in & out & refresh my stagnancy.

I have left the whole of society unrecorded. Tidmarsh, Cambridge, & now Rodmell: We had a queer little party here the other day—when the sinister & pedagogic Tom cut a queer figure. I cannot wholly free myself from suspicions about him—at the worst they only amount to calling him an American schoolmaster: a very vain man. He took me to Lear (unrecorded) & we both jeered & despised; & now he comes out in the Criterion with solemn & stately rebuke of those who jeer & despise.[4] I taxed him, lightly with this: he sat tight & said that he meant what he wrote: then what does he mean by what he says? God knows. There's something hole & cornerish, biting in the back, suspicious, elaborate, uneasy, about him: much would be liberated by a douche of pure praise, which he can scarcely hope to get. There was Philip Ritchie with his very clear cut nose. And shant I have a bath? as we've Dr Glover coming to discuss the P.S.S.[5] & then put on my new red dress?

4. VW had been with T. S. Eliot to the Phoenix Society's performance of *King Lear* at the Regent Theatre on Sunday 30 March. In 'A Commentary' (signed *Crites*) in the April 1924 number of the *Criterion*, Eliot wrote of it that it was 'almost flawless'. 'It is commonly said' he wrote, 'that *King Lear* is not a play to be acted; as if any play could be better in the reading than in the representation. It is more likely, to judge from the response of the audience, that *King Lear* is a work of such immense power that it offends and scandalizes ordinary citizens of both sexes.' The 'queer little party' was on 20 May when the Woolfs' dinner guests, Roger Fry and Philip Ritchie, were joined afterwards by Vanessa, Duncan, Lytton Strachey and Eliot. The Hon. Philip Charles Thomson Ritchie (1899-1927), eldest son of Lord Ritchie of Dundee, was about to leave Oxford and embark on a legal career; he was a new love of Lytton's.

5. Dr James Glover (1882-1926), the distinguished psychoanalyst, acting for the British Psycho-Analytical Society, was negotiating with LW the terms and arrangements whereby the Hogarth Press in 1924 undertook to distribute and henceforward publish the papers of the International Psycho-Analytical Library— a step which led to the Hogarth Press becoming the publishers of Freud's complete works in English translation (see *IV LW*, 163ff).

Leonard thinks less well of me for powdering my nose, & spending money on dress. Never mind. I adore Leonard.

Saturday 14 June

Back from Whitsun at Rodmell, & just off to sit in Gordon Sqre with Nessa & Angelica; so my diary will be defrauded; stifled by too much life. The unrecorded clogs my pen. Roger's story at the Etoile the other night was perhaps my most sensational piece of news. "Something dreadful has happened to me" he said, staring very steadily with his great wide open eyes. At which I, being frivolous, laughed. "But it was dreadful," upon wh. to the credit of my heart, it stopped beating, expecting cancer. And then he told me the story of the mad French peasant woman who shot herself for love of him on the cliff at Havre looking towards England. "And so my last chance of happiness is gone" said Roger. And so we walked town Tottenham Court Rd in the pouring rain, I protesting affection, & Roger saying that he was fated; he was cursed; he had never had more than 3 weeks happiness in his life. "I have pleasure —I enjoy my friends—but no happiness." I see what he means. And he's so young, he says—& so fond of women. To which Nessa adds, pertinently, that he'll recover, & do it again. For of course we cant help becoming cynical & merry. To hear us, gulls like Ott. (who's been here contaminating the June night) would think we were heartless. But how long can Roger love a woman without driving her mad? This creature thought he laughed at her, seeing that he dyed vests yellow & sent them to her, telling her to turn to the East & put them on, as a cure for tuberculosis. And he sent her pictures of negro sculpture. For some reason, against my habit, I feel as if I should like to write a story of this.[1]

1. Roger Fry had met Josette Coatmellec in November 1922 at Dr Coué's clinic in Nancy. They fell in love, but she was obsessed by suspicious fancies which led to misunderstandings; these came to a climax when he sent her the photograph of a negro mask he had recently bought, which she interpreted as a cruel joke at her expense. His distraught letter of remonstrance and affection was written during the night of 31 March/1 April, but she had killed herself before it was sent. See *II RF Letters*, no. 544 (to Josette Coatmellec) and no. 547 (to VW); also Fry Papers, King's College Library, Cambridge, 'Histoire de Josette'. Describing Fry's gullibility in her biography of him, VW could not refrain from making some use of this story, though she qualifies it as legend. See *Roger Fry*, 1940, pp 247-8. Roger and VW dined at the Etoile in Charlotte Street (at that time a modest restaurant), and were to have gone to the theatre; but LW's diary notes that they came back early.

Saturday 21 June

I am oh so sleepy; in fact just woken from a hot drowse. This week is Apostles week, & we went to a disillusioned party last night, after which L. contemplated, seriously, some scientific form of suicide.[2] I have my moods too. If I weren't so sleepy, I would write about the soul. I think its time to cancel that vow against soul description. What was I going to say? Something about the violent moods of my soul. How describe them, even with a waking mind? I think I grow more & more poetic. Perhaps I restrained it, & now, like a plant in a pot, it begins to crack the earthenware. Often I feel the different aspects of life bursting my mind asunder. Morgan is too restrained in his new book perhaps. I mean, what's the use of facts at our time of life? Why build these careful cocoons [?]: why not say straight out—yes, but what?

I met Sydney Waterlow last night, & was monolithic on purpose,—a bad thing to be; but I feared gushing & depths, & intended to keep myself free. He no doubt prescribes speaking out. Murry is married again;[3] & I don't often think of Katherine with any vividness.

I look forward with a little alarm to Dadie coming, chiefly I think that it commits us more seriously. But that will wear off soon. It seems to me the beginning of ten years of very hard work, because, for one thing, I should hate failure, & not to fail, we must keep on pressing forward, thinking, planning, imagining, letter writing, asking Vita to write, &c &c Siegfried [Sassoon] to write, accepting Nancy Cunard;[4] I dont see how Marjorie will fit in, altogether, & rather anticipate some rearrangement. So far, no gossip & no soul. Yet I've seen—Bob, Desmond, Lytton, Sebastian, Dorothy Bussy, Mrs Eliot—this last making me almost vomit, so scented, so powdered, so egotistic, so morbid, so weakly; & I already stale & talk sore with the rest of our doings.

2. The Apostles' dinner was held on Thursday 19 June at the Connaught Rooms. On the following night Alix and Marjorie Strachey gave a party at 50 Gordon Square; and it was on this occasion (and *not* that referred to in *I VW Diary*, p 94) that Marjorie Strachey produced her version of Schnitzler's *Reigen* (*La Ronde*). The copulation scene, though taking place in the dark and at the rear of the stage, horrified some and embarrassed most. 'It was a great relief when Marjorie sang hymns.' (Vanessa Bell to Roger Fry, 22 June 1924. CH, Camb.)

3. On 24 April 1924, to Violet le Maistre (*c.* 1900-1931). Murry had accepted her stories for publication in his *Adelphi*; his role as critical editor had unexpectedly given way to that of lover.

4. Nancy Cunard (1896-1965), the extravagantly rebellious and capricious daughter of Lady Cunard, lived mostly in Paris; her free verse poem *Parallax* was printed and published by the Hogarth Press in April 1925 (*HP Checklist* 57).

I am writing, writing, & see my way clear to the end now, & so shall gallop to it, somehow or other. But I am invaded by drowsiness; & cant write out what I had in my head to write before tea; can't even remember what it was; but shall go down to the basement where L. is printing, & then round to Gordon Sqre & then home to dinner, & then finish Romeo & Juliet by the open window, in spite of the noise, with the lovely view, & so to sleep; & to wake & all the rest of it.

Thursday 3 July

This is Dadie's second day. I looked out of my window, dressing, yesterday & saw him in grey with black bowler, Leonard, & Grizzle marching to the pillar box. Marjorie is ill, which is all to the good: business is brisk; I sat in the basement two days ago & took £5. Undoubtedly business is increasing—all divine fun. But I have let Garsington languish like a decaying wreath on my pen.[1] That was last Sunday. And, treading close on Garsington were the enamelled Lady Colefax, actually in this room, like a cheap bunch of artificial cherries, yet, loyal, hard, living on a burnished plate of facts: as for example Wembley: "a man who was in Canada tells me" "I happened to know the Editor of the Daily Express' all the time slightly trembling, in fear;[2] inquisitive; not at all able to sink to the depths; but a superb skimmer of the surface; which is bright, I suppose, & foam tipped. I can't bring myself to despise this gull as I ought. But aristocrats, worldlings, for all their surface polish, are empty, slippery, coat the mind with sugar & butter, & make it slippery too. Solid Lord Berners, who might have [been] cleft from an oak knot, had to tell stories, could not endure silence, & much preferred laughter to thought: amiable characteristics, Clive says. To me, after a time, laborious & depressing. Good prim priggish bright eyed Peter [F. L. Lucas] is a cut above that. I met him at Clive's, & he sliced English literature up very prettily, with a pocket knife. (Here Dadie came in & I had to make him tea; then we walked in the square in the rain; then called on the Stracheys, & I heard a good deal about Lord Lytton's blue dressing gown from Lady Strachey.)

1. The Woolfs went to Garsington after tea on 28 June; according to LW's diary, Ralli, Tom Eliot and Lord Balniel were there. They returned home the following evening.
2. The Woolfs had been to the British Empire Exhibition at Wembley on 29 May; on 2 July a party of Canadian newspapermen was entertained there; the editor of the *Daily Express* from 1902-32 was the American-born Ralph D. Blumenfeld (1864-1948).

Saturday 5 July

Just back, not from the 1917 Club; but from Knole, where indeed I was invited to lunch alone with his Lordship.[3] His lordship lives in the kernel of a vast nut. You perambulate miles of galleries; skip endless treasures—chairs that Shakespeare might have sat on—tapestries, pictures, floors made of the halves of oaks; & penetrate at length to a round shiny table with a cover laid for one. A dozen glasses form a circle each with a red rose in it. What can one human being do to decorate itself in such a setting? One feels that one ought to be an elephant able to consume flocks & be hung about with whole blossoming trees—whereas one solitary peer sits lunching by himself in the centre, with his napkin folded into the shape of a lotus flower. Obviously, I did not keep my human values & my aesthetic values distinct. Knole is a conglomeration of buildings half as big as Cambridge I daresay; if you stuck Trinity Clare & King's together you might approximate. But the extremities & indeed the inward parts are gone dead. Ropes fence off half the rooms; the chairs & the pictures look preserved; life has left them. Not for a hundred years have the retainers sat down to dinner in the great hall. Then there is Mary Stuart's altar, where she prayed before execution. "An ancestor of ours took her the death warrant" said Vita.[4] All these ancestors & centuries, & silver & gold, have bred a perfect body. She is stag like, or race horse like, save for the face, which pouts, & has no very sharp brain. But as a body hers is perfection. So many rare & curious objects hit one's brain like pellets which perhaps may unfold later. I cut no very intelligent sight seer beside Geoffrey Scott,— There was Lady Gerald Wellesley, & we motored down through Kent, which Vita loves;[5] all very free & easy, supple jointed as the aristocrat is; no

3. Lionel Edward Sackville-West, 3rd Baron Sackville (1867-1926), Vita's father, lived at Knole, one of the largest and finest baronial houses in England. Begun in 1456, it was greatly extended in the early seventeenth century by Thomas Sackville, 1st Earl of Dorset, to whom it was presented by his kinswoman, Queen Elizabeth. Vita's mother, the volatile half-Spanish Lady Sackville, had left Knole and her husband in 1919.

4. It had fallen to Thomas Sackville to deliver the death-warrant to Mary Queen of Scots on the eve of her execution at Fotheringay in 1586; in recognition of the delicacy with which he performed this painful duty, Mary presented him with a carved wooden triptych of saints and the procession to Calvary, which is still preserved in the chapel at Knole.

5. Geoffrey Scott (1883-1929), a nephew of C. P. Scott the celebrated editor of the *Manchester Guardian* and author of the influential book *The Architecture of Humanism* (1914); after New College, Oxford, he had worked in Italy as assistant to Bernard Berenson, as an architect, and as a diplomat. Vita first met him in

inhibitions, no false reserves; anything can be said; but as usual, that fatal simplicity or rigidity of mind which makes it seem all a little un-shaded, & empty. More mind, my God—[6] (I'm too jangled even to quote correctly). As a setting & preparation I always feel this, or Ottoline's, or any aristocrat's that I know, to be perfection. But one waits, & nothing happens. Not but what Harold [Nicolson], sitting on the iron bar before the great burning logs, gently butting the tassel from the baldaquin, or whatever its called, with his forehead, wasn't trusty & honest & vigorous. He wore a blue velvet jacket. I liked him better than the suaver & suppler Geoffrey. I rather suspect Geoffrey suspected me; smelt me to be of his herd, & not the aristocrats, & caught himself winking at me, like a couple of ragamuffins, & did not like to be reminded of his ragamuffin days. He referred bitterly to Florence & Berensons & that awful society. But its the breeding of Vita's that I took away with me as an impression, carrying her & Knole in my eye as I travelled up with the lower middle classes, through slums. There is Knole, capable of housing all the desperate poor of Judd Street,[7] & with only that one solitary earl in the kernel.

Marjorie has pneumonia; & we are likely to be worked off our feet. MSS pour in; & this press becomes a serious business.

Saturday 2 August

Here we are at Rodmell, & I with 20 minutes to fill in before dinner. A feeling of depression is on me, as if we were old & near the end of all things. It must be the change from London & incessant occupation.[1] Then, being at a low ebb with my book—the death of Septimus,—I

Rome in 1911; in 1918 he had married the widowed Lady Sibyl Cutting, daughter of the Earl of Desart and owner of the Villa Medici, Fiesole, where the previous autumn a sudden and intense love affair had sprung up between him and Vita, from which she was now disengaging herself. Dorothy Violet Wellesley, *née* Ashton (d. 1956), step-daughter of the Earl of Scarborough and an heiress, had married the second son of the 4th Duke of Wellington in 1914 (he was to succeed as 7th Duke in 1943). She had written poetry since childhood.

After lunch at Knole, VW was driven the short distance to Long Barn, the country home of Harold and Vita Nicolson, which she now saw for the first time.

6. 'More brain, O Lord, more brain!' George Meredith, *Modern Love*, xlviii.
7. Judd Street, WC1, runs between Brunswick Square and St Pancras Station and was one of the slum areas of Bloomsbury.
1. The Woolfs went to Monks House on Wednesday 30 July. During the four weeks in which her diary had been neglected, Marjorie Joad was still absent and VW had indeed been incessantly occupied by both work and people.

begin to count myself a failure. Now the point of the Press is that it entirely prevents brooding, & gives me something solid to fall back on. Anyhow, if I can't write, I can make other people write: I can build up a business. The country is like a convent. The soul swims to the top. Julian has just been & gone, a tall young man, who, inveterately believing myself to be young as I do, seems to me like a younger brother: anyhow we sit & chatter, as easily as can be. Its all so much the same—his school continues Thoby's school.[2] He tells me about boys & masters as Thoby used to. It interests me just in the same way. He's a sensitive, very quick witted, rather combative boy; full of Wells, & discoveries, & the future of the world. And, being of my own blood, easily understood—going to be very tall, & go to the Bar, I daresay. Nevertheless, in spite of the grumbling with which this began, honestly I don't feel old; & its a question of getting up my steam again in writing. If only I could get into my vein & work it thoroughly deeply easily, instead of hacking out this miserable 200 words a day, And then, as the manuscript grows, I have the old fear of it. I shall read it & find it pale. I shall prove the truth of Murry's saying, that there's no way of going on after Jacob's Room.[3] Yet if this book proves anything, it proves that I can only write along those lines, & shall never desert them, but explore further & further, & shall, heaven be praised, never bore myself an instant. But this slight depression—what is it? I think I could cure it by crossing the channel, & writing nothing for a week. I want to see something going on busily without help from me: a French market town for example. Indeed, have I the energy, I'll cross to Dieppe; or compromise by exploring Sussex on a motor bus. August ought to be hot. Deluges descend. We sheltered under a haystack today. But oh the delicacy & complexity of the soul— for, haven't I begun to tap her & listen to her breathing after all? A change of house makes me oscillate for days. And thats life; thats wholesome. Never to quiver is the lot of Mr Allinson [Allison], Mrs Hawkesford, & Jack Squire. In two or three days, acclimatised, started, reading & writing, no more of this will exist. And if we didn't live venturously, plucking the wild goat by the beard, & trembling over precipices, we

2. Julian Bell was sixteen, and was at Leighton Park School; Thoby Stephen had been at Clifton College, Bristol.
3. In the *Nation & Athenaeum* of 10 March 1923, in a review of L. H. Myers' *The Orissers* and Michael Sadleir's *Desolate Splendour* entitled 'Romance', Murry wrote of the lack of interest in plot or story among the 'most original minds' of the younger generation who have chosen prose-fiction for their medium—citing 'a D. H. Lawrence, a Katherine Mansfield, a Virginia Woolf', and said that as a consequence 'the novel has reached a kind of impasse' (see *M & M*, p 109).

should never be depressed, I've no doubt; but already should be faded, fatalistic & aged.

Sunday 3 August

Now its already going, my silver mist, & I don't quite recognise myself of yesterday. L. has been telling me about Germany, & reparations, how money is paid. Lord what a weak brain I have—like an unused muscle. He talks; & the facts come in, & I can't deal with them. But by dint of very painful brain exercises, perhaps I understand a little more than Nelly of the International situation. And L. understands it all—picks up all these points out of the daily paper absolutely instantly, has them connected, ready to produce. Sometimes I think my brain & his are of different orders. Were it not for my flash of imagination, & this turn for books, I should be a very ordinary woman. No faculty of mine is really very strong.

But its a question of work. I am already a good deal pulled together by sticking at my books: my 250 words of fiction first, & then a systematic beginning, I daresay the 80th, upon the Common Reader, who might be finished in a flash I think, did I see the chance to flash & have done with it. But there's a lot of work in these things. It strikes me, I must now read Pilgrim's Progress: Mrs Hutchinson. And should I demolish Richardson? whom I've never read. Yes, I'll run through the rain into the house & see if Clarissa is there. But thats a block out of my day, a long long novel. Then I must read the Medea. I must read a little translated Plato.[4]

Addison 1672-1719
Defoe 1659-1731
Pepys 1660
Evelyn 1660

Friday 15 August

Into all these calculations, broke the death of Conrad, followed by a wire from the Lit. Sup. earnestly asking me kindly to do a leader on him, which flattered & loyal, but grudgingly, I did; & its out;[5] & that number of the Lit. Sup. corrupted for me (for I cant, & never shall be

4. Editions of John Bunyan's *The Pilgrim's Progress* (see *Holleyman*, VS I, p 30): Samuel Richardson's *Clarissa Harlowe* (*Holleyman*, MH V, p 6); and Euripides' *The Medea* (*Holleyman* VS III, p 17 & VS V, p 75) were among the Woolfs' books sold after LW's death. VW had bought a copy of *Memoirs of the Life of Colonel Hutchinson . . . by his widow Lucy* in Brighton in 1918 (see *I VW Diary*, 3 September 1918).
5. Joseph Conrad died near Canterbury on 3 August 1924 aged sixty-seven. VW's valedictory essay upon him appeared in the *TLS* of 14 August 1924 (Kp C252).

able to, read my own writings. Moreover, now little Walkley's on the war path again I expect a bite next Wednesday[6]). Yet I have never never worked so hard. For, having to do a leader in 5 days, I made hay after tea—& couldn't distinguish tea hay from morning hay either. So doesn't this give me two extra hours for critical works anyhow (as Logan calls them)? So I'm trying it—my fiction before lunch, & then essays after tea. For I see that Mrs Dalloway is going to stretch beyond October. In my forecasts I always forgot some most important intervening scenes: I think I can go straight at the grand party & so end; forgetting Septimus, which is a very intense & ticklish business, & jumping Peter Walsh eating his dinner, which may be some obstacle too. But I like going from one lighted room to another, such is my brain to me; lighted rooms; & the walks in the fields are corridors; & now to day I'm lying & thinking. By the way, why is poetry wholly an elderly taste? When I was 20, in spite of Thoby who used to be so pressing & exacting, I could not for the life of me read Shakespeare for pleasure; now it lights me as I walk to think I have 2 acts of King John tonight, & shall next read Richard the 2nd. It is poetry that I want now—long poems. Indeed I'm thinking of reading [Thomson's] The Seasons. I want the concentration & the romance, & the words all glued together, fused, glowing: have no time to waste any more on prose. Yet this must be the very opposite to what people say. When I was 20 I liked 18th Century prose; I liked Hakluyt, Merimée. I read masses of Carlyle, Scott's life & letters, Gibbon, all sorts of two volume biographies, & Shelley. Now its poetry I want, so I repeat like a tipsy sailor in front of a public house.

We went to Charleston, & the Keynes' (so they are now called) with Robertson in attendance came here.[7] Lydia (I called her Rezia by mistake)

6. In the *Times* of 30 July 1924, A. B. Walkley devoted his usual Wednesday column to a discussion of 'Character in Fiction. Miss Virginia Woolf's Paper', which, based on the one she had read to the Cambridge Heretics in May, she had now published in the July number of the *Criterion* (Kp C251). 'Mr Bennett and Miss Woolf . . . say in effect that the novel, to be a good novel, *must* be a novel of character; that only the creation of character *counts.* . . . Miss Woolf pursues a path too difficult for my feet' (see *III VW Letters*, no. 1489). But her simple observation that 'on or about December, 1910, human character changed' prompted Walkley to wonder whether this 'prodigious event escaped Old Moore'? There were no further bites; no Wednesday essay by A.B.W. appeared in August— presumably he was on holiday.

7. Dennis Holme Robertson (1890-1963), economist, Fellow of Trinity College, Cambridge (1914-38), and later Reader and Professor at that University. He had been a pupil of Maynard Keynes before the war. With Lydia Lopokova, they came to tea at Monks House on 9 August.

leaves crumbs sticking to her face. And Maynard is grown very thick &
opulent; but I like him for his innocency. At Charleston theres the fat
boy in split blue cotton trousers—Quentin that is; almost a street sight,
now that hes back, fatter than ever.[8] Julian rather nervous & fine drawn
in comparison; & old Roger lean, brown, & truculent, attacking first
Shaw, then Conrad, & taking L.'s journalism as literally & bellicosely
as usual. O these Quakers! I don't think he's very happy though, &
that affair at Havre gnaws at him, in the midst of family life, I've no
doubt.

I dont often trouble now to describe cornfields & groups of harvesting
women in loose blues & reds & little staring yellow frocked girls. But
thats not my eyes' fault: coming back the other evening from Charleston,
again all my nerves stood upright, flushed, electrified (whats the word?)
with the sheer beauty—beauty abounding & superabounding, so that
one almost resents it, not being capable of catching it all, & holding it
all at the moment. This progress through life is made immensely interesting by trying to grasp all these developments as one passes. I feel as if
I were putting out my fingers tentatively on (here is Leonard, who has
ordered me a trap in which to drive Dadie to Tilton tomorrow[9]) either
side as I grope down a tunnel, rough with odds & ends. And I dont
describe encounters with herds of Alderneys anymore—though this
would have been necessary some years ago—how they barked & belled
like stags round Grizzle; & how I waved my stick & stood at bay; &
thought of Homer as they came flourishing & trampling towards me:
some mimic battle. Grizzle grew more & more insolent & excited &
skirmished about yapping. Ajax? That Greek, for all my ignorance, has
worked its way into me.

Mayor is printing her second edition, Stephen doing very well, Leys
publishing. Nancy Cunard estimating, Mrs Devonshire . . . rejecting;
business very brisk all round, I issuing a circular to all exhibitors at the
Royal Academy of Duncan's book.[10] Marjorie meanwhile convalesces,

8. Between preparatory and public schools, Quentin was sent for the summer term
   to a French family, the Pinaults, where his intellectual and gastric appetites were
   liberally provided for.
9. Tilton was the neighbouring farm house to Charleston; Maynard Keynes had
   rented it for the summer, and was later to acquire it and its land on a 99-year
   lease.
10. F. M. Mayor, *The Rector's Daughter* (*HP Checklist* 49); Leslie Stephen, *Some
    Early Impressions* (*HP Checklist* 53);Norman Leys, *Kenya*, with an Introduction
    by Professor Gilbert Murray (*HP Checklist* 48); Nancy Cunard, *Parallax* (*HP
    Checklist* 57); Mrs Devonshire unidentified; Roger Fry, *Living Painters—Duncan
    Grant* (*HP Checklist* 31).

presumably, & the question of her future with us comes up to be decided.

Sunday 7 September

It is a disgrace that I write nothing, or if I write, write sloppily, using nothing but present participles. I find them very useful in my last lap of Mrs D. There I am now—at last at the party, which is to begin in the kitchen, & climb slowly upstairs. It is to be a most complicated spirited solid piece, knitting together everything & ending on three notes, at different stages of the staircase, each saying something to sum up Clarissa. Who shall say these things? Peter, Richard, & Sally Seton perhaps: but I don't want to tie myself down to that yet. Now I do think this might be the best of my endings, & come off, perhaps. But I have still to read the first chapters, & confess to dreading the madness rather; & being clever. However, I'm sure I've now got to work with my pick at my seam, if only because my metaphors come free, as they do here. Suppose one can keep the quality of a sketch in a finished & composed work? That is my endeavour. Anyhow, none can help & none can hinder me any more. I've been in for a shower of compliments too from The Times, Richmond rather touching me by saying that he gives way to my novel with all the will in the world. I should like him to read my fiction, & always suppose he doesn't.

We had Dadie twice to stay; Clive & Mary yesterday; I slept a night at Charleston; L. went to Yorkshire: rather an odd disjointed wet summer, with people dropping in, Nelly rather moping, but loyal, Asheham offered us one evening by Mr Gunn, as he was poking his corn cocks, & looking at their blackness. I was tempted after 24 hours to buy it. We might get it for £1,500. But then it is dark & damp; & the loveliness might not quite compensate. The garden here flourishes. We put off deciding. We could let it of course, which we could not this, so that to fear being tied is no doubt foolish. Norman Leys was here one night;[1] making it quite plain that only certain sorts of people could pass the eye of his needle; & paring one down very quick; one of these good sturdy uncompromising men, whom M[argaret]. Ll[ewelyn]. D[avies]. would like, very able, trusty; paying no attention to art of any kind, & enforcing his virtue at every turn—but it is virtue of course. "They

1. Dr Norman Maclean Leys, MB, DPH (d. 1944), had spent sixteen years in the Public Health services in East and Central Africa; his book *Kenya*, to be published by the Hogarth Press in November 1924 (*HP Checklist* 48), dealt with the problems arising from the control of the black by the white race in East Africa.

belong to the gentlemanly side of the family..." Distrusts Oxford. Wishes to write as clearly as he can, hopes to live in the East end & educate working men. Wife spends £150 on garden; this distressing, but her only pleasure. Doesn't like taking fees, wh. mean that children go without boots. Thought me Thackeray's daughter & was only reassured when I cleared away dinner, & talked of religion, morality, his quarrel with the Colonial office, how he was besieged; protests too much in short; but a very nice man.

Monday 15 September

Here I am waiting for L. to come back from London, & at this hour, having been wounded last year when he was late, I always feel the old wound twingeing.[2] He has been seeing Nancy Cunard, so I expect a fair gossip. Vita was here for Sunday, gliding down the village in her large new blue Austin car, which she manages consummately. She was dressed in ringed yellow jersey, & large hat, & had a dressing case all full of silver & night gowns wrapped in tissue. Nelly said "If only she weren't an honourable!" & couldn't take her hot water. But I like her being honourable, & she is it; a perfect lady, with all the dash & courage of the aristocracy, & less of its childishness than I expected. She left with us a story which really interests me rather.[3] I see my own face in it, its true. But she has shed the old verbiage, & come to terms with some sort of glimmer of art; so I think; & indeed, I rather marvel at her skill, & sensibility; for is she not mother, wife, great lady, hostess, as well as scribbling? How little I do of all that: my brain would never let me milk it to the tune of 20,000 words in a fortnight, & so I must lack some central vigour, I imagine. Here I am, peering across Vita at my blessed Mrs Dalloway; & can't stop, of a night, thinking of the next scene, & how I'm to wind up. Vita, to attempt a return, is like an over ripe grape in features, moustached, pouting, will be a little heavy; meanwhile, she strides on fine legs, in a well cut skirt, & though embarrassing at breakfast, has a manly good sense & simplicity about her which both L. & I find satisfactory. Oh yes, I like her; could tack her on to my equipage for all time; & suppose if life allowed, this might be a friendship of a sort. The clock strikes 7, & I wonder if I hear Leonard, above the grey wild wind, talking to Nelly in the kitchen. Grizzle pricks a ear; lies flat again. He works & works. Here has the postman been, making

2. See above, 15 October 1923.
3. This was *Seducers in Ecuador* which the Hogarth Press published in November 1924 (*HP Checklist* 52). See also *III VW Letters*, no. 1497, to V. Sackville-West.

me choke a little, born sentimentalist that I am, by hoping so honestly & sincerely that Mr Woolf would address the ILP at Lewes on the League of Nations? This sort of thing counts: Does Murry, the professor of the soul, talk to postmen about the League of Nations? I like their trust & admiration; & the swing from Knole & Lord Sackville's invitation (J's R his favourite novel) to postmen getting up the local meetings, which suddenly seem to me, matters of the highest importance. All this confirms me in thinking that we're splinters & mosaics; not, as they used to hold, immaculate, monolithic, consistent wholes. How I scribble; & what use will this be for my great memoir writing age?

With Vita we discussed the murder of Mr Joshua,[4] Ottoline, literature. Then she took us to Charleston—& how one's world spins round—it looked all very grey & shabby & loosely cut in the light of her presence. As for Monks House, it became a ruined barn, & we picnicking in the rubbish heap. And then I regained my zest for life about an hour later. Now to the house, waiting for L.

Monday 29 September

A fortnight later: writing partly to test my new penkala (professing fountain qualities) partly to exorcise my demon. Only Karin & Ann: only a hole blown in my last chapter. There I was swimming in the highest ether known to me, & thinking I'd finish by Thursday; Lottie suggests to Karin we'd like to have Ann: Karin interprets my polite refusal to her own advantage & comes down herself on Saturday, blowing everything to smithereens. More & more am I solitary; the pain of these upheavals is incalculable; & I cant explain it either. *She* saw nothing. "Disturbing the flow of inspiration?" she said this morning, having shouted outside the door till I had to fetch cotton wool. And its down in ruins my house; my wings broken; & I left on the bare ground. Odd, very odd, how violent this has become. I dread even going back to London. True, I'm in the crisis, & if this last chapter spoils, the book spoils. But what cares Karin! Thats the rub. She slightly chortles to plant

4. On 5 September 1924 Albert Michael Joshua, a 54-year-old retired financier, married with two daughters (one of whom had dined at Hogarth House; see above, 17 January 1920), had been found shot dead in a flat in Prince of Wales Mansions, Battersea Park. Irene Victoria Maud Mercer, a 23-year-old servant employed at the flat, was found dead in the same room, a service revolver in her hand. It appeared at the inquest, on 9 September, that Mercer had known Joshua as a Mr Basil Montagu; and she wrote to him as 'My dear Husband'. The verdict was that Mercer killed Joshua and afterwards shot herself while in a state of unsound mind.

us with some of her burdens & makes off well pleased at having got her way. Didn't I years ago record in one of these very volumes that she'd get what can be got by asking, nothing more?[5] It is a case of spiritual deafness: she hears nothing of peoples thoughts; that is why she is, as she says unhappy; & its an affliction, not her fault; certainly our misfortune. Here I am with my wrecked week—for how serene & lovely like a Lapland night was our last week together[6]—feeling that I ought to go in & be a good aunt—wh. I'm not by nature: ought to ask Daisy what she wants; & by rights I fill these moments full of Mrs Dalloway's party for tomorrows writing. The only solution is to stay on alone over Thursday, & try my luck. A bad night (K.'s doing again) may partly account. But how entirely I live in my imagination; how completely depend upon spurts of thought, coming as I walk, as I sit; things churning up in my mind & so making a perpetual pageant, which is to me my happiness. This brew cant sort with nondescript people. These wails must now have ending, partly because I cannot see, & my hand shakes, having carried my bag from Lewes, where I sat on the castle top, where an old man was brushing leaves, & told me how to cure Lumbago; you tie a skein of silk round you; the silk costs 3 pence. I saw British canoes, & the oldest plough in Sussex 1750 found at Rodmell, & a suit of armour said to have been worn at Seringapatam.[7] All this I should like to write about, I think.

And of course children are wonderful & charming creatures. I've had Ann in talking about the white seal, & wanting me to read to her. And how Karin manages to be so aloof I can't think. There's a quality in their minds to me very adorable: to be alone with them, & see them day to day would be an extraordinary experience. They have what no grown up has—that directness—chatter, chatter chatter, on Ann goes,

5. See *I VW Diary*, 24 August 1918.
6. Cf. Wordsworth, 'To a Young Lady' (1805):
> 'But an old age serene and bright,
> And lovely as a Lapland night,
> Shall lead thee to thy grave.'

Karin had departed in the morning, leaving Ann and her nurse Daisy to stay on another night.
7. Two dug-out canoes designated as 'Ancient British Canoes' and exhibited in the Keep of Lewes Castle. The plough to which VW refers is part of a double exhibit described in a guide to the castle as 'a plough and rake... probably the oldest remaining in Sussex, used about 1750 on Northease Farm, near Rodmell'; both items are now at Wilmington Priory, the Sussex Archaeological Society's agricultural museum. The armour is a suit of chain mail 'worn by an Indian Prince at the Siege of Seringapatam when the city was captured by the British under General Harris in 1799'.

in a kind of world of her own, with its seals & dogs; happy because she's going to have cocoa tonight, & go blackberrying tomorrow: the walls of her mind all hung round with such bright vivid things, & she doesn't see what we see. But I'm forgetting Marjorie & only scribble till, as I hope in 15 minutes, the gate goes & L. comes. We have lost £100 a year, & he need no longer attend the office—a great gain. Now I hope for his book.[8] I also begin to cherish dreams of retiring to a lovely house in the country, & there writing—once we get the press on its feet, & Dadie attendant. This recalls Marjorie.[9] I thought her flimsy & cheap in 1917, enough, at first, with this harping on the niceness or nastiness of young men, which becomes so dreary. Then she said, I've left Cyril. The upshot of the affair is that we have to engage her as sec. at £3 a week. She depends absolutely on that. Then where is she to live? in Bloomsbury, with a girl— Its all chaotic & precipitous, & like a modern novel; but I suppose she will marry Tom Marshall.[10]

LW returned to Tavistock Square on 2 October, and VW followed two days later.

Friday 17 October

It is disgraceful. I did run up stairs thinking I'd make time to enter that astounding fact—the last words of the last page of Mrs Dalloway; but was interrupted. Anyhow I did them a week ago yesterday. "For there she was." & I felt glad to be quit of it, for it has been a strain the last weeks, yet fresher in the head; with less I mean of the usual feeling that I've shaved through, & just kept my feet on the tight rope. I feel indeed rather more fully relieved of my meaning than usual—whether this will stand when I re-read is doubtful. But in some ways this book

8. LW had become literary editor of the *Nation & Athenaeum* in April 1923. In his autobiography (*III LW*, 141) he wrote that after four years it was agreed that he might reduce his hours and his salary; but it appears from VW's note here and from her December letter to Margaret Llewelyn Davies (*III VW Letters*, no. 1518) that some reduction took place towards the end of 1924. He tried to resign entirely in March 1926, but in fact continued until 1930. His book, *After the Deluge*, was not published until 1931.

9. Marjorie Joad came to Monks House for the night of Friday 26 September and left next morning, when Karin and Ann and Daisy came.

10. Thomas Humphrey Marshall (b. 1893), economist and social scientist. His family had lived in Brunswick Square and was acquainted with the Stephens. With the intention of entering the Foreign Office he was studying in Germany when war broke out, and spent four years in internment there. He was a Fellow of Trinity College, Cambridge, and later taught at the London School of Economics.

is a feat; finished without break from illness, wh. is an exception; & written really, in one year; & finally, written from the end of March to the 8th of October without more than a few days break for writing journalism. So it may differ from the others. Anyhow, I feel that I have exorcised the spell wh. Murry & others said I had laid myself under after Jacob's Room. The only difficulty is to hold myself back from writing others. My cul-de-sac, as they called it, stretches so far, & shows such vistas.[1] I see already The Old Man.

But enough, enough—yet of what should I write here except my writing? Odd how conventional morality always encroaches. One must not talk of oneself &c; one must not be vain &c. Even in complete privacy these ghosts slip between me & the page. But I must here break off to go to the post, down that wonderful lamplit street, which has become more lovely more unreal through my double windows. And I sit shielded within. This house is now perfect. The studio the best study I've ever had.

The thought of Katherine Mansfield comes to me—as usual rather reprehensibly—first wishing she could see Southampton Row, thinking of the dulness of her death, lying there at Fontainebleau—an end where there was no end, & then thinking yes, if she'd lived, she'd have written on, & people would have seen that I was the more gifted—that wd. only have become more & more apparent. Indeed, so I suppose it would. I think of her in this way off & on—that strange ghost, with the eyes far apart, & the drawn mouth, dragging herself across her room. And Murry married again to a woman who spends an hour in the W.C. & so the Anreps have turned them out.[2] Murry whines publicly for a flat in the Adelphi. Thats a sordid page of my life by the way, Murry. But I stick to it; K. & I had our relationship; & never again shall I have one like it.

Lytton dined here the other night—a successful evening. Oh I was right to be in love with him 12 or 15 years ago. It is an exquisite symphony his nature when all the violins get playing as they did the other night; so deep, so fantastic. We rambled easily. He is in love again with Philip Ritchie. And hurt, a little; still capable of pain; but knows it now ridiculous, which hurts him too. & he feels it. For when I asked if we could help he was touched. We talked of his writing, & I think now he will write another book; of mine; of the School of Proust, he said; then of Maynard;

1. For *cul-de-sac* read *impasse*; see above 2 August 1924, n 3.
2. Murry had been living in rooms in Boris Anrep's house in Pond Street, Hampstead. In the summer of 1924 after his second marriage he bought an old coastguard station in Dorset, but needed a London *pied-à-terre*—which he acquired in Chelsea.

one side of him detestable; should have married Barbara; grown fat; of Nessa's picture, which he may buy (I want to see Nessa at this moment, & she's gone to Norfolk to look at a house, & I hope she won't take it, & leave London & Charleston & live till she dies, with her children painting in Norfolk & I here, & L. may go to India—[3]thats been brooding over me since I came back & he told me at tea the first afternoon, Saturday, how he'd been asked to go by the ILP & wanted very much to go, & take a week off to see Hambantota which a little hurt me. But I said to myself this is a side of life I've not lain on. I must face that too. Still nothing has been heard, though I still a little dread the mornings post, but this is concealed from L.—if he went, it would be after the Election, in Nov. Yes, after the Election, for owing to the defeat of the Govt. in the Campbell Case, we are now condemned to a dose of lies every morning: the usual yearly schoolboys wrangle has begun.[4] If I were still a feminist, I should make capital out of the wrangle. But I have travelled on—as K.M. said to me, she saw me as a ship far out at sea. But K.M. always *said* affectionate admiring things to me, poor woman, whom in my own way I suppose I loved. Human affections are not to be called by very strong, or rather very positive names, I think. Heres poor old Jacques writing to me, & Gwen wants to come & see me, after 11 years: a relationship revived by the art of the pen, across France.[5] I rather

3. Vanessa's lease of Charleston was coming to an end, and she had been offered the option of a renewal at an increased rental plus rates. She heard of an 18th century house near King's Lynn to be sold for £1250, and thought it might be more advantageous to own rather than to rent a country house for her family's use in summer and school holidays. In the event she decided to remain at Charleston. LW spent the last two and a half years of his time in the Colonial Service in southern Ceylon as Assistant Government Agent in charge of Hambantota Province for which he always retained a profound attachment.

4. The Campbell Case had its origin in the publication of an allegedly seditious article in the Communist newspaper, the *Workers' Weekly* of 25 July 1924. On 7 August John R. Campbell, the paper's acting editor, had been charged with incitement to mutiny for 'feloniously, maliciously and advisedly endeavouring to seduce divers persons serving in the Navy, Army and Air Force from their allegiance'. On 15 August the charge was withdrawn and in the House of Commons the Liberal opposition wanted to know why. The Attorney General, Sir Patrick Hastings, said the charge was dropped because Campbell could not be proved to be responsible for the paper's policy—nor did he want to make Campbell a martyr for the Communist cause. On 9 October the Labour Government was defeated by 166 votes on a Liberal request for an inquiry into the case. Ramsay MacDonald had threatened on the previous day that his Government would go to the country if defeated. Accordingly a General Election was held on 29 October.

5. See above, 22 August 1922, n 15. Gwen Raverat, whom VW had not seen since before the war, came to England for a visit in mid-October 1924.

dread revivals: partly vanity; you're fatter, less beautiful; changed; so self-conscious [?] am I; & then—the effort. Seeing people, now I see them so easily, is an effort. Why ———

Phil Baker is standing as a Labour candidate.[6] Irene will have his teeth filed & get him in—(a scrap of *real* dialogue). Did I put down my progress towards Perpetual Immortality (to quote one of Peggy Webling's wishes as a child—a Brief I'm doing, or should be doing?[7]) I asked Todd £10 for 1,000 words: she orders 4 articles at that fee:[8] Harper wishes me (I think) to write an American Browns & Bennetts; & Vogue, (via Dadie) is going to take up Mrs Woolf, to boom her: &—&—&— So very likely this time next year I shall be one of those people who are, so father said, in the little circle of London Society which represents the Apostles, I think, on a larger scale. Or does this no longer exist? To know everyone worth knowing. I can just see what he meant; just imagine being in that position—if women can be. Lytton is: Maynard; Ld Balfour; not perhaps Hardy. Which reminds me I ought to dash in Mrs Hardy in a nursing home, having had her tumour cut out; with Miss Charlotte Mew.[9] Nothing very exciting, even as a boast not very exciting now. H. remembers your father: did not like many people, but was fond of him; talks of him often. Would like to know you. But I cant easily fit into that relation; the daughter grateful for old compliments to her father. Yet I should like to see him; to hear him— say something. But what? One or two words about a flower, or a view, or a garden chair, perhaps.

(It strikes me that in this book I *practise* writing; do my scales; yes & work at certain effects. I daresay I practised Jacob here,—& Mrs D. & shall invent my next book here; for here I write merely in the spirit—

6. Philip Noel-Baker contested the Handsworth Division of Birmingham; he was not elected.

7. VW's anonymous review of *Peggy: the Story of One Score Years and Ten* by Peggy Webling appeared under 'Books in Brief' in the *Nation & Athenaeum* of 8 November 1924 (Kp C256.2).

8. Dorothy Todd became editor of British *Vogue* in 1922; her idea was that the magazine should not only be the essential authority on high fashion, but a stimulating guide to the arts in general, and to this end she sought out and actively encouraged contributions of an *avant-garde* tendency both from France and England. This policy, while leading to a highly sophisticated and lively production, failed to bring the commercial success the American owners required, and her contract was terminated in 1926. *Harper's Bazaar* published no contributions from VW at this time.

9. Charlotte Mary Mew (1869-1928), whom Thomas Hardy considered the best woman poet of her day, and VW presumably met at the bedside of his second wife Florence.

great fun it is too, & old V. of 1940 will see something in it too. She will be a woman who can see, old V.: everything—more than I can I think. But I'm tired now.)

Saturday 1 November

I must make some notes of work; for now I must buckle to. The question is how to get the 2 books done. I am going to skate rapidly over Mrs D. but it will take time. No: I cannot say anything much to the point, for what I must do is to experiment next week; how much revision is needed, & how much time it takes. I am very set on getting my essays out before my novel. Yesterday I had tea in Mary's room & saw the red lighted tugs go past & heard the swish of the river: Mary in black with lotus leaves round her neck. If one could be friendly with women, what a pleasure—the relationship so secret & private compared with relations with men. Why not write about it? truthfully? As I think, this diary writing has greatly helped my style; loosened the ligatures.

We had a party the other night—S. Sassoon; R. Mortimer, Duncan, Vanessa. Nancy Cunard should have come—the little anxious flibberti-gibbet with the startled honest eyes, & all the green stones hung about her. We met at Raymond's, & she slipped into easy desperate-sounding chatter, as if she didn't mind saying everything—everything—had no shadows no secret places—lived like a lizard in the sun, & yet was by nature for the shade. And I should be re-reading her poem to choose a title. As usual, I am, or think myself, snowed under with work to do; & this is cut into by hours of solid pleasure—going to the pictures tonight; & Suggia on Monday.[1] For its music I want; to stimulate & suggest.

We went to Hamspray on a wet misty day, & saw what the view might be in the sun; a flat meadow with trees in groups like people talking leading to the downs. We walked to the top with Carrington; but the young men, P. Ritchie & Senhouse, are a little simple minded—for Lytton likes that sort, & thus blankets himself.[2] Carrington was as if

1. Guilhermina Suggia (1888-1950), the celebrated Portuguese cellist, accompanied by her compatriot José Viana da Mota, gave a recital at the Wigmore Hall on 3 November 1924.
2. Lytton Strachey, with Carrington and Ralph Partridge, had moved from Tidmarsh to Ham Spray House, Hungerford, during the late summer; the Woolfs made their first visit on 25 and 26 October. Roger Henry Pocklington Senhouse (1900-1970), educated at Eton and Magdalen College, Oxford, was the inseparable companion of Lytton's newest love, Philip Ritchie, and was thus included in Lytton's frequent invitations to the latter.

recently beaten by Ralph. Is she really rather dull, I asked myself? or merely a sun flower out of the sun? We came home in the rain, & a man stopped L. to ask if his dog was a bitch: an angler, he was, & I wanted to ask had he caught a fish. We travelled down with Sydney.[3] Being rather ashamed of my temper—for one should never wall off people on theory—I was affable, yet discreet. Talked the whole time, but did not suggest future meetings. We hit it off successfully I think. Did I want John Franklin to be lenient to Mrs Dalloway? Not, I think, very seriously, & I see no harm in being faithful to old semi-friendships. His little boy is what he cares for, I imagine; & there was less protestation than usual. Murry is "tremendous" on Keats & Sh[akespea]re; Lawrence "tremendous" too; but a megalomaniac. They started a publishing house, like ours; which went smash, or never started, which had killed Kot's hopes; & Lawrence, who thought the whole of London would flock after him to Mexico, has retired there with Brett alone.[4] All this Sydney sees clearly & comicly, but intimates that there are depths beneath. I rather think the poor monster is clambering out, though. Now, for goodness sake, let me read a little— It is reading, not writing, that suffers in London—

Tuesday 18 November

Lady Colefax interrupts. I ask her to call me Virginia—so there.

What I was going to say was that I think writing must be formal. The art must be respected. This struck me reading some of my notes here, for, if one lets the mind run loose, it becomes egotistic: personal, which I detest; like Robert Graves. At the same time the irregular fire must be there; & perhaps to loose it, one must begin by being chaotic, but not appear in public like that. I am driving my way through the mad chapters of Mrs D. My wonder is whether the book would have been better without them. But this is an afterthought, consequent upon

3. To reach Ham Spray House, the Woolfs travelled on the Great Western Railway from Paddington to Hungerford; Sydney Waterlow would have continued to Pewsey for his home at Oare. His son, John Conrad, was now aged eight. 'John Franklin' unidentified.

4. Murry's book *Keats and Shakespeare* was not published until 1925. By October 1924 dissension among the sponsors of the *Adelphi*, which had increasingly become a vehicle for Murry's own views and Katherine Mansfield's literary remains, had become such that Koteliansky resigned his position, and his aspirations, as business manager. D. H. and Frieda Lawrence, with Brett, had left London to return to New Mexico in March 1924.

learning how to deal with her. Always I think at the end, I see how the whole ought to have been written.

Lady Colefax has made me tremble. I cannot write. We were, I was rather, at Mary's farewell party last night, & suffer today—[5]having, first, broken my watch, at 3.15 owing to a policeman calling; I having hotted water over the fire in the basement, being infinitely cold & as if rolled in sand, which misery still persists. The upper classes pretended to be clever. Duff Cooper, Lady Diana & all that set, as they say; & my chief amusement came from seeing them as a set. That is the only merit of these parties, that individuals compose differently from what they do in private. One sees groups; gets wholes; general impressions: from the many things being combined. No doubt Proust could say what I mean— that great writer whom I cannot read when I'm correcting, so persuasive is he. He makes it seem easy to write well; which only means that one is slipping along on borrowed skates. So Henry James gives one an unreal impetus; witness my writing after reading him, & Miss Bosanquet.

Dadie came back yesterday & we had a jolly afternoon—oh infinitely better than a party at River House!—lie though I did to Mary on the telephone, doing up Freud.[6] I in two jackets, for it is freezing, & hair down; he in shirtsleeves. Thus one gets to know people; sucks the marrow out, not poised on the edge of a chair on the slippery floor, trying to laugh, & being spurred by wine & sugar cakes. Clive of course changes into an upper class man very loud, familiar, & dashing at once. Lytton sits in his own green shade, only emerging when the gentle youths come in. Philip Ritchie thinks rather too highly of himself, as notice from Lytton always makes them. I was impressed by Nessa, who went to this party for which we were all titivating & dressing up, in her old red brown dress which I think she made herself. (Thinking it over, I believe its getting the rhythm in writing that matters. Could I get my tomorrow mornings rhythm right—take the skip of my sentence at the right moment—I should reel it off; —there is a good deal in this which I should like to think out; its not style exactly—the right words—its a way of levitating the thought out of one— Thank God I hear L.'s key: Grizzle gets up & stands still: now wags; & then trots to the door. A very cold damp foggy night.) But I was saying that I admired Nessa's utter independence of what people say, which triumphs, over all the tubular cropheads. Elizabeth

5. The St John Hutchinsons were moving from River House, Hammersmith to 3 Albert (now Prince Albert) Road, Regent's Park.
6. Volumes I & II of Freud's *Collected Papers* were published by the Hogarth Press in November 1924 (*HP Checklist* 44).

Saturday 13 December

Ponsonby, no doubt I meant to add.[1] But that is all faded out. And this diary may die, not of London, but of the Press. For 14 days we have been in the thick of a long press revolution—Dadie going Marjorie going, Marjorie staying, Angus Davidson coming.[2] That is the final result, but achieved only at the cost of 40 million words. For my own part, I could never see Dadie as a permanent partner, Dadie in his silver grey suits, pink shirts, with his powdered pink & white face, his nerves, his manners, his love of praise. Angus, however, after 3 days, already seems to me permanent & dependable. As I always talk of money here, & compliments & rebuffs, first I will own that my pamphlet is the worst seller of them all, then that Harper's offer me "at least £50" for a Times leader article! And once upon a time I was trying to get £15 out of Jack Squire! So I am suggesting 3 articles a year, to Richmond; & this, if it fructifies, will help us on the road to giving up the Nation, to which goal I look always, though the place has many perquisites.

I am now galloping over Mrs Dalloway, re-typing it entirely from the start, which is more or less what I did with the V.O. a good method, I believe, as thus one works with a wet brush over the whole, & joins parts separately composed & gone dry. Really & honestly I think it the most satisfactory of my novels (but have not read it coldbloodedly yet) The reviewers will say that it is disjointed because of the mad scenes not connecting with the Dalloway scenes. And I suppose there is some superficial glittery writing. But is it "unreal"? Is it mere accomplishment? I think not. And as I think I said before, it seems to leave me plunged deep in the richest strata of my mind. I can write & write & write now: the happiest feeling in the world.

A London winter is full of bright rooms, passages through dark streets to scenes of brilliancy; but I only recall tea's with Ethel Sands, a lunch with Ly Colefax, Sybil by the way she is now, a party last night at Gumbo [Marjorie Strachey]'s, which being undress & easy going gave me a good deal of pleasure. Ray is precisely like a very fine tabby, which, having been castrated, has grown to an enormous size, & never moves.

1. Elizabeth Ponsonby (1900-1940), daughter of Arthur Ponsonby (later Lord Ponsonby of Shulbrede) minister in the recent Labour government, was one of the dashing set labelled by the newspapers the 'Bright Young People'.
2. Rylands had hoped to be able to work at the Hogarth Press and on his Cambridge Fellowship dissertation concurrently, but found it too much. He suggested that Angus Henry Gordon Davidson (b. 1900), a friend and graduate of Magdalene College, Cambridge, who had been writing art criticism for the *Nation & Athenaeum*, might succeed him.

She sits smiling out of her green blue cats eyes. She is sending us, rather to my trepidation, her new novel. There was also Julia Strachey whom I cross examined; the gifted wastrel.[3] Leys & Vita are both in great demand, Simkin ordering them urgently this morning, & Angus going off in a hurry. But I will not let the Press entirely devour this page. I am rather cross with Marjorie [Joad], about her objecting to my criticism of her private life; & then taking 3 weeks holiday, which will leave us very little, & heaven knows when. But then she seems in a state of nerves—terrified of getting ill, terrified of leaving us, jumpy, unhappy, now on edge, now obsequious, having Tom Marshall about the place, & Ralph Wright & Cyril to divorce,[4] which, to my thinking, distract her mind from her work, & lessen my chances of selling my books. But the thing to aim at is an impersonal, amicable business relation I am sure, now we have Angus, less sympathy & more work.

This quarrel has been made up

Whatever they may say, Vita & Clive & Lytton, people crowd to the press, & can't be beaten off. Bernadette Murphy was ready to come. Angus dropped like ripe fruit from the tree. Vita explains that the Heir of Redcliffe, her cousin, implores her to resist the contamination of Bloomsbury, personified in the serpent destroyer, V.W. I half like, half mind this.[5]

Monday 21 December

Really it is a disgrace—the number of blank pages in this book! The effect of London on diaries is decidedly bad. This is I fancy the leanest of them all, & I doubt that I can take it to Rodmell, or if I did, whether I could add much. Indeed it has been an eventful year, as I prophesied; & the dreamer of Jan. 3rd has dreamt much of her dream true; here we

3. Ray Strachey's next novel was not published by the Hogarth Press. Her step-daughter, Julia Frances (b. 1901) was the only child of Oliver Strachey and his first wife Ruby Mayer, from whom he was divorced in 1908. Brought up largely in the homes of well-intentioned relatives and at Bedales, she was now sharing a Chelsea flat with another young woman, and attempting to earn a living. She was to become a writer of unusual character and quality if of scant quantity.
4. Ralph Wright had become a partner in Birrell and Garnett's bookshop, thus enabling it to move to more convenient premises at 30 Gerrard Street, near the 1917 Club; he was one of Marjorie's several lovers. Although she kept up the fiction about Joad, she was never either married to, or divorced from, him.
5. A joke name, derived from the novel by C. M. Yonge, for Edward Sackville-West, who stood to inherit the Sackville titles and properties when Vita's father and uncle should die. Bernadette Murphy had acted as secretary to the London Group in 1920.

are in London, with Nelly alone, Dadie gone it is true, but Angus to replace him. What emerges is that changing houses is not so cataclysmic as I thought; after all one doesn't change body or brain. Still I am absorbed in "my writing", putting on a spurt to have Mrs D. copied for L. to read at Rodmell; & then in I dart to deliver the final blows to the Common Reader, & then—then I shall be free. Free at least to write out one or two more stories which have accumulated. I am less & less sure that they *are* stories, or what they are. Only I do feel fairly sure that I am grazing as near as I can to my own ideas, & getting a tolerable shape for them. I think there is less & less wastage. But I have my ups & downs. As for fame & money, Clive's long article on me is out in The Dial.[6] £50, apparently, from Harper. Clearly, as L. said, we are safe to make, both of us, as much as we want by our pens. Never again, I daresay, shall we agitate about getting £15 from Jack Squire.

So much of my time goes talking—talking to strays in the basement, to particular people like Ethel Sands, Elena Richmond, Vita, up here, that when I write, I tend to meditate; to sing my own praises, & sum up the months work.

How sharply society brings one out—or rather others out! Roger the other night with Vita for instance.[7] He became the nonconformist undergraduate at once, the obstinate young man, (I could see him quite young with his honest uncompromising eyes) who will *not* say what he does not believe to be true. The effect on Vita was disastrous; & pure honesty is a doubtful quality; it means often lack of imagination. It means self assertiveness, being rather better than other people; a queer trait in Roger to unearth after so many years of smooth intercourse. For the most part he is so sympathetic. His Quaker blood protests against Vita's rich winy fluid; & she has the habit of praising & talking indiscriminately about art, which goes down in her set, but not in ours. It was all very thorny until that good fellow Clive came in, & addressed himself to conciliate dear old obtuse, aristocratic, passionate, Grenadier like Vita. Then came Sprott; a dull dog if ever there was one.

We have also seen Aldington, who calls like a tradesman for orders;[8]

6. 'Virginia Woolf' by Clive Bell appeared in the December 1924 number of *The Dial*, New York.
7. They dined with the Woolfs on Friday 19 December.
8. E. G. (Richard) Aldington (1892-1962), poet, novelist, and critic. A friend of Ezra Pound, he had preceded T. S. Eliot as assistant editor of *The Egoist*. With Lady Ottoline Morrell and VW, he was one of the sponsors of the Eliot Fund (see above, 19 July 1922, n 13), and although Eliot had declined to take advantage of it, subscriptions were still coming in, and it was possibly in this connection that Aldington called at 52 Tavistock Square.

a bluff, powerful, rather greasy eyed, nice downright man, who will make his way in the world, which I dont much like people to do. All young men do it. No young women; or in women it is trounced; in men forgiven. Its these reflections I want to enmesh, in writing; or these are among them.

Marjorie & I kissed—there above the little grave we kissed again with tears.[9] My coldness, she said, had made it impossible for her to work. We explained, standing in the doorway. I like her; I like her inner integrity, after cutting through that rather cheap, bargain counter like surface.

All our Bloomsbury relationships flourish, grow in lustiness. Suppose our set to survive another 20 years, I tremble to think how thickly knit & grown together it will be. At Christmas I must write & ask Lytton if I may dedicate the common reader to him.[10] And thats the last of my books to be dedicated, I think. What do we talk about? I wish I could write conversations.

With Elena we discussed women's dress; she sitting there so matronly & ornate, in a S. Kensington way, with pearls, & a tiger trimmed black coat, all black, substantial, & middleaged.

"I love driving. I went with my grandmother on a driving tour, with Kentish horses. We did about 20 miles a day. I was at a party the other night when everyone said how charming Mrs Carnegie (you remember Mrs Chamberlain, Virginia?) looked, dressed in a fitting pink dress, cut low: every single woman in the room was dressed in a chemisette dress of georgette."[11] Dadie was a great success. "That enchanting creature" she called him, relieved I think to meet a human being here.

Vita talked about criticism. Ly G. Wellesley wants to found a 2nd Hawthornden prize for poets only. I said it should be for critics. What are critics, said Vita; & added, being engagingly a student of reviews of her own books, a little ink steeped indeed, that no two critics took the same view. This started Roger on aesthetic criticism, constructive criticism.

We go over the same things, undoubtedly. The press however is always casting up wreckage. People come most days. I enjoy my printing afternoons, & think it the sanest way of life—for if I were always writing, or merely recouping from writing, I should be like an inbreeding rabbit,

---

9. From Tennyson, *The Princess*, ii, introductory song.
10. No letter about the matter survives, but the book *is* dedicated to Lytton Strachey.
11. Joseph Chamberlain's widow (his third wife the American Mary Endicott) married the rector of St Margaret's, Westminster, the Rev. W. H. Carnegie, in 1916. VW had known the Chamberlains in her Kensington youth.

—my progeny becoming weakly albinos. A man called Peter Miller met at Gumbo's confirmed me in this the other night. One meets a good many men now. Theres a little thrush like creature called Tomlin who wants to sculpt me.[12] This afternoon they cut down the tree at the back: the tree I used to see from my basement skylight.

The Woolfs went to Monks House on Christmas Eve, taking Angus Davidson with them. VW had again collaborated with Quentin Bell in the production of a Christmas Supplement to the Charleston Bulletin, *entitled* 'The Dunciad', *recording apocryphal scenes in the life of Duncan Grant, but the two households did not meet; the weather was appalling, and the river Ouse overflowed its banks.*

12. Stephen Tomlin (1901-1937), youngest son of the High Court judge Sir Thomas (later Lord) Tomlin, abandoned his study of the Law at Oxford to become a sculptor. A man of exceptional charm, humour, and sympathy, he had, through a visit to his bookshop, become friends with Bunny Garnett and thus with *his* friends in Bloomsbury (See David Garnett, *The Familiar Faces*, 1962, p 1ff). VW was eventually prevailed upon to sit for him. Peter Miller has not been identified.

ABBREVIATIONS
AND
APPENDIXES

ABBREVIATIONS

CH, Camb.	Charleston Papers deposited in the Library of King's College, Cambridge
Holleyman	Holleyman & Treacher Ltd: *Catalogue of Books from the Library of Leonard and Virginia Woolf, taken from Monks House, Rodmell, and 24 Victoria Square, London, and now in the possession of Washington State University.* Privately printed, Brighton, 1975
Holroyd	Michael Holroyd: *Lytton Strachey. A Biography*. Revised edition, Penguin Books, 1971
HP Checklist	*A Checklist of the Hogarth Press 1917-1938*. Compiled by J. Howard Woolmer. With a short history of the Press by Mary E. Gaither, Hogarth Press, London, 1976
Kp	B. J. Kirkpatrick: *A Bibliography of Virginia Woolf*. Revised edition, Hart-Davis, London, 1967
LW	Leonard Woolf. Five volumes of his *Autobiography*, Hogarth Press, London.
I LW	*Sowing: . . . 1880-1904*. 1960
II LW	*Growing: . . . 1904-1911*. 1961
III LW	*Beginning Again: . . . 1911-1918*. 1964
IV LW	*Downhill all the Way: . . . 1919-1939*. 1967
V LW	*The Journey not the Arrival Matters: . . . 1939-1969*. 1969
M & M	Robin Majumdar and Allen McLaurin: *Virginia Woolf. The Critical Heritage*, Routledge & Kegan Paul, London, 1975
MHP, Sussex	*Monks House Papers*. University of Sussex Library Catalogue, July 1972
RF Letters	*Letters of Roger Fry*. Edited by Denys Sutton. Chatto & Windus, London, 1972
I RF Letters	Volume I, 1878-1913
II RF Letters	Volume II, 1913-1934
QB	Quentin Bell: *Virginia Woolf. A Biography*. Hogarth Press, London, 1972
I QB	Volume I: *Virginia Stephen*, 1882-1912
II QB	Volume II: *Mrs Woolf*, 1912-1941
TLS	*Times Literary Supplement*
VW	Virginia Woolf
VW Diary	*The Diary of Virginia Woolf*. Edited by Anne Olivier Bell. Hogarth Press, London.
I VW Diary	Volume I: *1915-1919*. 1977

VW Letters	*The Letters of Virginia Woolf.* Edited by Nigel Nicolson. Hogarth Press, London.
I VW Letters	Volume I: *The Flight of the Mind* (1888-1912), 1975
II VW Letters	Volume II: *The Question of Things Happening* (1912-1922), 1976
III VW Letters	Volume III: *A Change of Perspective* (1923-1928), 1977

NOTE

The Uniform Edition of the Works of Virginia Woolf, published by the Hogarth Press, is used for reference purposes.

APPENDIX I

Biographical Outlines of Persons
Most Frequently Mentioned

BELL, Clive (Arthur Clive Heward Bell, 1881-1964), art critic, married Vanessa Stephen in 1907, and as VW's brother-in-law played a notable part in her life. At Trinity College, Cambridge, he was a friend of VW's brother Thoby Stephen. His marriage had since 1914 been a matter of convenience and friendship; for some years now Mary Hutchinson had held pride of place in his affections. Clive Bell's publications up to the present period include *Art* (1914), *Peace at Once* (1915), *Ad Familiares* (1917) and *Pot-Boilers* (1918).

BELL, Vanessa ('Nessa'), *née* Stephen (1879-1961), painter, VW's elder sister and, after LW, the most important person in her life. She married Clive Bell in 1907, but from about 1914 and until her death she was, in terms of sentiment, the wife of Duncan Grant. A curriculum vitae and brief bibliography is contained in the catalogue of the Arts Council Exhibition: *Vanessa Bell: a Memorial Exhibition of Paintings*, 1964, with an introduction by Ronald Pickvance; see also S. P. Rosenbaum, *The Bloomsbury Group*, 1975, p 420; Richard Shone, *Bloomsbury Portraits*, 1976.

CARRINGTON, Dora de Houghton (1893-1932), painter; known invariably as Carrington. She had been at the Slade before the war with Barbara Bagenal, Dorothy Brett, and Mark Gertler, who passionately loved her and was driven to despair by her equivocations and the discovery of her (to him inexplicable) devotion to Lytton Strachey. This had taken a domestic form in 1917 at The Mill House, Tidmarsh, where she acted as Lytton's housekeeper and hostess, and he as her tutelary genius and sympathetic friend. After the war this ménage had been enlarged by the inclusion of Ralph Partridge, who loved her and whose manly strength and capabilities both attracted and reassured Lytton.

ELIOT, Thomas Stearns (1888-1965), American-born poet, educated at Harvard and Oxford. In 1915 he married Vivienne Haigh-Wood and, after teaching, he joined the London staff of Lloyds Bank where he was to remain from 1917-25. In 1917, too, he became assistant editor of *The Egoist* and published his first book of poems, *Prufrock and Other Observations*. VW first met him in November 1918 and six months later the Hogarth Press published his *Poems*, and subsequently *The Waste Land* (1923) and his essays *Homage to John Dryden* (1924).

FORSTER, Edward Morgan, 'Morgan' (1879-1970), novelist, educated at King's College, Cambridge, 1897-1902, an Apostle. Living for the most part with his mother at Weybridge in Surrey, he was a rather elusive familiar in Bloomsbury. He had travelled in Italy and Greece, and spent six months in India (1912/13). From 1915 until the war had ended he held a post in the Red Cross in Alexandria. VW set particular store by his reactions to her novels; all his own novels, except *A Passage to India* (1924) and *Maurice* (1971), had been published by 1910.

FRY, Roger Eliot (1866-1934), art critic and painter, descended from generations of Quakers, gained first class honours in Natural Sciences at King's College, Cambridge, where he became an Apostle. He abandoned science for the study and practice of art, and became an established and respected figure in the museum and art world in England, France and America. He had married in 1896, but his wife developed a thickening of the skull; she slowly went mad, and in 1910 was consigned to a mental home. In that year, a slight earlier acquaintance with Vanessa burgeoned into close friendship with her and Clive Bell, and they and their circle became enthusiastic supporters of Fry's efforts to introduce the work of the Post-Impressionists to London and, in 1913, to establish the Omega Workshops. He fell in love with Vanessa and she, for a while, with him—a love she transmuted into lifelong friendship. VW's *Roger Fry. A Biography* was published in 1940. See also *Letters of Roger Fry*, 2 volumes, 1972, edited by Denys Sutton.

GARNETT, David ('Bunny', b. 1892). During the war he had served for a period in 1915 with a Quaker Relief Unit in France; then, from September 1916, he and Duncan Grant had lived at Charleston and, as pacifists, worked at nearby Newhouse Farm, Firle. In 1919 he entered into partnership with Francis Birrell to establish a new and secondhand bookshop Birrell & Garnett, in Taviton Street, not far from Gordon Square. His first book, *Lady into Fox*, was awarded the Hawthornden Prize in 1923.

GRANT, Duncan James Corrowr (b. 1885), painter, only child of Major Bartle Grant whose sister was Lady Strachey; Duncan spent much of his youth with the Strachey family. VW probably met him in Paris in 1907 with the Bells. He became their neighbour when she and her brother lived in Fitzroy Square, and in 1911 an occupant of their house in Brunswick Square. From about 1914 he had been, in all but name, husband to Vanessa Bell and remained so until her death in 1961.

HUTCHINSON, Mary, *née* Barnes (1889-1977), a first cousin once removed of Lytton Strachey, married in 1910 the barrister St John Hutchinson. Since 1914-15 she had been the most important person in Clive Bell's life.

KEYNES, (John) Maynard (1883-1946), economist, scholar of Eton and of King's College, Cambridge, an Apostle, a Fellow of the College and University lecturer in Economics. In 1911, with Duncan Grant and LW, he became one of the 'inmates' of Adrian and Virginia Stephen's house at 38 Brunswick Square. In January 1915 he was appointed to a post in the Treasury. He served as the British Treasury's chief representative at the Paris Peace Conference in 1919, but resigned in protest against the conditions to be imposed upon Germany. His polemic, *The Economic Consequences of the Peace*, begun that summer at Charleston, was published in December 1919.

MacCARTHY, (Charles Otto) Desmond (1877-1952), literary journalist and editor, graduate of Trinity College, Cambridge, and an Apostle. He had known the Stephen family since before Sir Leslie's death; in 1906 VW had attended his wedding to Mary (Molly) Josefa Warre-Cornish, a daughter of the Vice-Provost of Eton and, like her, a niece by marriage of 'Aunt Anny'— Lady Anne Thackeray Ritchie. In 1920 he became literary editor of the *New Statesman*, for which he had been drama critic, and began his weekly column in that paper, "Books in General", under the pseudonym "Affable Hawk". *Remnants*, a collection of articles by MacCarthy, was published in 1918.

MANSFIELD, Katherine, adopted name of the New Zealand-born writer Kathleen Mansfield Beauchamp (1888-1923); she married in 1918 John Middleton Murry, with whom she had been living since 1912. She had met the Woolfs probably towards the end of 1916. Her long short story *Prelude* (1918) was the third publication of the Hogarth Press.

MURRY, John Middleton (1889-1957), literary critic, editor and author, married in 1918 Katherine Mansfield. He was a leading luminary in that world of literary journalism and promotion which VW called 'the underworld'. In 1919 he became editor of the *Athenaeum*, and in the same year the Hogarth Press published his poem *The Critic in Judgment*. Among his publications up to the present period are *Still Life* (1916), *Dostoevsky: A Critical Study* (1916) and *Poems: 1917-1918* (1918).

STEPHEN, Adrian Leslie (1883-1948), VW's younger brother, with whom she had lived, not very harmoniously, at 29 Fitzroy Square after Vanessa's marriage in 1907, and then in 1911 until her own, at 38 Brunswick Square. After attending Trinity College, Cambridge (1902-05), he studied Law, but remained without profession or vocation until five years after his marriage in 1914 to Karin Costelloe, when he and his wife became medical students as a preliminary to becoming psychoanalysts.

STEPHEN, Karin Elizabeth Conn, *née* Costelloe (1889-1953), had graduated with distinction in Philosophy from Newnham College, Cambridge, where in 1914-15 she held a research fellowship. In 1914 she married Adrian Stephen and with him in 1919 became a medical student. She was a stepdaughter of

Bernard Berenson, niece of Logan Pearsall Smith and of Alys Russell (first wife of Bertrand Russell); her sister Rachel was married to Oliver Strachey.

STRACHEY, (Giles) Lytton (1880-1932), critic and biographer, a contemporary and friend of both Thoby Stephen and LW at Trinity College, Cambridge, and like the latter an Apostle. After her brother's death in 1906, Lytton became one of VW's close friends and in 1909 he briefly contemplated marrying her. *Eminent Victorians* by Lytton Strachey was published in 1918.

SYDNEY-TURNER, Saxon (1880-1962) was contemporary and close friends with Thoby Stephen, LW and Lytton Strachey at Trinity College, Cambridge, where he took a double first in classics and was an Apostle. A life-long devotee of the opera, particularly of Wagner, he had accompanied VW and her brother Adrian to Bayreuth in 1909. On leaving Cambridge he had entered the Civil Service and was at the present time, and until his retirement, in the Treasury. His peculiar and eccentric character is described in *I LW*, 103-108 and 114-119. VW made him the subject of an essay (unpublished) entitled 'One of Our Great Men', MHP, Sussex, MH/A 13c.

WATERLOW, Sydney Philip Perigal (1878-1944), scholar of Eton and of Trinity College, Cambridge. In 1900 he entered the Diplomatic Service, and served in Washington. In 1905 he resigned, but on the outbreak of war was re-employed by the Foreign Office on a temporary basis; he was re-appointed in 1920 after assisting at the Paris Peace Conference; he finally retired in 1939 as British Minister in Athens and a KCMG. VW met him through the Clive Bells, probably in 1910; in 1911 after the breakdown of his first marriage, he proposed to her. He married Margery Eckhard in 1913.

APPENDIX II

'The Plumage Bill' by Virginia Woolf

From The Woman's Leader, *23 July 1920*

If I had the money and the time I should, after reading "Wayfarer", in the *Nation* of July 10th, go to Regent Street, buy an egret plume, and stick it—is it in the back or the front of the hat?—and this in spite of a vow taken in childhood and hitherto religiously observed. The Plumage Bill has been smothered; millions of birds are doomed not only to extinction but to torture; and "Wayfarer's" comment is, "What does one expect? They have to be shot in parenthood for child-bearing women to flaunt the symbols of it, and, as Mr Hudson says, one bird shot for its plumage means ten other deadly wounds and the starvation of the young. But what do women care? Look at Regent Street this morning!" One can look at Regent Street without leaving one's room. The lower half of the houses is composed of plate glass. One might string substantives and adjectives together for an hour without naming a tenth part of the dressing bags, silver baskets, boots, guns, flowers, dresses, bracelets and fur coats arrayed behind the glass. Men and women pass incessantly this way and that. Many loiter and perhaps desire, but few are in a position to enter the doors. Most of them merely steal a look and hurry on. And then there comes on foot, so that we may have a good look at her, a lady of a different class altogether. A silver bag swings from her wrist. Her gloves are white. Her shoes lustrous. She holds herself upright. As an object of beauty her figure is incomparably more delightful than any other object in street or window. It is her face that one must discount, for, though discreetly tinted and powdered, it is a stupid face, and the look she sweeps over the shop windows has something of the greedy petulance of a pug-dog's face at tea-time. When she comes to the display of egret plumes, artfully arranged and centrally placed, she pauses. So do many women. For, after all, what can be more etherially and fantastically lovely? The plumes seem to be the natural adornment of spirited and fastidious life, the very symbols of pride and distinction. The lady of the stupid face and beautiful figure is going to-night to the opera; Clara Butt is singing Orpheus; Princess Mary will be present; a lemon-coloured egret is precisely what she wants to complete her toilet. In she goes; the silver bag disgorges I know not how many notes; and the fashion writers next day say that Lady So-and-So was "looking lovely with a lemon-coloured egret in her hair".

But since we are looking at pictures let us look at another which has the advantage of filling in certain blank spaces in our rough sketch of Regent Street in the morning. Let us imagine a blazing South American landscape.

In the foreground a bird with a beautiful plume circles round and round as if lost or giddy. There are red holes in its head where there should be eyes. Another bird, tied to a stake, writhes incessantly, for red ants devour it. Both are decoys. The fact is that before "the child-bearing woman can flaunt the symbols of parenthood" certain acts have to be devised, done, and paid for. It is in the nesting season that the plumes are brightest, So, if we wish to go on making pictures, we must imagine innumerable mouths opening and shutting, opening and shutting, until—as no parent bird comes to feed them—the young birds rot where they sit. Then there are the wounded birds, trailing leg or wing, as they flutter off to droop and falter in the dust. But perhaps the most unpleasant sight that we must make ourselves imagine is the sight of the bird tightly held in one hand while another hand pierces the eyeballs with a feather. But these hands—are they the hands of men or of women? The Plumage Bill supporters say that the hunters "are the very scum of mankind". We may assume that the newspapers would have let us know if any of the other sex had been concerned in it. We may fairly suppose then that the birds are killed by men, starved by men, and tortured by men—not vicariously, but with their own hands. "A small band of East End profiteers" supports the trade; and East End profiteers are apt also to be of the male sex. But now, as "Wayfarer" says, the birds "have to be shot in parenthood for child-bearing women to flaunt the symbols of it".

But what is the nature of this compulsion? Well, men must make their livings, must earn their profits, and must beget children. For though some people say that they can control their passions, the majority maintain that they should be protected from them rather than condemned for them. In other words, it is one thing to desire a woman; quite another to desire an egret plume.

There remains, however, a body of honourable and disinterested men who are neither plume hunters, profiteers, nor women. It is their duty, as it is within their power, to end the murder and torture of the birds, and to make it impossible for a single egret to be robbed of a single plume. The House of Commons took the matter up. The Plumage Bill was sent to Standing Committee C. With one exception each of its sixty-seven members was a man. And on five occasions it was impossible to get a quorum of twenty to attend. The Plumage Bill is for all practical purposes dead. But what do men care? Look wherever you like this morning! Still, one cannot imagine "Wayfarer" putting it like that. "They have to be shot for child-begetting men to flaunt the symbols of it. . . . But what do men care? Look at Regent Street this morning!" Such an outburst about a fishing-rod would be deemed sentimental in the extreme. Yet I suppose that salmon have their feelings.

So far as I know, the above, though much embittered by sex antagonism, is a perfectly true statement. But the interesting point is that in my ardour to confute "Wayfarer", a journalist of admitted humanity, I have said more about his injustice to women than about the sufferings of birds. Can it be that it is a graver sin to be unjust to women than to torture birds?

APPENDIX III

'The Intellectual Status of Women'

The publication in 1920 of Arnold Bennett's Our Women *and its attendant publicity led Virginia Woolf to consider 'making up a paper on Women, as a counterblast to Mr Bennett's adverse views' (see 26 September). No such paper has survived, if it was ever begun, but a counterblast was fired. It was discharged through the correspondence columns of the* New Statesman *in which Desmond MacCarthy, as the columnist 'Affable Hawk', had discussed Bennett's book in terms which Virginia Woolf found too provocative to ignore. He agreed with Bennett that 'no amount of education and liberty of action will sensibly alter' the fact that women are inferior to men in intellectual power, and that women's indisputable 'desire to be dominated is ... a proof of intellectual inferiority'. The offending article, which also gave a brief notice to* The Good Englishwoman *by Orlo Williams, appeared on 2 October 1920. Virginia Woolf's protest was published the following week under the heading:* The Intellectual Status of Women.

Sir,— Like most women, I am unable to face the depression and the loss of self respect which Mr Arnold Bennett's blame and Mr Orlo Williams' praise— if it is not the other way about—would certainly cause me if I read their books in the bulk. I taste them, therefore, in sips at the hands of reviewers. But I cannot swallow the teaspoonful administered in your columns last week by Affable Hawk. The fact that women are inferior to men in intellectual power, he says, "stares him in the face". He goes on to agree with Mr Bennett's conclusion that "no amount of education and liberty of action will sensibly alter it". How, then, does Affable Hawk account for the fact which stares me, and I should have thought any other impartial observer, in the face, that the seventeenth century produced more remarkable women than the sixteenth, the eighteenth than the seventeenth, and the nineteenth than all three put together? When I compare the Duchess of Newcastle with Jane Austen, the matchless Orinda with Emily Brontë, Mrs Heywood with George Eliot, Aphra Behn with Charlotte Brontë, Jane Grey with Jane Harrison, the advance in intellectual power seems to me not only sensible but immense; the comparison with men not in the least one that inclines me to suicide; and the effects of education and liberty scarcely to be overrated. In short, though pessimism about the other sex is always delightful and invigorating, it seems a little sanguine of Mr Bennett and Affable Hawk to indulge in it with such certainty on the evidence before them. Thus, though women have every reason to hope that the intellect of the male sex is steadily diminishing, it would be unwise, until they have more evidence than the great war and the great peace supply, to announce it as a fact. In conclusion, if Affable Hawk sincerely wishes to discover a great poetess, why does he let himself be fobbed off with a possible authoress of the Odyssey? Naturally, I cannot claim to know Greek as Mr Bennett and Affable Hawk know it, but I have often been told that Sappho was a woman, and that Plato and Aristotle placed her with Homer and Archilocus among the greatest of their poets. That Mr Bennett can name fifty of the male sex who are indisputably her superiors is therefore a welcome surprise, and if he will publish their names I will promise, as an act of that submission which is so dear to my sex, not only to buy their works but, so far as my faculties allow, to learn them by heart.— Yours, etc.,

Virginia Woolf

'Affable Hawk' remained unconvinced, proved reluctant to allow even Sappho her laurels and concluded, on the question of education, with the following points: "(1) that unfavourable in many respects as the conditions of women have been in the past, they have not been more unfavourable than many men possessing extraordinary intellectual powers have overcome; (2) that in directions to which those conditions were less unfavourable (literature, poetry, music and painting), they have hardly attained, with the possible exception of fiction, the highest achievements reached by men; (3) that, in spite of education, in pursuits requiring pure intellect they have not rivalled men. This does not imply, however, that a small percentage of women are not just as clever as any clever men, just as good artists, just as good correlators of facts, only that it seems that they fall short of the few men who are best of all." Virginia Woolf returned to the fray in the issue of 16 October.

Sir,—To begin with Sappho. We do not, as in the hypothetical case of Burns suggested by "Affable Hawk", judge her merely by her fragments. We supplement our judgment by the opinions of those to whom her works were known in their entirety. It is true that she was born 2,500 years ago. According to "Affable Hawk" the fact that no poetess of her genius has appeared from 600 B.C. to the eighteenth century proves that during that time there were no poetesses of potential genius. It follows that the absence of poetesses of moderate merit during that period proves that there were no women writers of potential mediocrity. There was no Sappho; but also, until the seventeenth or eighteenth century, there was no Marie Corelli and no Mrs Barclay.

To account for the complete lack not only of good women writers but also of bad women writers I can conceive no reason unless it be that there was some external restraint upon their powers. For "Affable Hawk" admits that there have always been women of second or third rate ability. Why, unless they were forcibly prohibited, did they not express these gifts in writing, music, or painting? The case of Sappho, though so remote, throws, I think, a little light upon the problem. I quote J. A. Symonds:

"Several circumstances contributed to aid the development of lyric poetry in Lesbos. The customs of the Aeolians permitted more social and domestic freedom than was common in Greece. Aeolian women were not confined to the harem like Ionians, or subjected to the rigorous discipline of the Spartans. While mixing freely with male society, they were highly educated and accustomed to express their sentiments to an extent unknown elsewhere in history— until, indeed, the present time."

And now to skip from Sappho to Ethel Smyth.

"There was nothing else [but intellectual inferiority] to prevent down the ages, so far as I can see, women who always played, sang and studied music, producing as many musicians from among their number as men have done," says "Affable Hawk". Was there nothing to prevent Ethel Smyth from going to Munich? Was there no opposition from her father? Did she find that the playing, singing and study of music which well-to-do families provided for their daughters were such as to fit them to become musicians? Yet Ethel Smyth was born in the nineteenth century. There are no great women painters, says "Affable Hawk", though painting is now within their reach. It is within their reach—if that is to say there is sufficient money after the sons have been educated to permit of paints and studios for the daughters and no family reason requiring their presence at home. Otherwise they must make a dash for it and disregard a species of torture more exquisitely painful, I believe, than any that man can imagine. And this is in the twentieth century. But, "Affable Hawk" argues, a great creative mind would triumph over obstacles such as these. Can he point to a single one of the great geniuses of history who has sprung from a people stinted of education and held in subjection, as for example the Irish or the Jews? It seems to me indisputable that the conditions which make it possible for a Shakespeare to exist are that he shall have had predecessors in his art, shall make one of a group where art is freely discussed and practised, and shall himself have the utmost of freedom of action and experience. Perhaps in Lesbos, but never since, have these conditions been the lot of women. "Affable Hawk" then names several men who have triumphed over poverty and ignorance. His first example is Isaac Newton. Newton was the son of a farmer; he was sent to a grammar school; he objected to working on the farm; an uncle, a clergyman, advised that he should be exempted and prepared for college; and at the age of nineteen he was sent to Trinity College, Cambridge. (See D.N.B.) Newton, that is to say, had to encounter about the same amount of opposition that the daughter of a country solicitor encounters who wishes to go to Newnham in the year 1920. But his discouragement is not increased by the works of Mr Bennett, Mr Orlo Williams and "Affable Hawk".

Putting that aside, my point is that you will not get a big Newton until you have produced a considerable number of lesser Newtons. "Affable Hawk" will, I hope, not accuse me of cowardice if I do not take up your space with an enquiry into the careers of Laplace, Faraday, and Herschell, nor compare the lives and achievements of Aquinas and St Theresa, nor decide whether it was Mill or his friends who was mistaken about Mrs Mill. The fact, as I think we shall agree, is that women from the earliest times to the present day have brought forth the entire population of the universe. This occupation has taken much time and strength. It has also brought them into subjection to men, and incidentally—if that were to the point—bred in them some of the most lovable and admirable qualities of the race. My difference with "Affable Hawk" is not that he denies the present intellectual equality of men and women. It is that he, with Mr Bennett, asserts that the mind of woman is not sensibly affected by education and liberty; that it is incapable of the highest achievements; and that it must remain for ever in the condition in which it now is. I must repeat that the fact that women have improved (which "Affable Hawk" now seems to admit), shows that they may still improve; for I cannot see why a limit should be set to their improvement in the nineteenth century rather than in the one hundred and nineteenth. But it is not education only that is needed. It is that women should have liberty of experience; that they should differ from men without fear and express their difference openly (for I do not agree with "Affable Hawk" that men and women are alike); that all activity of the mind should be so encouraged that there will always be in existence a nucleus of women who think, invent, imagine, and create as freely as men do, and with as little fear of ridicule and condescension. These conditions, in my view of great importance, are impeded by such statements as those of "Affable Hawk" and Mr Bennett, for a man has still much greater facilities than a woman for making his views known and respected. Certainly I cannot doubt that if such opinions prevail in the future we shall remain in a condition of half-civilised barbarism. At least that is how I define an eternity of dominion on the one hand and of servility on the other. For the degradation of being a slave is only equalled by the degradation of being a master.— Yours, etc.,

Virginia Woolf

At this 'Affable Hawk' withdrew, saying that "If the freedom and education of women is impeded by the expression of my views, I shall argue no more".

INDEX

Baker, Ida Constance (Leslie Moore, L.M.): 45 & n

Balfour, Arthur James, 1st Earl of: 113 & n, 319

Balzac: 184

Banks, Harold, revolutionary: 36-7

Barbellion, W. N. P.: 32 & n

Barclay, Florence, novelist: 340

Baring (family): 144

Barker, Miss, teacher of dancing: 85

Barker's, Kensington store: 239

Bath, Lady: 275, 276 & n

Bayreuth: VW's resolution at, 221 & n

Beanstalk Lane, near Charleston: 199 & n

Beatrice, Lady, née Gascoyne-Cecil, see Ormsby-Gore

Beckford, William: 163

Bedales School: 197

Bedford Estate: 284 & n

Bedford Music Hall: Marie Lloyd at, 107 & n

Beerbohm, Max: caricatures Lytton, 110 & n; has not read VW, 135; nor complimented her, 216

Beethoven: string quartets, 114 & n; ref: 14

Behn, Aphra: 339

Bell (family): 225, 278, 289 & n

Bell, Angelica: riding on Roger's foot, 73; Vanessa draws for, 79; very white, 94; performs womanly act, 260; in road accident, 298-9; ref: 39, 207, 221, 303

Bell, Clive: for Biographical Note see Appendix I; 'my poor parrokeet', 6; sells Roger's ideas, 10-11 & n; objective at Memoir Club, 23; getting middle-aged, 27-8; in Paris with Mary, 36; and VW's field day, 47; underrates Katherine Mansfield, 55; advises VW to approach America, 58; Lytton's view of, 64; yellow like a canary, 73; the Spanish affair, 87 & n, 90; on Mrs Raven-Hill, 89 & n; gritty and bawling, 91; too appalling, 92; 'that little man', 100; dissipated, deprecating, 135; writes to VW, all bubble and muddle, 137-8; too many cocktails, 146; he and Roger far apart, 151; Vanessa's attitude to, 156-7; 'knows nothing whatever' about painting, 159; what a sprightly journalist! 160 & n; 'my old lover', 171; polishes VW's manners, 172-3; to set up at 50 Gordon Square, 183 & n; faded and fly-blown, 185; 'Clive & I . . . much alike', 195; *Jacob's Room* a masterpiece, 210; 'proudest moment of his life', 223; a cry from his room, 224-5; phones up ashamed, 247; his article on VW, 259 & n, 325 & n; bald as a turkey's egg, 263; instant upper class man, 322; ref: viii, 13, 15, 54, 63, 71, 81, 104, 123, 141, 142, 158, 170, 187, 190, 191, 202, 216, 217, 221, 234, 246, 249, 258, 260 & n, 262, 264, 265, 274, 277, 278, 289, 291, 297, 299, 305, 312, 324; *Civilization*, 101; *Legend of Monte Sibilla*, 274n; *Poems*, 96 & n, 144; *Potboilers*, 54 & n

Bell, Julian: with French lesson, 73; and a temperature, 94; at boarding school, 159 & n; a continuation of Thoby, 308 & n; ref: 39, 52, 129, 221, 311

Bell, Quentin: declares Angelica 'very white', 94; coming home nightly, 159 & n; with gas leak, 221; means to be a painter, 246; collaborates with VW, 278, 327; fatter than ever, 311 & n; ref: 129

Bell, Vanessa: for Biographical Note see Appendix I; her charms resplendent, 6; plumbs emotional depths at Memmoir Club, 23; VW's discomfort unsuspected by, 26; friends too seldom gathered, 27; fails to phone, 38; presents from abroad, 39; on brink of ruin, 40 & n; and 'mad Mary', 47 & n; at wits' end over Roger's show, 50; thinks younger generation callous, 51; of the open air, 52; her great party, 54 & n; underrates Katherine Mansfield, 55; broaches new studio, 58 & n; advises VW on Mary, 69; invents Major Grant and hay-boxes, 71 & n; creates brightness in heart of darkness, WV 73; quarrels with, 75; draws for Angelica, 79; to be retained, 81; approves of *Monday or Tuesday*, visits Cambridge, 98; her hopes for Clive, 101; a shabby old moth, 104; tells pack of troubles, 104-5; antique simplicity of, 156-7; tête-à-tête with, 159; and Mary Hutchinson, 182-3; her passive ferocity, 195; regrets Kitty Maxse, but . . ., 207; dines with Clive and VW,

'Charleston time', 69 & n; notice to leave, 104; by bus to, 195; Woolfs not well received at, 260; shabby in Vita's presence, 314; *ref*: 57, 67, 101, 137, 202, 265, 278, 282, 310, 311, 312, 318

Charleston Bulletin, periodical: 278, 327

Chart, Annie, cook: 39 & n

Chatto & Windus, publishers: 34

Chaucer: 185 & n, 189 & n, 196, 198, 205, 242, 259

Chekhov, Anton: LW translating, 75 & n; costs of printing, 86; Kot's ms books lost, 99 & n; Murry attacks 'our Tchekhov', 123 & n; his letters, 141 & n; *ref*: 32, 72 & n, 108, 110, 118, 124, 151; *The Cherry Orchard*, 53 & n

Chelsea: 30 & n, 87, 190, 224

Chelsea, All Saints Church: tablet to Henry James: 30 & n

Chiddingly, Sussex, 198

Chrissie *see* MacLaren, Christabel

Christow, Devon: 229 & n

Clare College, Cambridge: 306

Cleeve House, Seend: 221

Clifford, Mrs W. K.: 12 & n, 16; *Miss Fingal*, 12 & n

Clifford's Inn: 78, 283 & n

Clutton-Brock, Arthur: 57 & n, 58

Clutton-Brock, Evelyn, 57 & n, 58

Coade Son & Budgen: 283, 284n, 288

Coatmellec, Josette: and Roger Fry, 303 & n

Cock Club: 86 & n, 90, 96

Cole, George Douglas Howard: a Webb in embryo, 40-1; *ref*: 40n

Cole, Margaret, *née* Postgate: a Webb in embryo, 40-1; *ref*: 40n

Colefax, Sir (Henry) Arthur: 180 & n

Colefax, Lady, *née* Sibyl Halsey: Clive turned against, 137 & n; a bore, 180; a black fox, 185 & n; Valéry *chez*, 210 & n; kindly glass eyed, 275; enamelled, 305; *ref*: 181, 183, 191, 246, 274, 288, 321, 322, 323

Coleridge, Mary Elizabeth: 73 & n

Coleridge, S. T.: 77 & n, 81, 129-30 & n

Coliseum, The London: 199

Collins, Mr (fict); 192 & n

Colonial Office: 313

Commercio Restaurant: 187

Congreve, William: *Love for Love*, 103 & n, 104

Conrad, Joseph: VW struggling with *The*

Rescue, 49 & n; and standing firm, 52; to write dialogue on, 259 & n; *TLS* wire on his death, 309 & n; *ref*: 261, 265, 311; *The Rescue*, 49 & n

Constable & Co., publishers: offer for Hogarth Press, 212 & n

Constant, Benjamin: *Adolphe*, 104

Contemporary Review: 71 & n, 151, 181

Cooper, Alfred Duff: 322

Cooper, Lady Diana: 289 & n, 322

Cooperative Stores: 111

Corelli, Marie: leads to suicide, 168; *ref*: 169 & n, 340; *The Mighty Atom*, 169 & n

Cornford, Frances: 272 & n

Cornish (family): 23 & n

Cornwall: with Lytton's troupe to? 92; anticipated, 100; VW incurably romantic about, 103; reading list for, 104; lines written in, 105; *ref*: 100, 249

Costelloe (family): 36 & n

Cotman, John Sell: 113

Craig, Edith, theatrical producer: 174 & n

Craig, Dr Maurice: 76 & n, 99

Crawford, Marion: 132 & n

Criterion, periodical: Eliot on *King Lear* in, 302 & n; *ref*: 170n, 178, 204, 256

Crome, John: 113

Cromer, Katherine, Countess of: outrageous banter with, 14; repetitions, 73; 'a little middle class' after all, 117; in charwoman's bonnet, 144; *ref*: 14n, 114, 117n, 182

Cromwell Road, No. 33, home of Kitty Maxse: 206 & n

Crosse, Felix Warren: 20 & n

Crowninshield, Francis (Frank) Welch, editor of *Vanity Fair*: 249 & n

Cunard, Nancy: 304 & n, 311, 313, 320; *Parallax*, 304n

Curzon, Lady Cynthia: 36 & n

Daily Express: 305 & n

Daily Herald: 28, 128 & n

Daily Mail: 116 & n

Daily News: 116 & n, 123, 127, 128, 209 & n

Daisy, nurse to Ann Stephen: 315 & n

Dalloway, Clarissa (fict): 272, 312

Dalloway, Richard (fict): 312

Dalloways, The (fict) in *The Voyage Out*: 65

349

124-5; VW no longer afraid of, 140; supple as an eel, starting magazine, written poem, 170-1; recites *The Waste Land*, 178; the 'Eliot Fund' begun, 183 & n; and continued, 204; slightly malevolent, 187; and *Ulysses*, 189, 200, 202-3; appearance and manner, 203-4; and *Nation* post, 236, 238, 239, 240; conversation piece, 256-7; to be published by Press, 259; drunk to perfection, 278 & n; Tom the magisterial, 292 & n; suspicions about him and *King Lear*, 302 & n; *ref*: 19, 21, 70, 76, 78, 116, 170n, 182, 192, 277, 299; *Prose and Verse*, 116n; *Prufrock and Other Observations*, 68n; *The Sacred Wood: Essays on Poetry and Criticism*, 76n, 78n, 79n; *Sweeney Agonistes*, 68n; *The Waste Land*, 171 & n, 178, 257n

Eliot, Vivienne, *née* Haigh-Wood: 19, 247 & n, 256-7, 304

Elsie, a Rodmell girl: 3 & n

Emerson, Ralph Waldo: 262

Emilia (fict), character in *Othello*: 243

Enfield, Doris Edith, *née* Hussey: talking Stracheyese, 32; tea with recalls VW's youth, 78; writes in style of Lytton, 181 & n; irritates VW, 184; a Victorian seamstress, 223; *ref*: 20 & n, 90 & n, 182; *A Lady of the Salons. The Story of Louise Colet*, 131n

Enfield, Ralph Roscoe: 90n, 184

English Review, periodical: Maynard and Lytton to buy? 183 & n, further speculation upon, 185

Etoile, restaurant: 303 & n

Euripides: 196, 206, 275, *The Medea*, 309 & n

Evans, Charles Seddon: 11 & n, 12, 213n

Evelyn, John: VW's pickle over in *TLS*, 74 & n; *ref*: 69, 70, 73, 261

Fabians: 143 & n

Fagan, James Bernard: *The Flame*, 284 & n

Fanshawe, Lady: 262 & n

Faraday, Michael: 341

Farrell, Sophie: 36n, 38

Fergusson, Dr D. J.: on the habits of lice, 16, forbids work, 157-8, pronounces VW's pulse 'insane', 160, right lung 182, 185, discussion over VW, 189,

threatens tonsils, 227; *ref*: 17n, 131

Field, periodical: 66 & n, 127 & n

Fielding, Henry: 97; *The Virgin Unmasked*, 97n

Findlay, Professor Joseph and Mrs, of Manchester: 101, 102n

Firle, Sussex: 133

Firle Beacon: 58

Fisher, Herbert Albert Laurens: distinguished, yet empty, 32 & n, his political work and character, 112-14; *ref*: 112n, 114n, 122; *An Unfinished Autobiography*, 112n

Fisher, Hervey: 122 & n

Fisher, Mary (Aunt Mary): on a donkey, 113 & n; *ref*; 122

Fisher, Mr, at Rodmell Rectory: 95

Fitzgerald, Edward: queer individuality of, 168; *Letters and Literary Remains of Edward Fitzgerald*, 168n

Fitzroy Square: 277, 291

Flanders, Mrs (fict): 94

Florence: 115, 307

Forster, John: 253 & n

Forster, Edward Morgan: for Biographical Note *see* Appendix I; his normal day one of pure light, 6; his diary, 27 & n; asks VW to review for *Daily Herald*, 28 & n; his reliance on LW, 33; his story 'might boom', 52; but not suddenly, 53; goes to India . . . 96 & n; critical letter from, 138-9; home—with no Rajah and no novel, 171-2; reads memoir, 178; his character, his novel, and Hardy, 203-4; letter on *Jacob's Room*, 209 & n; buttoned like a hairdresser, 230; detached as a saint, 241; couples VW with Lawrence, 242; based on hidden rock, 269; novel finished, 289 & n, 291; on VW and the soul, 292; too restrained in new book? 304; *ref*: 19, 25, 33n, 36, 42, 54, 115, 138n, 171n, 192, 202, 233, 298; *A Passage to India*, 289, 291; *Pharos and Pharillon*, 233 & n; *The Story of the Siren*, 36 & n, 52 & n

Forster, Mrs (Morgan's mother): 270 & n

France: 10, 71, 140, 156, 167, 265, 318

Franck, César: 233 & n

Franklin, John (unidentified): 321

Freshfield, Augusta Charlotte, *née* Ritchie: 143 & n, 221

Freud, Sigmund: 135 & n, 322 & n;

Collected Papers, vols. I and II, 322n

Fritham House, New Forest: 166 & n

Fry, Margery: 207 & n, 258

Fry, Pamela *see* Diamand, Pamela

Fry, Roger: for Biographical Note *see* Appendix I; letter about *Night and Day*, 5; his house, and apparent wilfulness, 10 & n; sold in America by Clive, 10-11 & n; speaks on modern art, 21 & n; objective at Memoir Club, 23; his show—a misfire, 48 & n; his pictures like ugly girls, 49-50; his 'open air', 52; work in view for Press, 72 & n; Angelica on his foot, 73; and Murry, 74, 139 & n; his book out, 78 & n; sumptuous but rudimentary, 80-1; attractive quality of imagination, 94; lectures Cambridge Heretics, 98 & n; on keeping up to mark, 106; entirely without meanness, 107; restoring Mantegnas, 108 & n; VW not a fake, 109; his woodcuts, 109 & n, 144; sees masterpieces ahead, 150; suspects Clive's friendships, 151; gives lecture, 177 & n, 229 & n; hair flying, with portraits of Logan, 187-8; painting assiduously, grown querulous, 260; his pictures, his vitality, 289; dreads British Parish, 290; rampant to paint Woolfs, 298; and Josette Coatmellec, 303 & n; a truculent Quaker, 311; disastrous with Vita, 325; *ref:* 18, 55, 91, 93, 110, 111, 120 & n, 121, 122, 126, 145, 149, 151n, 172, 178, 183, 187n, 188n, 189, 199, 223, 257, 258, 326; *Living Painters—Duncan Grant*, 311n; *Twelve Original Woodcuts*, 109 & n, 144; *Vision and Design*, 78n, 80

Fyfe, H. Hamilton: praises LW in *Daily Mail*, 116 & n

Gandarillas, Juana: a lady in the continental style, 107; *ref:* 87n, 92, 141, 157

Gardiner, Dr Matthew Henry, of Richmond: 141 & n

Garnett, David ('Bunny'): for Biographical Note *see* Appendix I; enthuses over *Jacob's Room*, 209; asks VW to be godmother, 223 & n; praises her in *Dial*, 259 & n; is abused in *Adelphi*, 266 & n; *ref:* 18, 25

Garnett, Edward: 184 & n; *Friday Nights*, 184 & n

Garsington Manor, home of Philip and Ottoline Morrell: gossip about, 7; VW visits, 179-80; origins of Eliot Fund, 183 & n; weekend at, 243-5; *ref:* 67, 179n, 187, 305

Gaskell, Mrs: 263; *Wives and Daughters*, 263

Gay, John: *Beggar's Opera*, 72 & n, 212, 216; 'Women and Wine', 216

General Election: 212, 318 & n

General Strike: foreboding of, 111 & n

George IV: to be done by Lytton? 114, 115, 163

George V: 46

Gerhardt, Elena: 298 & n

Germany: 100 & n, 140, 309

Gertler, Mark: gives VW gooseflesh, 149; his company and character, 150; 'the pigsty', 158; *ref:* 149n

Gibbon, Edward: 115, 210, 310

Gilman, Emma, Nelly Boxall's niece: 173 & n

Gladstone, W. E.: 139, 176

Glover, Dr James: 242n, 302 & n

Goha Le Simple, *see* Adès, Albert and Josipovici, Albert

Goldie *see* Dickinson, Goldsworthy Lowes

Goldman, unidentified financier: 101

Gordon, General: 176

Gordon Square (a social entity): the pleasure of leaving, 36; begins again, 38; Norton daren't face, 76; *ref:* 48, 80, 107

Gordon Square (the London Square): 88, 120, 211, 260, 284, 285, 303, 305

Gordon Square, No. 37: 183n, 221

Gordon Square, No. 41: 79 & n, 106

Gordon Square, No. 46: VW spends night at, 55; blaring and brazen, 92; party scene described, 223-4; is become a centre, 238-9; continues to excite, 246; *ref:* 13 & n, 15, 21, 33, 38, 73, 99, 233, 277

Gordon Square, No. 50: Vanessa's new home, 23 & n; its astonishing brightness, 73; Clive to set up at, 183 & n; *ref:* 36n, 38-9, 182, 222, 224, 289n, 297

Gordon Square, No. 51, home of Lady Strachey and daughters: 23 & n

Gorki, Maxim: *Reminiscences of Leo Nicolayevitch Tolstoi*, 34 & n

Goss, John, baritone: 174, 175n

meretricious fille de joie, 28; in Paris with Clive, 36; hates and fears VW, 54; scented, tinted, 63; Lytton on, 64; to be steered clear of, 69; straight faced before VW's jokes, 77; fallen off her perch, 87 & n; liked slightly better, 90; finds separation intolerable, 100-1; her low opinion of VW's work, 135; not on visiting terms, 137; VW to settle quarrel, 138; solicitous, affectionate, 142; fine diplomatic game, 146; Vanessa on, 157; on desert island with 158; interprets *The Waste Land*, 178; dines alone with VW, further diplomacy, 182-3; in grey silk stockings, 202; in lemon coloured trousers, 223; her shriek, 225; her instinctive nature, 233-4; worships canary, 263; would roast VW, 289; tea with, 320; her farewell, 322; *ref*: 15, 33, 71, 104, 171, 172, 181 & n, 191, 195, 216, 237, 239, 257, 258, 262, 277, 278, 291, 312
Hutchinson, St John: 64 & n
Huxley, Aldous: to be canonised? 44; summed up by VW, 49 & n; *Crome Yellow* and Ottoline, 180 & n; in canary coloured socks, 216; *ref*: 19, 52, 142; *Leda and Other Poems*, 44 & n; *Crome Yellow*, 180 & n
Hyde Park Gate, No. 22: VW's memoir, 121n; *ref*: 122, 166

Ibsen, Henrik: 196
Iford, Sussex: 270
I.L.P. (Independent Labour Party): 314, 318
Ireland: violence in, 73; shootings & hangings, 100; Herbert Fisher and, 112 & n; *ref*: 122, 127n, 157
Isle of Wight: 252
Italy: 27, 39, 71, 88, 140

Jack *see* Hills, John Waller
James, Henry: VW intent upon, 27 & n; *TLS* article on attacked, 29 & n; reconsidered, 30; and Eliot's development, 68 & n; VW on *The Wings of the Dove*, 136; on his ghost stories, 142 & n; and VW's use of 'lewd', 151; *ref*: 115, 149, 152, 262, 292 & n, 322; *The Wings of the Dove*, 136
Jebb, Sir Richard Claverhouse: 206 & n, 225

Joad, C. E. M.: cocksure, with Marjorie, 213-14; scenes with Marjorie, 276; avoided by Bertrand Russell, 294; *ref*: 213n, 292, 316, 324
Joad, Marjorie *see* Thomson, Marjorie
John, Augustus and Dorelia: slightly gross & elderly, 149 & n
John Bull, periodical: 253 & n
John O'London's Weekly, periodical: 207 & n
Johnson, Dr Samuel: 161, 203
Johnstone, James, surgeon: 173 & n
Jones, Alice Louisa: 262 & n
Jones, Duncan *see* Duncan-Jones, Arthur
Jones, Philip Hugh: 262 & n
Jonson, Ben: *Epicoene, or The Silent Woman*, 238 & n
Joshua, Albert Michael: 314 & n
Joshua, Catherine Marie: 7, 8 & n
Josipovici, Albert: *Le Livre de Goha le Simple*, 56 & n
Jowitt, William and Lesley: 146 & n
Joyce, Giorgio: 256 & n
Joyce, James: and damned egotistical self, 14; admired by Eliot, 67; his method explained, 68; better than VW? 69; a callow board school boy, 199; his intention, 203; *ref*: 114, 161, 187, 204, 256 & n; *Ulysses*, disliked more and more, 195-6; last immortal chapter 197; a misfire, 199; J. C. Squire and, 202; *ref*: 68 & n, 125, 188, 193, 200 & n, 205
Joyce, Nora, *née* Barnacle: 256 & n

Ka *see* Arnold-Forster, Katherine
Keats, John: VW and Eliot on, 104; Shelley and, 130 & n; *ref*: 88, 297; *Lamia*, 130 & n; *Letters*, 104
Kelvin, Lord: 147 & n
Kensington Gardens: 174
Kensington High Street: 239
Kent House, Knightsbridge: 46 & n, 181 & n
Kew, Royal Botanical Gardens: spring at, 21; *ref*: 7, 295
Keynes, John Maynard: for Biographical Note *see* Appendix I; toasts Duncan, is unmoved by success, 18; his book a work of morality, 33; on brink of ruin, 40 & n; VW spends night in his bed, 55; opinion of *Queen Victoria*, 64; VW's vivid vision of, 69; on Norton's

Maitland, Florence, *née* Fisher, see Darwin
Florence
Mallock, William Hurrell: *Memoirs of
Life and Literature*, 66 & n
Mallory, Mrs, tennis champion: 133 & n
Malthouse, Mr, Rodmell publican: 59 & n
Malvolio (fict): 139
Manchester: an account of, 101-3; *ref*: 95,
100, 148
Manchester, University of: 101, 102 & n
Mannheimer, Charlotte, *née* Abrahamson,
cousin of LW: 42n
Manning-Sanders, Ruth: 159 & n, 160,
161, 178 & n: *Karn*, 159n
Manorbier, Pembrokeshire: 197 & n
Mansfield, Katherine, *née* Kathleen Beauchamp (Mrs J. M. Murry): for Biographical Note *see* Appendix I;
praised in *Athenaeum*, VW winces,
28 & n; back in England, 34 & n; no
word from, 36; and no answer from,
41; sends note, 43 & n; 'interview'
with—two hours of priceless talk, 43-
6; praises Conrad, 52; farewell deferred, 55; and conducted, 61-2; VW glad
to hear her abused, 78-9; 'insincere-
sincere' letter to, 80; why indecent?,
82; swims from triumph to triumph,
87; and the Bibesco scandal, 91 & n;
loses Kot's mss, 99 & n; robbed of
Hawthornden, 116; so clever . . . so
disagreeable, 138; to burst upon the
world, 161 & n; soaring . . . but put in
her place, 170-1; back in London, 194
& n; her death—rivalry and friendship recollected, 225-7; 'no competitor'
now, 228; posthumous life, 237-8;
about feeling deeply, 247-8 & n;
'Lord' in her sense, 250 & n; Murry's
revelations, 253 & n; 'used to write all
day', 263; not often thought of, 304;
that strange ghost, 317; VW's love
for, 318 *ref*: 43n, 45n, 46n, 48, 49,
226n, 257; *Bliss*, 78n, 192; *The Doves'
Nest and Other Stories*, 248 & n, 250n;
The Garden Party and Other Stories,
161n; *The Man Without a Temperament*, 43n, 44; *Prelude*, 44 & n
Mantegna: 108 & n
Margesson, Catherine: 181 & n
Marlborough, Duchess of, *née* Gladys
Deacon: 76 & n, 152 & n
Marie Louise, H.H. Princess: 46 & n

Marlowe, Christopher: 196
Marlowe Society (Cambridge): 230n
Marsh, Edward ('Eddie'): 104 & n, 229n,
297
Marshall, Thomas Humphrey ('Tom'):
316 & n, 324
Martin, Mrs: Monks House lent to, 104
& n
Marvell, Andrew: 114
Mary ('mad Mary'), housemaid: 40n, 47
& n
Mary, Aunt *see* Fisher, Mary
Mary Queen of Scots: 306 & n
Masefield, John: 163 & n
Mason, J. H., printer and typographer:
172 & n
Massingberd, Stephen: 162 & n
Massingham, H. W. ('Wayfarer'): offers
LW *Nation* post, 34; wipes out bitterness, 38 & n; another offer for LW,
42 & n; VW's arrow launched against,
58 & n; gratifying to refuse, 93; forgiven, 212 & n; *Nation* sold over his
head, 227; to start new paper, 229;
delaying at Monte Carlo, 232 & n;
fairly certain to prevail, 233; full
speed ahead, 236; to go in a month,
237; badly treated? 241; *ref*: 229n,
337, 338
Mathew *see* Matthaei, Louise
Matthaei, Louise Ernestine: life devastated, 94 & n; *ref*: 4 & n
Maxse, Katherine (Kitty), *née* Lushington:
on *Night and Day*, 5; worldly wishes
for VW, 144; her death . . . and
her memory, 206-7; *ref*: 5n, 206n,
207n
Maxse, Leopold: and Kitty's death, 206-7;
ref: 206n
Mayor (family): 67, 97, 175 & n, 181
Mayor, Beatrice ('Bobo'), *née* Meinertzhagen: a little stupid, 97; her play
rehearsed, 174-5; a damp owl, 223; a
vague affair, 228; *ref*: 97n, 156, 157,
172, 174n, 175
Mayor, Flora MacDonald: 292 & n
May's, removal firm: 293 & n
Mecklenburgh Square: Adrian sits alone
in, 292; *ref*: 277
Meinertzhagen, Elizabeth (Betty Potter):
comes cropper, 97 & n; loves VW, 173;
at rehearsal, 174 & n; limp and stagnant,
228; *ref*: 98

357

Mansfield in *Athenaeum*, 28 & n; asks VW to write for *Athenaeum*, 36; KM and VW on, 44, 46; and KM, an odd couple, 62; a suggested victim, 63; VW rejects work from, 66; the manners of the underworld? 70 & n; his quest, 74; KM advertised by, 78; promulgating doctrines, 87; born queer, 88; the Bibesco Scandal and Katherine, 91 & n; "a damned swindler", 123 & n; Eliot on, 124-5; ignorant on ballet, 137 & n; sneers at Roger Fry, 139 & n; 'the pigsty', 158; pleading and whining, 180; Round Robin for his removal, 183; slobbers over E. Garnett, 184 & n; thinks VW a back number, 190; drags VW in for praise, 196 & n; at Katherine's death, 228; his alleged duplicity, 245 & n; a jigger insect, 249; like a revivalist preacher, 252-3; 'We're enemies', 296-7 & n; married again, 304 & n; 'no way of going on after *Jacob's Room*', 308 & n, 317; the professor of the soul, 314; whining for a flat, 317 & n; *ref*: 5 & n, 16, 34, 48, 49, 52, 67, 171, 191, 194, 227, 257, 266; *Aspects of Literature*, 78n, 184n; *Cinnamon and Angelica*, 44 & n; 'The Defeat of the Imagination', 44 & n; *Keats and Shakespeare*, 321 & n; *The Problem of Style*, 123n, 124

Murry, Katherine *see* Mansfield, Katherine

Myers, Leopold, and wife: 246, 247 & n, 250, 251

Nation: post on offered to LW, 34; flattering review of VW in, 38 & n; Hogarth Press books advertised in, 53; Eliot reviewed in, 79 & n; read between coffee and cigarette, 169; LW accepts post on, 181 & n; anti-Murry, 183; sold, 227; acquired by Maynard and group, 229 & n; uncertainty about, and the Wee Frees, 232 & n; and Eliot, 236, 239; hangs over us, 237; literary editorship offered to LW, 240 & n; VW contributes 'To Spain', 241 & n; *New Statesman* rivalry, 252, 265; and Henderson's policy, 268; can Woolfs give it up? 282; and Plumage Bill, 337; *ref*: 208, 238, 243, 244, 248, 249, 251, 260, 269, 316n, 323

Nation (New York): Joyce reviewed in, 200 & n

National Gallery: part of field day, 47; *ref*: 257

Nesbitt, Cathleen: 229 & n

Nessa *see* Bell, Vanessa

Nevinson, H. W.: 297 & n

Newcastle, Duchess of: 339

New Forest: 143 & n, 252

Newhaven, Sussex: 134

Newnes, Sir George: 142 & n

New Leader, ILP weekly: 194 & n

Newman, Cardinal: 202

Newnham College, Cambridge: 197, 231, 341

New Republic: praises VW, 42 & n; VW talking to editor, 298 & n; *ref*: 135, 288

New Statesman: Desmond succeeds Squire on, 9; numberless projects for, 10; VW reviews *Love for Love* for, 103 & n; Desmond on VW in, 108 & n; VW on women in, 157 & n, 339-42; skims reviews in, 169; and *Nation* rivalry, 252, 265, 268; *ref*: 243

New Statesman, Office, Great Queen Street: 116

Newton, Isaac: 341

New York Times: wants monthly article by LW, 212

Nicolson, Harold: down right bluff, 236; incurably stupid, 239; trusty and honest and vigorous, 307; *ref*: 235

Nicolson, Mrs *see* Sackville-West, Vita

Niemeyer, Otto Ernst: 90 & n

1917 Club: merit of, 6; VW speaks at, 21 & n; revolutionary Mr Banks at, 36-7; opens new rooms, 181 & n; *ref*: 6n, 7, 11, 25, 30, 35, 71, 79, 87, 117, 152, 175, 184, 213, 229, 306

Nisbet, James, publisher: 13 & n

Noble, Celia (Mrs Saxton Noble): 46 & n, 181n

Noble, Saxton William Armstrong, armaments manufacturer: 46 & n

Noel-Baker, Irene: 25-6 & n, 319

Noel-Baker, Philip: 26 & n, 319 & n

Norman, Herman Cameron: 165 & n

Northcliffe, A. C. W. Harmsworth, 1st Viscount: 254 & n

Northcliffe, Lady: 254 & n

Northease, Sussex farm: 64

Norton, Henry Tertius James: his crisis traced far back, 76-7; 'an Apostle in

359

around her, 122; 'my foe', 236; *ref:* 93
& n, 238
Rubens Hotel: 48 & n
Russell (family): 148
Russell, Alys, *née* Pearsall Smith (Aunt
Lou): death at her dance, 51 & n
Russell, Bertrand ('Bertie'): a fervid egoist,
146-8; on himself . . . and others, 293-
5; *ref:* viii, 146n, 147n, 148n, 252 & n,
265, 268, 294n, 295n
Russell's, Sussex bakers: 85
Russell Square: 174
Russian Famine Fund: 140
Rylands, George Humphrey Wolferston
('Dadie'): young kitten, 258 & n; a
corn flower, 266; at Bindon Abbey,
267; might join Press, 268, 271;
considerable grit, 300; awaited with
alarm, 304; never a permanent partner,
323 & n; that enchanting creature, 326;
ref: 273, 278, 281, 305, 311, 312, 316,
319, 325

Sackville-West, Edward: peevish shop
girl, 243-4 & n
Sackville-West, Lionel Edward, 3rd Baron
Sackville: 306 & n, 314
Sackville-West, Vita: (Mrs Harold Nicolson) thinks VW the best woman writer,
187; meets VW, 216-17; a book every
other day, 225; detests scrolloping
honours, 232; a pronounced Sapphist,
235; incurably stupid, 239; asked to
write for Press, 304; a perfect body,
206; vision of her, 307; in new car . . .
an 'honourable', 313; and Bloomsbury
contamination, 324 & n; disastrous
effect of Roger, 325; *ref:* 187n, 221,
314, 324, 326; *Seducers in Ecuador,*
313n
Sainsbury, Dr Harrington: proscribes
going abroad, 170; the lung question,
182, 185; semi-legal discussion over
VW, 189; *ref:* 170n
St Davids, Lady: 138 & n
St Ives, Cornwall: heartache at, 15; Kitty
Maxse's engagement, 206 & n; childhood, 217; and poetry, 246
St John's Wood: 117, 254
St Pancras Infirmary: 47
St Simon: 114
Salisbury, Robert, Marquess of: biography

of, 161 & n; Lytton on, 163; and the
Gordon crisis, 176; *ref:* 26 & n
Salisbury, Lady: 163
Sands, Ethel: 210 & n, 211, 212, 235, 237,
240, 288, 290, 291, 300, 323, 325
Sanger, Anna Dorothea ('Dora'), *née*
Pease: and Mr Banks the revolutionary,
36-7; can't face death, 99; escorted by
countrywoman, 197; *ref:* 36n, 100,
192, 198, 199, 200, 201, 216
Sanger, Charles Percy: 'a Sanger evening',
9; silent about death, discouraging
about Russian, 99; on Greek bedrooms,
197; hops on dry perches, 201; knows
life's hardship, 286; Bertrand Russell
on, 293; *ref:* 9n, 20, 86, 192, 198, 199,
200, 216
Sanger, Daphne: 197 & n, 198, 200, 201
Sappho: 340, 341
Sargent, John Singer: 117
Sassoon, Siegfried: not a welcome sight at
Rodmell, 62; a good fellow, 287; asked
to write for Press, 304; *ref:* 63n, 287n,
320
'Saturday Westminster' *see Westminster
Gazette*
Saunders, Florence, of Playwrights
Theatre: 174
Saxe, Hilda, piano teacher: 292
Schiff, Mr and Mrs Sydney: 52 & n
Schubert: quintet—notes for a story,
24 & n
Scott, Cyril, composer: 213 & n
Scott, Geoffrey: intelligent sightseer, 306
& n, 307
Scott, Walter: 'masterly'—has VW by
hair, 164; *ref:* 161, 245, 310; *The
Antiquary,* 164; *Old Mortality,* 161 &
n, 164
Scott-Chad, Cecil: engaged to Gerald
Duckworth, 78 & n
Segesta, Sicily: 243 & n
Selby-Bigge, Sir Amherst, and family:
64 & n
Seligman, Mrs, unidentified: 180
Senhouse, Roger: 320 & n
Seringapatam: 315 & n
Seton, Dr David Elphinstone: and Julia
Stephen's death, 300; *ref:* 301n
Seton, Sally (fict): 312
Sevigné, Madame de: 64
Shakespeare: life like, 273; chairs he might
have sat on, 306; VW couldn't read

363

see Appendix I; reads memoir, 23; urges Katherine to stick it out, 45; Murry's influence, 74; without a core, 87 & n; drops VW in hot water, 90; absurdly over emphatic, 91; not his own man, 93; nor an Apostle, 94 & n; the Waterlow tragedy, 143 & n; gives VW gooseflesh, 149; shocks Gertler, 150; wants to come back, 158; lost his belief in Murry, 183; a feather bed, 190-1; and Katherine Mansfield, 194; Murry's alleged duplicity, 245 & n; VW monolithic with, 304; on Murry and Lawrence, 321 & n; *ref*: 45n, 86, 124, 145, 149, 184, 191n, 192, 193

Watts, George Frederic: his drawing of mother, 36 & n; and Ellen Terry naked, 255; *ref*: 21n, 113 & n, 117, 255n; 'Una and the Red Cross Knight', 113n

Wayfarer *see* Massingham, H. W.

Webb, Beatrice: displays shark-like teeth, 20; her diary, 93 & n; *ref*: 20n

Webb, Sidney: 20 & n

Webbs, The: lunch with, 20; LW dines with, 143 & n; ask LW to edit book, 152; *ref*: 40, 99

Webling, Peggy: 319 & n

Wedgwood, Josiah (J. W.): 7, 8n

Wee Frees, The: 232 & n, 233

Weiss, Professor Frederick Ernest and Mrs, of Manchester: 101, 102 & n

Weller, Miss: and Dickens, 254

Wellesley, Lady Dorothy: 306 & n, 326

Wellington, Duke of: 102

Wells, H. G.: 63, 161, 260, 293

Wembley *see* British Empire Exhibition

Wemyss, Rosslyn ('Rosie') Erskine, 1st Baron Wester Wemyss: 89 & n

West, Rebecca: 257 & n, 282

Westminster: 32, 51

Westminster Gazette, daily newspaper: 98, 123, 143, 208, 268

Weybridge: 171 & n, 178, 249

Whaddon Chase, hunting dispute: 19 & n

Whistler, James Abbott McNeill: 223 & n

Whitall, James: possible recruit for Press, 189-90, 198; *ref*: 190n, 208, 210, 213 & n

White Hart Inn, Lewes: 269

Whitehead, Rev. Alfred: 294, 295n

Whitehead, Alfred North: 294, 295n

Whitham, John Mills: 24 & n

Whitham, Sylvia, *née* Milman: 24 & n

Whitton, The Old Manor House: 46n

Wigmore Hall: 39, 143, 233

Wilde, Oscar: 97; *A Florentine Tragedy*, 97n

Wilkinson, Clennel Anstruther: 15 & n

Williams, Alice, *quo* Mrs Sydney Waterlow: 143 & n

Williams, Orlo: 339, 341; *The Good Englishwoman*, 339

William IV: 89 & n

Wilmington, Sussex: 282

Wilmot, Catherine: 57; *An Irish Peer on the Continent, 1801-1803*, 57n

Wilson, Romer: 156 & n; *The Death of Society*, 116 & n, 117

Wimborne, Lady: 255

Winchester (school) 144

Wittering, Eleanor Farm: 64, 187, 202

Woburn Square, No. 35: 272, 274

Woman's Leader: 337

Women's Co-operative Guild (WCG): 22 & n, 94, 142 & n

Woolf, Clara: to America?, 38; *ref*: 26n

Woolf, Edgar and Sylvia: 15 & n

Woolf, Leonard. Divided thus: (1) Character, health, occupations and financial situation. (2) Literary work. (3) Political activities.

(1) *Character, health, occupations and financial situation*: doubts concerning removal to London, viii, 250; LW a gardener, 4, 138, 155; a chairmender, 5; publishes—but stays calm, 8; suffers from itch, 16; 'curious family crisis', 26, 38; mouse in his bed, 28; calms E. M. Forster, 33; observations on MacCarthy, 33; on Leopold Campbell-Douglas, 39 & n; his evening ruined, 50; his arm swollen, 50; naked in kitchen, 54; scheme for Press, 56; in search of Lottie, 59; admired by Partridge, 63; on VW's feelings for Mary Hutchinson, 63; critical of Strachey, 64; and of T. S. Eliot, 67; envied by VW, 68, 69; satisfied by his book, 80; gift to VW, 81; depressed, 88, 232, 285, 304; learns Russian, 88, 89, 90; on Clive Bell, 92, 137-8; on Mr Brenton of Barnes, 118; gastric cold, 118; bored by Madge Vaughan, 122; saddened by Murry, 124; by VW, 133; his rise, 137; catches a mouse,

144; housework, 148; on Roger Fry, 150; unsociable, 157, 237; anxiety concerning servants, 173, possible income, 179; on Mirrlees family, 185; on *Jacob's Room*, 186; a celebrity? 187; too much ego in VW's cosmos, 191 & n; similarity between VB and LW, 195; suffers from extreme clarity, 222; edits *Nation*, 240, 260; thinks VW and Lopokova 'sillies', 266; on R. Mortimer, 266; would resign *Nation*, 278; has flu, 290; on reparations, 309; reduced salary, 316; to visit India? 318

(2) *Literary work*: his book published, 8; Memoir Club contributions, 26, 77; to work on *Nation*, 34 & n; journalism, 66; *Contemporary Review*, 71 & n; new status, 71; stories published by Hogarth, 72 & n; a book for Snowden, 74 & n; translating Chekhov, 75; review of Eliot, 77; stories printing, 93; success anticipated 98; plan for book, 111-12; stories well reviewed, 116 & n; sales, 118; new post on *Contemporary Review*, 144 & n; work on *Labour Monthly*, 151; for Webbs, 152; for *Criterion*? 170; replaces Brailsford, 181 & n; Squire rejects story, 190; on Turkey, 212; rivalry with MacCarthy, 252; *Socialism and Co-operation*, 261 & n; on journalism, 268; on E. M. Forster, 269

(3) *Political activities*: Mrs Webb on his career, 20; work on *Nation*, 34 & n, 42, 181 & n; candidature, 36 & n, 42, 101-3, 148, 210 & n; Webbs and Fabians, 143 & n; Lewes ILP, 314

Works by LW referred to: *Empire and Commerce in Africa*, 5 & n; *Socialism and Cooperation*, 74 & n; *Stories of the East*, 72 & n, 110, 111 & n, 116 & n

Woolf, Marie (Mrs Sidney Woolf): 200, 201

Woolf, Philip Sidney: 88 & n, 182 & n, 200

Woolf, Virginia. Entries are divided into eight sections thus: (1) Early life and relationships. (2) Character, personality and health. (3) Literary activity and opinions. (4) Relationship with LW. (5) Public affairs and political activities. (6) Diversions, art and music. (7) Domestic (house hunting, house-keeping, shopping, etc., and financial). (8) The Hogarth Press.

(1) *Early life and relationships*: her youth compared to that of Miss Hussey, 78; attachment to Clive Bell, 89; to Madge Vaughan, 121-2; South Kensington, 144; Stella Duckworth's engagement, 190 & n; Kitty Maxse, 206 & n; Kate Stephen, 234-5; events of 1913, 283 & n; death of Mrs Stephen, 300

(2) *Character, personality and health*: as revealed in Diaries, viii-ix; her accuracy, viii; state of tranquillity, 3-5; vanishing charms, 6; literary vanity, 9, 10, 63; thirty-eighth birthday, 13; infected by lice? 15; confessions of snobbery, 15-16, 57, 235-6; depressed by criticism, 29 & n, 30-1, 106-10, 135; and toothache, 30; relationship with Katherine Mansfield, 55, 61, 78-9, 80, 116, 225-7 (*see also*: Mansfield, Katherine); dental treatment, 58, 176; relationship with Mary Hutchinson, 63, 69, never laughed at VW's jokes, 77, quarrel with, 137-8, 142, a far more instinctive nature, 233-4 (*see also*: Hutchinson, Mary); with lower classes, 64; threat of headache, 70; doubts and discontents, 73; learning Russian, 88-9; 'settling in too soundly', 88; on death, 99, 168, public tragedies, 100, Manchester dons 102; laudatory quotations, 115 & n, 187; reflections on Miss Green, 120; ill health, 125-6; strain of writing, 129; encouragements to write, 131; 'fidgets' 133-4; looking well, 146; influenza, 156; not to travel, 170; flirtation with Clive Bell, 172-3; doctors disagree, 182, 185, 189; Hussey, her faults, 184; celebrity, 187; 'too much ego', 191 & n; disruptive visitors, 191-2, 314-15; headache, 193, 194; perfect satisfaction 212; childless, 221; elderly, 222; depressed, 232; an unpleasant time, 237; shy, 238; snubbed by Squire, 239; an editor's wife, 241; must leave Richmond, 249, 250, 251; alive and energetic, 251; famous? 259; restrained

267; a psychological crisis, 270-1; diary as a therapeutic, 276; relationship with Adrian Stephen, 277; reflections on former madness, 283; good health, 285; charms of London, 301; Press as a therapeutic, 308, 326; change of scene, 308; 'Perpetual Immortality', 319; friendships with women, 320

(3) *Literary activity and opinions*: development as a writer, vii; diaries and letters, ix; second edition of *Voyage Out*, 13, and of *Night and Day*, 13

Jacob's Room, plans for, 13-14, 28, 30; loss of impetus, 35-6; amused by, 40; interrupted at, 53, 57, 68-70, 73, 106 & n; progress, 56, 62, 67; seems rather good, 80; at a crisis, 86; last lap, 89; an eyesore, 92; Mrs Flanders in the orchard, 94; finished, 141; further work on, 170; copying, 176; for U.S.A. 178; criticism anticipated, 179, 208; finishing, 182; LW on, 186; proofs, 199; verge of publication, 205, 207, 208; reception, 209 & n; Roger Fry on 214

On *Voyage Out*, 17; on memoirs, 26-7, 28; on K. Mansfield, 28 & n, 44-5 & n, 46 & n, 55, 62 & n, 80, 138, 170-1; on Henry James, 29 & n, 136, 142 & n, 151-2, 322; *An Unwritten Novel*, 29, 30; a review attacked, 29 & n, 30, 31; on Bishop Berkeley, 33; on J. M. Keynes, 33; flattered by the *Nation*, 38, and in U.S.A., 42 & n; on Conrad, 49 & n, 52, 265, 309 & n; on Aldous Huxley, 49 & n; on Chekhov, 53 & n, 75; on *The Plumage Bill*, 53, (see Appendix II); on *Don Quixote*, 55; *Goha le Simple*, 56 & n; the *Trachiniae*, 59, 63; reviewing for *TLS*, 63, 65-6; on *Queen Victoria*, 65; on *Ulysses*, 67, 68, 188-9, 193, 195, 197, 199-200, 202-3; on Evelyn, 69, 70, 74 & n; on *Our Women* (Bennett), 70 & n (see Appendix III); on D. H. Lawrence, 75; on Coleridge, 77; Strachey on Eliot, 79; Dorothy Worthworth, 92; *Monday or Tuesday*, 96, 108 & n, 109-10, 111-12, 116 & n, 125; Romer Wilson, 117; criticism in the *Dial*, 118 & n; Patmore, 120

The Common Reader ('*Reading*'), planned 120 & n; work on delayed, 156, 172, 188; Greek studies for, 213, 215, 275, 276, 299; plans for 242, 261-2; reading for, 309; dedicated to Strachey, 326 & n

Keynes on VW, 121 & n; Hardy obituary, 126 & n, 142, 145, 149, 150-1, 155 & n, 158, 204; strain of writing, 129; Leigh Hunt, 129-30; encouragement, 131; Dostoievsky and Turgenev, 145 & n; Peacock and Scott, 164 & n; reviews—written with care read without, 169; the *Criterion*, 170-1; *The Waste Land*, 178; the Eliot Fund, 183, 204 & n; *The English Review*, 185; V. Sackville-West on VW, 187

Mrs Dalloway ('*The Hours*'), writing too quickly, 189; left off, 190; develops, 207; aeroplane chapter, 211; manner of writing, 248; devil of a struggle, 249; progress, 259; weak dribble, 260; good in parts, 262; connecting 'caves', 263; Lopokova model for Rezia, 265; mad scene, 272, 321; dissatisfied with, 289; an interesting attempt, 292; the 'Dr' chapter, 299; timetable for, 301 & n; way clear to end, 305; death of Septimus, 307-8; to stretch beyond October, 310; the party, 312; can't stop, 313; work interrupted, 314-15; finished, 316; plans for revision, 320; galloping over, 323, 325

Murry's dismissive criticism, 190, 194; Thoreau, 191 & n; 'rocking oneself into writing', 193; praise from Murry, 196; schemes of work, 196, 205, 208, 211-12; contemporary English literature, 203; Proust, 234, 322; *The Silent Woman*, 238 & n; snubbed by Squire, 239; T. S. Eliot and the *Nation*, 239; *How It Strikes a Contemporary*, 240; *Urn Burial*, 245; Montaigne, 282, 284, 285, 287; Jane Austen, 288; Bosanquet (and others), 292; poetry—a mature taste, 310; use of Diary, 319; Plumage Bill, 337-8; capacity and status of women, 339-42

(4) *Relationship with LW*: VW on his equanimity, 8; seeks to please him, 54 & n; they discuss his book,